A-Z WARWICK

C000173310

REFERENCE

Motorway	**M6**	Car Park (selected)	**P**
Primary Route	**A46**	Church or Chapel	†
A Road	A5	Cycleway (selected)	🚲
B Road	B4455	Fire Station	■
Dual Carriageway		Hospital	**H**
One-way Street		House Numbers (A & B Roads only)	20 ... 40
Traffic flow on A Roads is also indicated by a heavy line on the driver's left.		Information Centre	🛈
Road Under Construction		Junction Name (M6 Toll only)	DUNTON INTERCHANGE
Opening dates are correct at the time of publication.		National Grid Reference	⁴30
Proposed Road		Park and Ride	Stratford **P+R**
City Centre Ring Road & Junction Numbers	①	Police Station	▲
Restricted Access		Post Office	★
Pedestrianized Road		Safety Camera with Speed Limit	**30** **V**
Track / Footpath		Fixed cameras & long term road works cameras. Symbols do not indicate camera direction.	
Residential Walkway		Toilet: without facilities for the Disabled / with facilities for the Disabled	▽ / ▽
Railway	Station / Heritage Station / Level Crossing / Tunnel	Viewpoint	☀ ⁂
		Educational Establishment	⬜
Built-up Area	HOOPER STREET	Hospital or Healthcare Building	⬜
Local Authority Boundary	–·–·–·–	Industrial Building	⬜
Posttown Boundary	———	Leisure or Recreational Facility	⬜
Postcode Boundary (within Posttown)	– – – –	Place of Interest	⬜
		Public Building	⬜
Map Continuation	**40** / Large Scale Centres **135** / Road Map Pages **144**	Shopping Centre or Market	⬜
Airport	✈	Other Selected Buildings	⬜

SCALE

Map Pages 6-134	1:16,896	Coventry City Centre Page 135	1:8,448	Stratford-upon-Avon Town Centre Pages 136-137	1:4,224
0	¼ Mile	0 100 200 Yards		0 50 100 Yards	
0 250 Metres		0 100 200 Metres		0 50 100 Metres	
3¾ inches (9.52cm) to 1mile		7½ inches (19cm) to 1mile		15 inches (38.1cm) to 1mile	
5.9cm to 1km		11.8cm to 1km		23.6cm to 1km	

A-Z Az AtoZ
registered trade marks of
Geographers' A-Z Map Company Ltd

www./az.co.uk

EDITION 3 2016
Copyright © Geographers' A-Z Map Co. Ltd.
Telephone: 01732 781000 (Enquiries & Trade Sales)
01732 783422 (Retail Sales)

© Crown copyright and database rights 2016 OS 100017302.

Safety camera information supplied by www.PocketGPSWorld.com.
Speed Camera Location Database Copyright 2016 © PocketGPSWorld.com

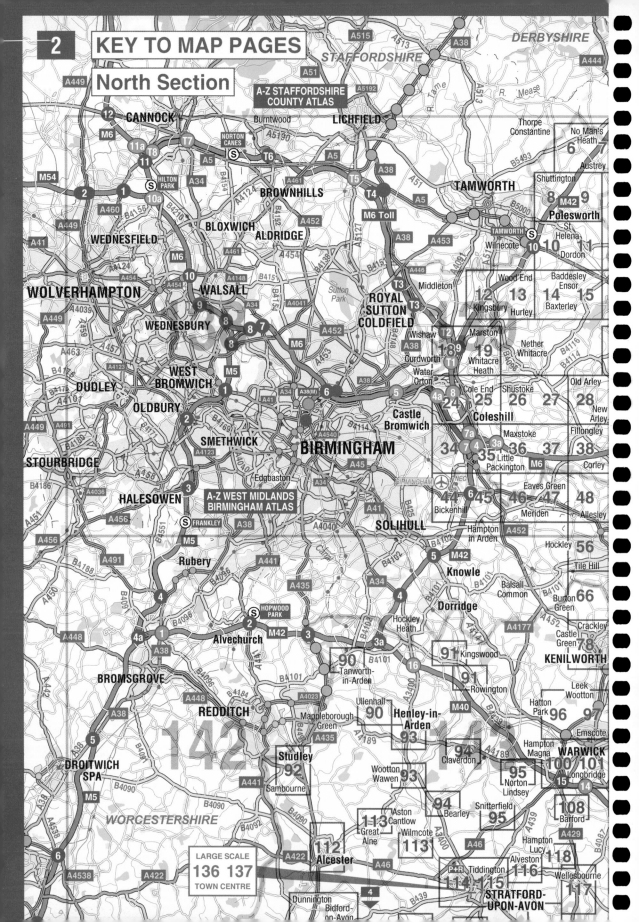

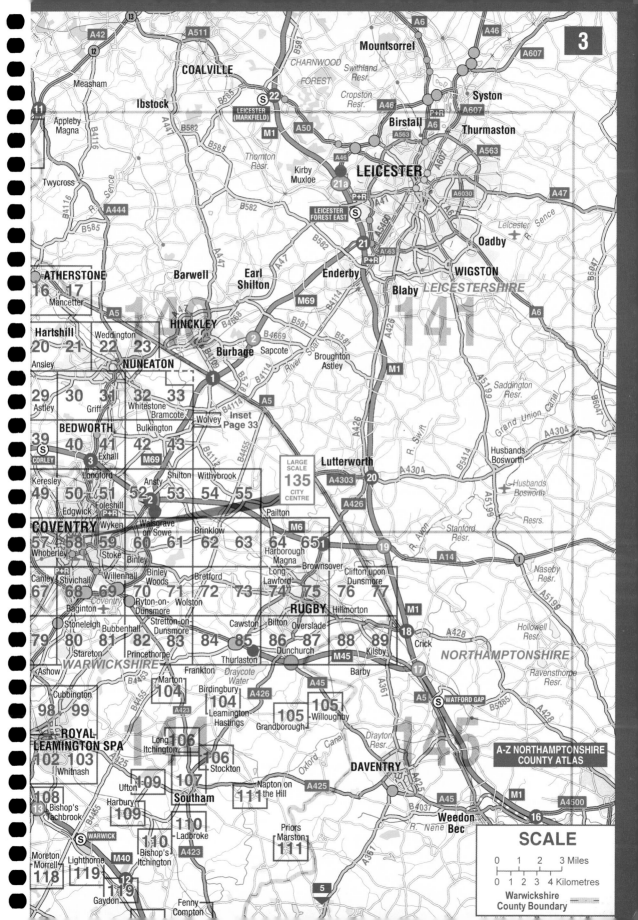

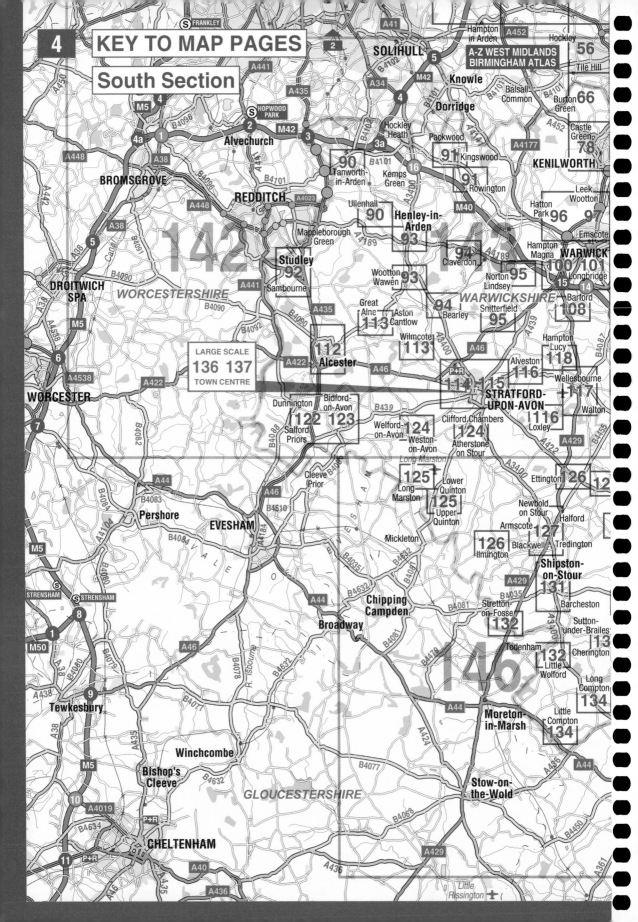

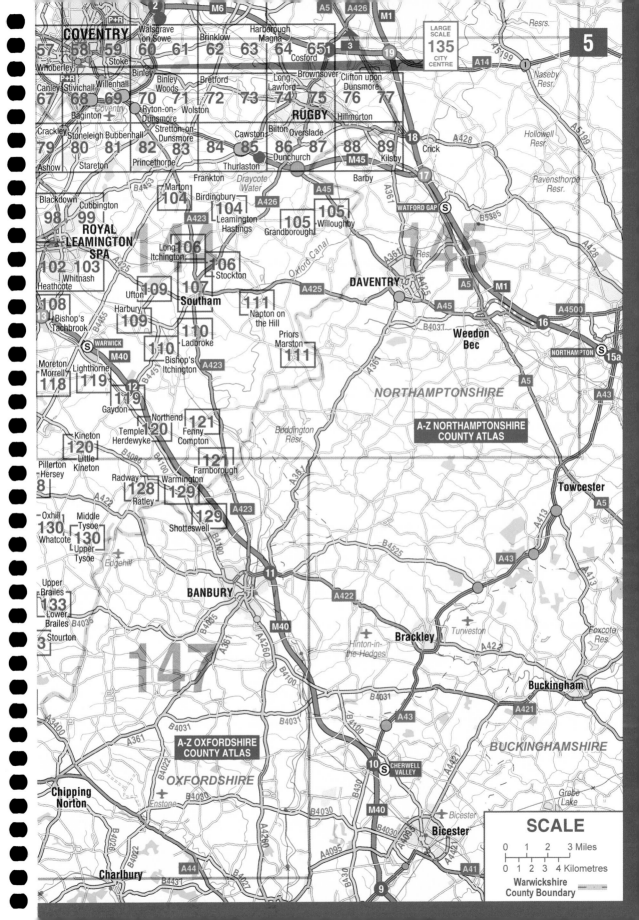

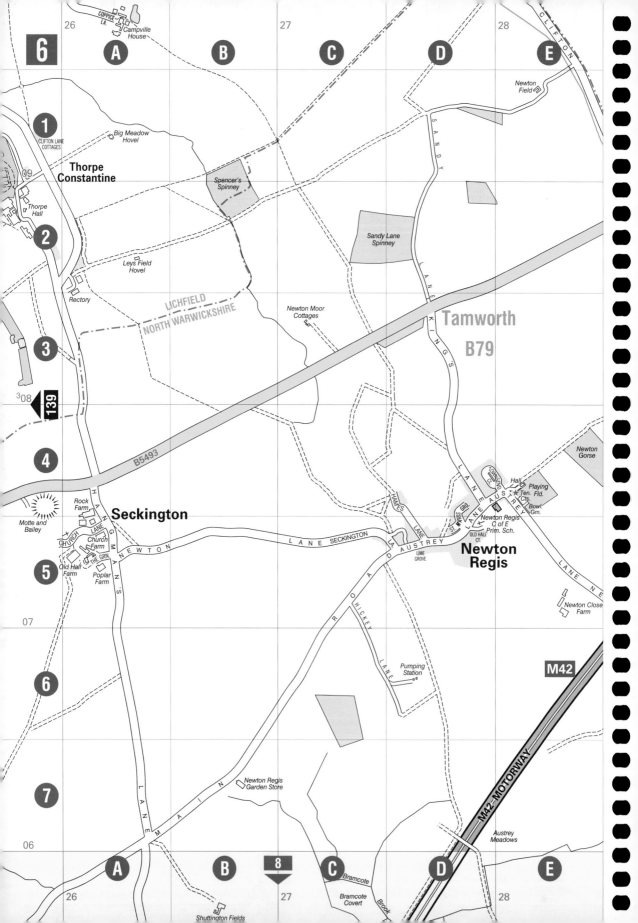

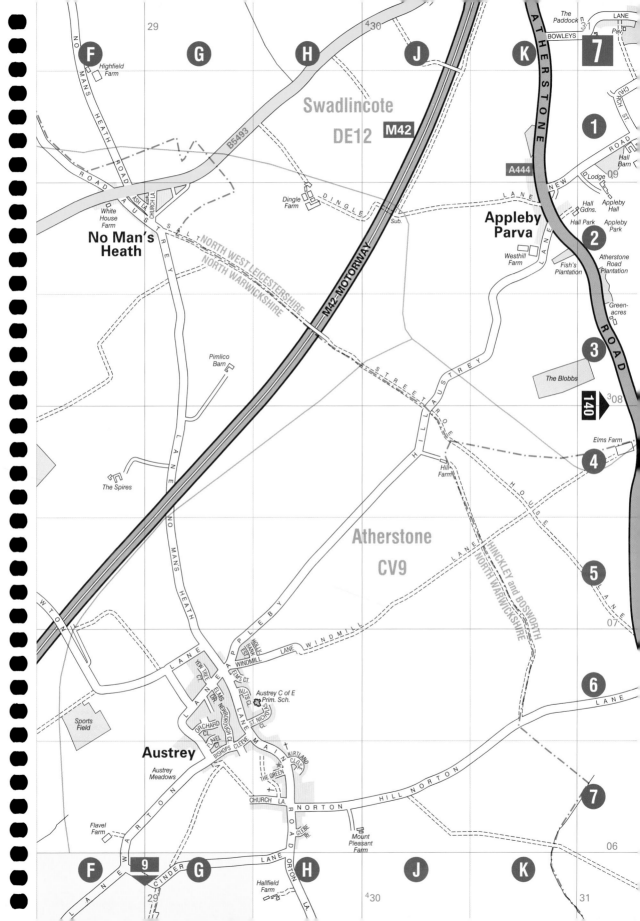

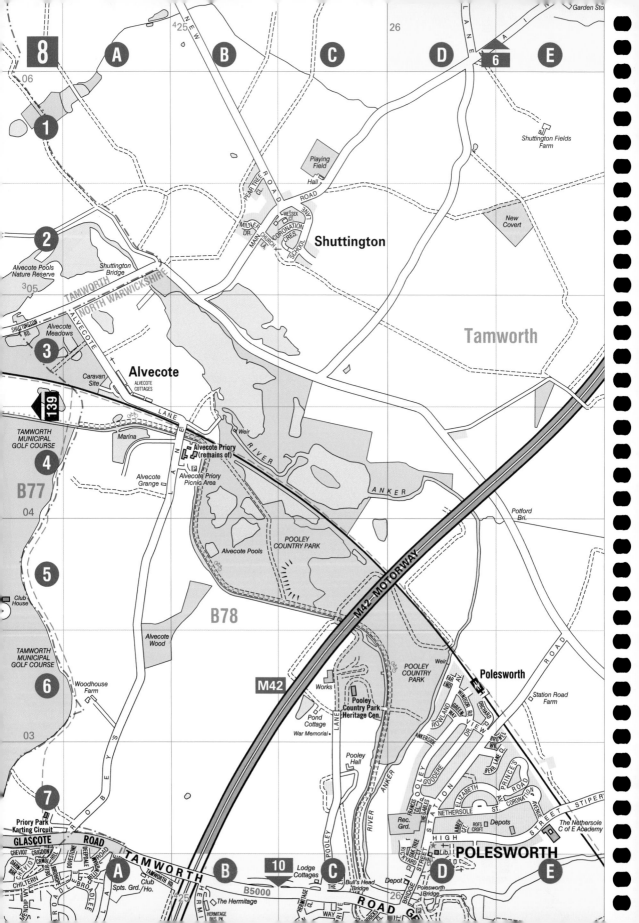

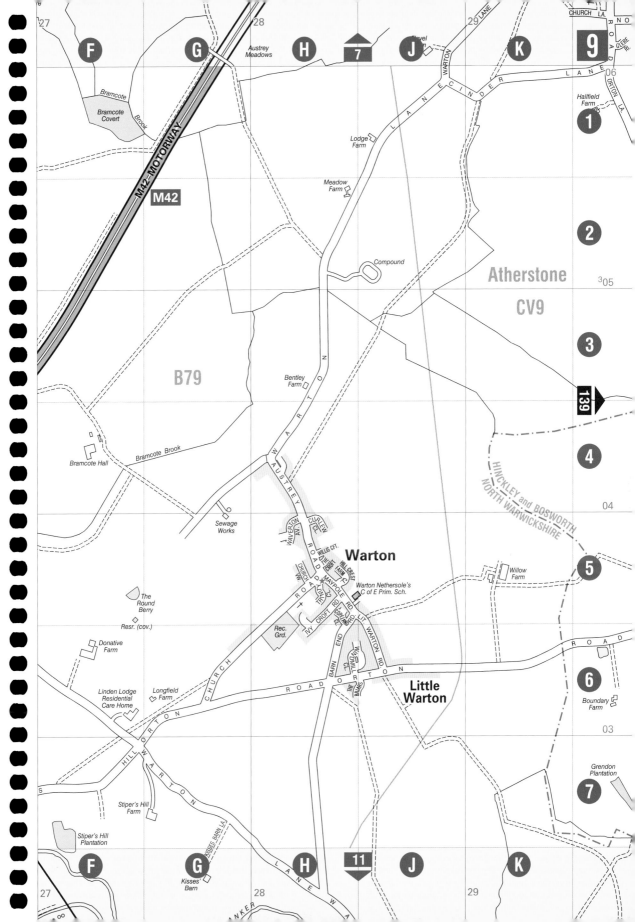

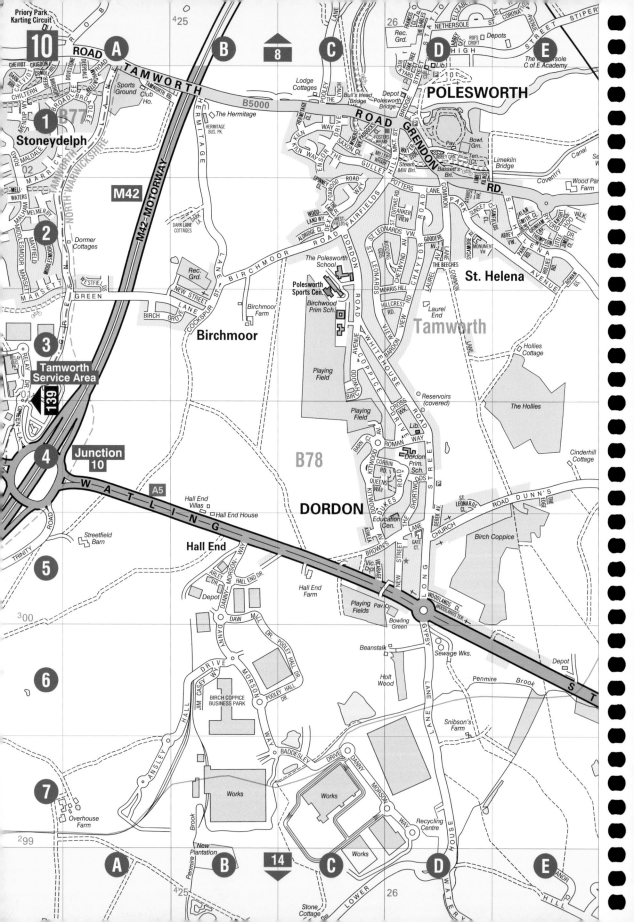

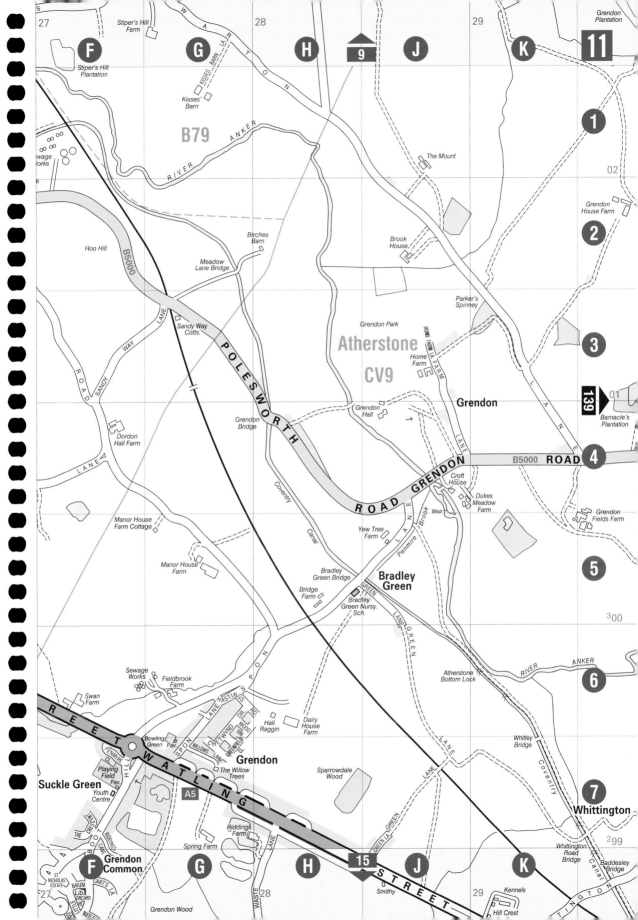

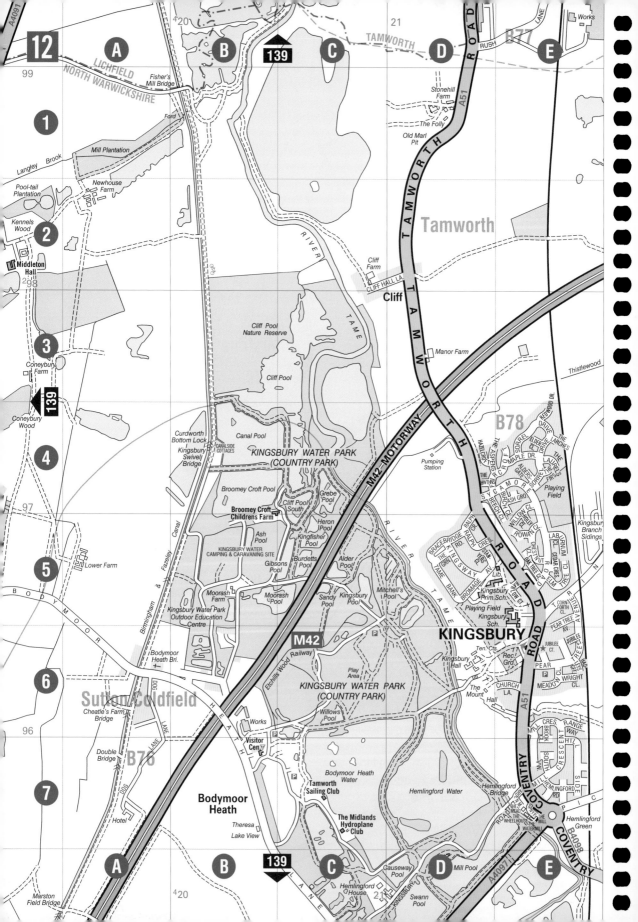

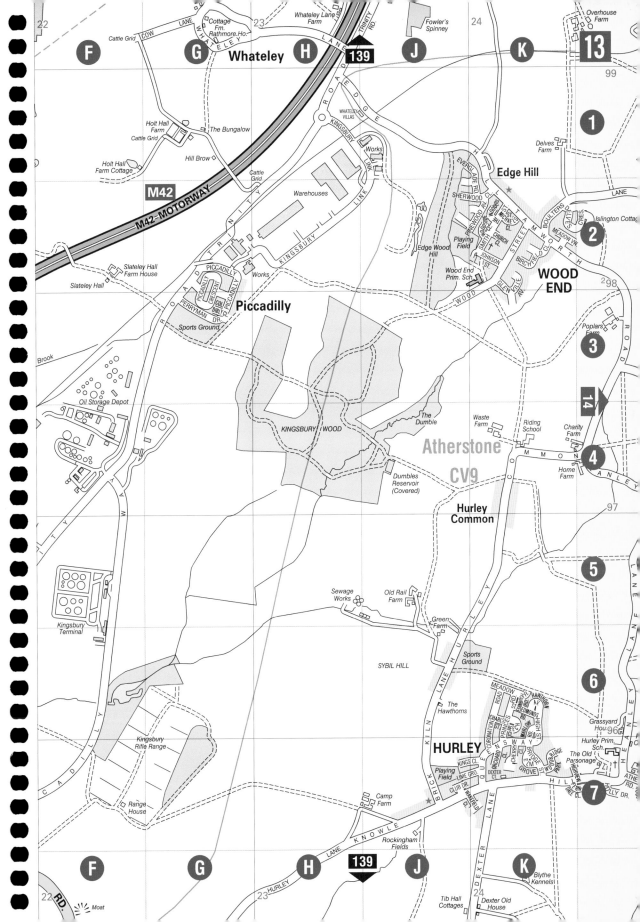

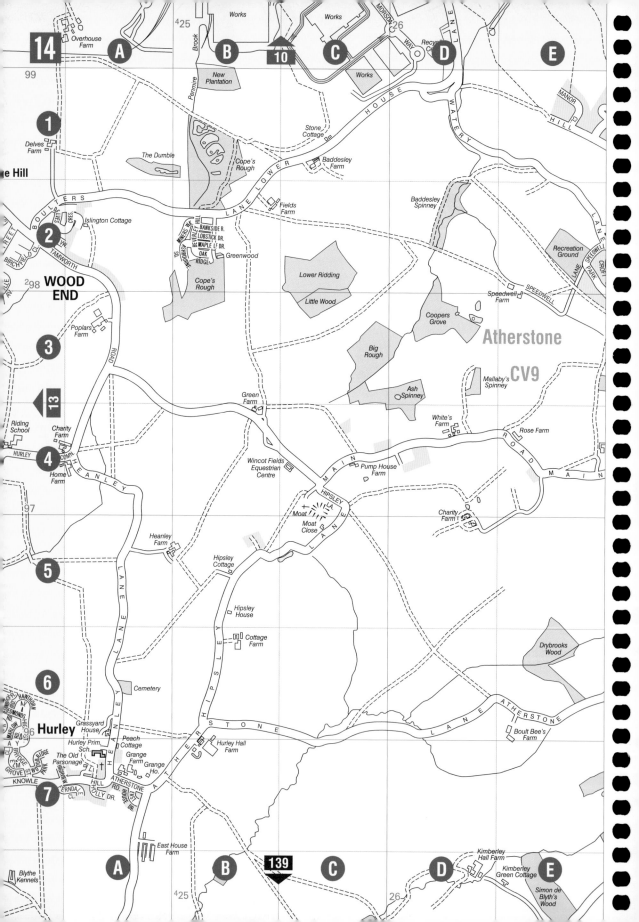

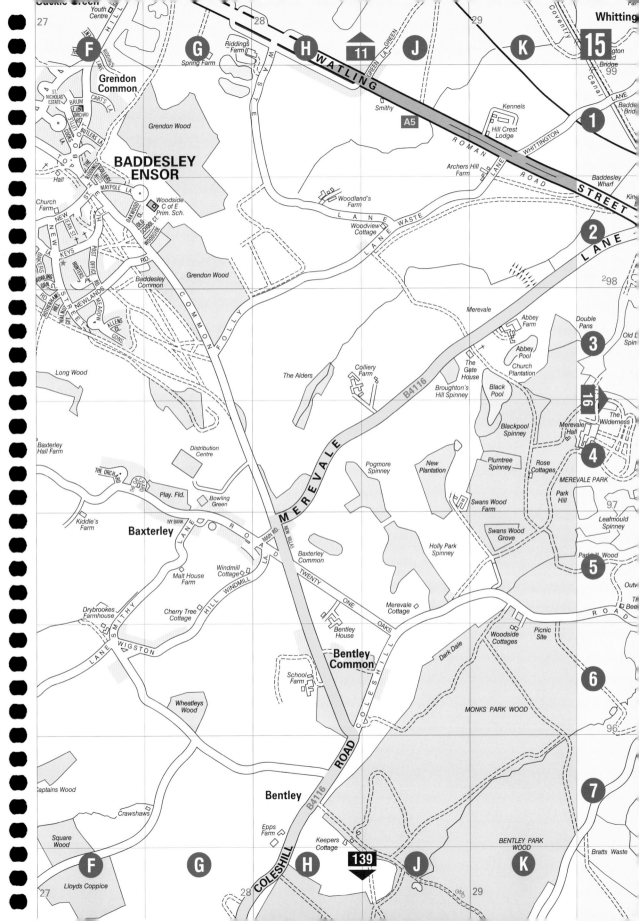

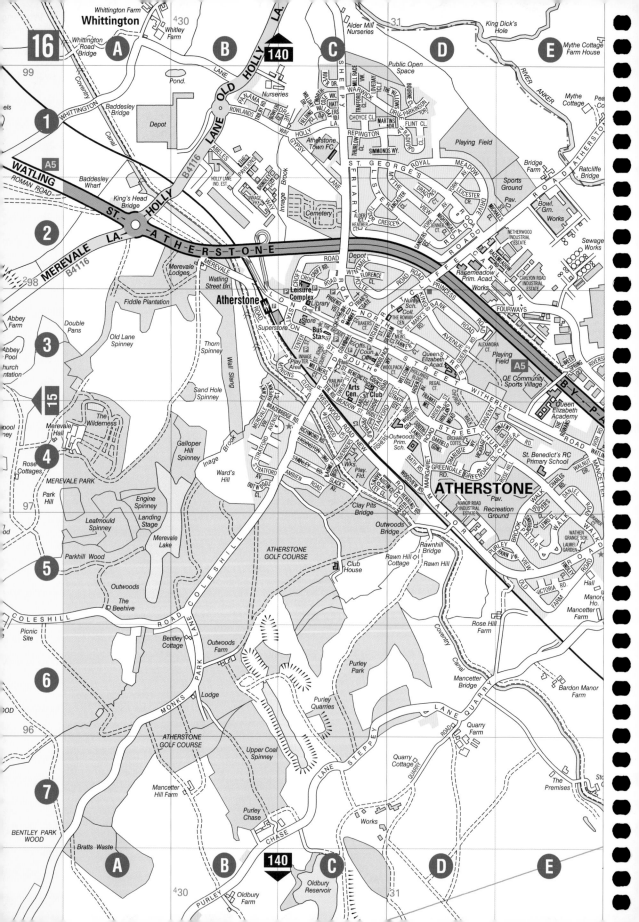

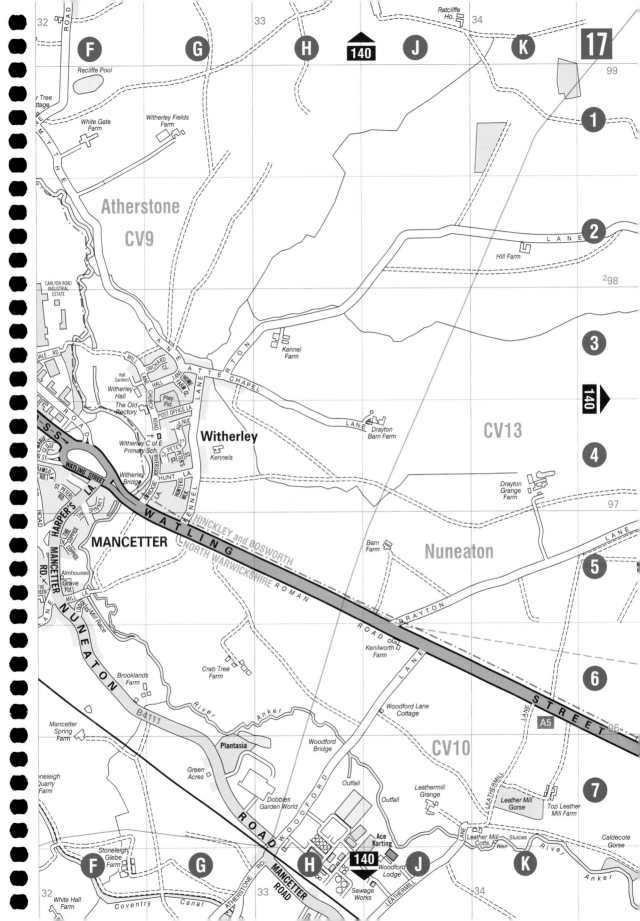

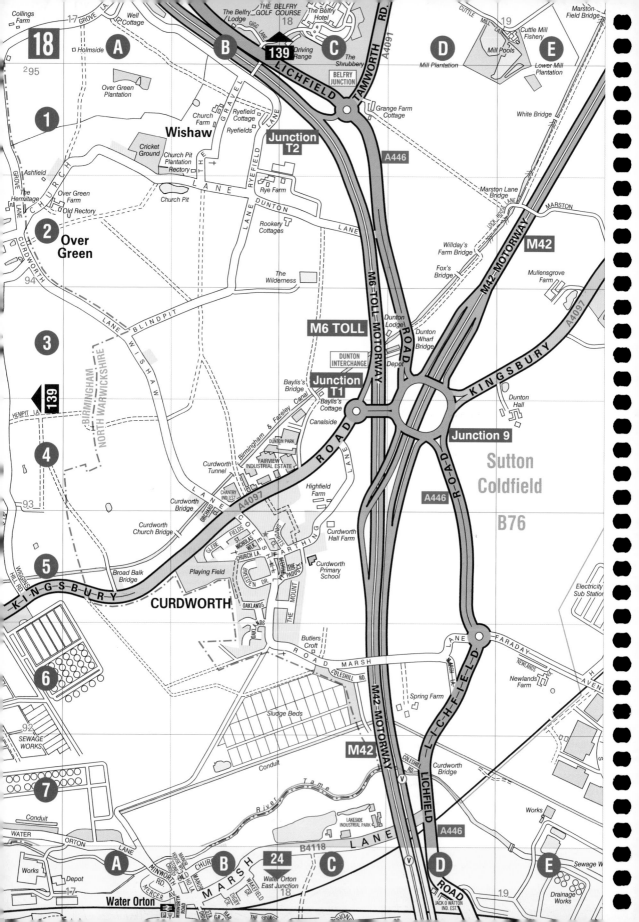

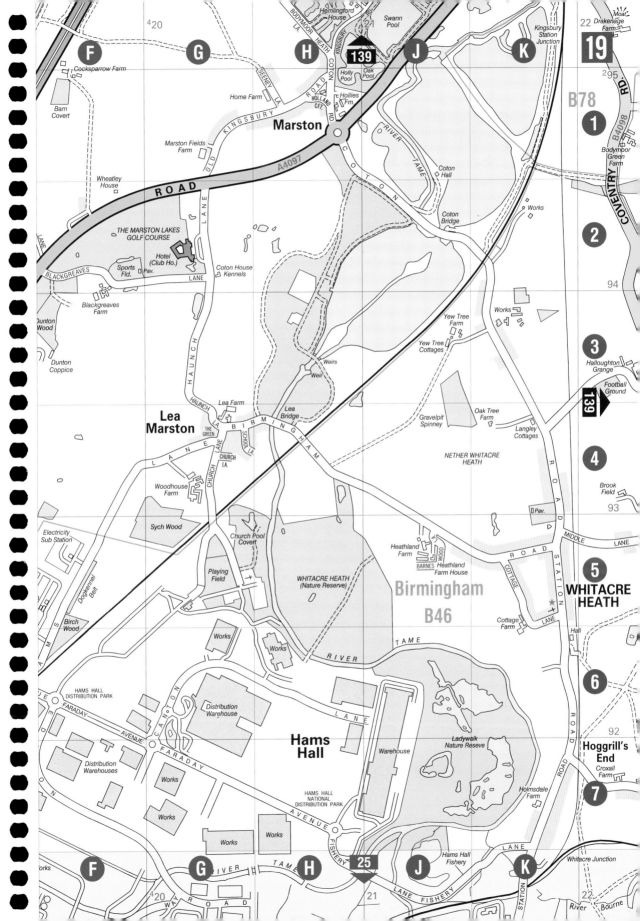

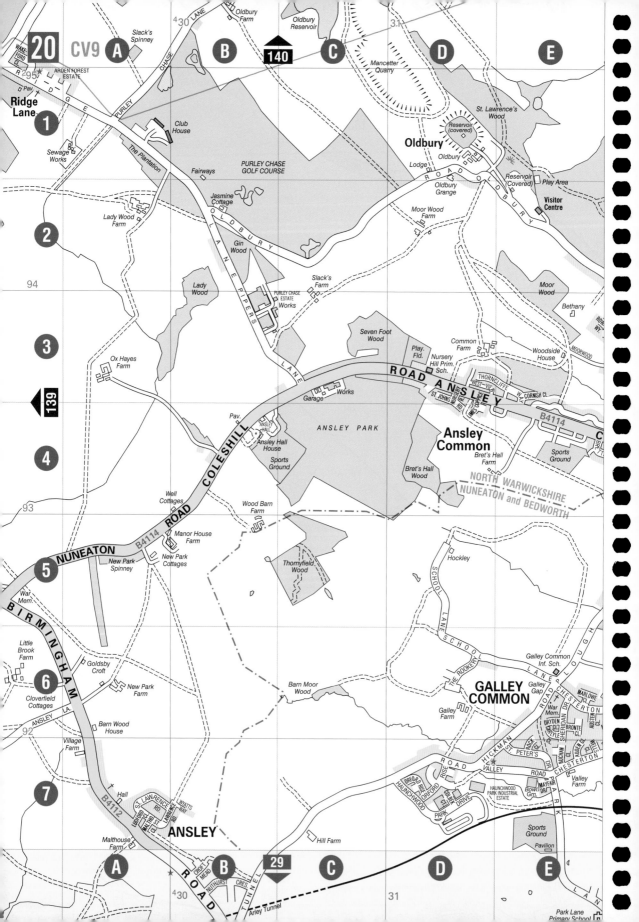

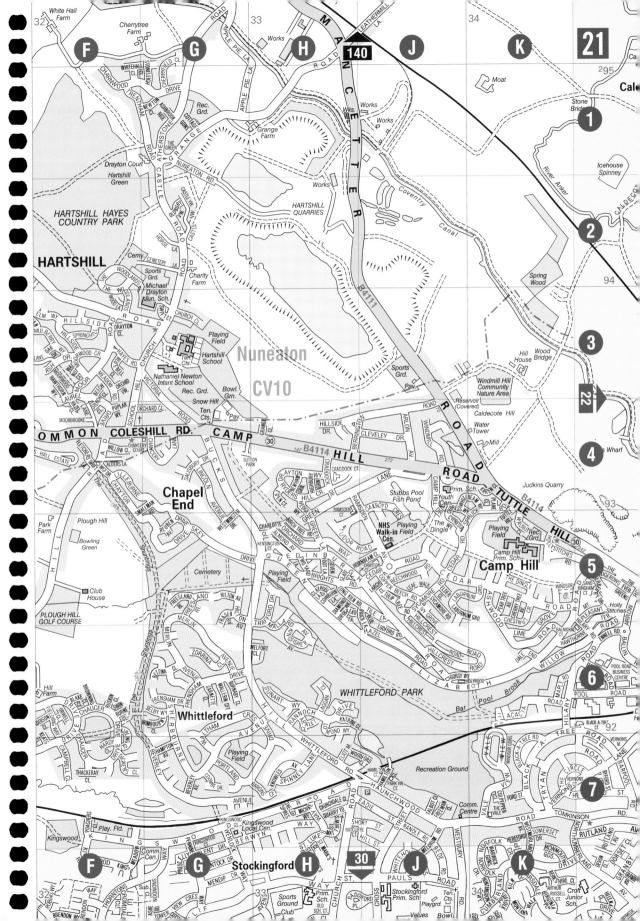

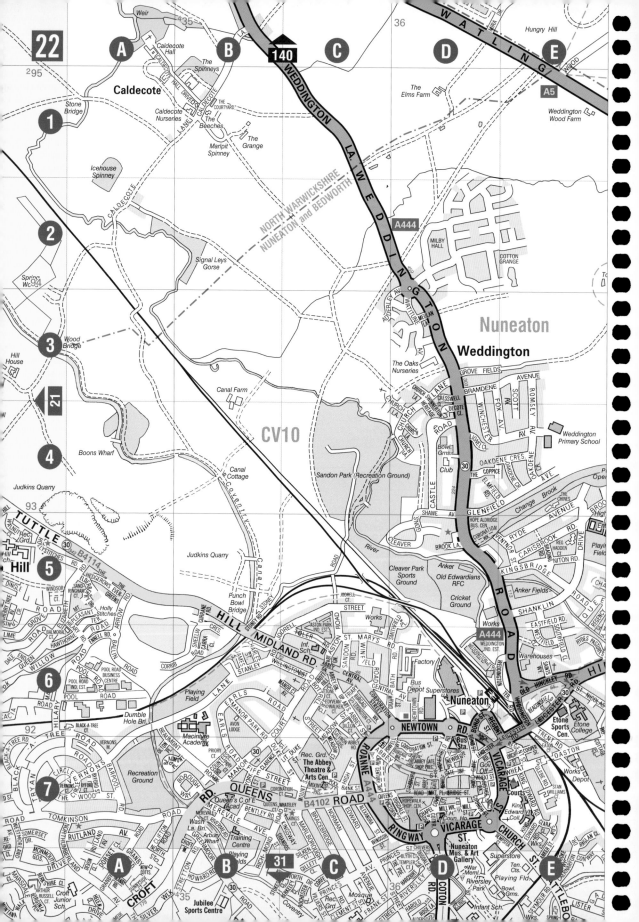

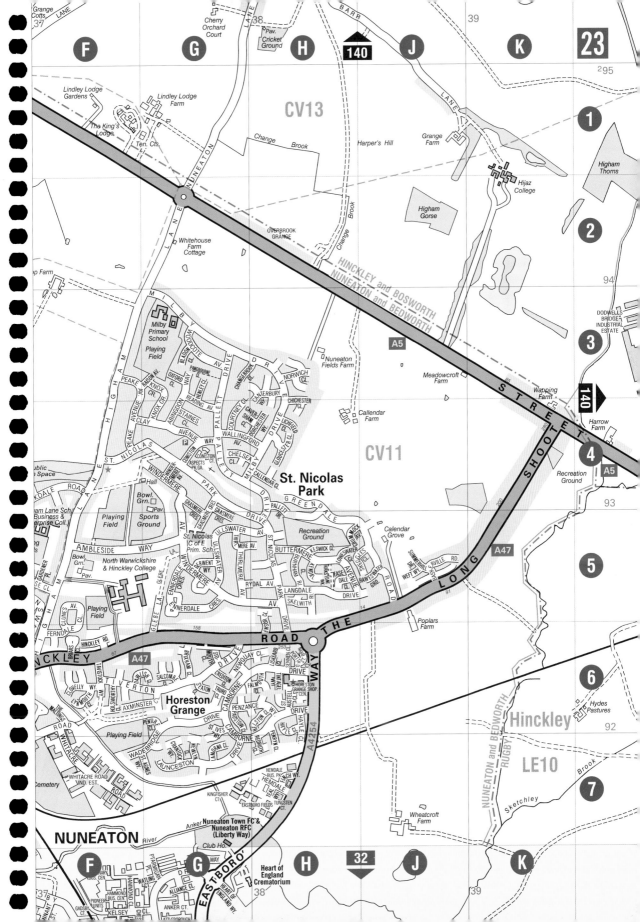

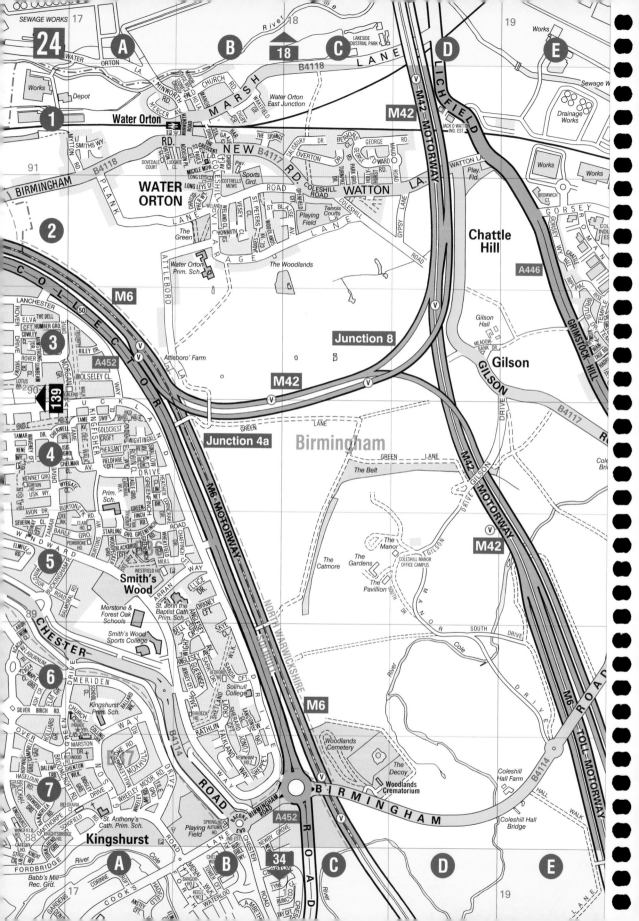

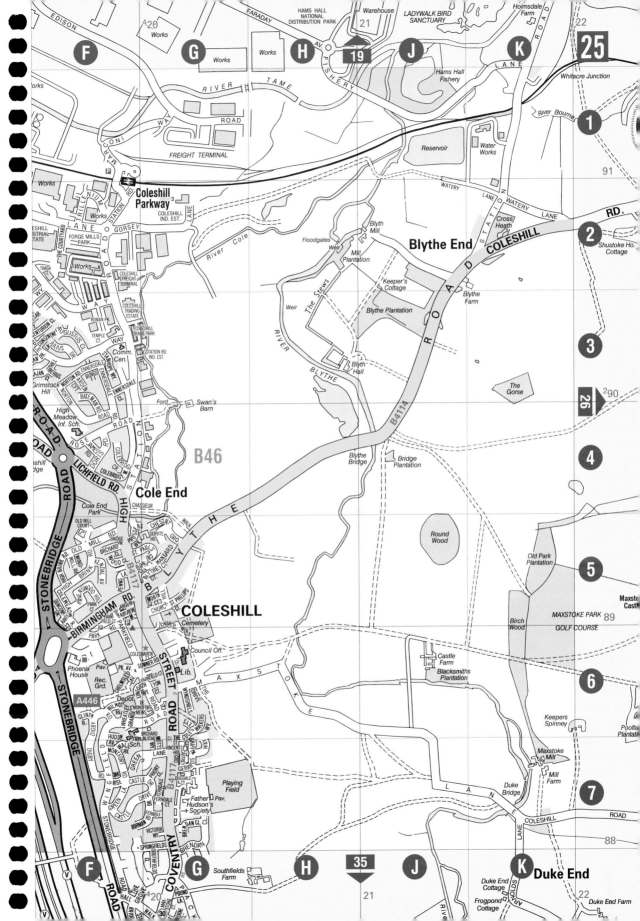

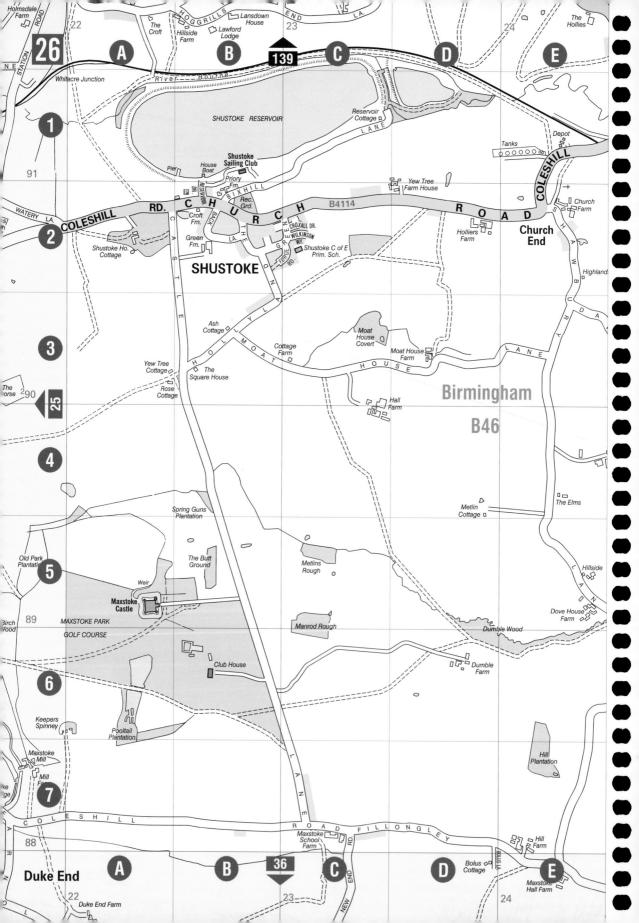

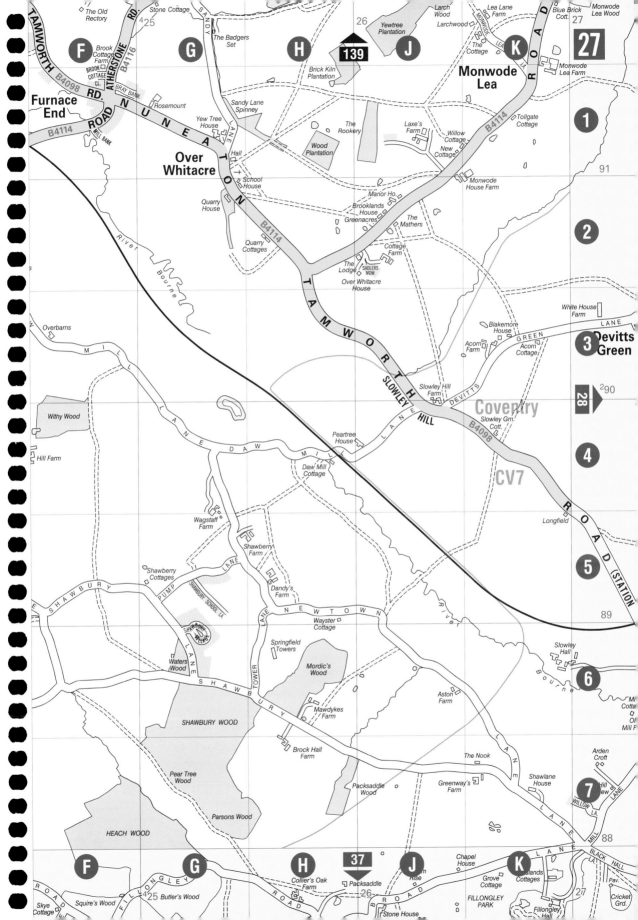

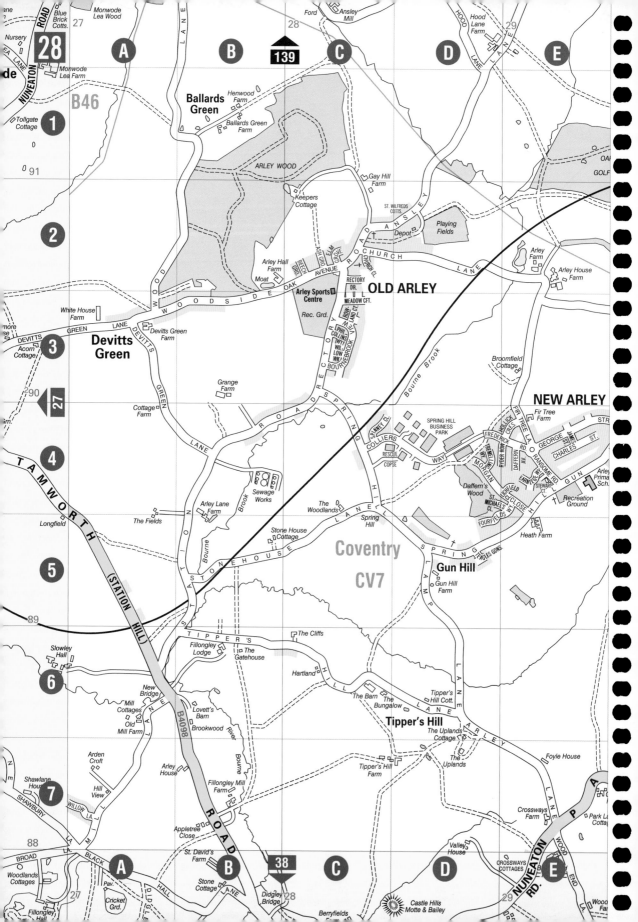

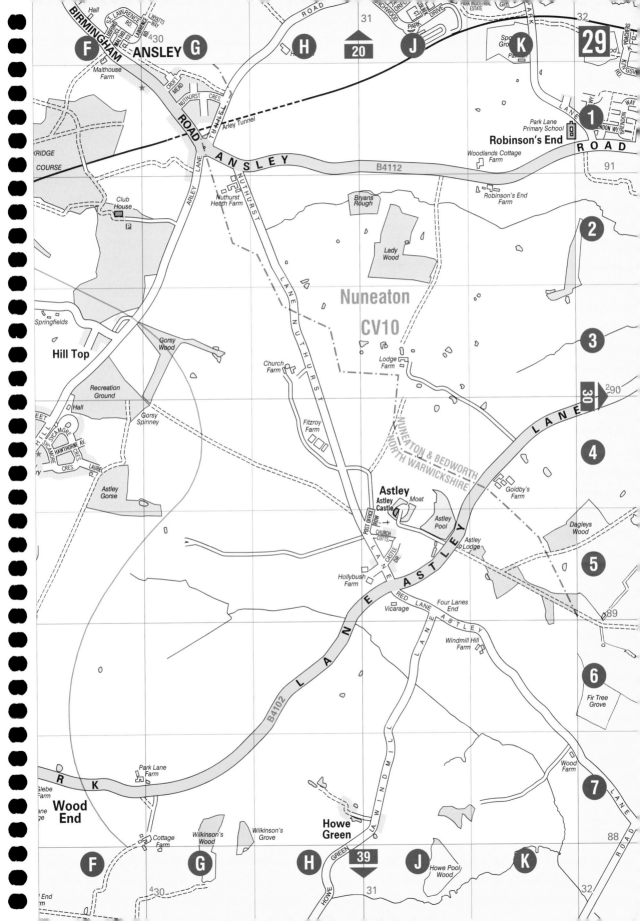

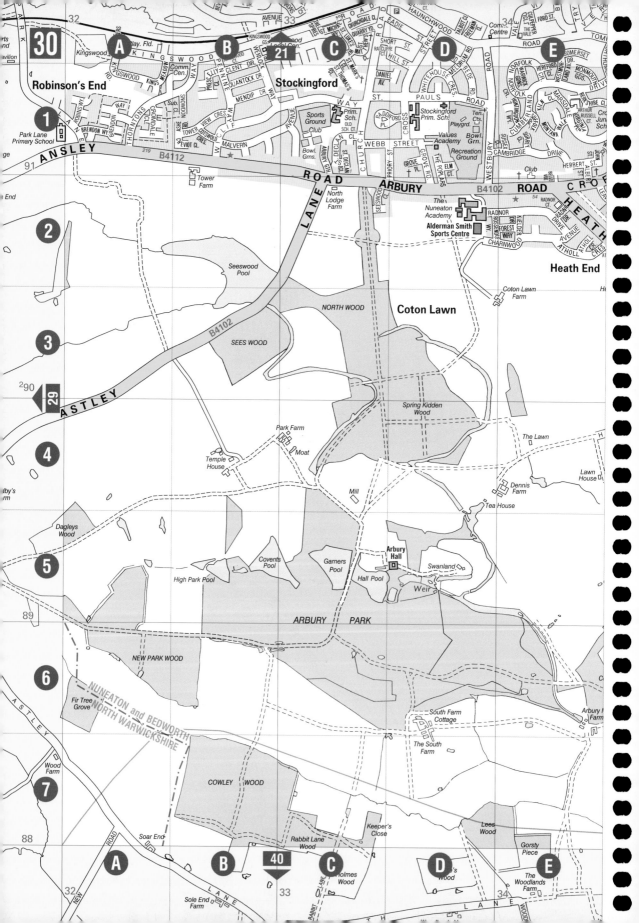

30

Robinson's End

Stockingford

Coton Lawn

Heath End

SEES WOOD

SEESWOOD POOL

NORTH WOOD

Spring Kidden Wood

Dagleys Wood

High Park Pool

Covents Pool

Garners Pool

Hall Pool

Swanland

Arbury Hall

Weir

ARBURY PARK

NEW PARK WOOD

Fir Tree Grove

NUNEATON and BEDWORTH
NORTH WARWICKSHIRE

Wood Farm

COWLEY WOOD

Rabbit Lane Wood

Keeper's Close

Holmes Wood

Lees Wood

Gorsty Piece

The Woodlands Farm

South Farm Cottage

The South Farm

Arbury Farm

Park Lane Primary School

Tower Farm

North Lodge Farm

Park Farm

Temple House

Moat

Mill

Coton Lawn Farm

The Lawn

Lawn House

Dennis Farm

Tea House

The Nuneaton Academy

Alderman Smith Sports Centre

Stockingford Prim. Sch.

Sports Ground Club

Prim. Sch.

Recreation Ground

Values Academy

A **B** **C** **D** **E**
1 **2** **3** **4** **5** **6** **7**

ANSLEY   B4112   ROAD   ARBURY   ROAD

ASTLEY

B4102

29

NEW ROAD

Sole End Farm

Soar End

RABBIT LANE

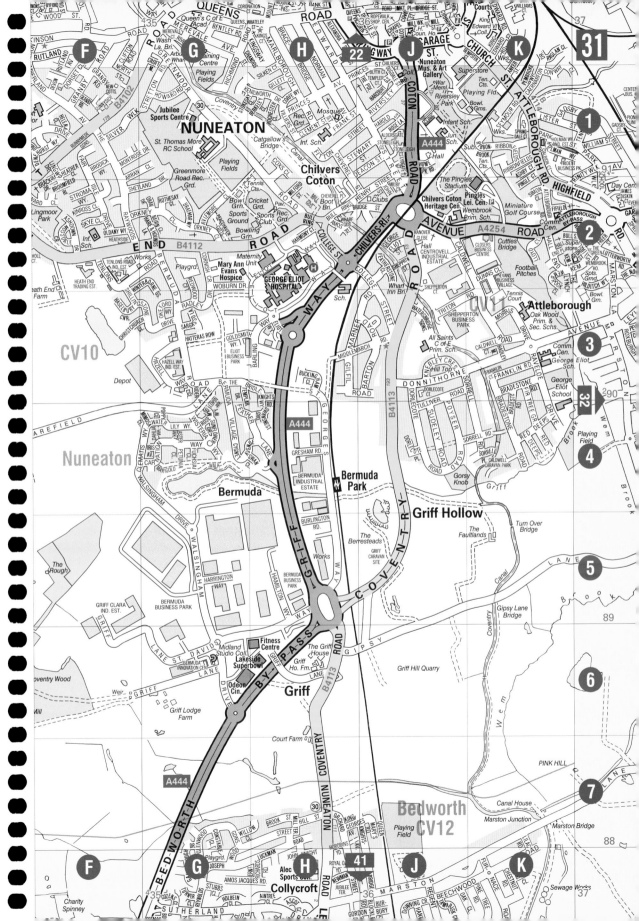

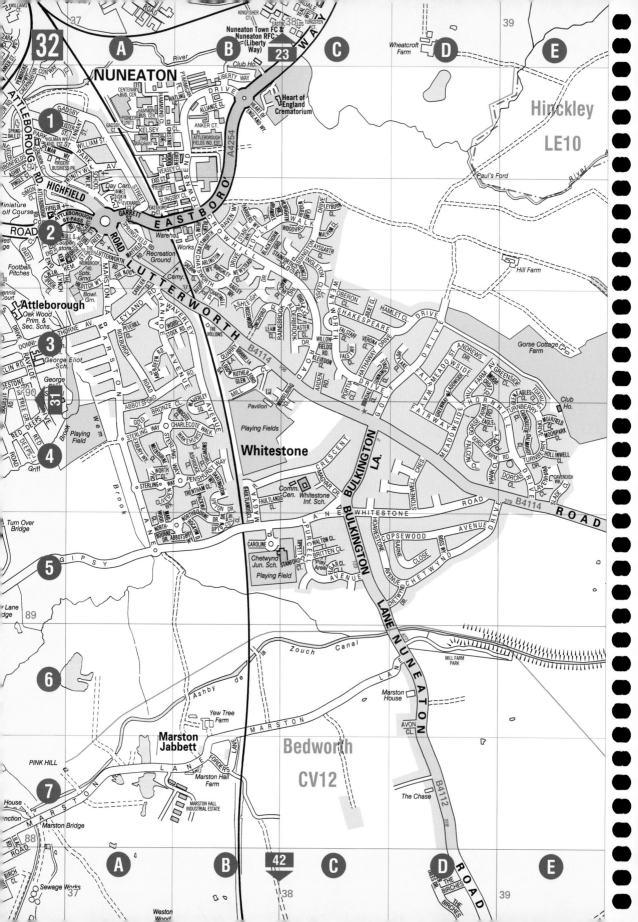

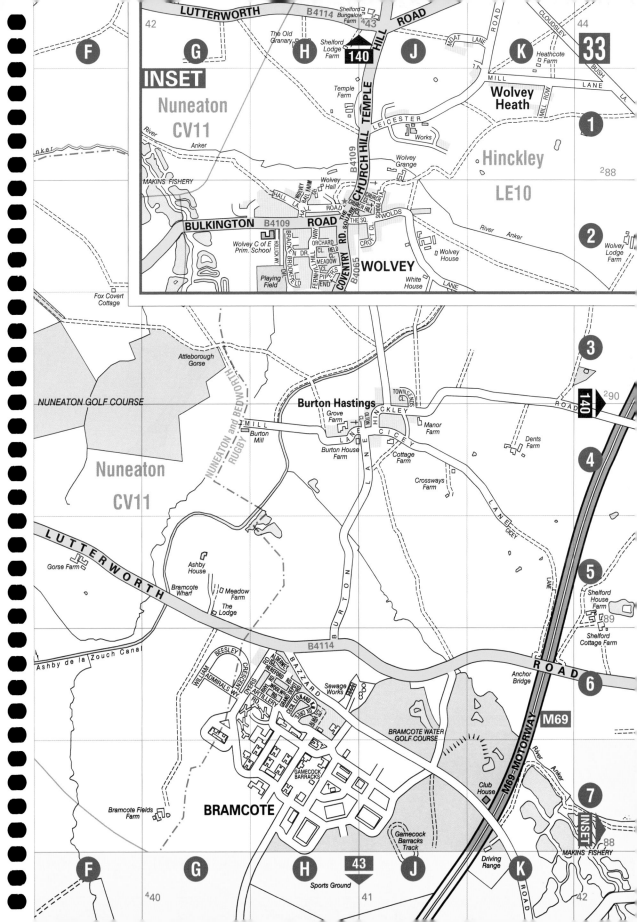

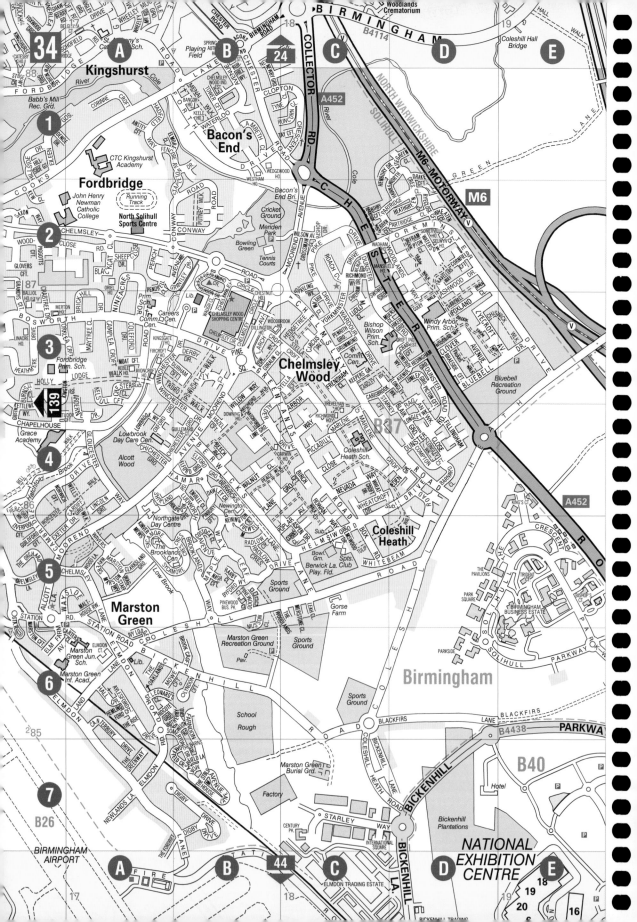

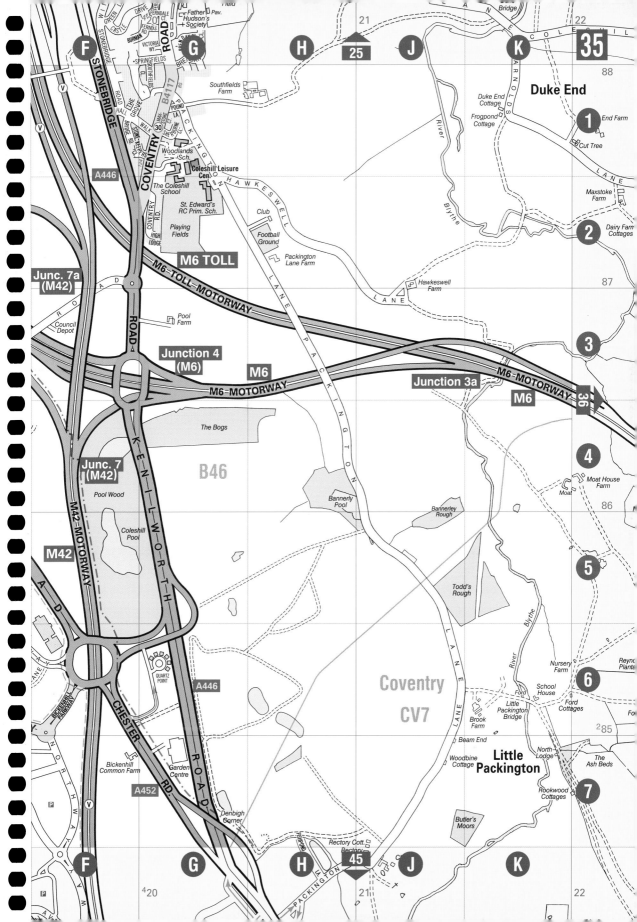

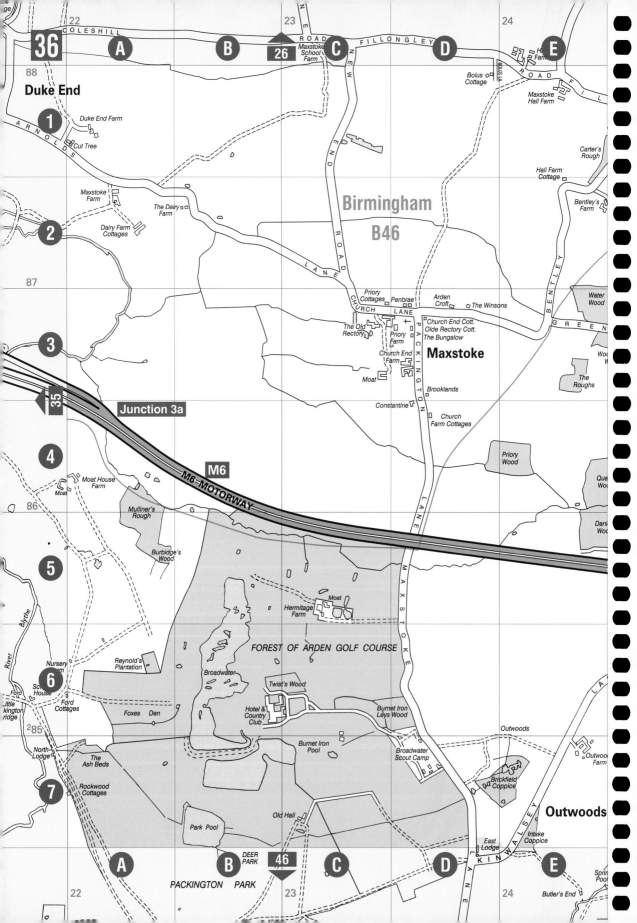

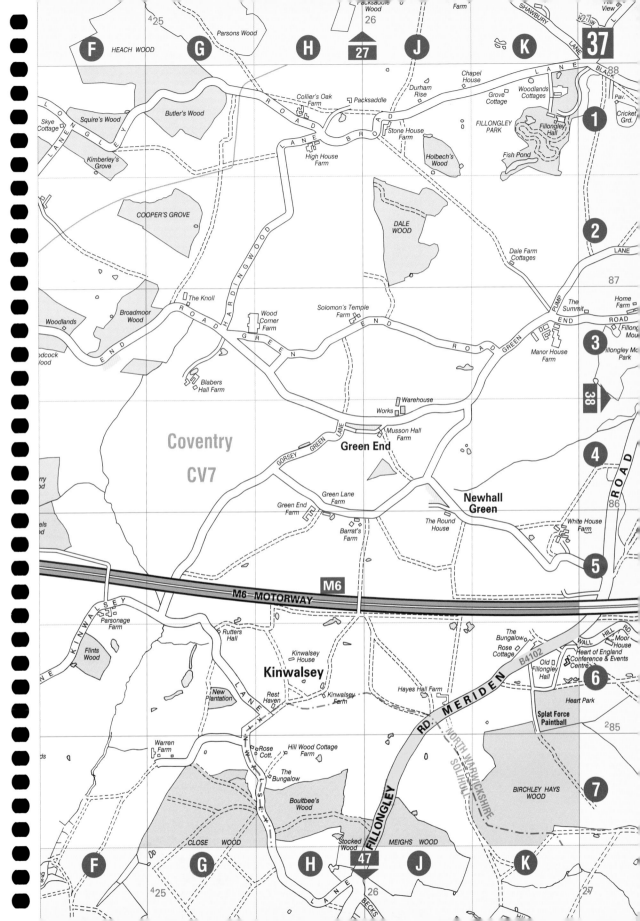

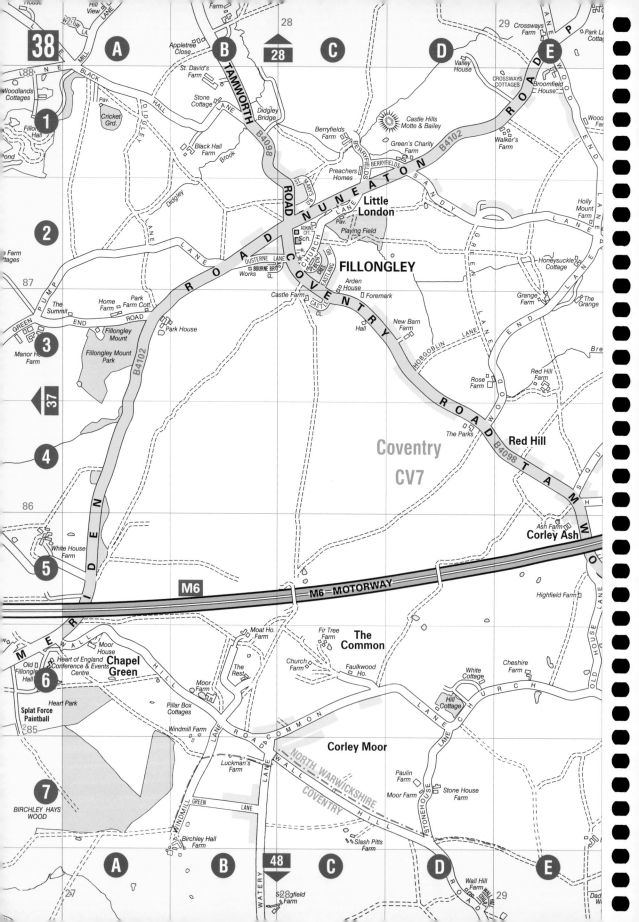

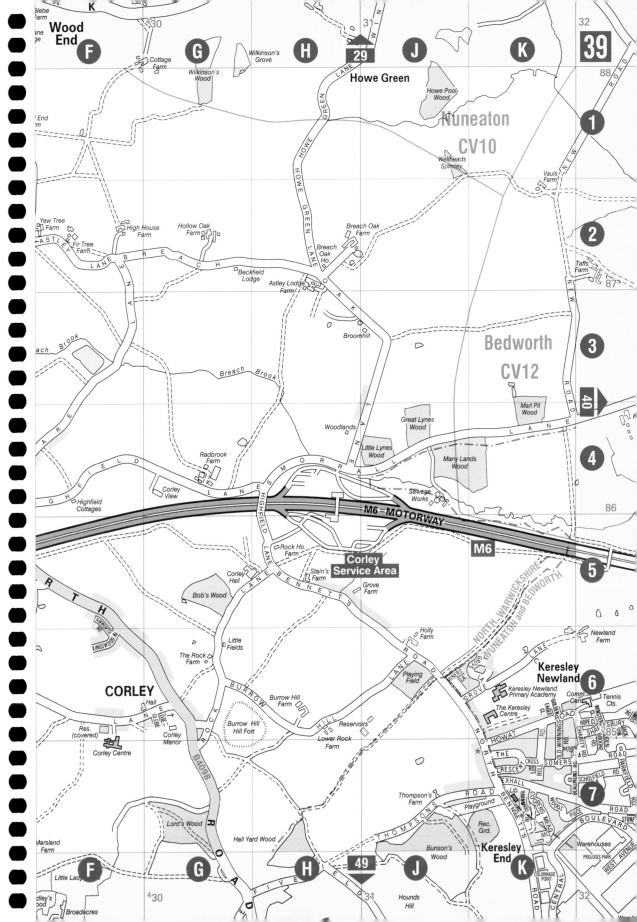

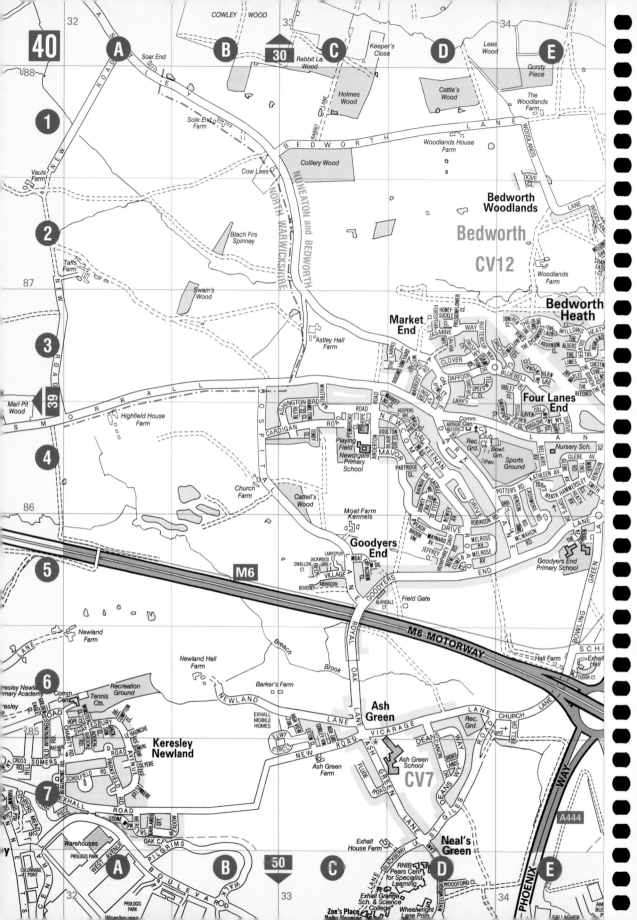

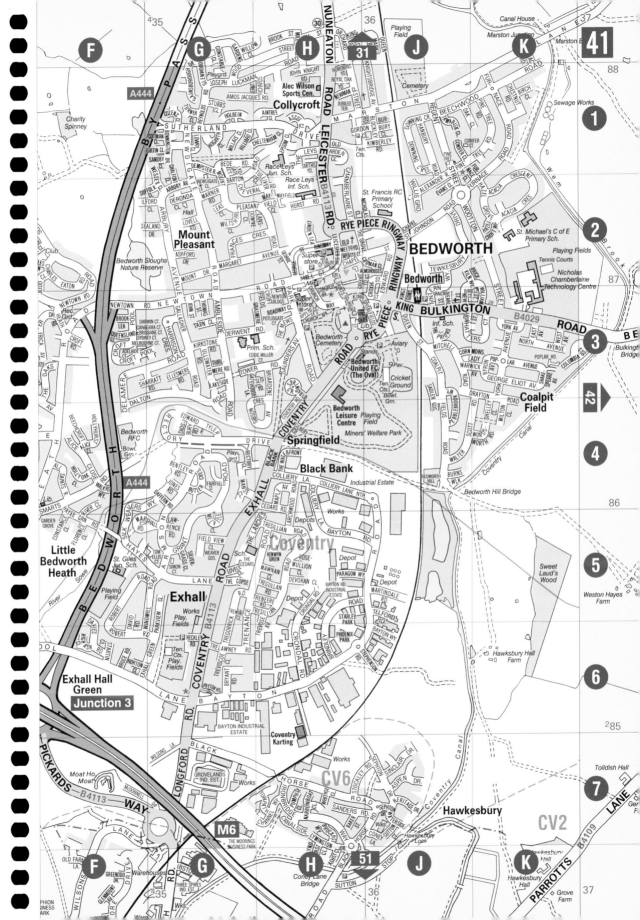

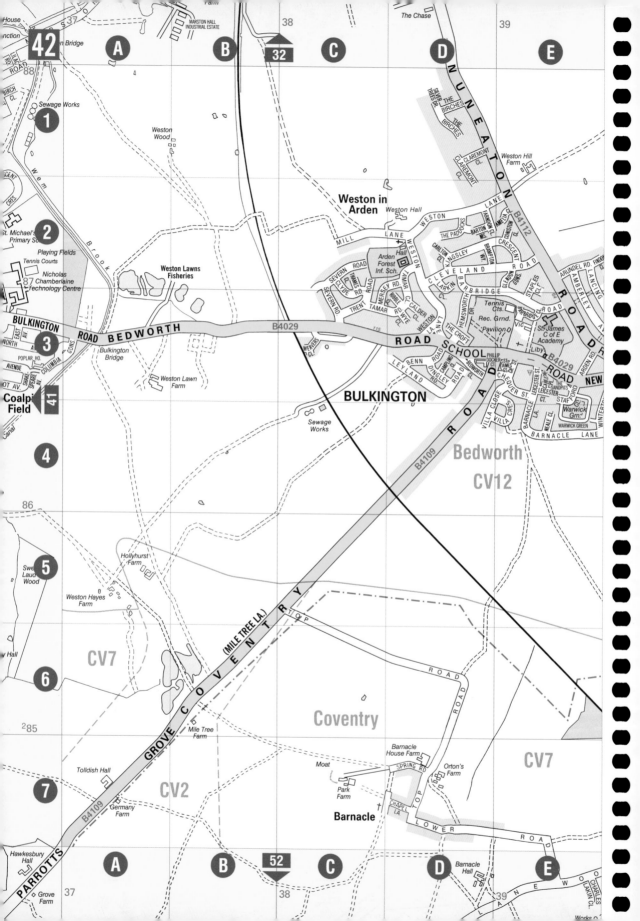

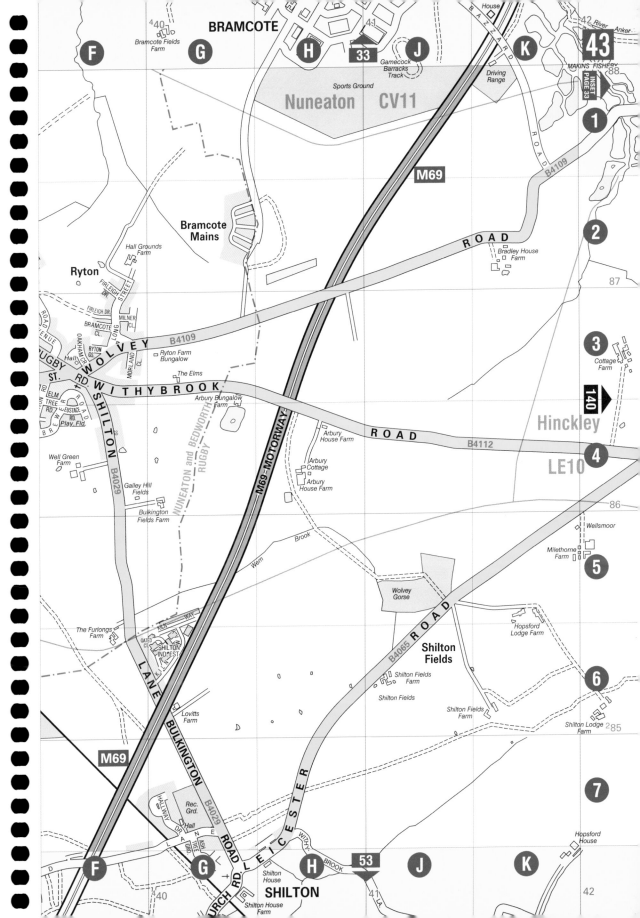

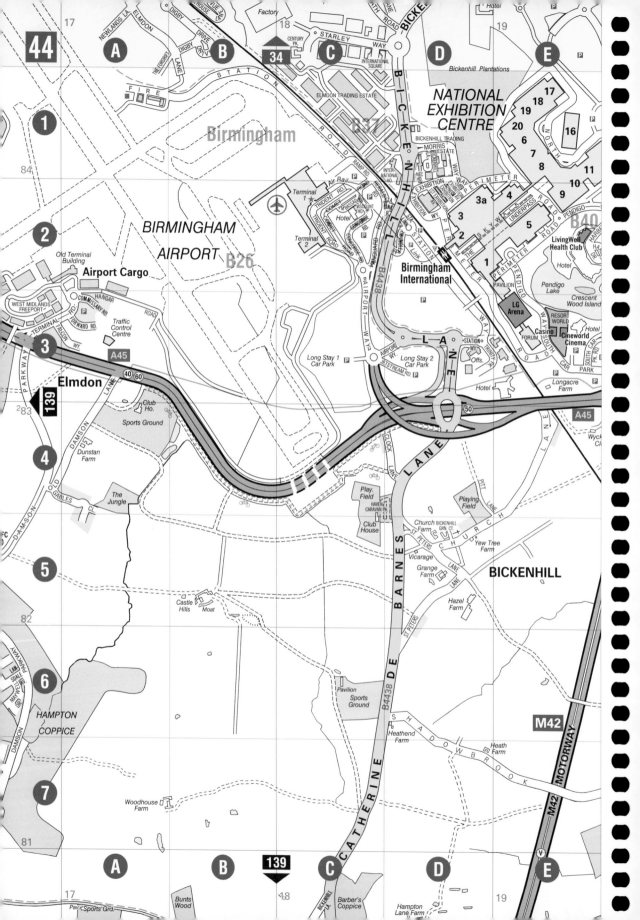

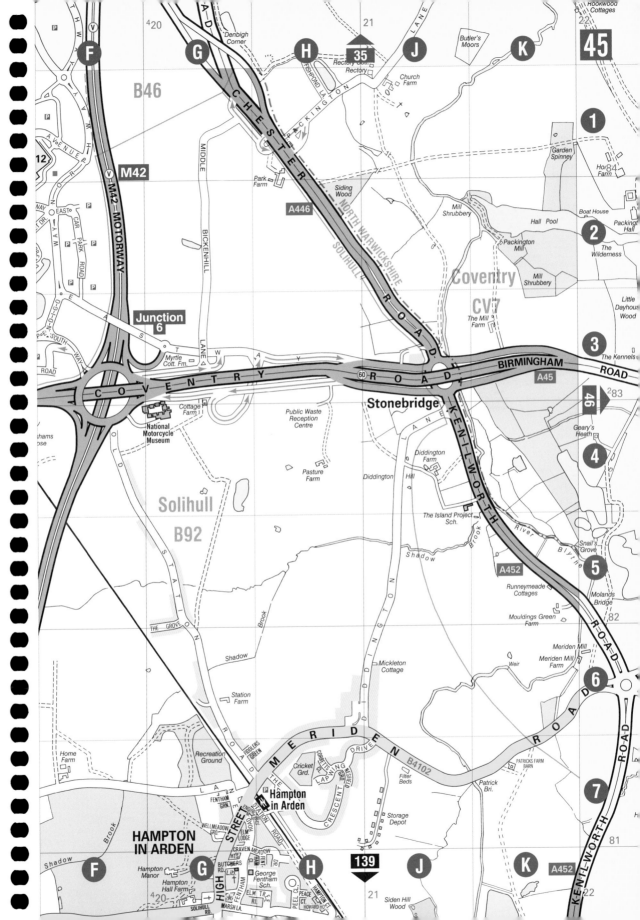

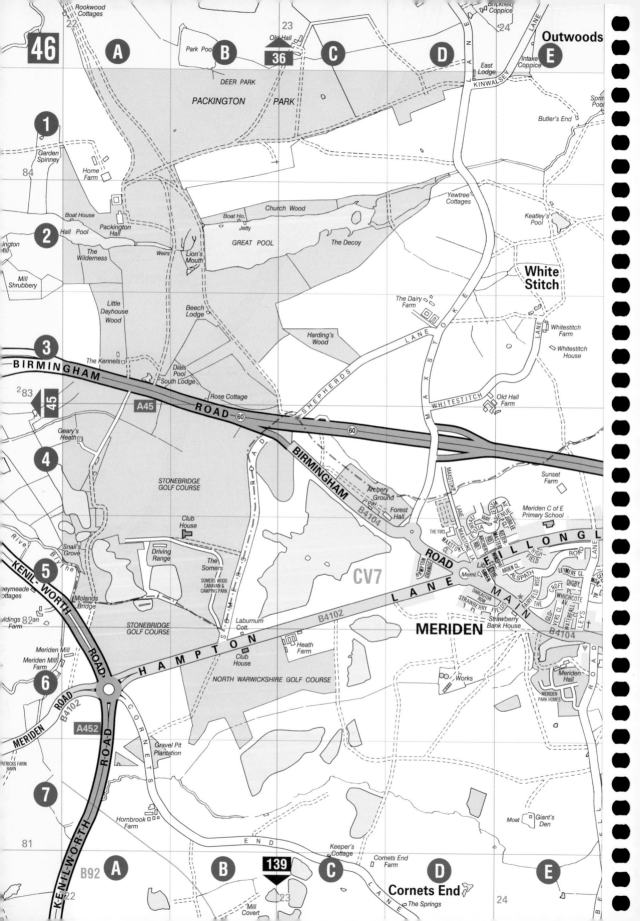

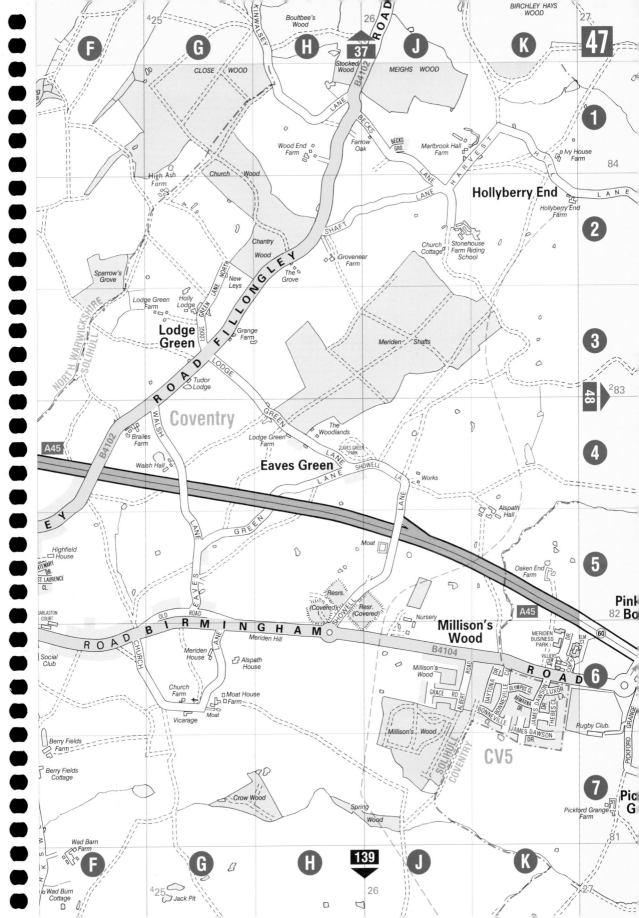

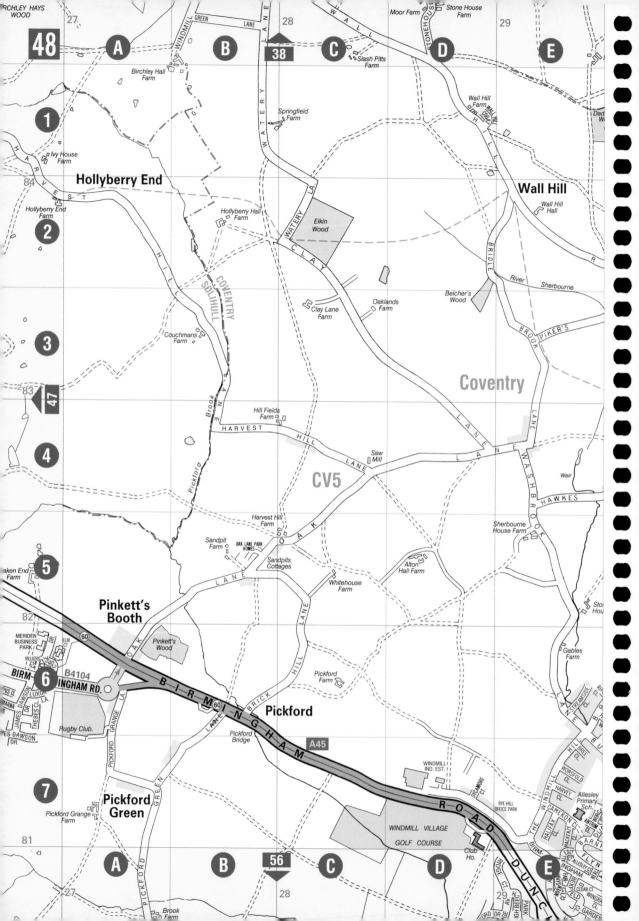

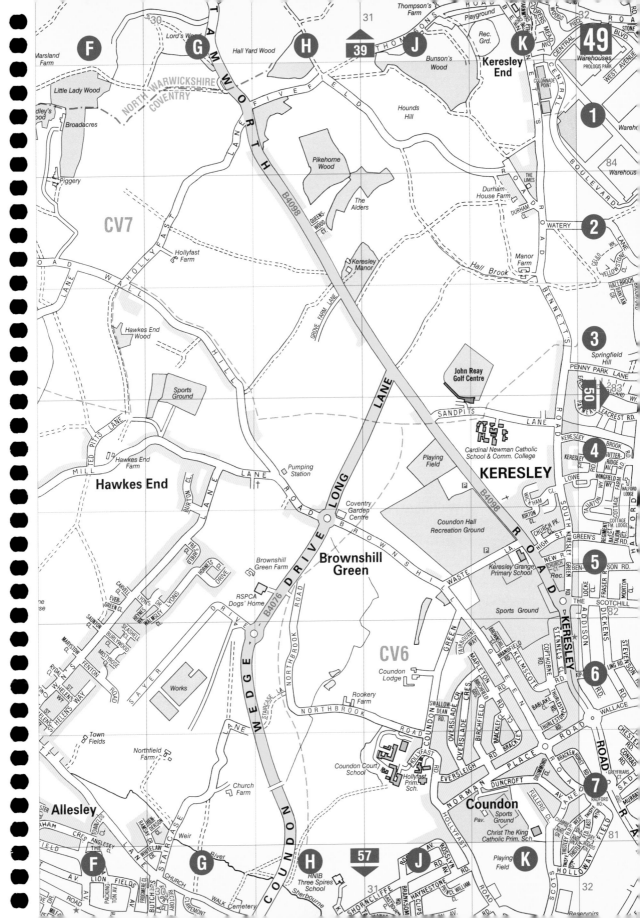

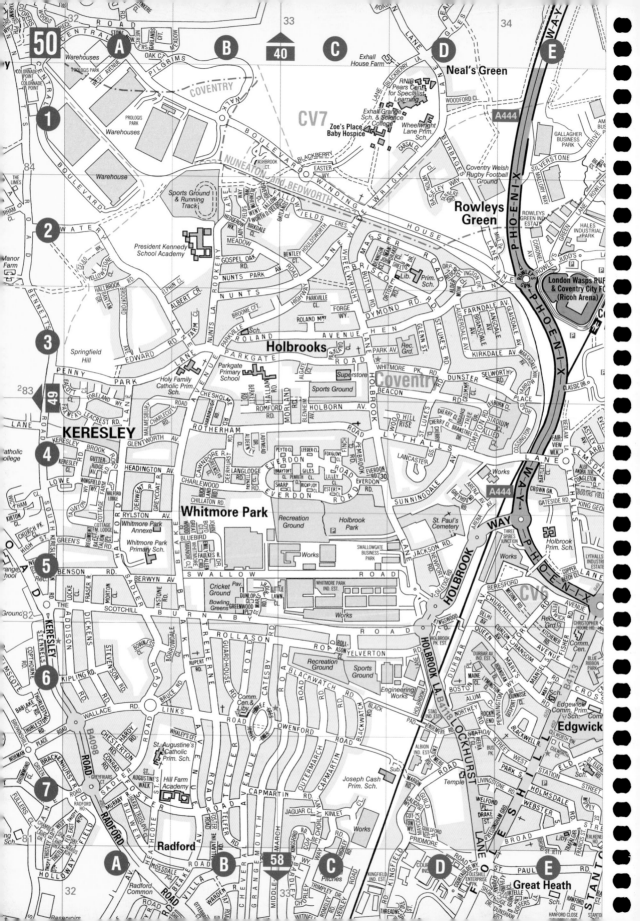

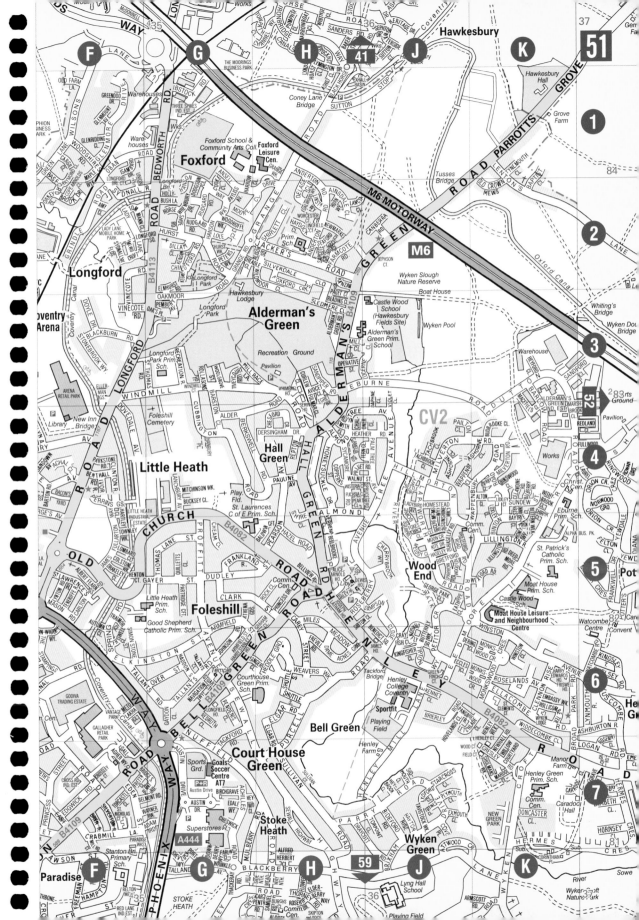

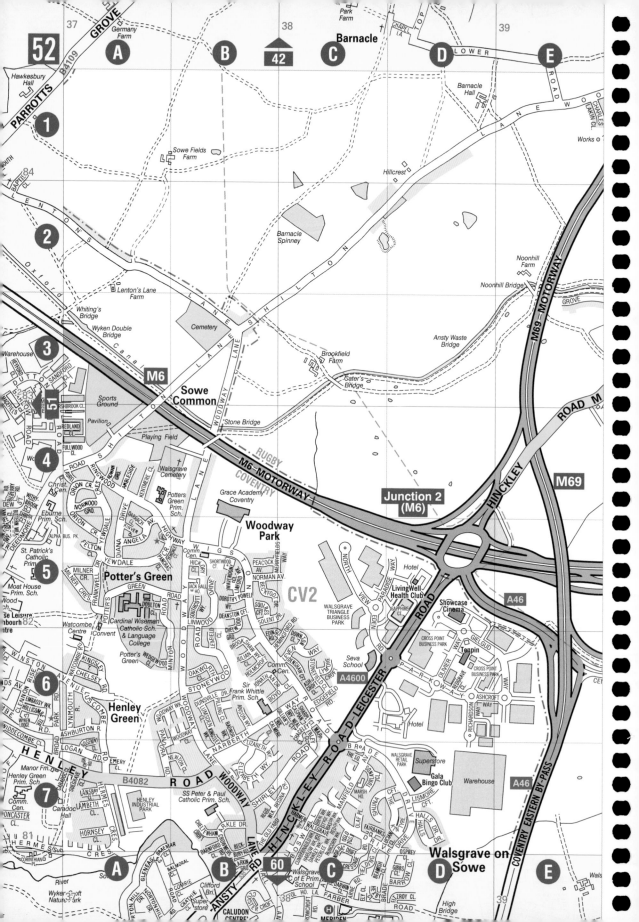

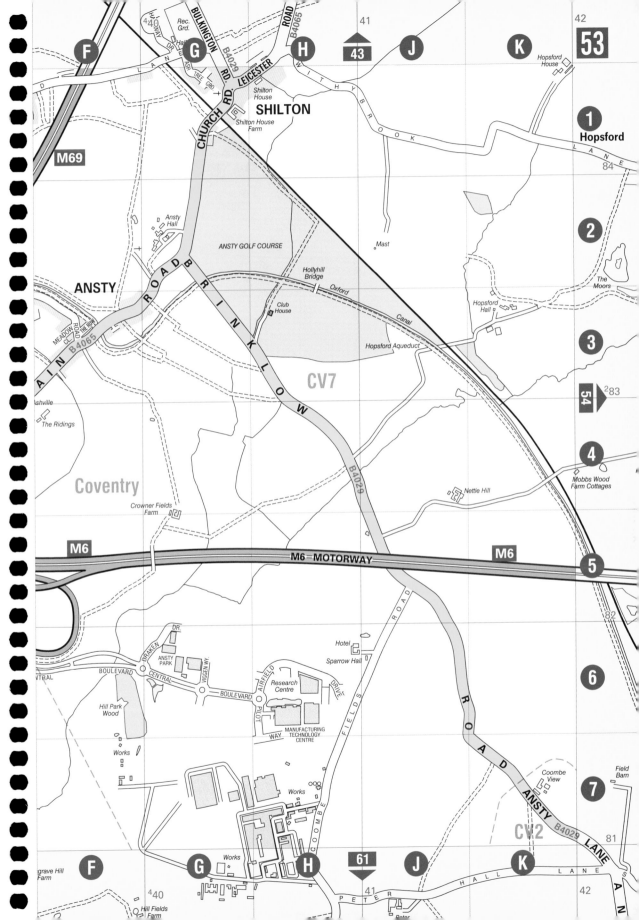

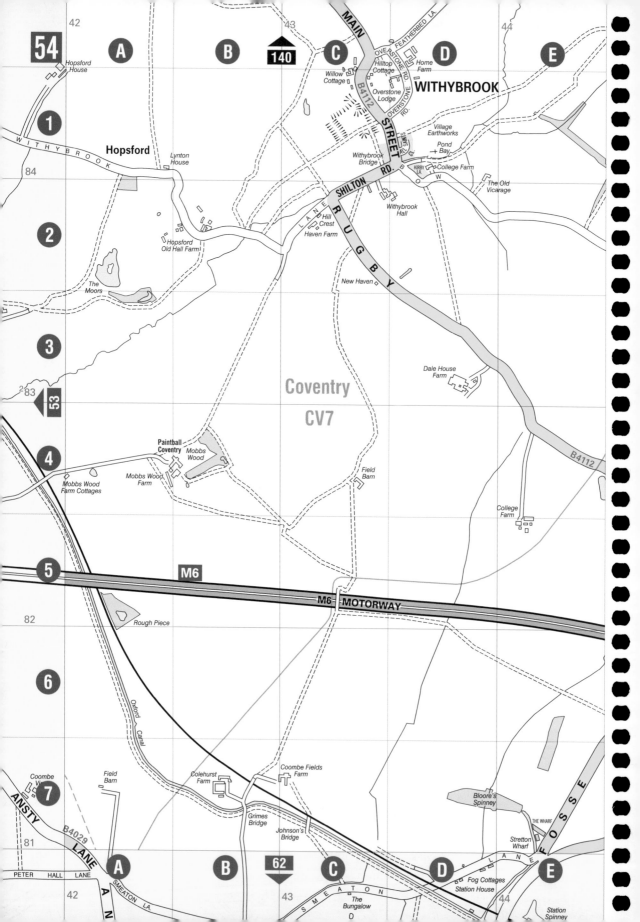

54

42 · 43 · ▲ 140 · 44

A · B · C · D · E

Hopsford House

WITHYBROOK

FEATHERBED LA.

Willow Cottage

Hilltop Cottage

OVERSTONE RD.

Home Farm

Overstone Lodge

1

WITHYBROOK

Hopsford

84

Lynton House

Withybrook Bridge

Village Earthworks

Pond Bay

KIRBY LA.

College Farm

MAIN STREET

OVERSTONE RD.

The Old Vicarage

SHILTON RD.

2

Hill Crest

Haven Farm

Withybrook Hall

Hopsford Old Hall Farm

The Moors

New Haven

RUGBY LANE

3

83

◀ **53**

Dale House Farm

Coventry

CV7

4

Paintball Coventry

Mobbs Wood

Mobbs Wood Farm

Field Barn

College Farm

Mobbs Wood Farm Cottages

B4112

5

M6

M6 MOTORWAY

82

Rough Piece

6

Oxford Canal

Field Barn

Coombe Fields Farm

Bloore's Spinney

Coombe Vi..

7

Colehurst Farm

THE WHARF

Stretton Wharf

ANSTY

B4029

LANE

Grimes Bridge

Johnson's Bridge

FOSSE LANE

PETER HALL LANE

SMEATON LA.

A · B · ▼ **62** · C · D · E

42 · 43 · 44

The Bungalow

Fog Cottages

Station House

Station Spinney

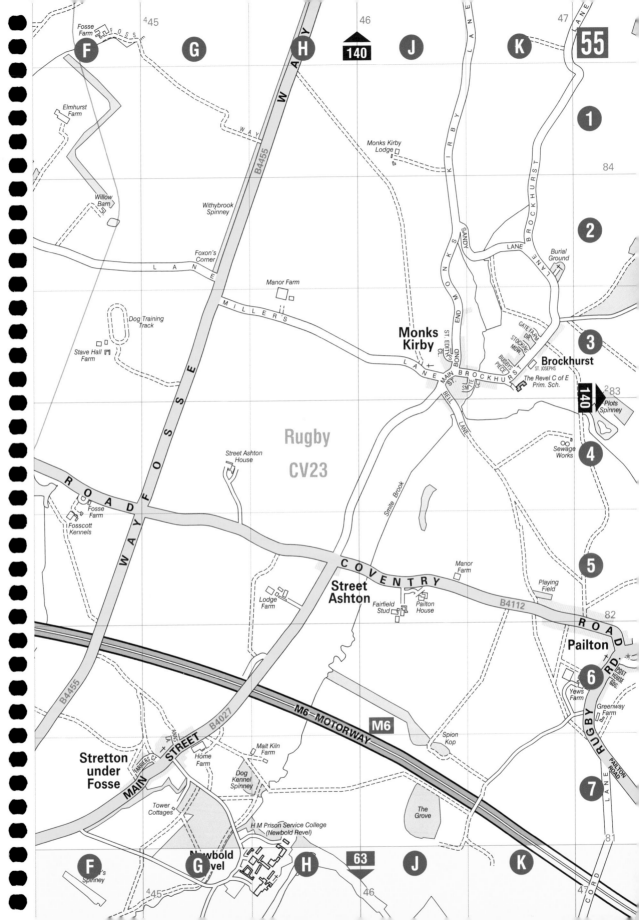

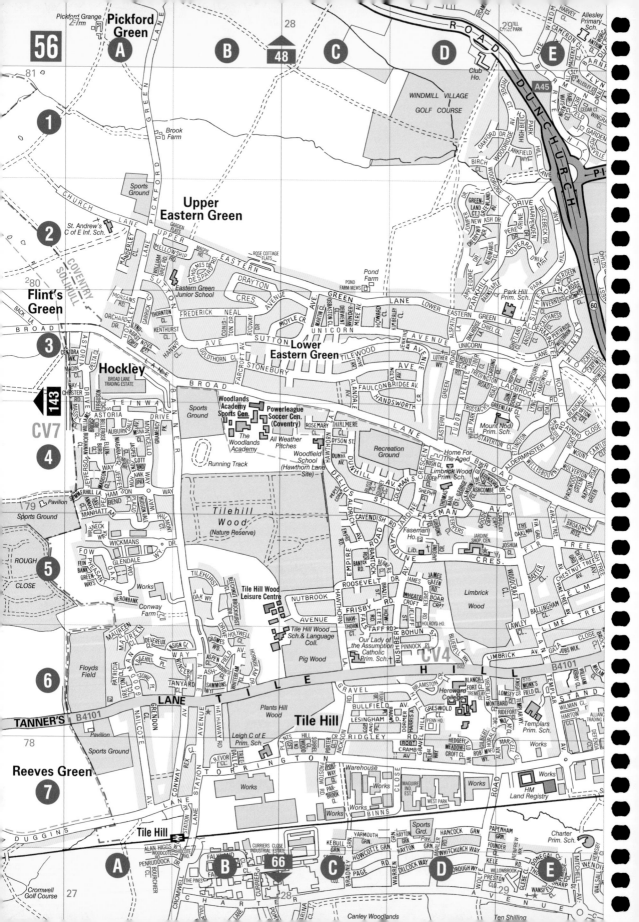

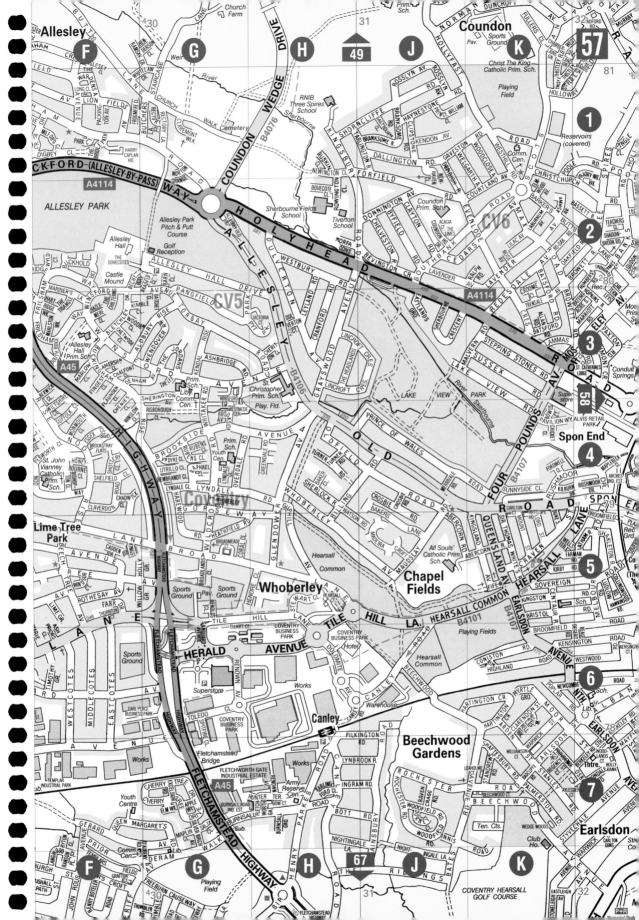

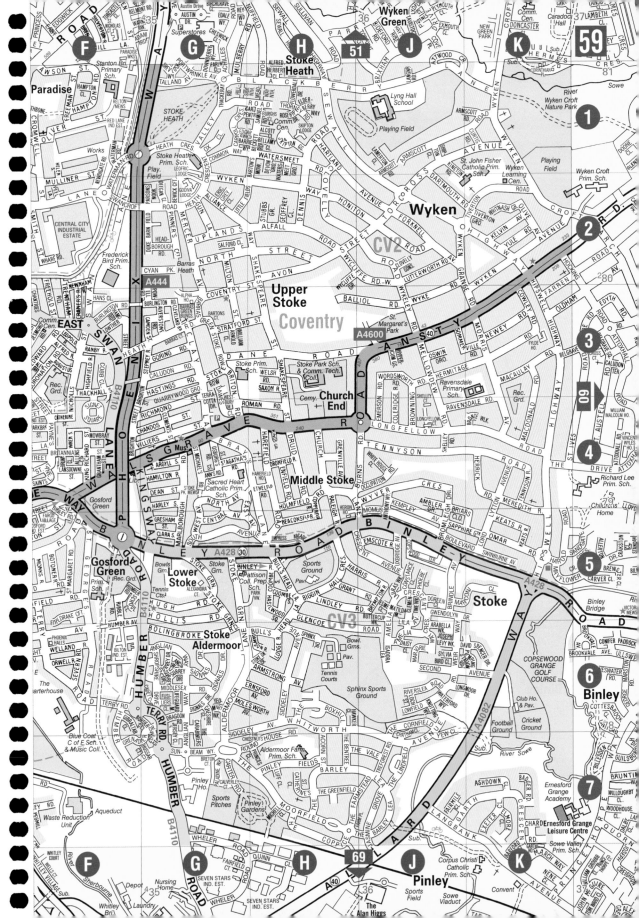

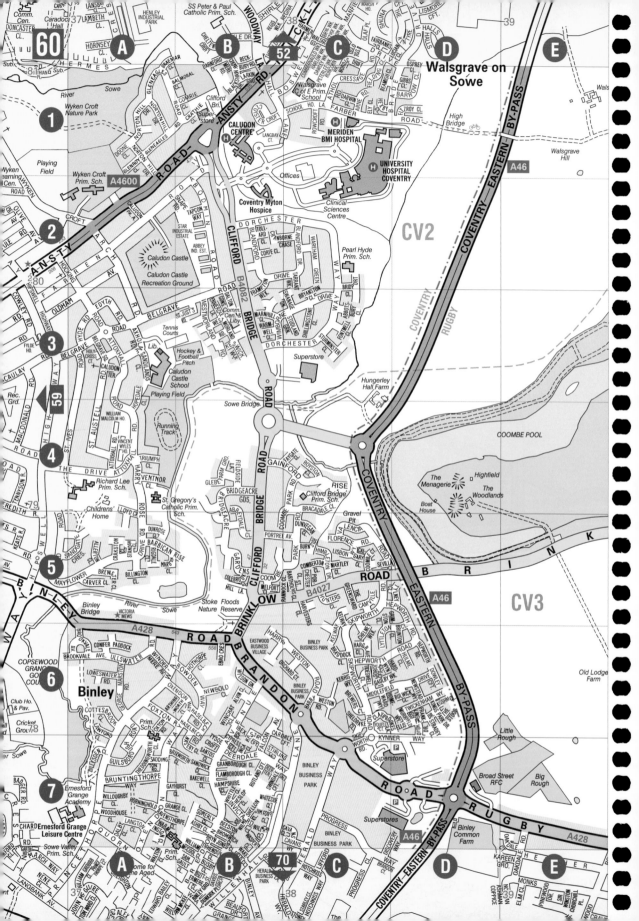

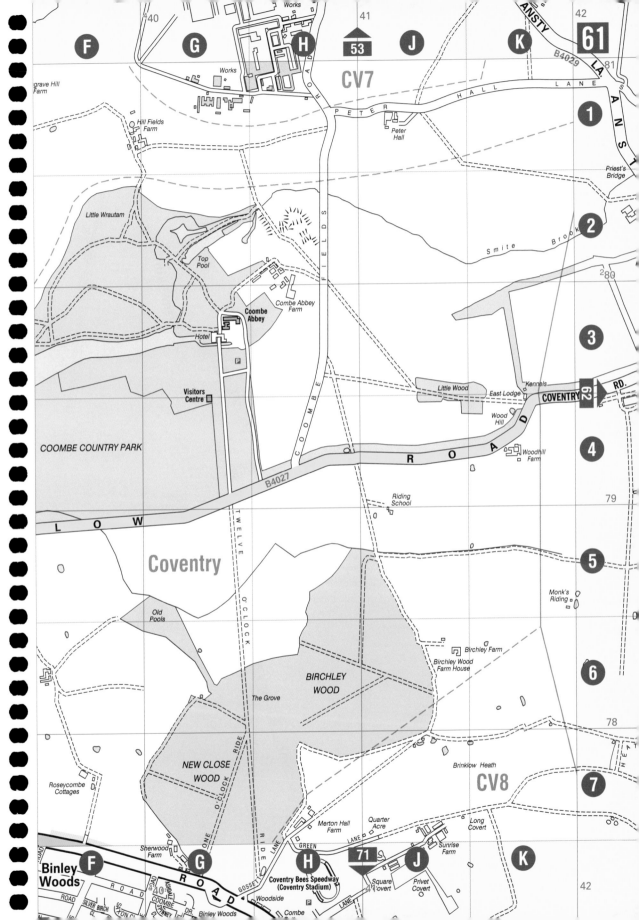

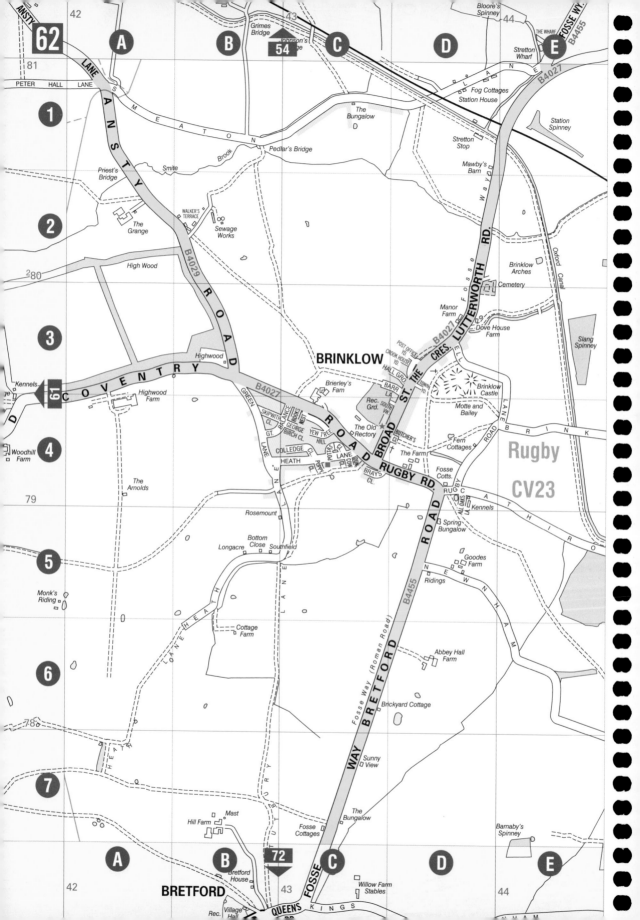

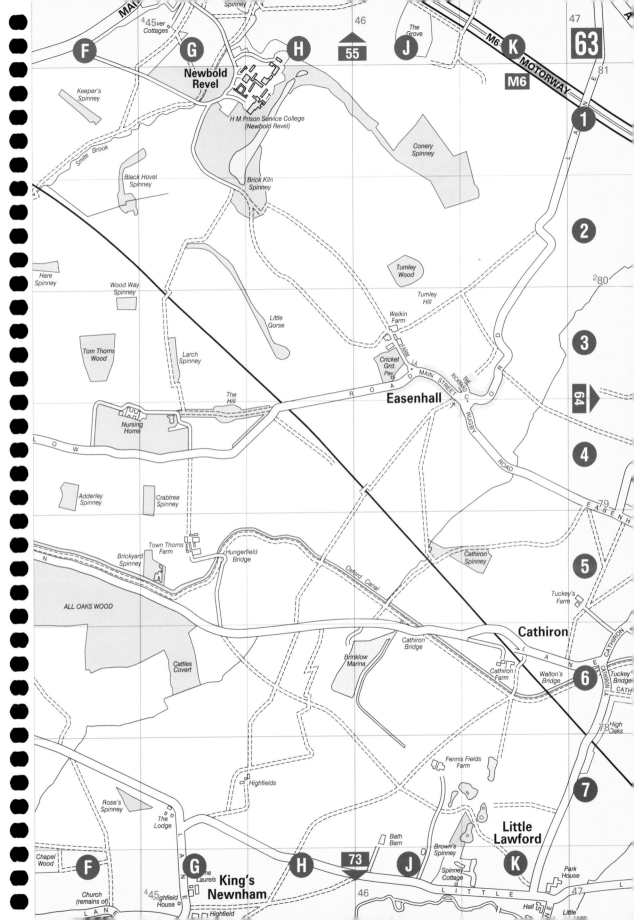

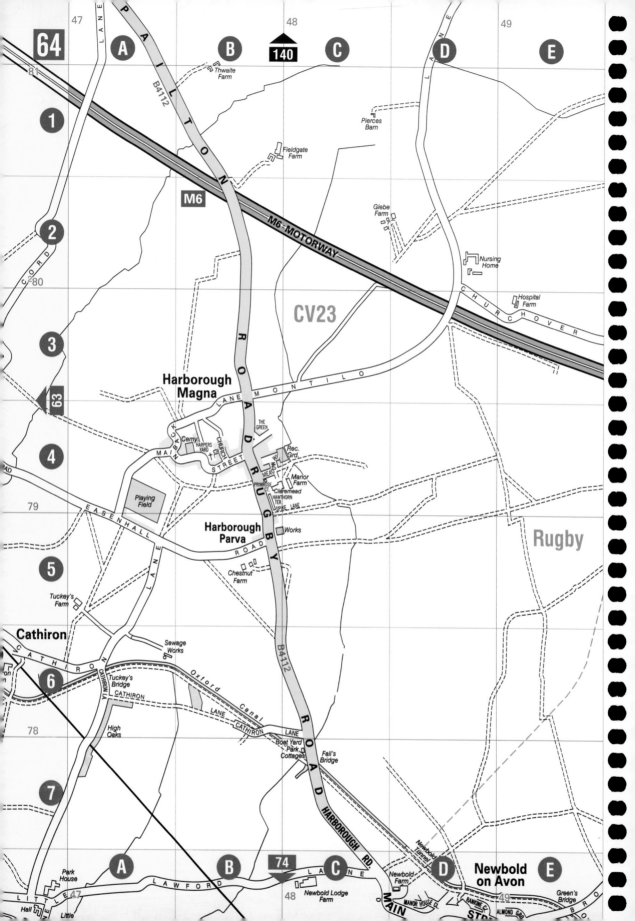

A   **B**   140   **C**   **D**   **E**

1

B4112

M6

M6-MOTORWAY

2

C-ORD

80

CV23

3

63

Harborough
Magna

LANE MONTILO

CHURCHOVER

Thwaite
Farm

Fieldgate
Farm

Pierces
Barn

Glebe
Farm

Nursing
Home

Hospital
Farm

4

BACK

CHURCH CL.

HARPERS
YARD

Cerny

MAIN STREET

THE
GREEN

Rec.
Grd.

MEAD

Manor
Farm

PRIMROSE

Claremead

HAWTHORN
TER.

SPIKE LANE

79

EASENHALL

Playing
Field

Harborough
Parva

ROAD

Works

Rugby

5

Chestnut
Farm

Tuckey's
Farm

LANE

RUGBY

B4112

6

Cathiron

CATHIRON

CATHIRON

Tuckey's
Bridge

CATHIRON

Sewage
Works

Oxford Canal

LANE

CATHIRON   LANE

Boat Yard
Park
Cottages

Fall's
Bridge

78

High
Oaks

ROAD

7

HARBOROUGH RD.

Newbold
Tunnel

Newbold
Farm

A   **B**   74   **C**   **D**   **E**

Park
House

LAWFORD

47   48   49

Hall

Little   Little

Newbold Lodge
Farm

MAIN

MANOR HOUSE CL.

RANINE CL.

ALMOND GR.

Newbold
on Avon

Green's
Bridge

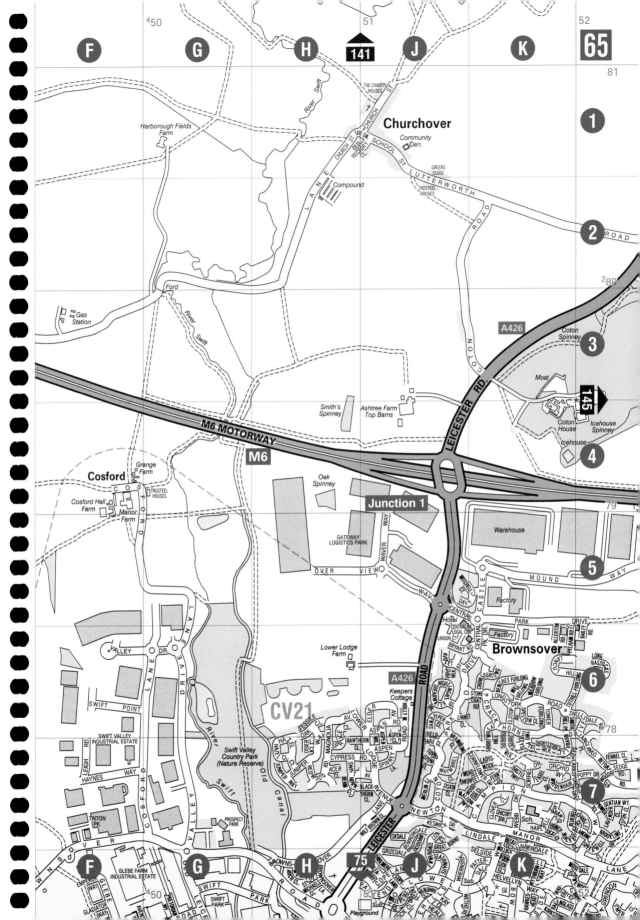

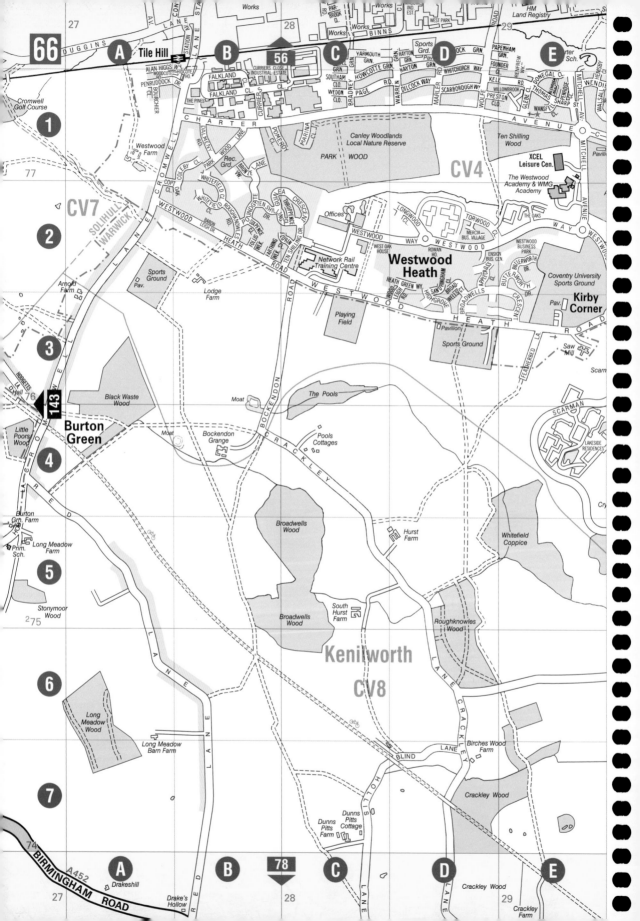

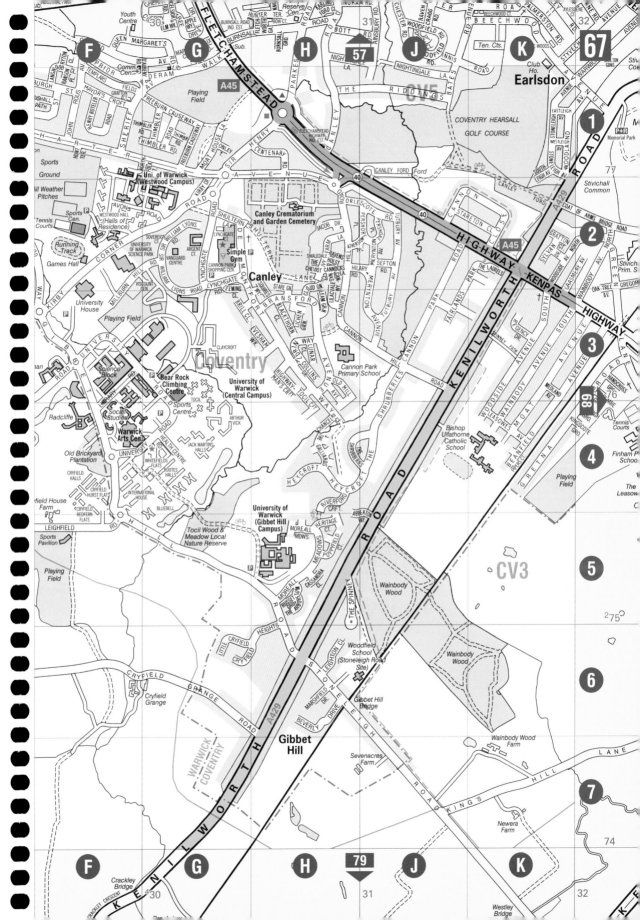

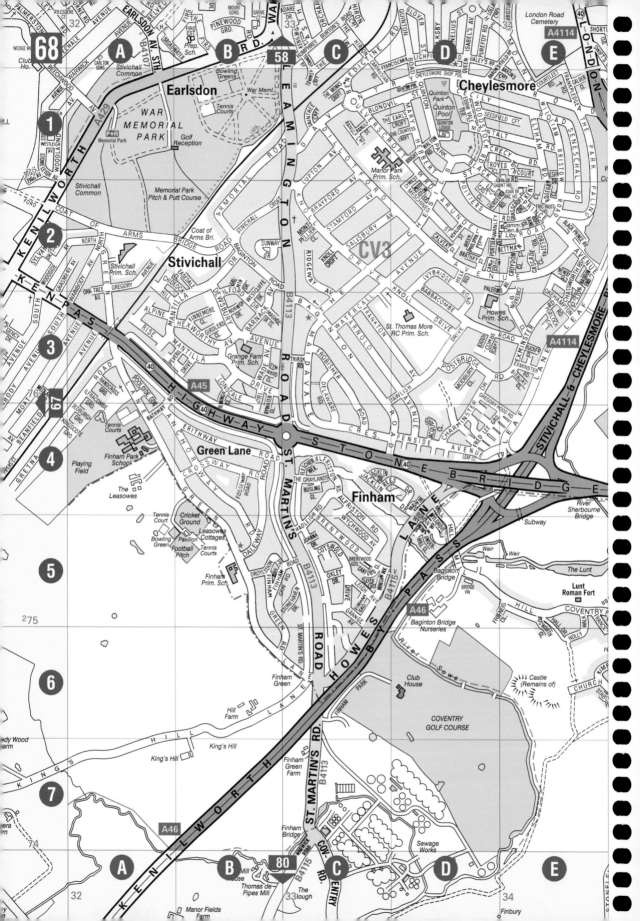

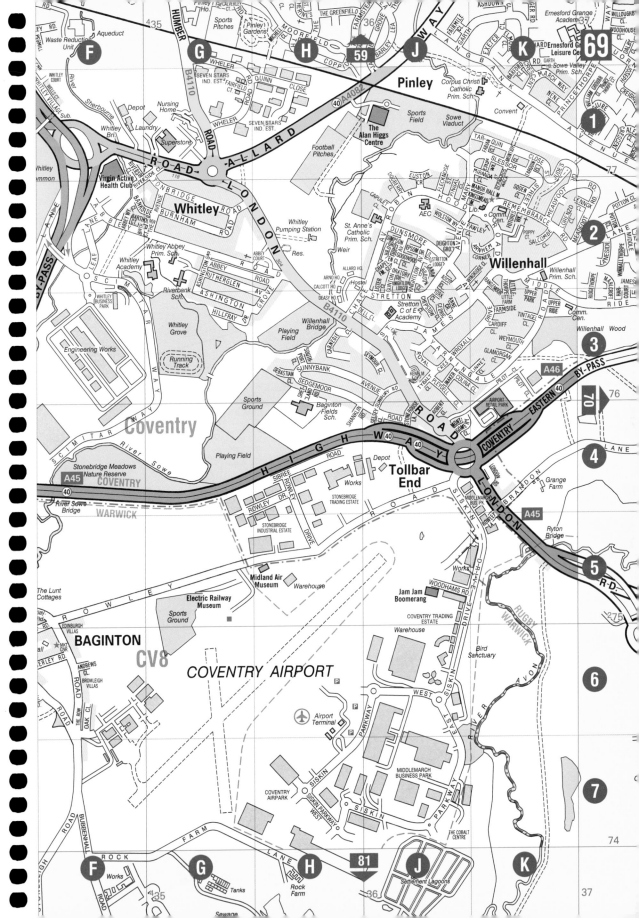

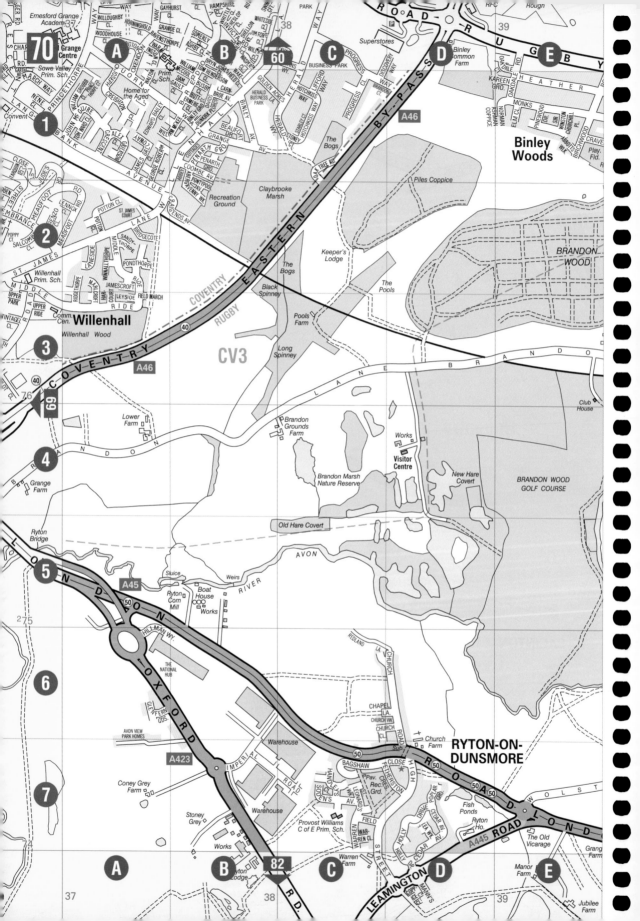

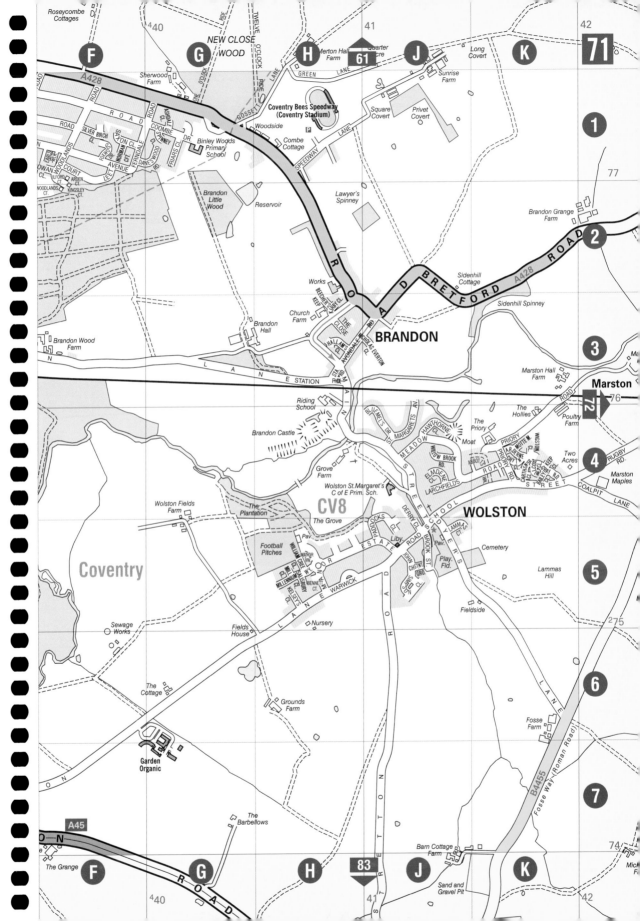

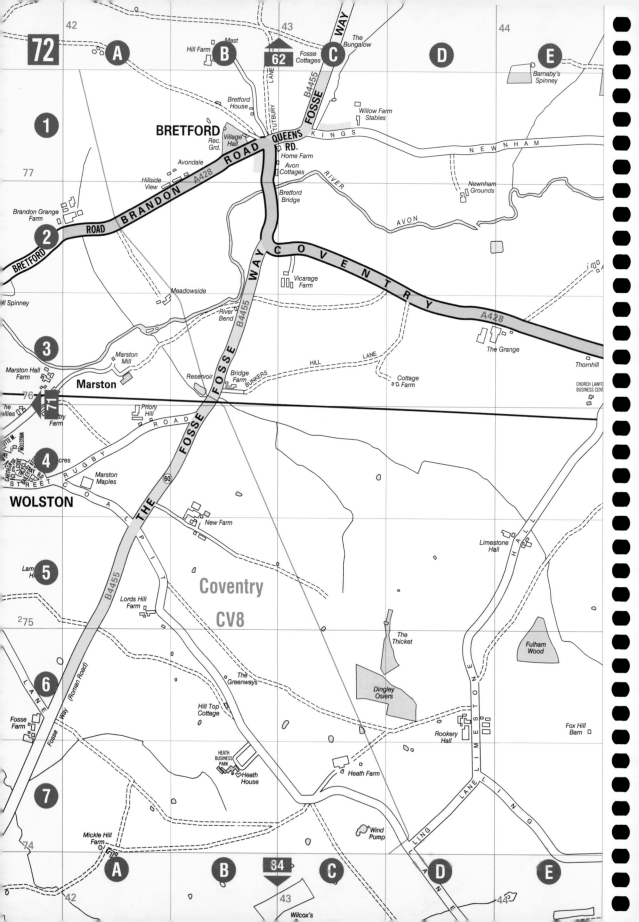

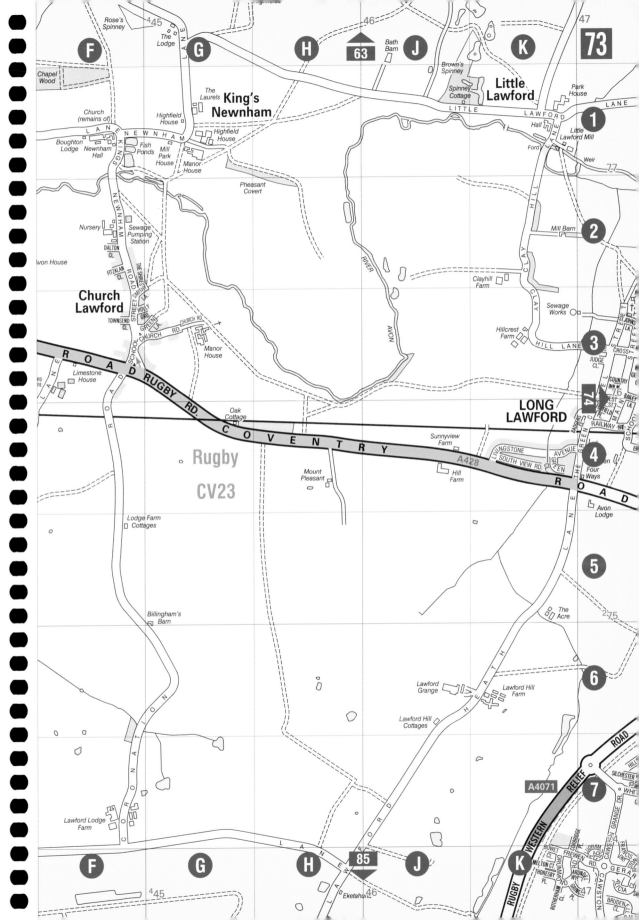

F **G** **H** 63 Bath Barn **J** **K**

Rose's Spinney
The Lodge
45
46
47

Chapel Wood

Brown's Spinney
Spinney Cottage

Little Lawford

Park House

The Laurels
King's Newnham

Church (remains of)

Highfield House

Highfield House

LITTLE LAWFORD LANE

LANE

Boughton Lodge
Newnham Hall

Fish Ponds

Mill Park House

Manor House

NEWNHAM

KINGS

Hall

Little Lawford Mill

Ford

Weir

77

1

Pheasant Covert

Nursery

Sewage Pumping Station

DALTON CL

FITZALAN CL

RIVER

AVON

CLAY HILL

Mill Barn

Clayhill Farm

Sewage Works

2

Avon House

Church Lawford

ROAD

THE SHRUBS

SMITH'S LA

HOLLY GRO

TOWNSEND CL

SCHOOL

STREET

GREEN LA

CHURCH RD.

CHURCH ROAD

Manor House

Hillcrest Farm

HILL LANE

CLAY

JUDGE CL

COUNTRY INN LA

MAIN STREET

ST JOHNS LA

CROSS FIELD

BAILEY

3

76

74

Limestone House

LANE

ROAD

Rugby

CV23

RUGBY RD.

COVENTRY

Oak Cottage

Mount Pleasant

Sunnyview Farm

Hill Farm

A428

LIVINGSTONE

SOUTH VIEW RD.

THE GREEN

LANE

AVENUE

RAILWAY ST.

BADGERS CFT

LONG LAWFORD

SCHOOL

ROAD

Four Ways

4

Avon Lodge

Lodge Farm Cottages

5

The Acre

275

Billingham's Barn

CAVENDISH LANE

Lawford Grange

HEATH

LANE

Lawford Hill Farm

Lawford Hill Cottages

6

ROAD

Lawford Lodge Farm

NEW

LANE

ROAD

RELIEF

WESTERN

RUGBY

SILCHESTER

A4071

7

BOWET

CONINGSBY

FREWEN

COMBROOK

CAWSTON

GRANGE DR

ROTHERHAM

MELTON CT

THORESBY

ARUNDEL

LUDHAM

AGER

FRANCIS RD

GERA

CAWSTON

BRUDEN

F **G** **H** 85 **J** **K**

45
46
47

Eketahuna

Rugby

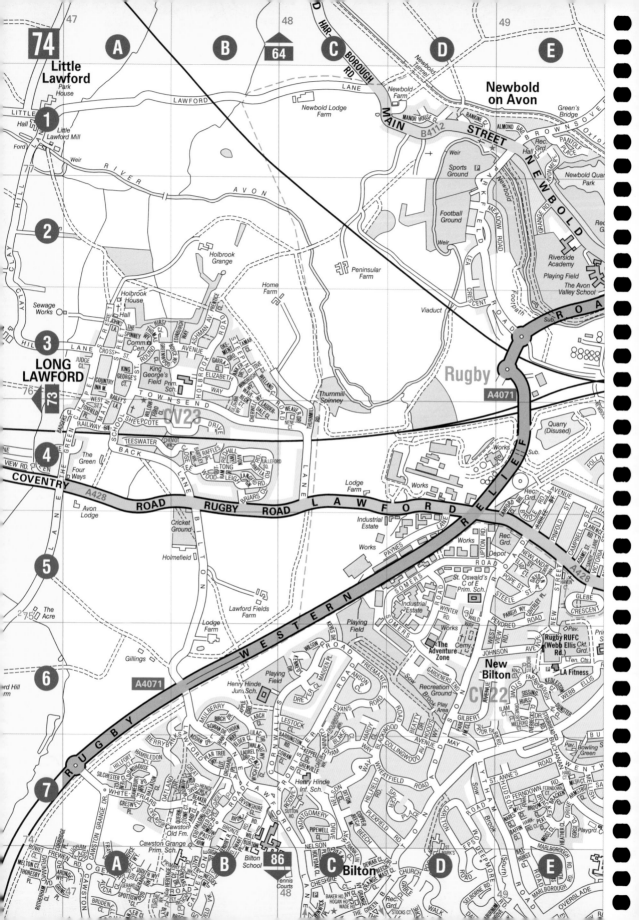

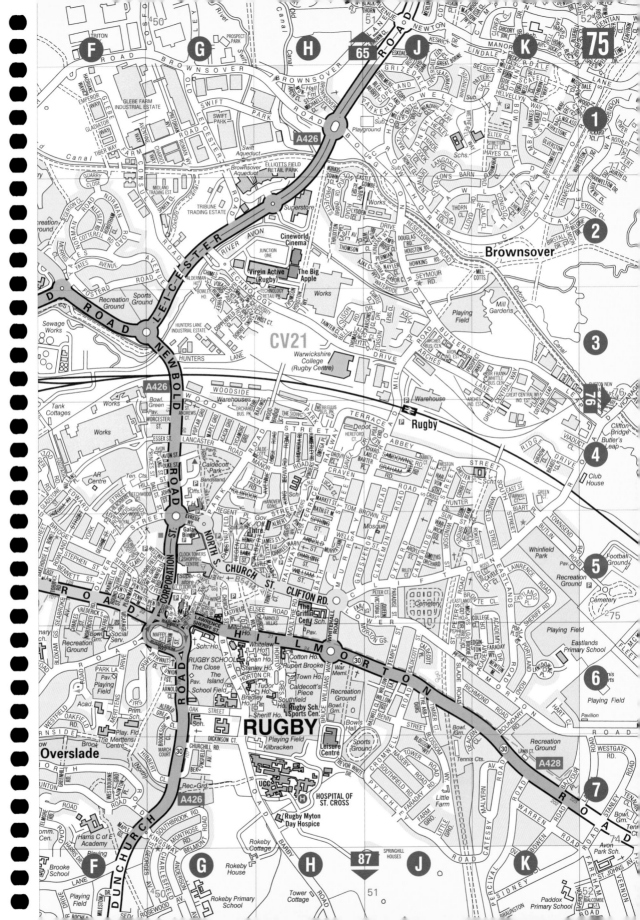

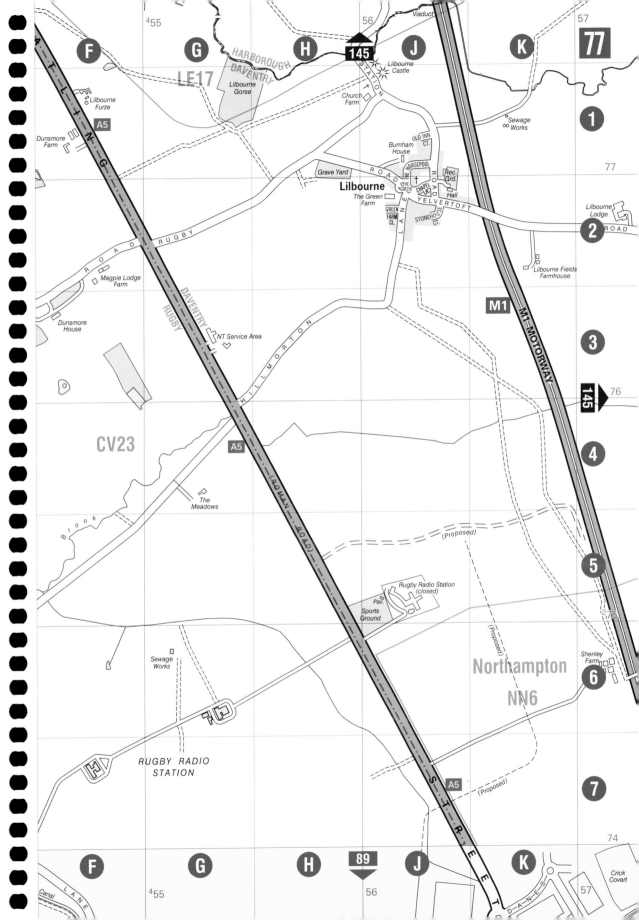

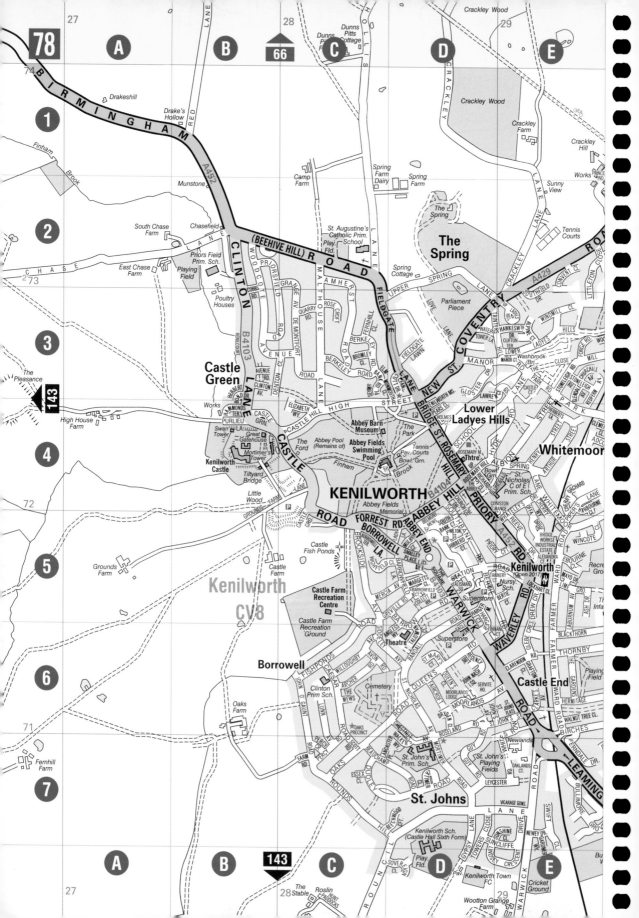

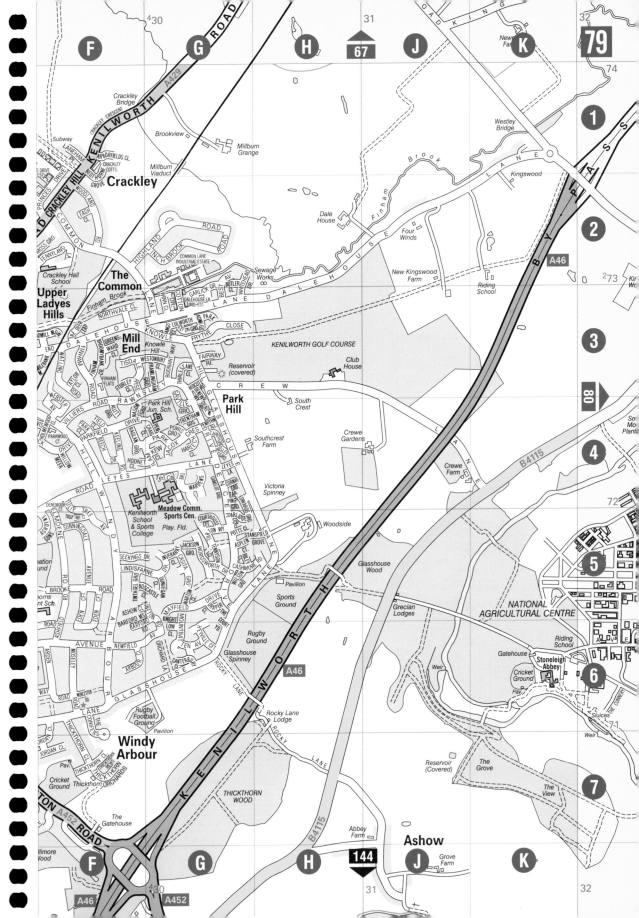

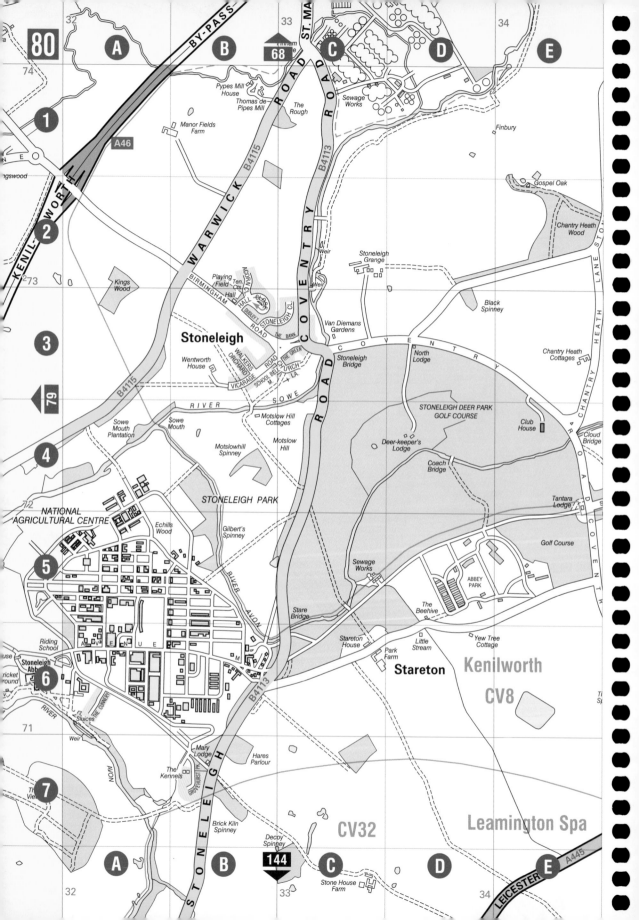

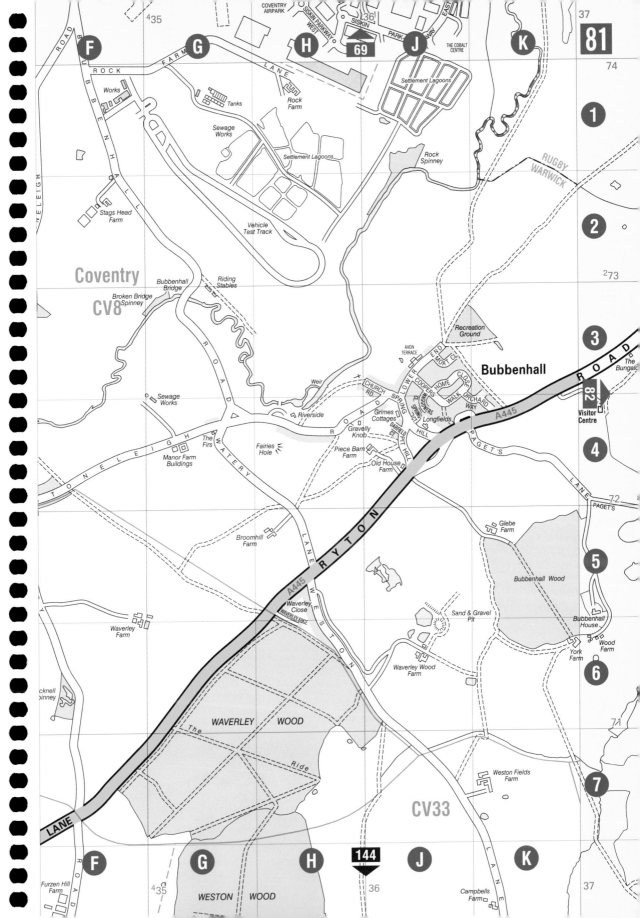

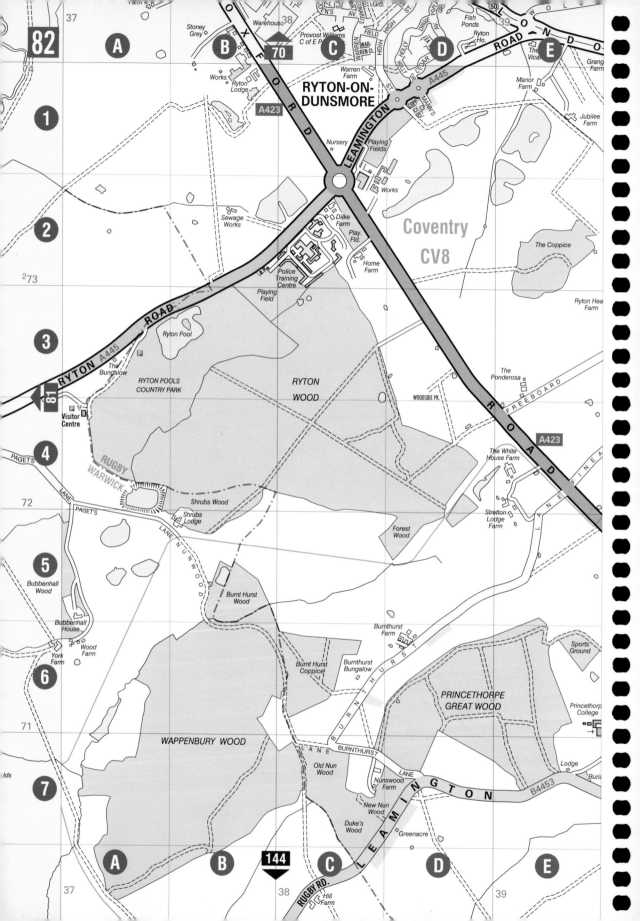

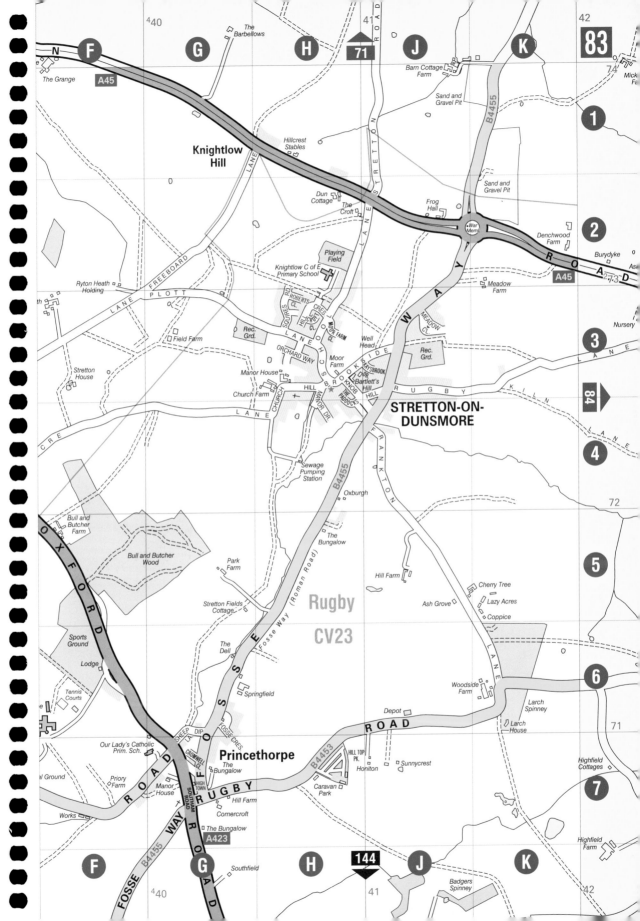

N

F **G** **H** 71 **J** **K**

74

1

The Grange

The Barbellows

A45

The Grange

Knightlow
Hill

Hillcrest
Stables

Barn Cottage
Farm

Sand and
Gravel Pit

STRETTON LANE

ROAD

Mick
Fa

2

Dun
Cottage

The
Croft

Frog
Hall

Sand and
Gravel Pit

War
Mem.

Denchwood
Farm

Burydyke

A45 273

Ash

Playing
Field

Knightlow C of E
Primary School

Meadow
Farm

FREEBOARD LANE

PLOTT LANE

Ryton Heath
Holding

ROBERTS CL.

SQUIRES LANE

HILLCRES CL.

MOOR FARM

Well
Head

Meadow
Cl.

Rec.
Grd.

WAYSIDE

MEADOW
CL.

3

Nursery

KILN LANE

Field Farm

Rec.
Grd.

ORCHARD WAY

Moor
Farm

BROOK

MAYBROOK

RUGBY

84

Stretton
House

CRE

Manor House

Church Farm

HILL

CHURCH LA.

MANOR DR.

THE PADDOCKS

Bartlett's
Hill

KNOB HILL

STRETTON-ON-
DUNSMORE

4

72

Sewage
Pumping
Station

Oxburgh

FRANKTON LANE

B4455

5

Bull and
Butcher
Farm

Bull and Butcher
Wood

Park
Farm

The
Bungalow

Hill Farm

Cherry Tree

Lazy Acres

Coppice

Ash Grove

Fosse Way (Roman Road)

FOSSE WAY

OXFORD

Rugby
CV23

Sports
Ground

Lodge

Stretton Fields
Cottage

The
Dell

Tennis
Courts

Springfield

Woodside
Farm

Larch Spinney

6

71

Depot

ROAD

Larch
House

Our Lady's Catholic
Prim. Sch.

SHEEP LA.

FOSSE CRES.

DIP

CROMWELL CL.

Princethorpe

The
Bungalow

B4453

HILL TOP
PK.

Honiton

Sunnycrest

Highfield
Cottages

7

al Ground

Priory
Farm

Manor
House

FOSSE WAY B4455

HIGH
TOWN

SOUTHAM ROAD

RUGBY

Hill Farm

Cornercroft

Caravan
Park

Highfield
Farm

Works

ROAD A423

The Bungalow

F **G** Southfield **H** 144 **J** **K**

Badgers
Spinney

440 41 42

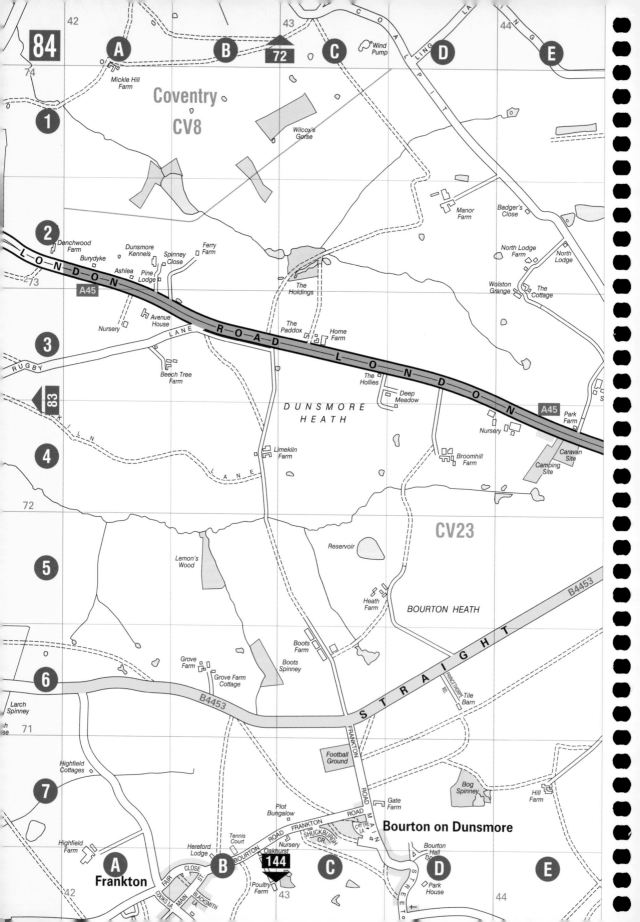

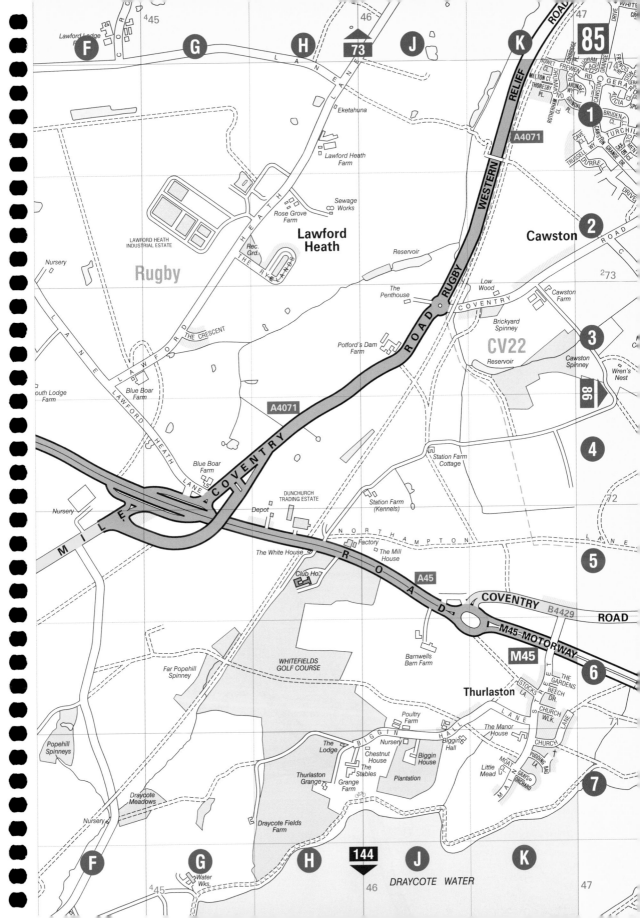

F
G
H
73
J
K

45
46
47

Lawford Lodge

Lawford Heath
Farm

Eketahuna

Sewage
Works

Rose Grove
Farm

A4071

1

**Lawford
Heath**

Nursery

LAWFORD HEATH
INDUSTRIAL ESTATE

Rec.
Grd.

THE RYELANDS

Reservoir

Cawston

2

Rugby

273

The Penthouse

Low
Wood

COVENTRY

Cawston
Farm

THE CRESCENT

Potford's Dam
Farm

ROAD

RUGBY

Brickyard
Spinney

CV22

Reservoir

Cawston
Spinney

3

Wren's
Nest

outh Lodge
Farm

Blue Boar
Farm

A4071

COVENTRY

Station Farm
Cottage

86

4

LANE

LAWFORD HEATH

Nursery

Blue Boar
Farm

Dunchurch
Trading Estate

Depot

Station Farm
(Kennels)

72

Nursery

MILEY

NORTHAMPTON

LANE

5

The White House

ROAD

Factory

The Mill
House

A45

COVENTRY

B4429

ROAD

Club Ho.

WHITEFIELDS
GOLF COURSE

M45 MOTORWAY

M45

6

Far Popehill
Spinney

Barnwells
Barn Farm

Thurlaston

THE
GARDENS

BEECH
DR.

CHURCH
WLK.

LANE

STOCKS LA.

STREET

Poultry
Farm

HALL

The Manor
House

CHURCH

Popehill
Spinneys

BIGGIN

The
Lodge

Nursery

Biggin
Hall

Biggin
House

Little
Mead

PUDDING BAG

GRAY'S
ORCHARD

MOAT CL.

PURLING LA.

Draycote
Meadows

Chestnut
House

The
Stables

Plantation

MAIL

LANE

7

Nursery

Thurlaston
Grange

Grange
Farm

Draycote Fields
Farm

Water
Wks.

45
46
DRAYCOTE WATER
47

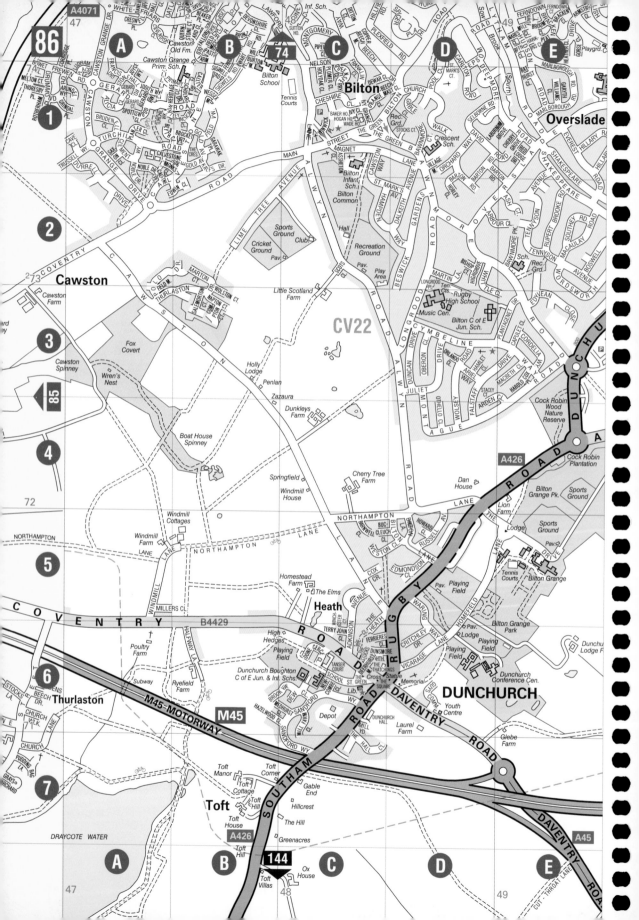

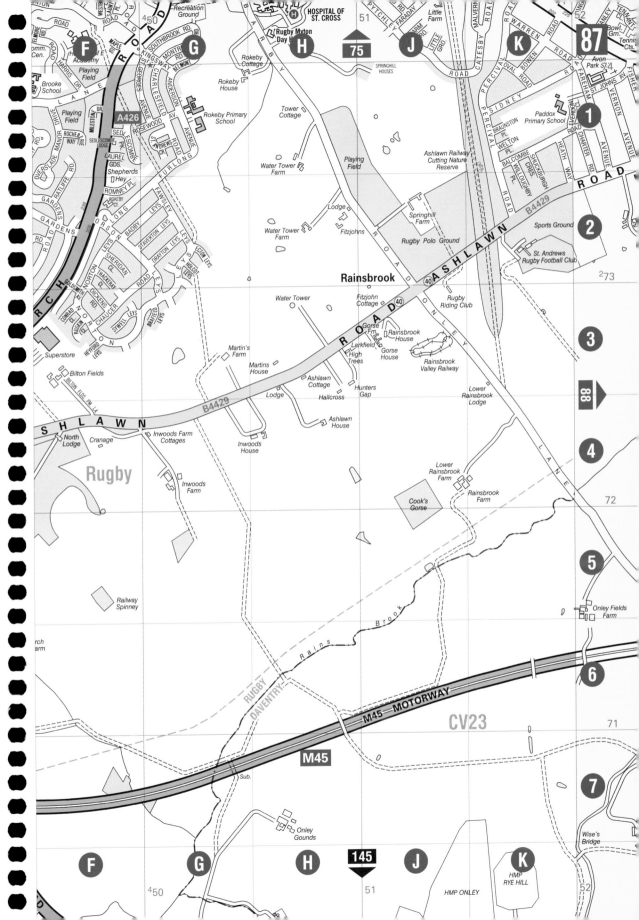

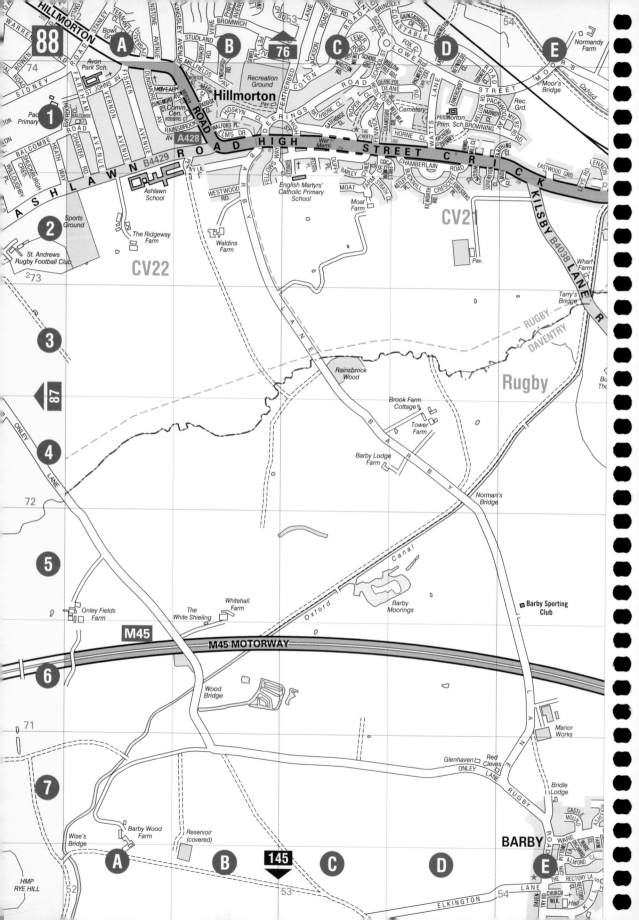

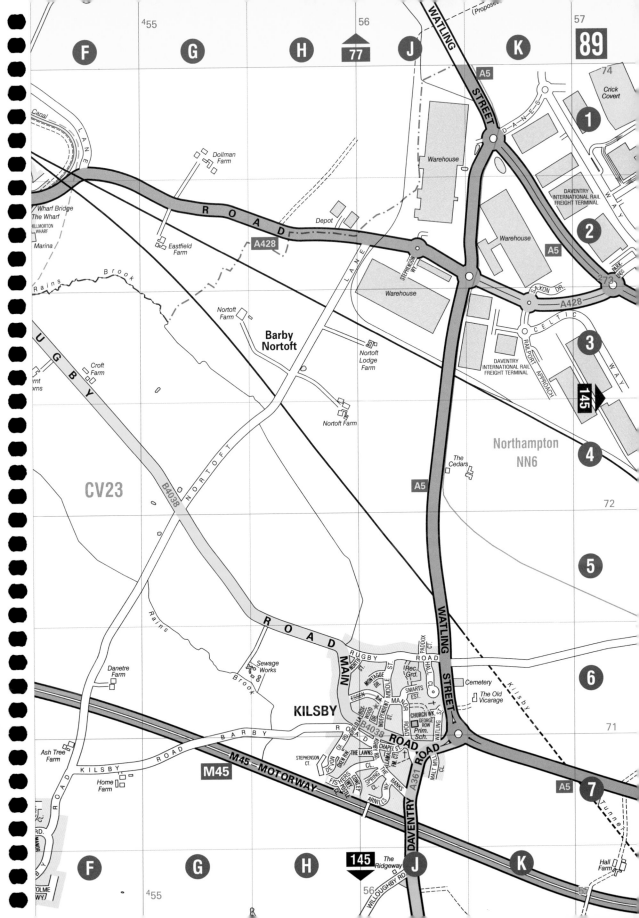

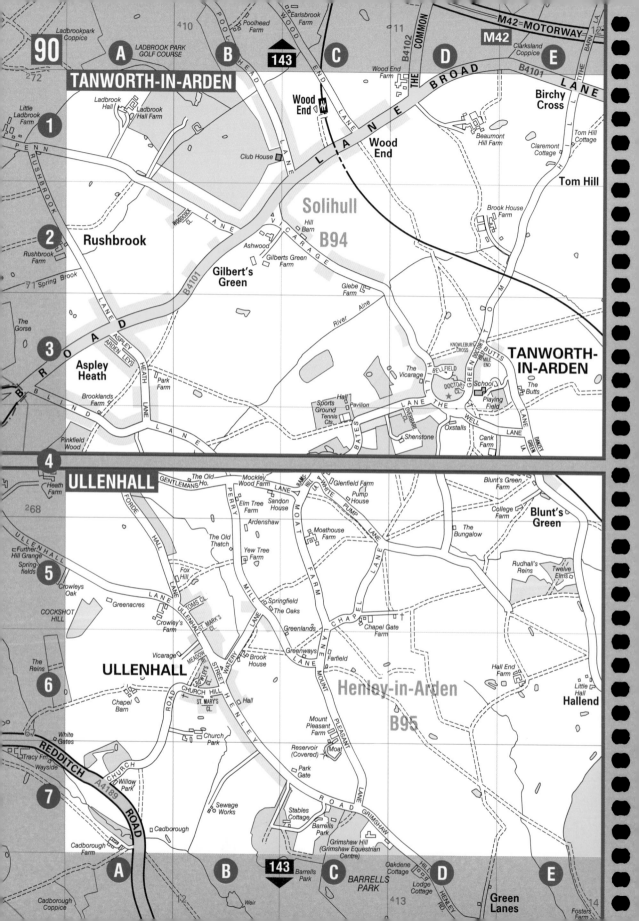

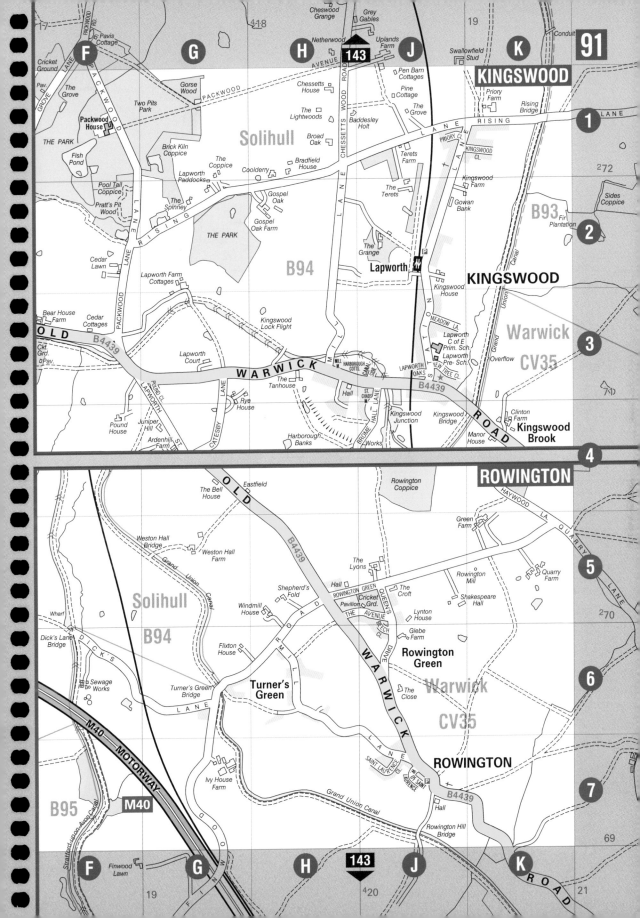

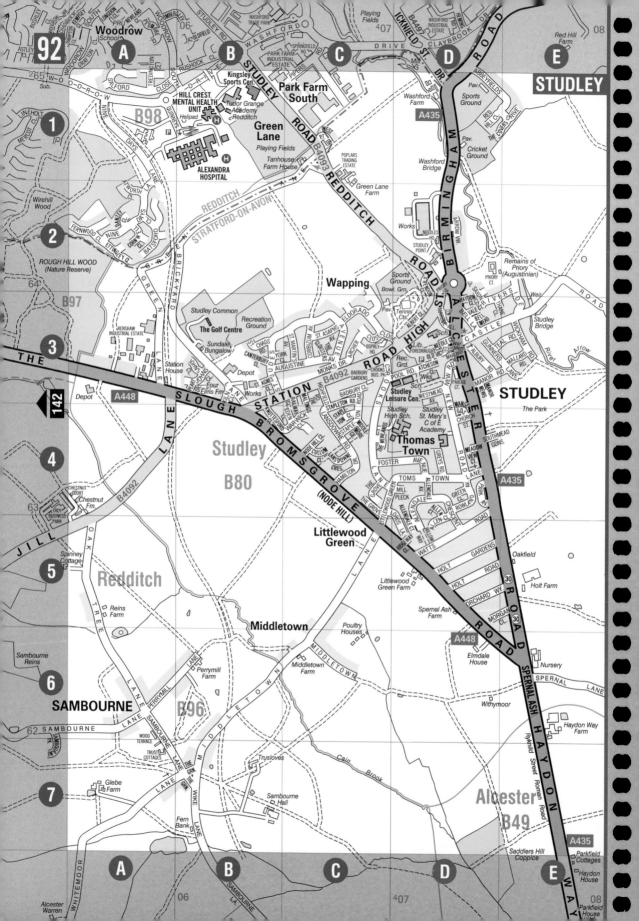

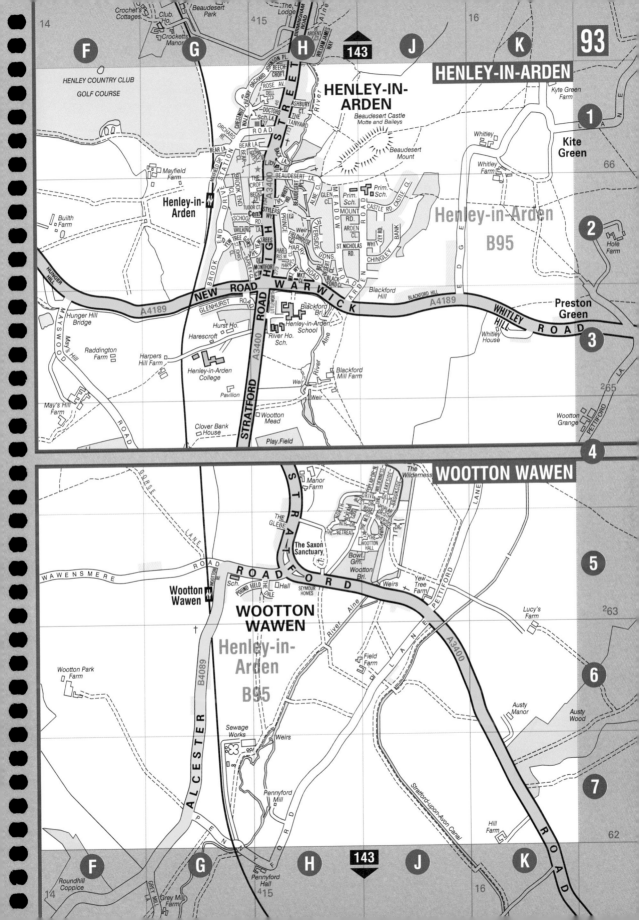

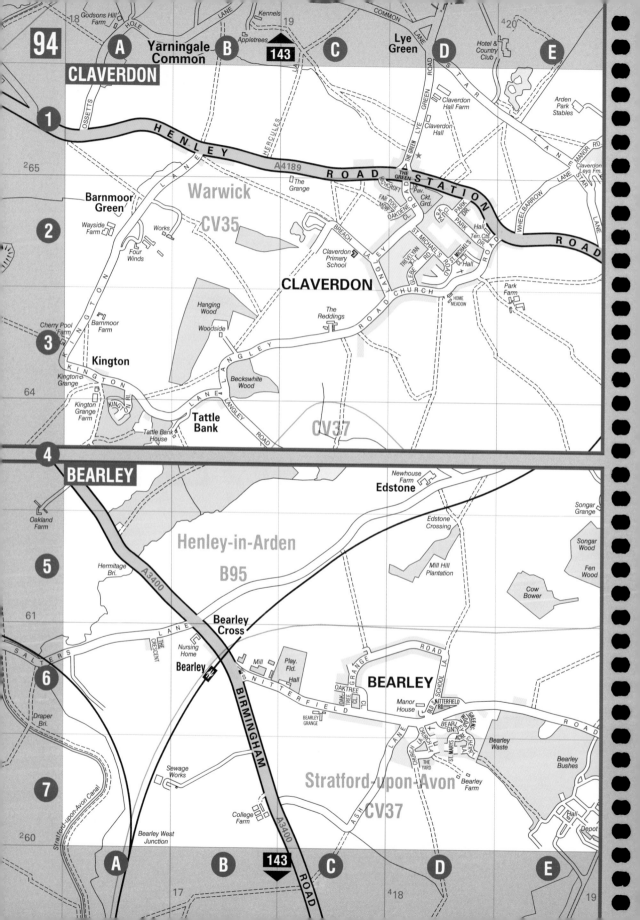

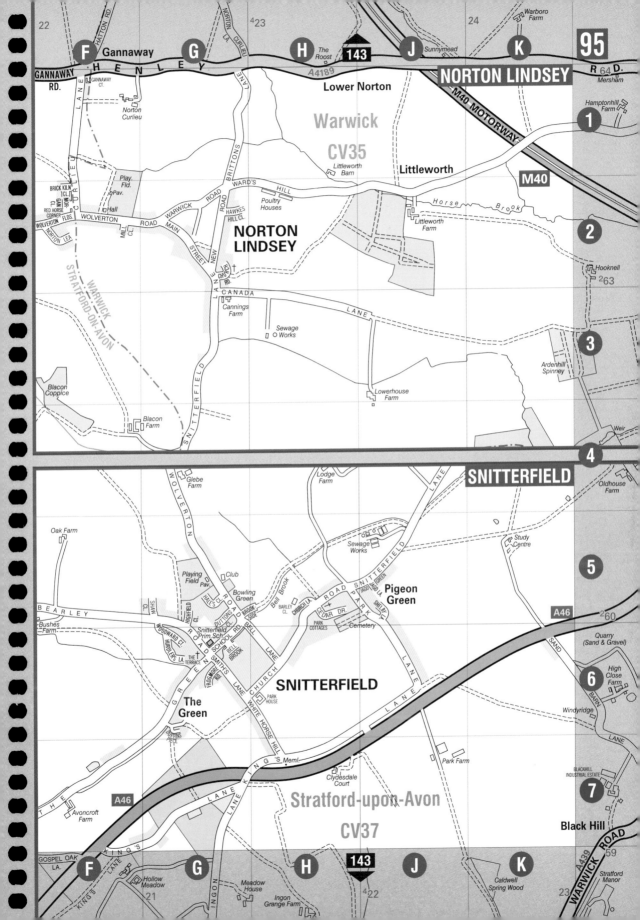

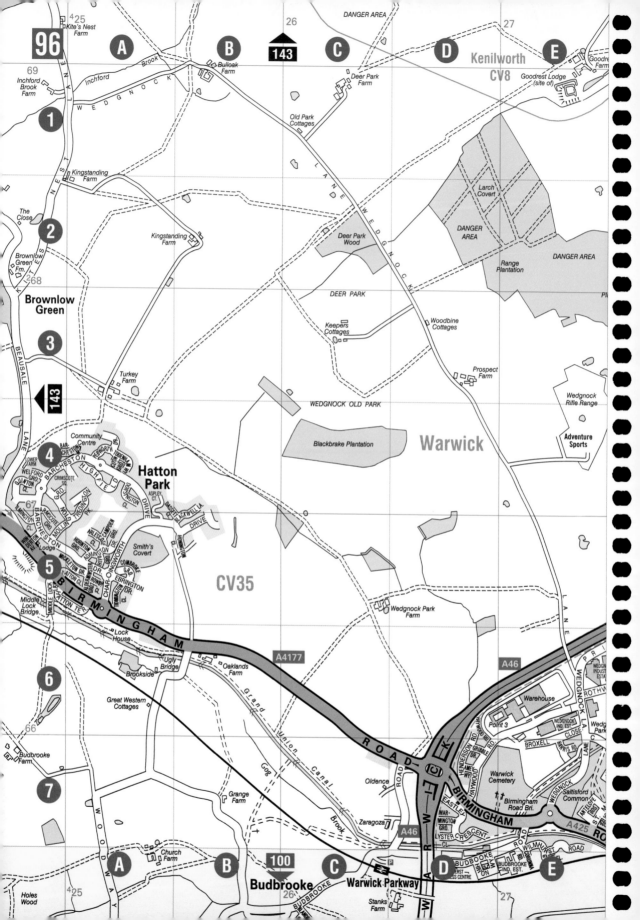

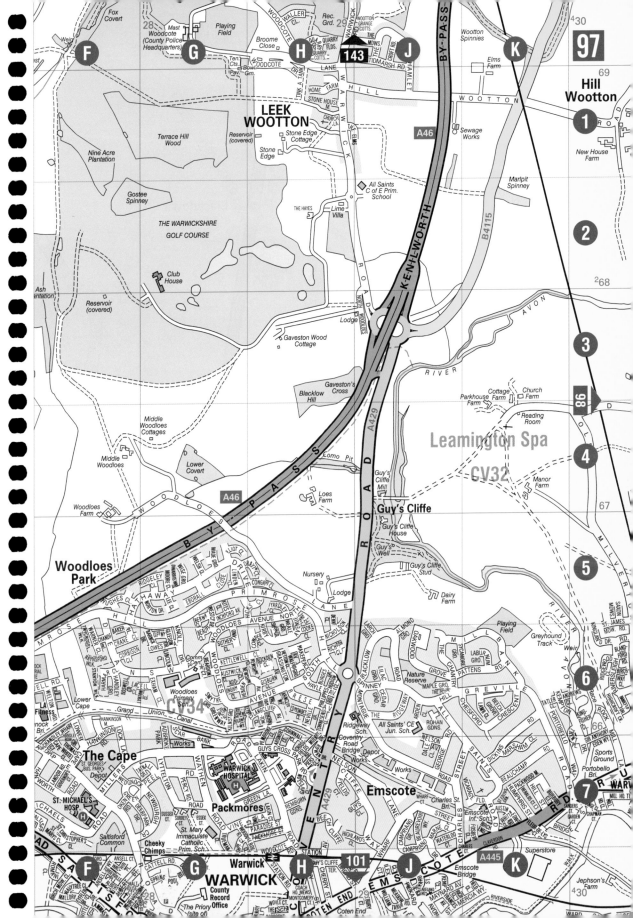

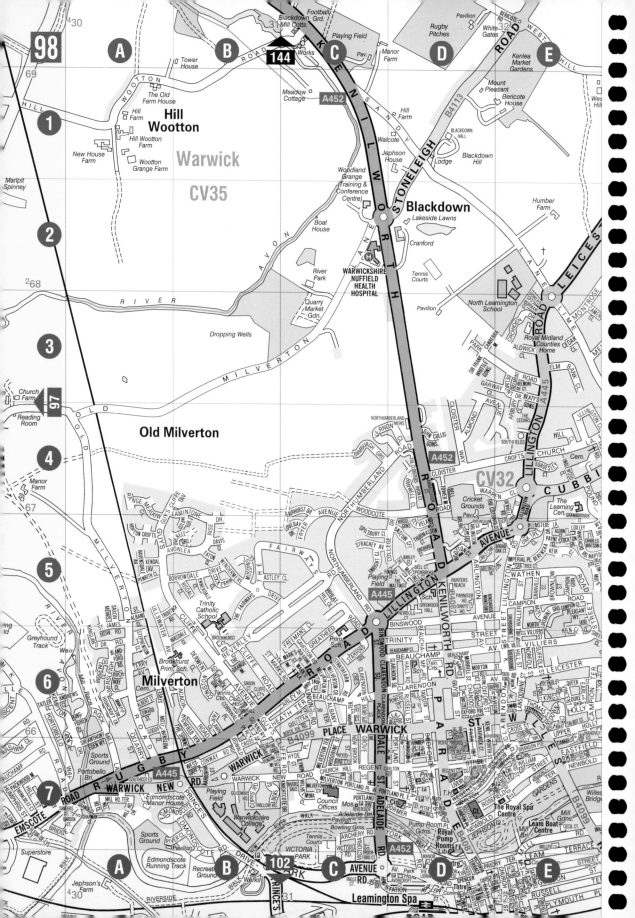

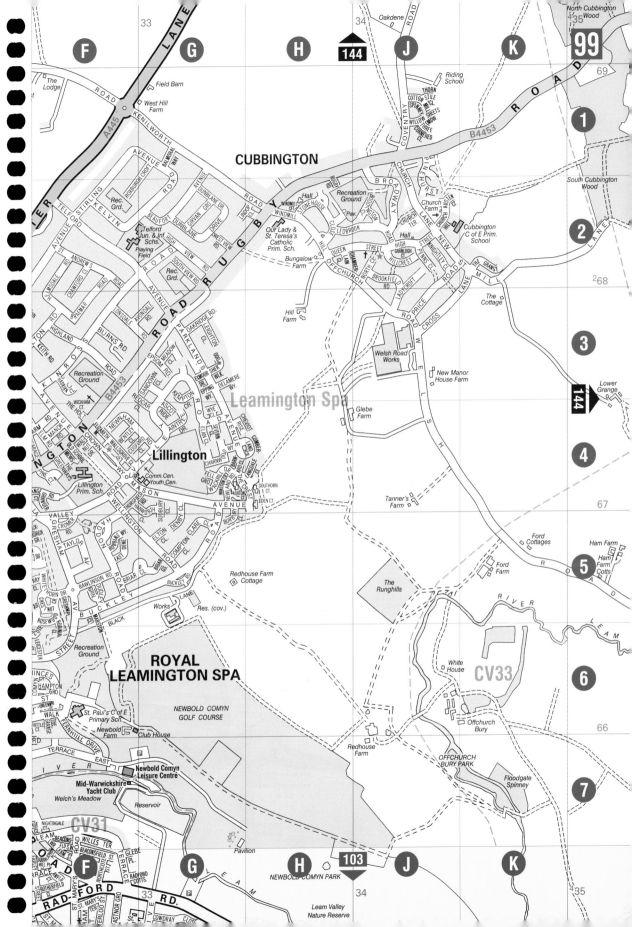

F　　G　　H　　144　　J　　K

North Cubbington Wood

33

34　Oakdene　ROAD

69

Riding School

1

THORN
COTTON STILE CL
SPINNEY SHEETS
WILLOW
THREE CORNERED CL

CUBBINGTON

COVENTRY ROAD　B4453

South Cubbington Wood

2

CHURCH TER
BROADWAY
Church Farm
Cubbington C of E Prim. School

268

KENILWORTH ROAD
A445
The Lodge
Field Barn
West Hill Farm

BALMORAL WAY
ROXBURGH CROFT
DUNBLANE DR
GIRVAN DRIVE
WEST VIEW RD
DUNBLANE
BEAUFORT
DUNBLANE
Telford Jun. & Inf. Schs.
Playing Field
Rec. Grd.
SOUTH VIEW RD
Rec. Grd.

RUGBY ROAD

Hall
STONE HOUSE CL
WINDMILL
Windmill
LEDBROOK
Our Lady & St. Teresa's Catholic Prim. Sch.
Bungalow Farm
QUEEN STREET
OFFCHURCH
CHAMBERS
LIN
HILL
TURTLE
CROFT
BROOKFIELD RD.
LADYCROFT
PRICE
Hall
HIGH
GRANLEIGH CT
HILLCREST

Recreation Ground
Pav.

CHURCH TER
CHURCH STREET
NEW STREET
HIGH STREET
PENNS CL
KNIGHTLEY RD
ROAD

CROSS

GRANGE MILL LANE

The Cottage

3

Leamington Spa

OAKRIDGE RD
LEIGHTON CL
ODAM
DELAMERE WY
EPPING WY
DENBY CL
Welsh Road Works
New Manor House Farm

WELSH

144
Lower Grange

ROAD

STIRLING
KELVIN
TELFORD
AVENUE
LANSDALE RD
CRAWFORD CL
ANDREWS RD
BRAEMAR
HIGHLAND
BURNS RD
CONSDALE
Recreation Ground
B4453
WICKHAM CT
THE HOLT
KEITH RD
NELSON
HAMILTON
KINGTON
PARKLAND
MEADOW
EPSOM CL
SANDOWN CL
REDCAR
ASCOT RIDE
KEMPTON
AINTREE DR
SEFTON CL
CURLEW
RISE
LUMMER
NEWNHAM
ELIZABETH
BENTLEY
WALSGRAVE
COSFORD
CHARNWOOD
CROWN WY
Lib
Comm. Cen.
Youth Cen.
Lillington Prim. Sch.
WINDRUSH
FELL GRO
NEWLAND
THE CREST
ASHTON CL
EDEN CT.
SOUTHORN
CL

Lillington

4

67

WILLES TER
MASON
WELLINGTON
HADDON
GRESHAM
TAYLOR
ROBINS WY
BANBURY
EAST
BRIAR
ELTON CL
COMPTON CL
DENBY CL
CLARE
BUCKLEY
AVENUE
ROAD
BURFORD
SUDBURY CL
Tanner's Farm

VALLEY RD
CROMER RD
GRESHAM
PINE CL
WHITETHORN DR
BUCKLEY
ROSEWOOD
NUT
RUBINA
LEICESTER
STREET
Recreation Ground
Redhouse Farm Cottage
BLACK
LANE
Works
Res. (cov.)

The Runghills

Ford Cottages
Ford Farm
Ham Farm
Ham Farm Cotts.

5

RIVER
LEAM

ROAD

White House

CV33

6

66

ROYAL LEAMINGTON SPA

PRINCES ST
HAMPTON ST
St. Paul's C of E Primary Sch.
Newbold Farm
NEWBOLD COMYN GOLF COURSE
Club House

Offchurch Bury

FERNHILL DRIVE
Newbold Comyn Leisure Centre
Mid-Warwickshire Yacht Club
Welch's Meadow
Reservoir
TERRACE EAST
OFFCHURCH BURY PARK
Redhouse Farm
Floodgate Spinney

7

RIVER

CV31
NIGHTINGALE
BEACONS
BEACONSFIELD ST
GLEBE TERRACE
RADFORD COTTS.
WILLES TER
ST MARY'S
RADFORD RD.
COWDRAY CLOSE
Pavilion

F　　G　　H　　103　　J　　K

33

34

NEWBOLD COMYN PARK

Leam Valley Nature Reserve

435

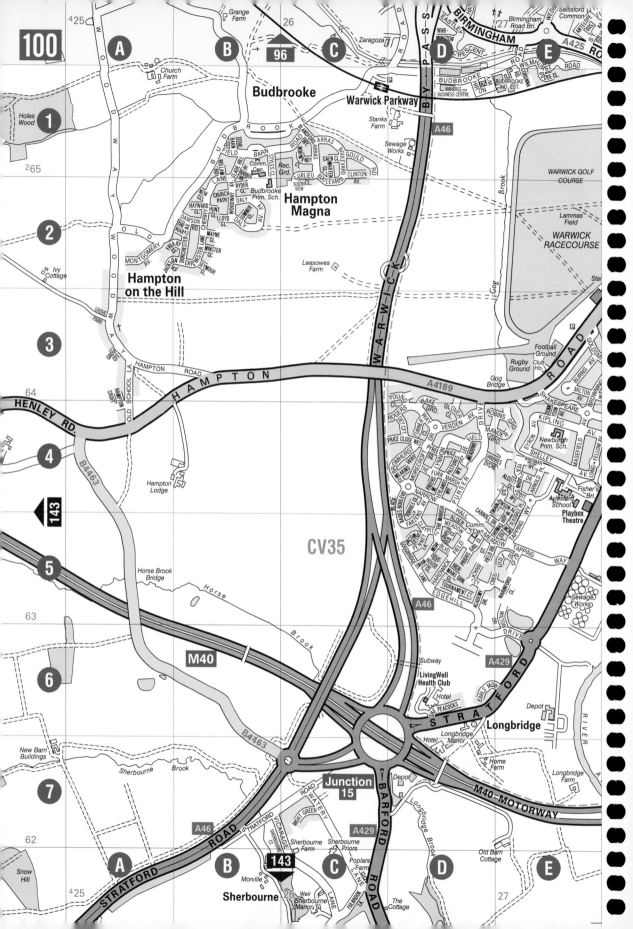

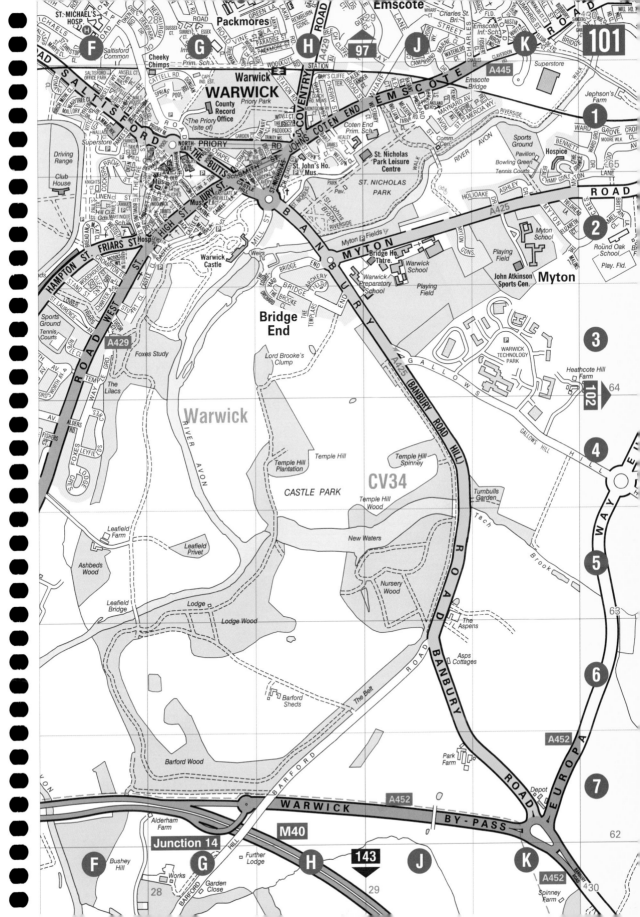

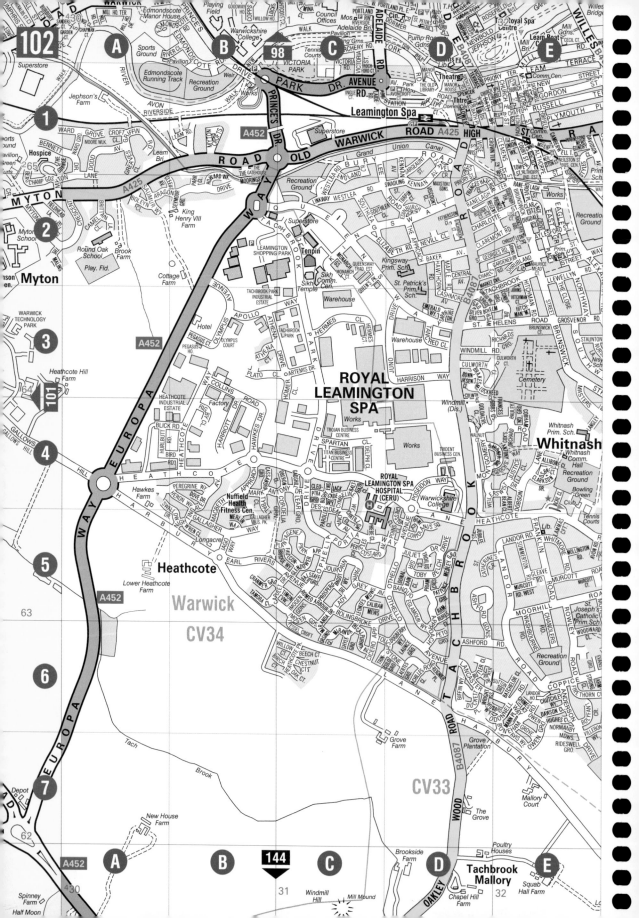

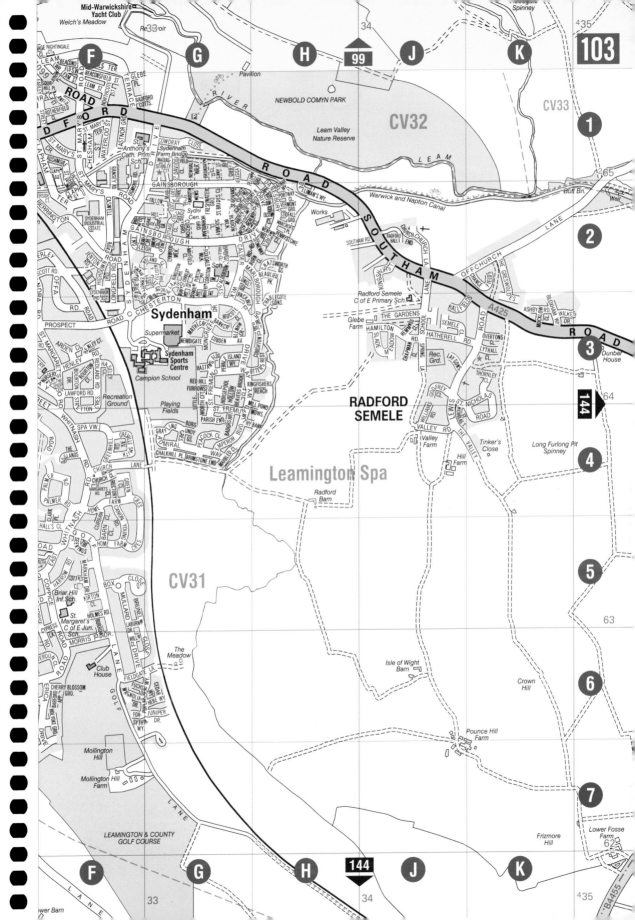

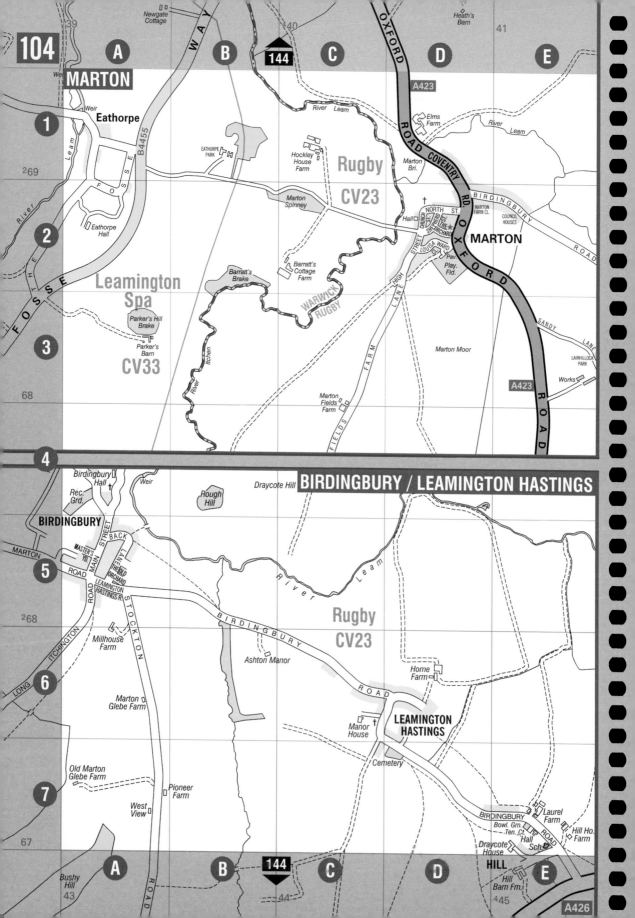

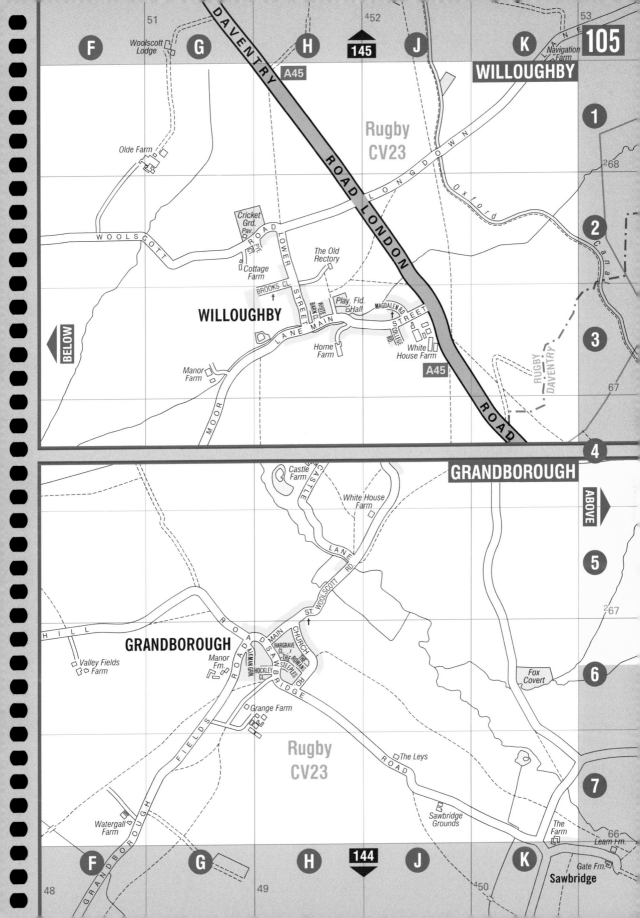

F **G** DAVENTRY **H** ▲ **145** **J** **K**

A45

Woolscott Lodge

Navigation Farm

51   452   53

1

Rugby CV23

268

Olde Farm

ROAD LONDON

LONGDOWN

Oxford

Canal

2

WOOLSCOTT

Cricket Grd. Pav.

ROAD

The Old Rectory

Cottage Farm

BELOW

LOWER STREET

BROOKS CL.

WHITE BARN CL.

MAGDALEN RD.

Play. Fld.
Hall

STREET

COLLEGE RD.

3

RUGBY DAVENTRY

67

WILLOUGHBY

MAIN

LANE

Home Farm

White House Farm

A45

Manor Farm

MOOR

ROAD

4

Castle Farm

CASTLE

White House Farm

ABOVE

5

LANE

WOOLSCOTT RD.

267

HILL

ST.

GRANDBOROUGH

ROAD

MAIN

NAYMAN GRN.

SAWBRIDGE

CHURCH

HARGRAVE CL.
THE ROWANS
THE STEEPLES

HOCKLEY CL.

Fox Covert

6

Valley Fields Farm

Manor Fm.

Grange Farm

FIELDS

Rugby CV23

ROAD

The Leys

7

GRANDBOROUGH

Watergall Farm

Sawbridge Grounds

The Farm

66

Leam Fm.

F **G** **H** ▼ **144** **J** **K**

Gate Fm.

Sawbridge

48   49   450

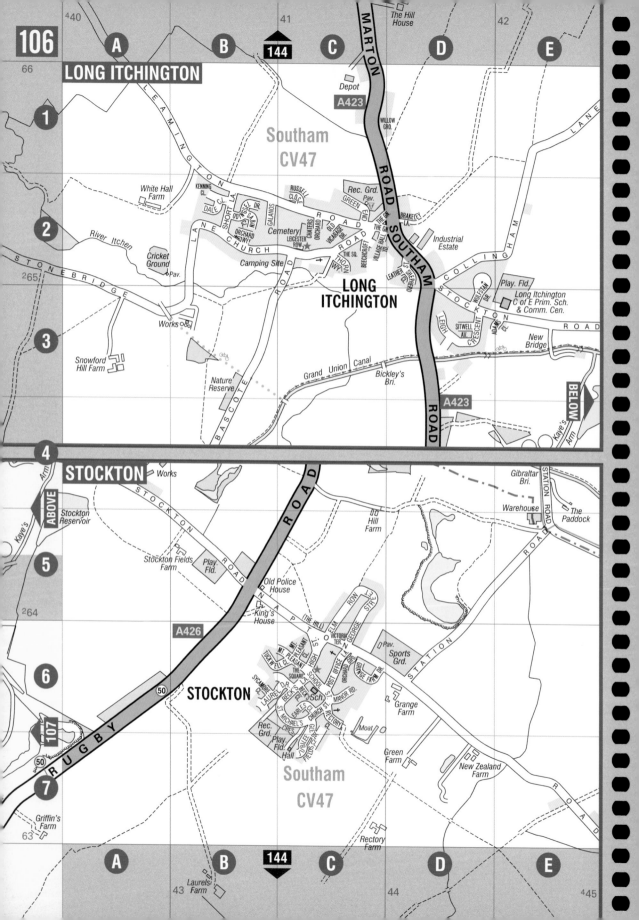

LONG ITCHINGTON

A B 144 C D E

440 41 42

66

Southam
CV47

1

A423

Depot

The Hill House

MARTON ROAD

Willow Gro.

White Hall Farm

KENNING CL.

SHORT LA.

ODINSEL DR.

DALE CL.

GALANOS

ORCHARD WY.

CHAMERS

RUSSELL CLOSE

GREEN END

Rec. Grd.
Pav.

THE GN.

THE GN.

BRAKELEY

SOUTHAM ROAD

Industrial Estate

2

River Itchen

LANE

CHURCH

GABB

ROAD

ORCHARD

ROAD

Cemetery

LEICESTER ROW

VICARAGE DR.

OLD

BEECHCROFT

THE SQ.

VILLAGE HALL

LEATHER

SILEHEAD

COLLINGHAM

Play. Fld.

Long Itchington
C of E Prim. Sch.
& Comm. Cen.

265

STONEBRIDGE

Cricket Ground

Pav.

Camping Site

HORN WY.

LONG ITCHINGTON

STOCKTON

WULSTAN DR.

SITWELL AV.

ADAMS CL.

LEIGH CRESCENT

ROAD

New Bridge

3

Works

Snowford Hill Farm

BASCOTE

Nature Reserve

Grand Union Canal

Bickley's Bri.

A423

ROAD

BELOW

Kaye's Arm

4 STOCKTON

144

66

Works

STOCKTON ROAD

Gibraltar Bri.

STATION ROAD

Warehouse

The Paddock

Kaye's Arm

ABOVE

Stockton Reservoir

Stockton Fields Farm

Play. Fld.

ROAD

Hill Farm

5

264

Old Police House

King's House

A426

MAP

(THE HILL)

ELM

ROW

1ST STREET

Victoria Ter.

GEORGE

Pav.

Sports Grd.

STATION

6

107

50

STOCKTON

RUGBY

50

SYCAMORE

LAUREL

HICKNELL CL.

MT. PLEASANT

MT. PLEASANT CL.

THE SQUARE

D.R.

BECK'S

CL.

SCHOOL

HIGH

ST.

VICTORIA

O

Sch.

POST OFFICE LA.

ORCHARD GRO.

VILLAGE FARM DR.

MANOR RD.

Grange Farm

50

7

ST. MICHAEL'S

CRES.

Rec. Grd.

Play. Fld.

Hall

ST. CHARLES

FULLER CL.

GLEBE FIELDS

CHURCH ST.

RECTORY

Moat

Green Farm

New Zealand Farm

Griffin's Farm

Southam
CV47

Rectory Farm

63

A B 144 C D E

43 44 445

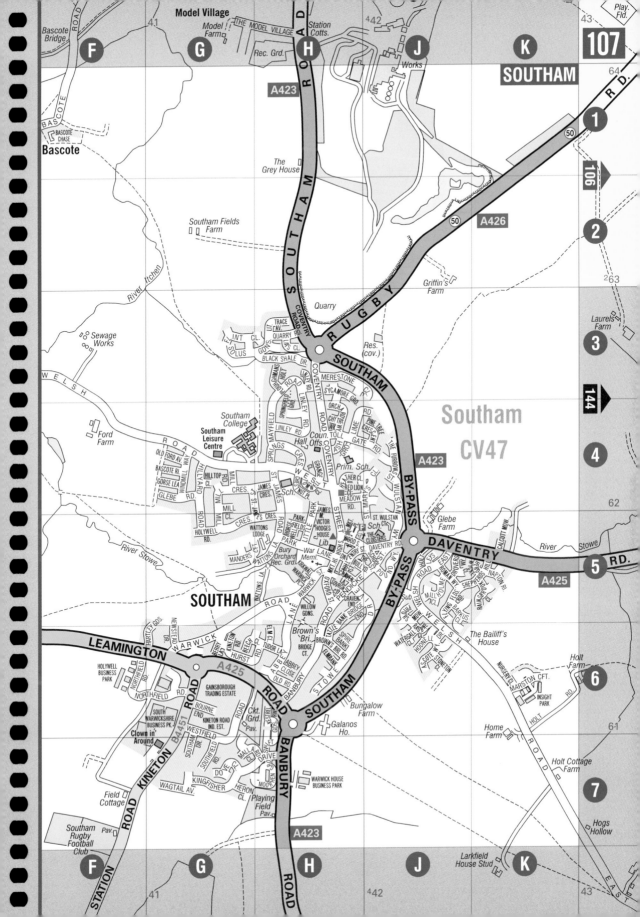

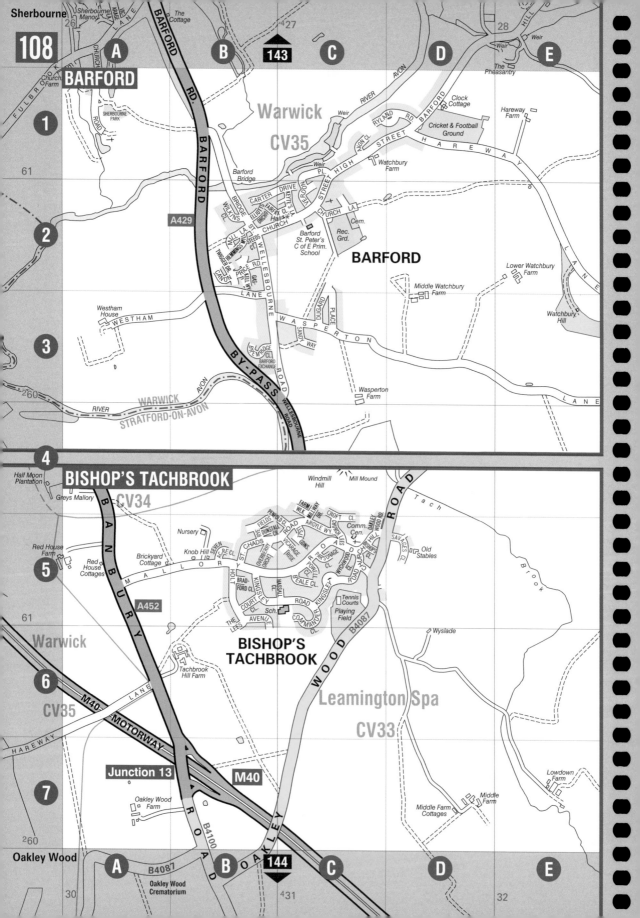

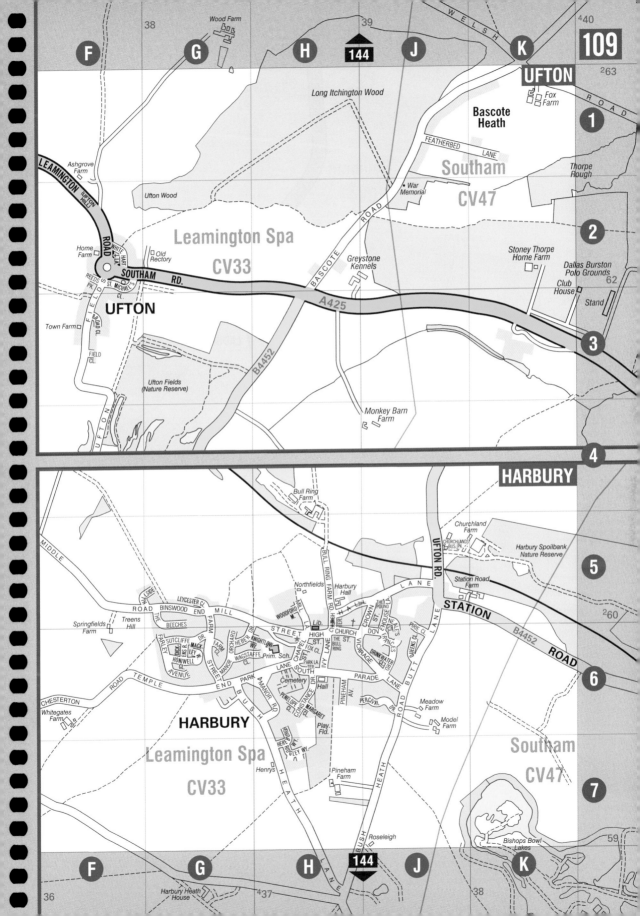

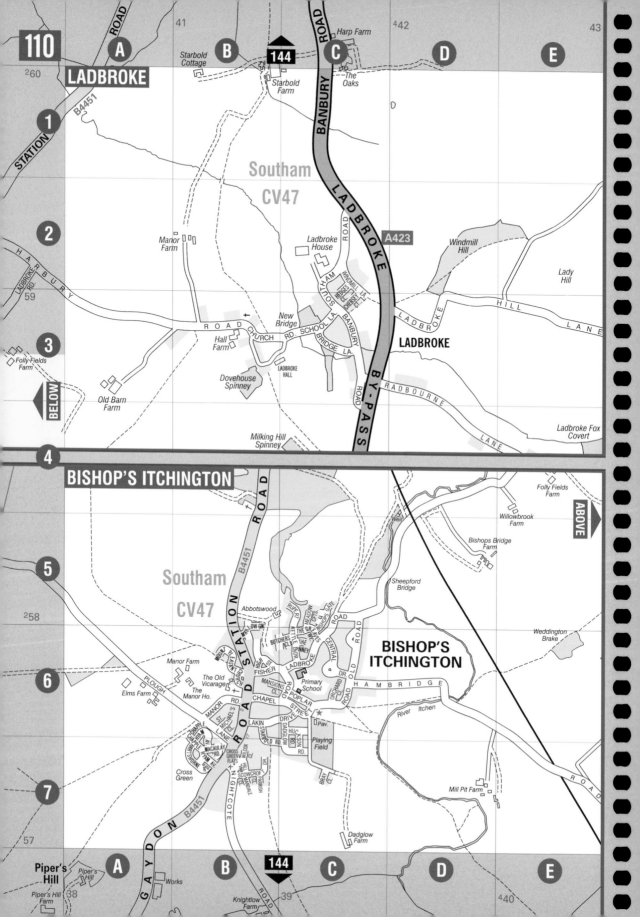

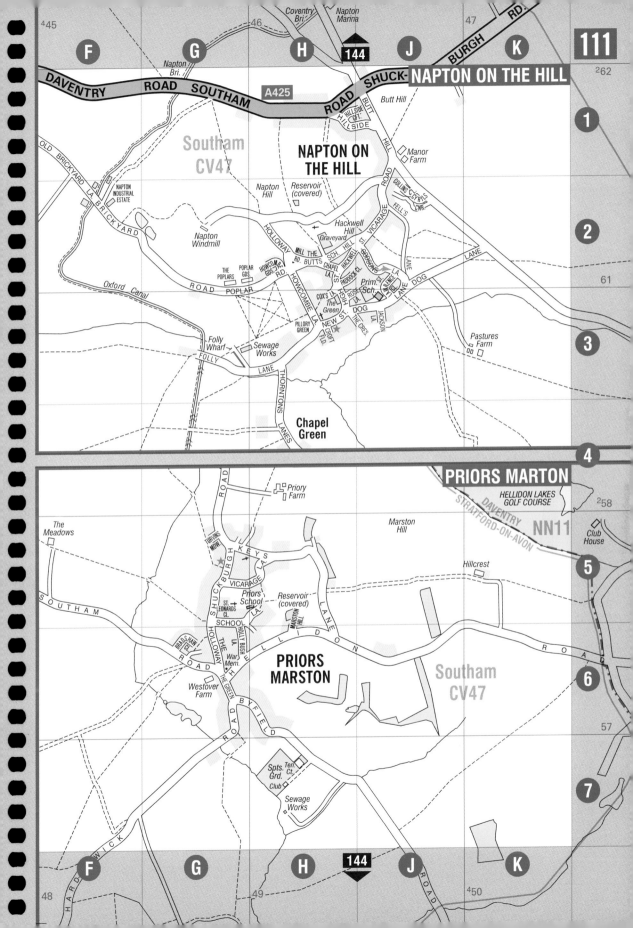

F G H 144 J K

NAPTON ON THE HILL

DAVENTRY ROAD SOUTHAM **A425** ROAD SHUCK-BURGH RD.

1

Napton Bri.
Coventry Bri.
Napton Marina
144
BURGH

Southam
CV47

NAPTON ON THE HILL

HILLSIDE CFT.
HILLSIDE
BUTT HILL
Butt Hill

Manor Farm

Napton Hill
Reservoir (covered)
Napton INDUSTRIAL ESTATE
OLD BRICKYARD LA. BRICKYARD

COLLIN'S CYD. CNR.
FELL'S
VICARAGE RD.

2

Napton Windmill
Hackwell Hill
Graveyard

Oxford Canal
ROAD POPLAR
THE POPLARS
POPLAR GDS
HOWCOMBE GDS. RD.
HOLLOWAY
MILL THE RD. BUTTS
SCH. LA.
CHAPEL LA.
HACKWELL ST.
GIBSON'S LA.
ROSE LA.
PADDOCK CL.
Prim. Sch.
DOG LANE
LANE
61

3

Folly Wharf
Sewage Works
FOLLY LANE
THORNTONS LANES
HOWCOMBE LA.
PILLORY GREEN
COX'S LA.
The Green
HIGH ST.
NEW ST.
CROFT RD.
THE CRES
DOG LA.
JACKSON LA.

Pastures Farm

Chapel Green

4

PRIORS MARTON

HELLIDON LAKES GOLF COURSE
DAVENTRY
STRATFORD-ON-AVON
258

Priory Farm

Marston Hill

NN11

Club House

The Meadows

TURVINS MDW.
KEYS LA.
VICARAGE
SHUCKBURGH
ST. LEONARDS CL.
Priors School
HOLLY BUSH LA.
SCHOOL
Reservoir (covered)
MARSTON HILL
ELLIDON LANE

Hillcrest

5

SOUTHAM ROAD
BRADSHAW CL.
THE HOLLOWAY
War. Mem.
THE GREEN

PRIORS MARSTON

Southam
CV47

6

Westover Farm
BYFIELD ROAD

57

HARDWICK ROAD
Spts. Grd.
Ten. Ct.
Club
Sewage Works

7

F G H 144 J K

445 46 47
48 49 450

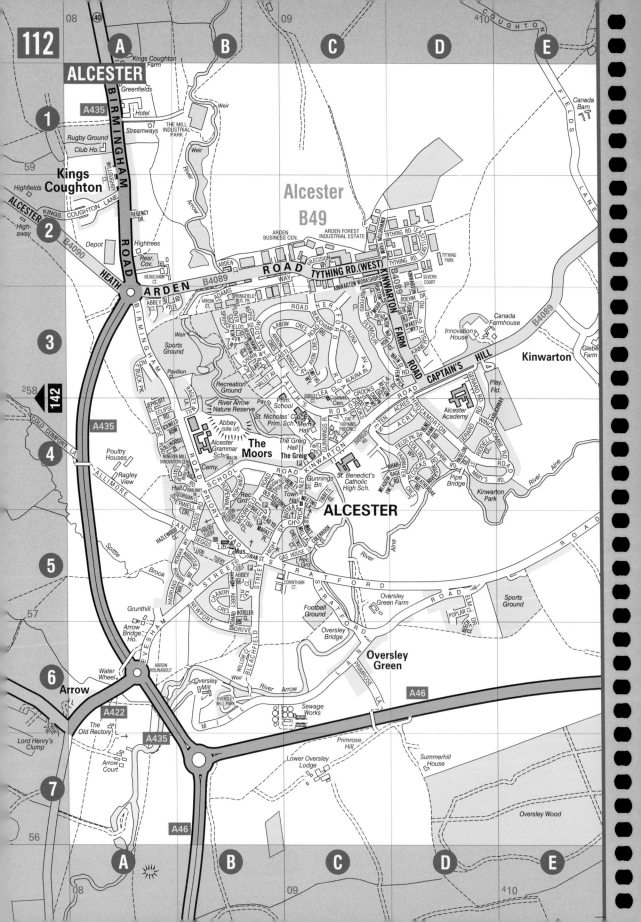

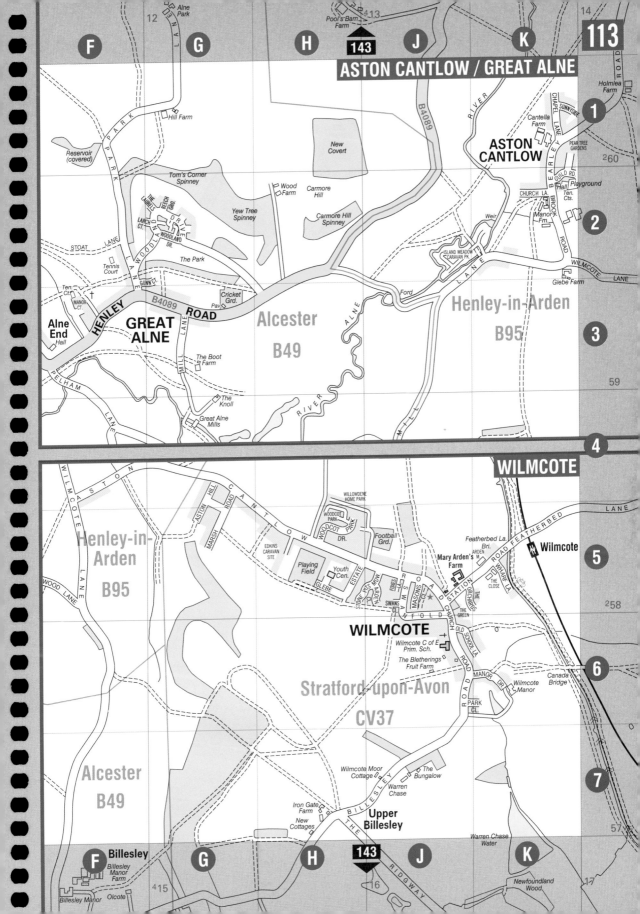

WILMCOTE

F G H J K

1 2 3 4 5 6 7

143

12 14

260

59

258

57

415 16 17

Alne Park

Pool's Barn Farm

413

Holmlea Farm

Sunnyside

Chapel Lane

Cantella Farm

Bearley

PEAR TREE GARDENS

ASTON CANTLOW

GUILD RD.

Hall

Ten. Cts.

Playground

CHURCH LA.

BROOK ROAD

Manor Fm.

WILMCOTE LANE

Glebe Farm

Hill Farm

New Covert

RIVER

B4089

Reservoir (covered)

PARK

Tom's Corner Spinney

Wood Farm

Carmore Hill

Carmore Hill Spinney

Weir

Island Meadow Caravan Pk.

MILL LANE

Yew Tree Spinney

THE LAURELS

BEECH GRO.

WOODLAND DRIVE

LARCH CT.

WOODLAND DR.

The Park

STOAT LANE

LANE

Tennis Court

GUNN CT.

Cricket Grd.

Pav.

Ford

RIVER ALNE

Henley-in-Arden B95

Ten. Ct.

MANOR CT.

HENLEY

B4089 ROAD

GREAT ALNE

Alcester B49

Alne End Hall

PELHAM LANE

The Boot Farm

MILL LANE

The Knoll

Great Alne Mills

RIVER

WILMASTON ROAD

WILMCOTE LANE

WOOD LANE

Henley-in-Arden B95

Alcester B49

ASTON HILL

MARSH

CANTLOW ROAD

WILLOWDENE HOME PARK

WOODCOT PARK

WOODCOT PARK DR.

Football Grd.

EDKINS CARAVAN SITE

Playing Field

GLEBE

Youth Cen.

ESTATE

STONE PITS MDW.

FOXES

MASONS

SWANS CL.

SWANS CL.

SONG... MDW.

MASNS MDW.

PENFOLD

SWAN RD.

ARDEN ROAD

CHURCH ROAD

Featherbed La.

Bri.

FEATHERBED ROAD

Wilmcote

WHARF LA.

Mary Arden's Farm

ARDEN M.

THE ORCHARDS

THE CLOSE

THE GREEN

WILMCOTE

Wilmcote C of E Prim. Sch.

The Bletherings Fruit Farm

Stratford-upon-Avon CV37

OLD SCHOOL LA.

Canada Bridge

MANOR DR.

Wilmcote Manor

STATION ROAD

PARK CL.

Wilmcote Moor Cottage

The Bungalow

Warren Chase

Iron Gate Farm

New Cottages

Upper Billesley

BILLESLEY

THE RIDGWAY

Warren Chase Water

143

Billesley

Billesley Manor Farm

Billesley Manor

Olcote

Newfoundland Wood

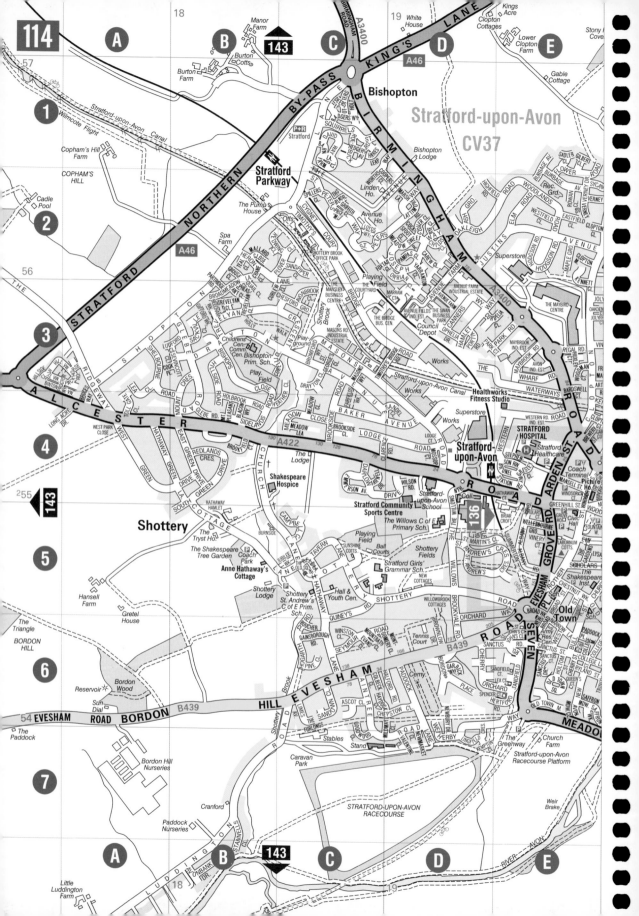

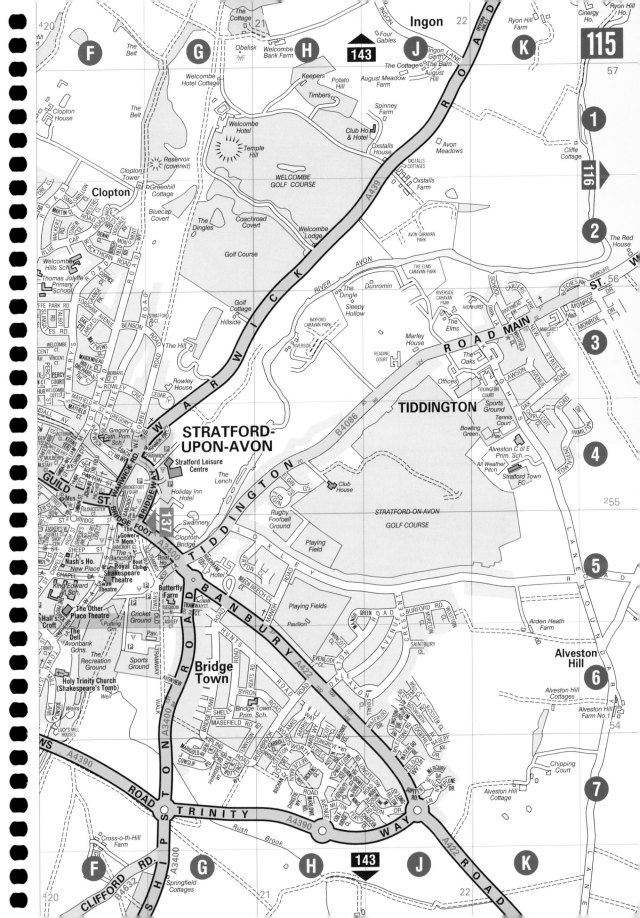

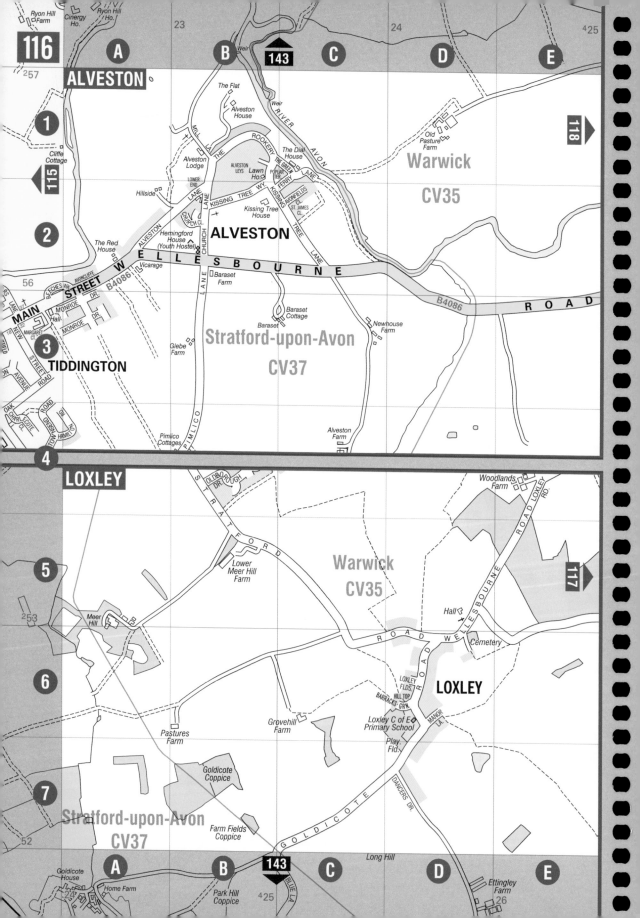

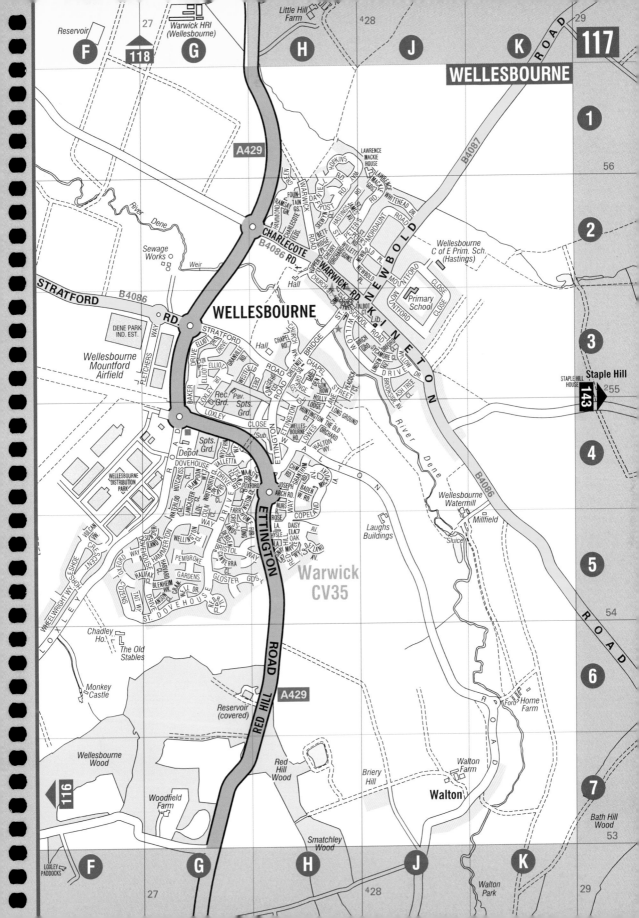

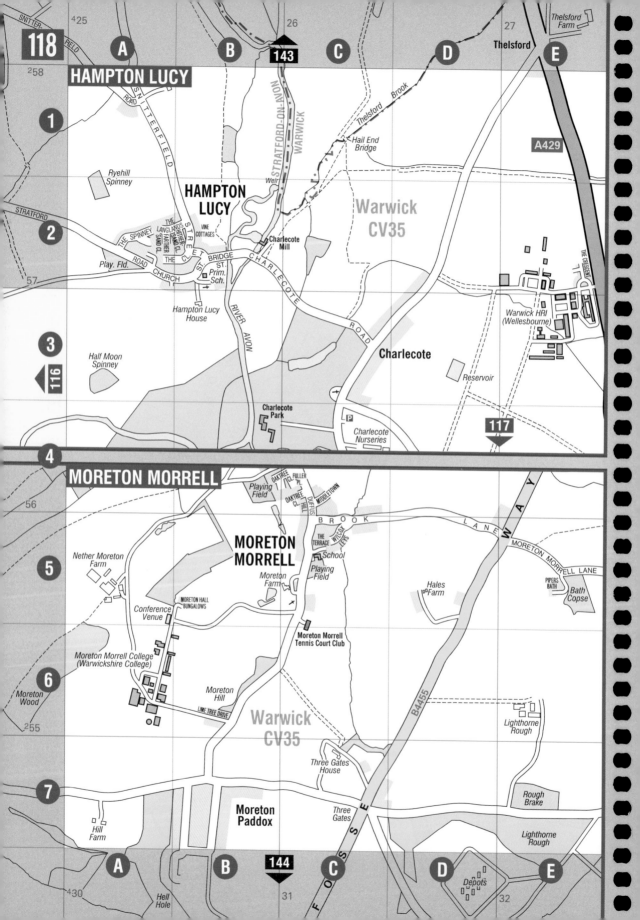

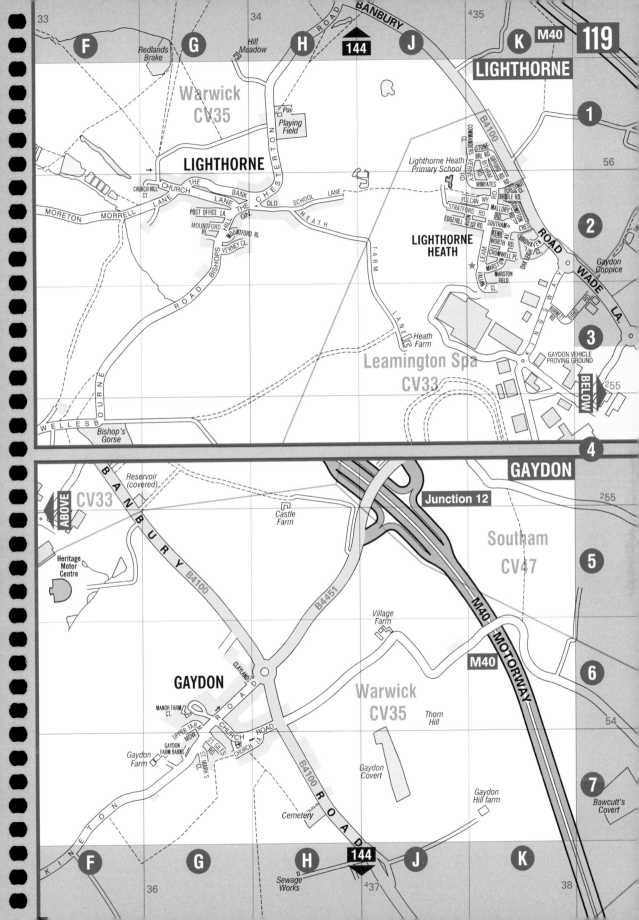

F **G** **H** **J** **K** M40

144

LIGHTHORNE

1

Redlands Brake

Hill Meadow

Warwick CV35

Pav
Playing Field

56

LIGHTHORNE

B4100

CHURCH HILL CT.

CHURCH LANE
THE BANK
THE GN.
POST OFFICE LA.
HILL

MOUNTFORD RL.
MOUNTFORD RL.
VERNEY CL.

MORETON MORRELL

CHESTERTON ROAD
OLD SCHOOL LANE

HEATH

FARM

Lighthorne Heath Primary School

COMMANDERS CT.
VERNEY CT.
STONE
BRI. RD.
BRYONY RD.
BITHAM RD.
WINYATES

CHESTNUT CL.
BRIDLE RD.

VULCAN WY.
STRATFORD RD.
MALLORY RD.
EDGEHILL RD.
SOUTHAM RD.

COMPTON RD.

LIGHTHORNE HEATH

KENIL.
WORTH RD.
CROMWELL PL.
OAK LEIGH

LEAM
MARSTON
FIELD.
FLINT CL.

CRES.
BIRD HAVEN CL.

MARSTON FIELD.

KINGSWAY

BURNETT RD.
BIRD RD.

2

ROAD
WADE LA.

Gaydon Coppice

3

Heath Farm

Leamington Spa CV33

GAYDON VEHICLE PROVING GROUND

BELOW

255

4

WELLESBOURNE

Bishop's Gorse

BISHOPS ROAD

GAYDON

Reservoir (covered)

ABOVE CV33

BANBURY ROAD B4100

Castle Farm

Junction 12

255

Heritage Motor Centre

B4451

Village Farm

M40

Southam CV47

5

M40 MOTORWAY

M40

54

6

GAYDON

MANOR FARM CT.

UPPER FARM MDW.
GAYDON FARM BARNS

Gaydon Farm

ST. MARK'S CL.
ST. GILES RD.

CLAYLANDS

CHURCH

CHURCH LA.

ROAD

Warwick CV35

Thorn Hill

Gaydon Covert

Gaydon Hill farm

7

Bawcutt's Covert

KINETON

B4100 ROAD

Cemetery

F **G** **H** **144** **J** **K**

Sewage Works

33 34 435 36 37 437 38

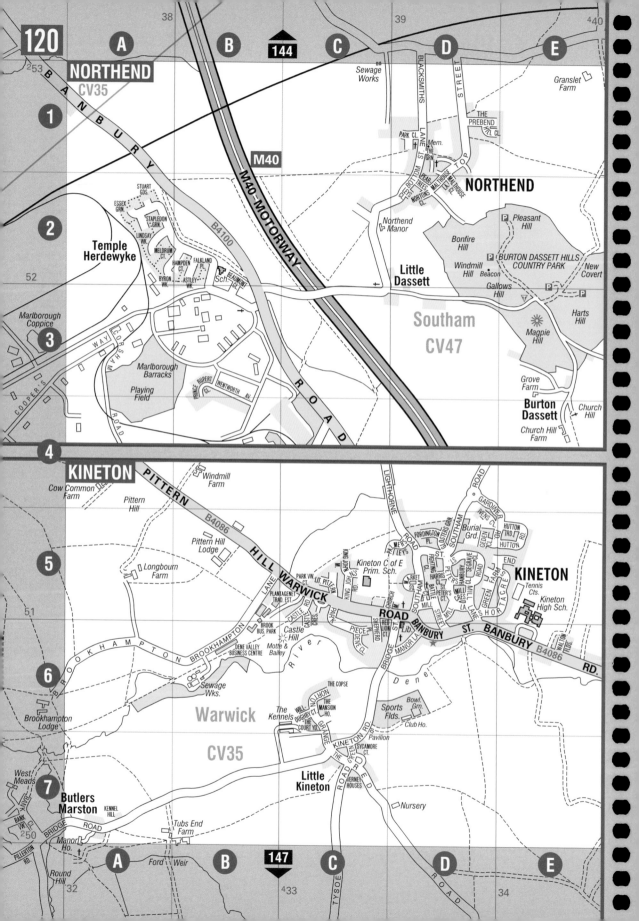

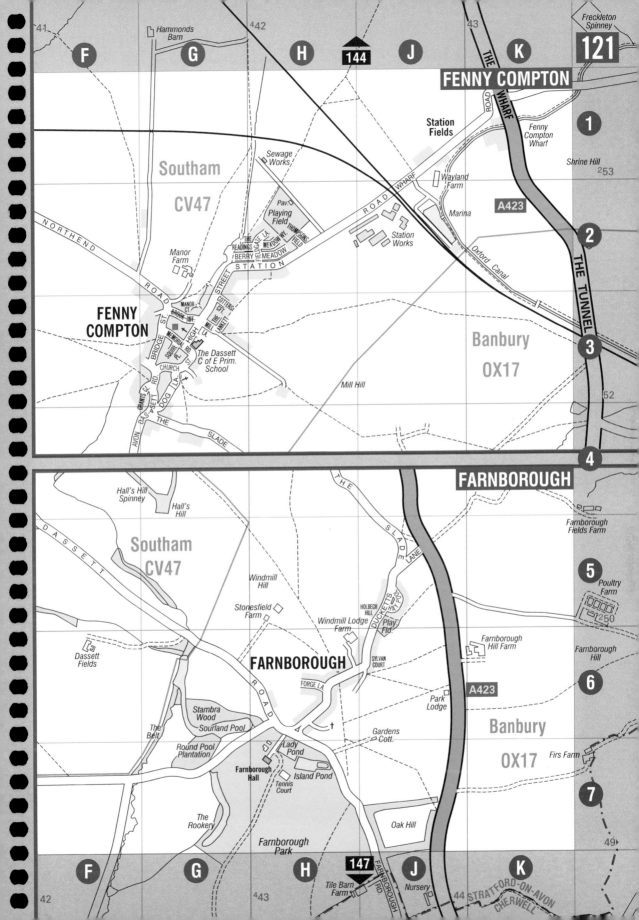

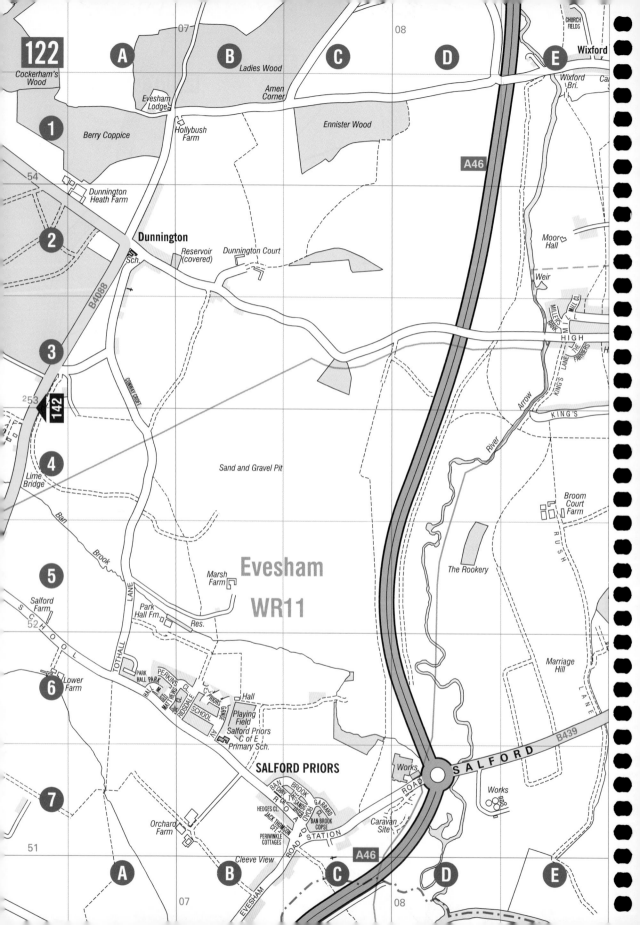

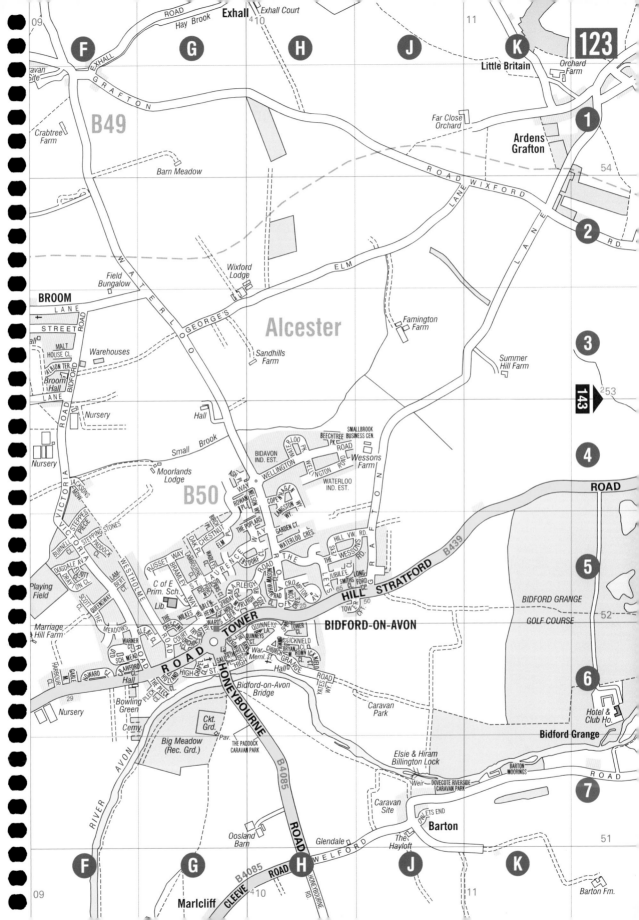

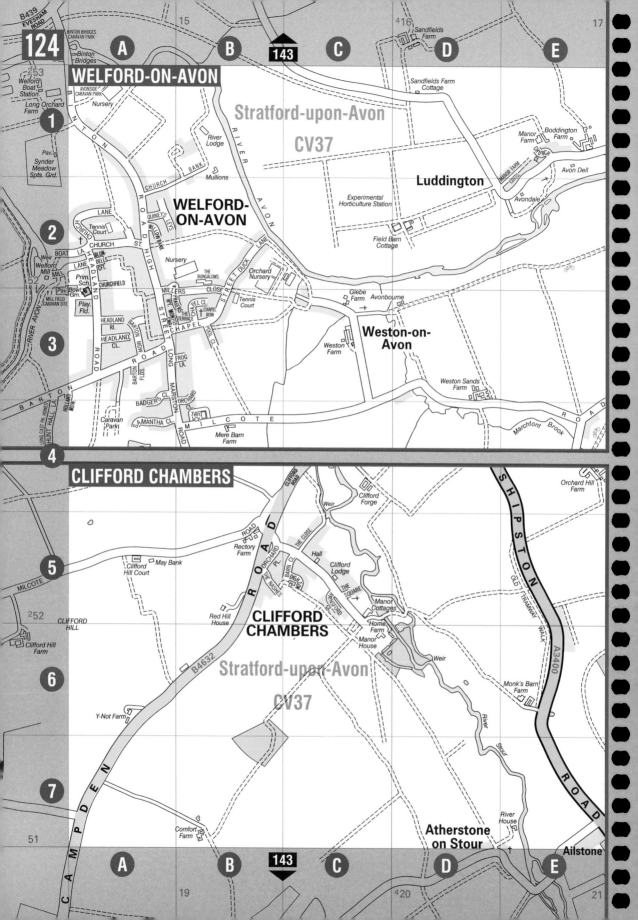

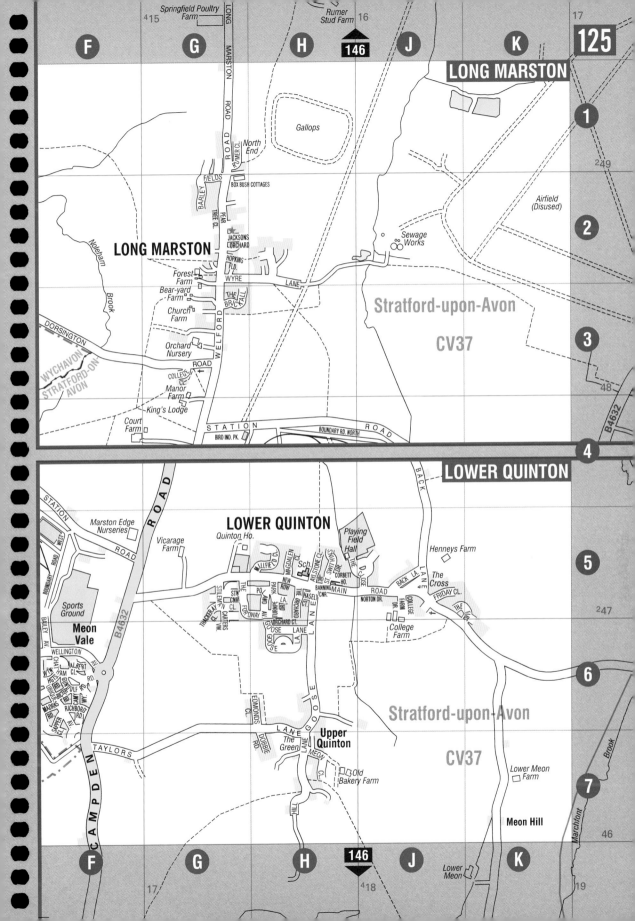

F **G** **H** **J** **K**

LONG MARSTON

Springfield Poultry Farm
415

Rumer Stud Farm
16 **146** 17

249

1

Gallops

North End

2

BARLEY FIELDS

BOX BUSH COTTAGES

PEAR TREE CL.

Airfield (Disused)

LONG MARSTON

★ JACKSONS ORCHARD

HOPKINS FLD.

Sewage Works

Forest Farm

WYRE LANE

Bear-yard Farm

THE BRICK HALL

Stratford-upon-Avon

Church Farm

WELFORD

CV37

3

Orchard Nursery

DORSINGTON

COLLEGE ROAD

Noleham Brook

WYCHAVON
STRATFORD-ON-AVON

Manor Farm

King's Lodge

48

Court Farm

STATION ROAD

BIRD IND. PK.

BOUNDARY RD. NORTH

B4632

4

LOWER QUINTON

BACK

STATION ROAD

LOWER QUINTON

Marston Edge Nurseries

Quinton Ho.

Playing Field Hall

Henneys Farm

Vicarage Farm

ROAD

STATION ROAD

MILLFIELD CL.

MAGDALEN

Sch.

AYLSTONE CL.

ST. SWITHINS

THE CLOSE

BACK LA.

The Cross

5

BOUNDARY ROAD

BAILEY AV.

B4632

Sports Ground

Meon Vale

NEW ROW

PO.

PARK LA.

THE ROPEWAY

STILEMANS

STN. CNR.

TIMBERBAY CL.

CARTERS VW.

ORCHARD CT.

THE CLOSE

GOOSE

CORBETT HO.

BANNING CNR.

HASELL CT.

ORCHARD

MAIN

ROAD

NORTON DR.

COLLEGE FARM DR.

College Farm

FRIDAY CL.

THE VALE

247

6

WELLINGTON AV.

CHATHAM CL.

ALBERT RD.

WTN.

HGT.

BROUGH CL.

DOVER CL.

ORFORD RD.

BICESTER RD.

JARVIS WY.

MADRAS RD.

RICHBORO RD.

SAPPER CL.

GOOSE LANE

EDMONDS CL.

DOBBIE RD.

The Green

Upper Quinton

MEON RD.

Old Bakery Farm

Lower Meon Farm

Marchfont Brook

TAYLORS

Stratford-upon-Avon

CV37

7

HILL

Meon Hill

46

CAMPDEN ROAD

Lower Meon

F **G** **H** **146** **J** **K**

17 418 19

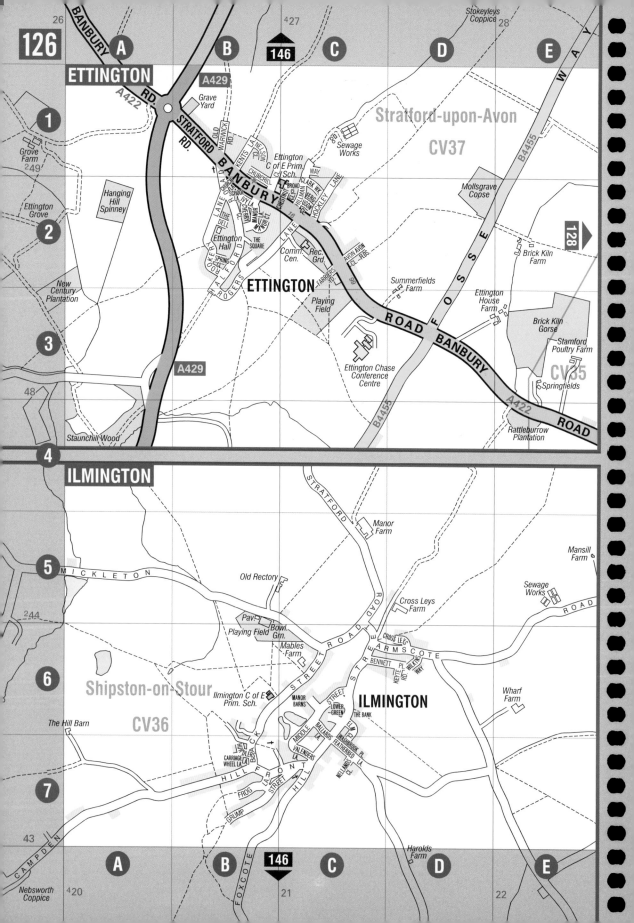

ETTINGTON

BANBURY RD.

A422

A429

146

Stratford-upon-Avon
CV37

Grove
Farm
249

Ettington
Grove

Hanging
Hill Spinney

New
Century
Plantation

Staunchill Wood

A429

Grave
Yard

OLD WARWICK RD.

KENTS LANE

NELSON CL.

CHURCHILL CL.

CHURCH LANE

SCHOOL LA.

THE DELL

ROKER SPRING CL.

ALFORD

ROGERS LA.

IVY LA.

KIRBY CL.

MANOR

Ettington
Hall

THE SQUARE

Ettington
C of E Prim.
Sch.

BROAD

CHESTNUT LA.

CLARK WK.

HERB

HILLMAN

HOCKLEY LANE

WAY

AUSTIN

Sewage
Works

ETTINGTON

Comm.
Cen.

Rec.
Grd.

Playing
Field

FARRIERS MDT.

AVON AVON CL. FLDS.

ROAD BANBURY

Ettington Chase
Conference
Centre

B4455

Summerfields
Farm

Ettington
House
Farm

Mollsgrave
Copse

Brick Kiln
Farm

128

Brick Kiln
Gorse

Stamford
Poultry Farm

CV35

Springfields

A422 ROAD

Rattleburrow
Plantation

FOSSE WAY

B4455

Stokeyleys
Coppice

48

ILMINGTON

STRATFORD

Manor
Farm

MICKLETON

Old Rectory

Pav!

Playing Field

Bowl.
Grn.

Mables
Farm

Cross Leys
Farm

STREET ROAD

CROSS LEYS

ARMSCOTE

BENNETT

PL.

WILKINS WAY

NEPTE RD.

Sewage
Works

ROAD

Mansill
Farm

Shipston-on-Stour

CV36

The Hill Barn

244

Ilmington C of E
Prim. Sch.

STREET ROAD

STREET

STREET

ILMINGTON

Manor
Barns

LOWER
GREEN

THE BANK

MIDDLE ST.

BALLARDS LA.

VALENDERS LA.

WASHBROOK PL.

FEATHERBED LA.

MELLOWS CL.

Wharf
Farm

HILL

FRONT STREET HILL

CRAB MILL LA.

CARRIAGE
WHEEL LA.

HUNTLERS LA.

FROG LA.

GRUMP

CAMPDEN

43

Nebsworth
Coppice

420

FOXCOTE

146

Harolds
Farm

21

22

A B C D E

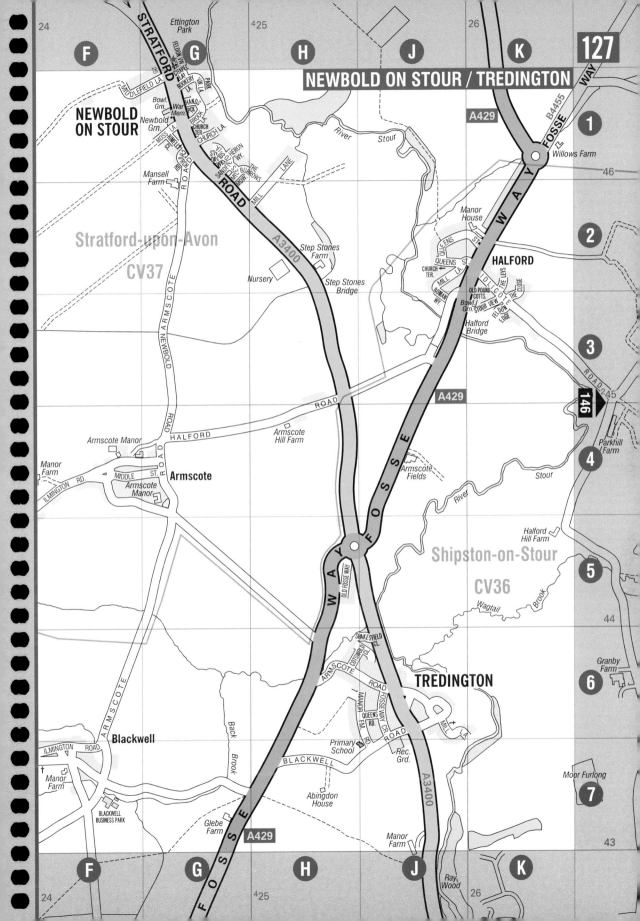

F G H J K

1
2
3
4
5
6
7

NEWBOLD ON STOUR

STRATFORD

Ettington Park

Bowl. Grn.
War. Mem.
Newbold Grn.

Mansell Farm

Stratford-upon-Avon CV37

NEWBOLD ROAD

A3400

Step Stones Farm

Nursery

Step Stones Bridge

River Stour

MILL LANE

Willows Farm

46

A429

Manor House

QUEENS ST.
QUEENS ST.
CHURCH TER.
ROMAN WY.

HALFORD

FOSSE WAY

B4455

MILL LA.
STOUR
OLD POUND COTTS.
Bowl. Grn.
STOUR VIEW
FELDON EDGE
THE LEYS
THE CLOSE
DILCOTE

Halford Bridge

Halford Hill Farm

ROAD 245

146

Parkhill Farm

ARMSCOTE ROAD

Armscote Manor

Manor Farm

ILMINGTON RD.

MIDDLE ST.

Armscote

Armscote Manor

HALFORD ROAD

Armscote Hill Farm

A429

Armscote Fields

River Stour

Shipston-on-Stour CV36

Wagtail Brook

44

Granby Farm

OLD FOSSE WAY

FOSSE WAY

A3400

SHAKESFIELD CL.
ARMSCOTE ROAD
MANOR FM.
QUEENS RD.
JOHNSON CR.
FOSSE WAY CR.
ROAD

TREDINGTON

MILL LA.

Primary School

Rec. Grd.

ILMINGTON ROAD

Blackwell

Back Brook

BLACKWELL

Abingdon House

Manor Farm

BLACKWELL BUSINESS PARK

Glebe Farm

A429

FOSSE WAY

Manor Farm

Moor Furlong

Ray Wood

43

F G H J K

24   425   26

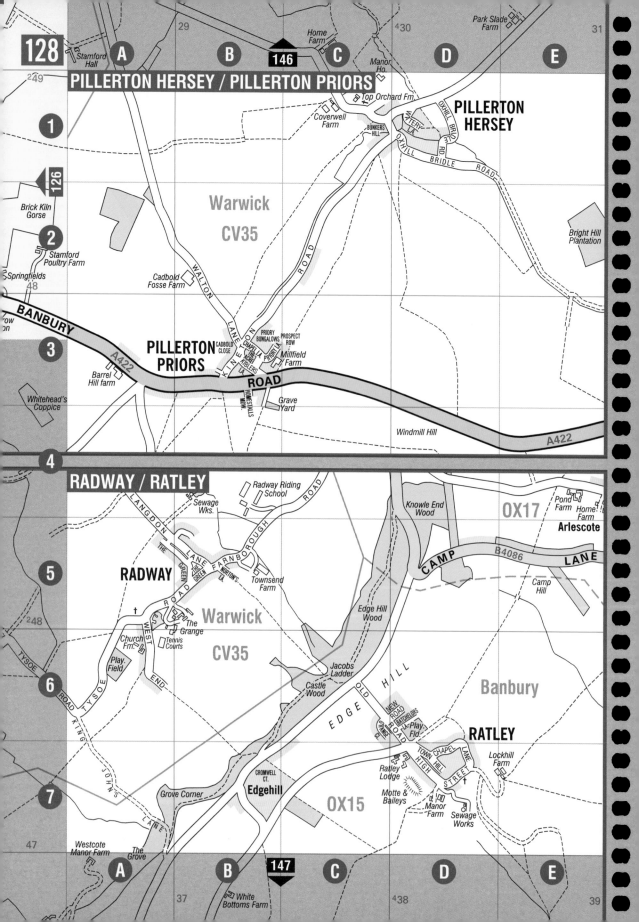

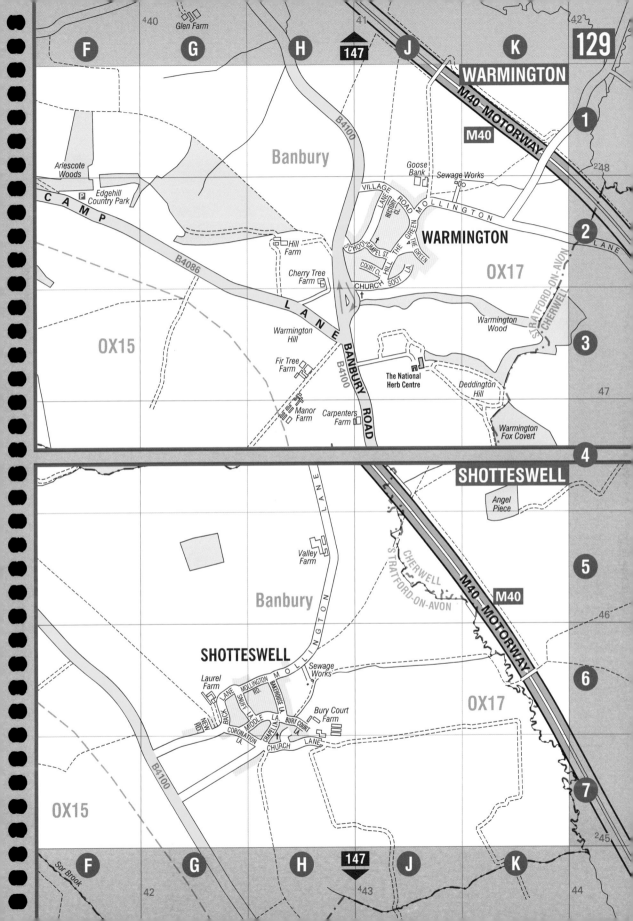

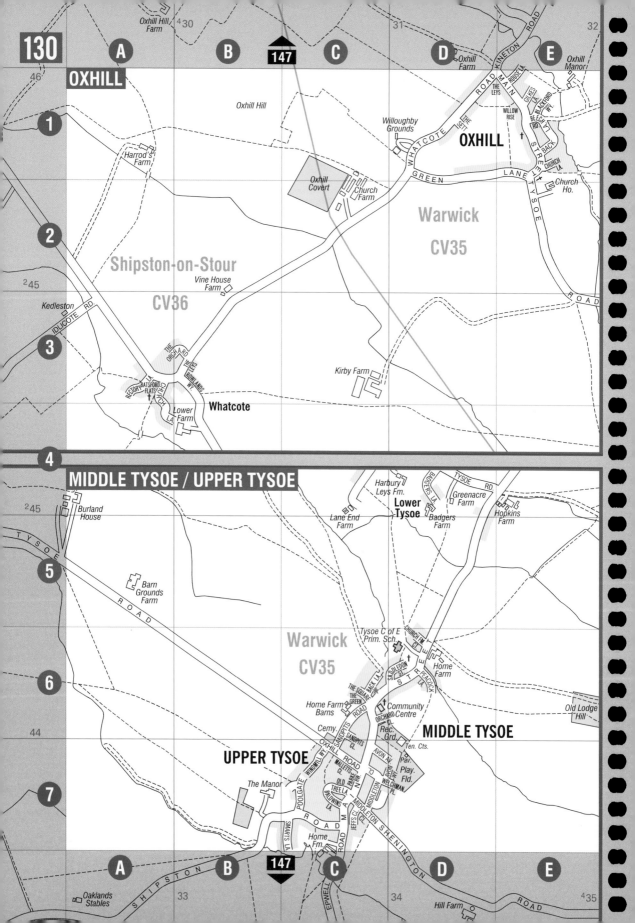

OXHILL

A **B** 147 **C** **D** **E**

Oxhill Hill Farm

30 31 32

46

Oxhill Hill

Willoughby Grounds

Oxhill Farm

Oxhill Manor

1

Harrod's Farm

THE SETT

WHATCOTE

KINETON ROAD

MAIN ST

ROUSE LA

GILKES LA

THE LEYS

WILLOW RISE

BEECH CL

BLACKFORD WY

BACK LA

CHURCH LA

OXHILL

Oxhill Covert

Church Farm

GREEN

LANE

TYSOE STREET

Church Ho.

2

Shipston-on-Stour

Vine House Farm

Warwick

CV35

CV36

245

Kedleston

IDLICOTE RD

ROAD

3

Kirby Farm

THE ORCHARD RD

THE LEYS

HOWLANDS WY

RECTORY LA

BATSFORD FLATS

CH RCH

BATSFORD LA

Whatcote

Lower Farm

4

MIDDLE TYSOE / UPPER TYSOE

A **B** 147 **C** **D** **E**

Burland House

245

Harbury Leys Fm.

Lane End Farm

TYSOE RD

Lower Tysoe

BADGERS LA

Greenacre Farm

Badgers Farm

Hopkins Farm

5

TYSOE

ROAD

Barn Grounds Farm

Tysoe C of E Prim. Sch.

CHURCH LA

Home Farm

SADDLEDON

PADDOCK

ST RE E

6

Warwick

CV35

Home Farm Barns

THE SQUARE

BACK LA

THE GREEN

ORCHARD RD

Community Centre

Old Lodge Hill

44

Cemy.

OXHILL ROAD

SANDPITS CL

SANDPITS

ORCHARD CL

Rec. Grd.

AVON AV

Pav.

Ten. Cts.

Play. Fld.

MIDDLE TYSOE

UPPER TYSOE

The Manor

WINDMILL WY

POOLGATE

OLD TREE LA

BALDWINS LA

MALLETTS CL

BANK CL

OLD TREE RD

MIDDLETON ROAD

AVON AV

WELCHMAN

JEFFS CL

7

ROAD

SHIPSTON

SLAWNS

Home Fm.

ROAD

EPNELL CL

MIDDLETON

SHENINGTON ROAD

Oaklands Stables

33 34 35

Hill Farm

A **B** 147 **C** **D** **E**

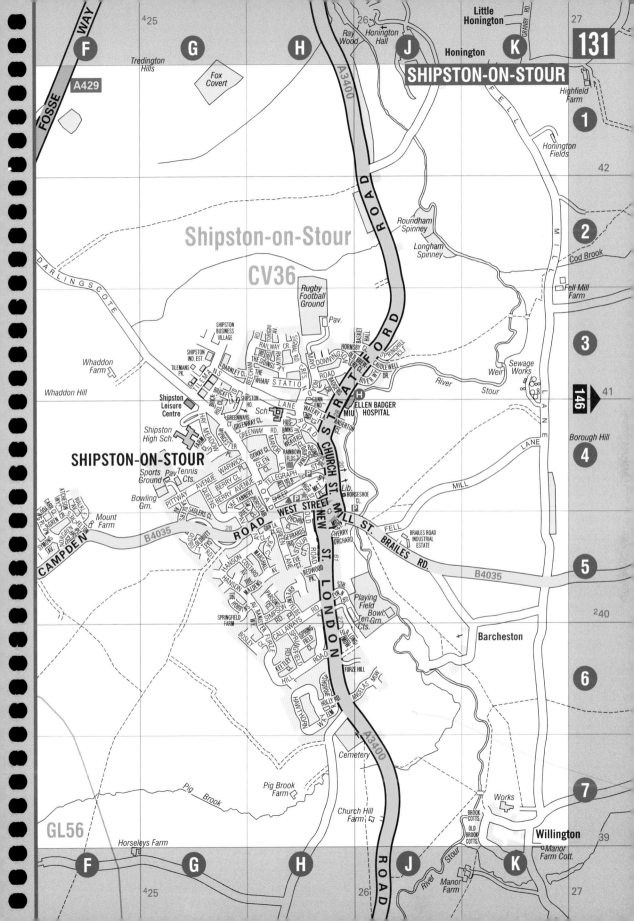

SHIPSTON-ON-STOUR

Grid references (top): F · G · H · J · K

Grid references (top labels): ⁴25 · 26 · 27

Little Honington

GRANBY RD

Honington

Honington Hall

Ray Wood

Highfield Farm

Honington Fields

42

FOSSE WAY

A429

Tredington Hills

Fox Covert

Shipston-on-Stour

CV36

DARLINGSCOTE

Roundham Spinney

Longham Spinney

Cod Brook

Fell Mill Farm

Rugby Football Ground

Pav.

Whaddon Farm

Whaddon Hill

SHIPSTON BUSINESS VILLAGE

SHIPSTON IND. EST.

TILEMANS PK.

Shipston Leisure Centre

River Stour

Weir

Sewage Works

STRATFORD ROAD

A3400

146

41

Borough Hill

Shipston High Sch.

HAY MEADOW

TAMM MEADOW

WORCESTER

WARWICK

BERRY CL.

QUEENS AVENUE

AVENUE

PITTWAY

Sports Ground

Pav

Tennis Cts.

Bowling Grn.

SHIPSTON-ON-STOUR

MILL LANE

ELLEN BADGER HOSPITAL

MIU

CHURCH ST.

MILL ST.

Lib.

HORSESHOE CL.

P

WEST STREET

NEW ST.

CHERRY ORCHARD

BRAILES RD.

BRAILES ROAD INDUSTRIAL ESTATE

FELL LANE

Mount Farm

CAMPDEN ROAD

B4035

SYMONS

CARRS

OLDMILL

SADLERS CL.

HANSON AV.

CASTARD

THE MEADOWS

MARSHAL

REDWOOD PK.

THE ROBBINS

SPRINGFIELD FARM

BOSLEY

CALLAWAYS

SPRINGFIELD RD.

FURZE

KETTLER HILL

SIMPSON RD.

PARSONS

FIR LONG

STH. VIN.

A3400

Playing Field

Bowl.

Ten.Grn.

Cts.

B4035

²40

Barcheston

FURZE HILL

ANGELAS MDW.

HOLLY RD.

HAWTHORN W. FM.

Works

Cemetery

Pig Brook Farm

Pig Brook

Church Hill Farm

BROOK COTTS.

OLD BROOK COTTS.

River Stour

Manor Farm

Willington

Manor Farm Cott.

39

GL56

Horseleys Farm

Grid references (bottom): F · G · H · J · K

Grid references (bottom labels): ⁴25 · 26 · 27

1 · 2 · 3 · 4 · 5 · 6 · 7

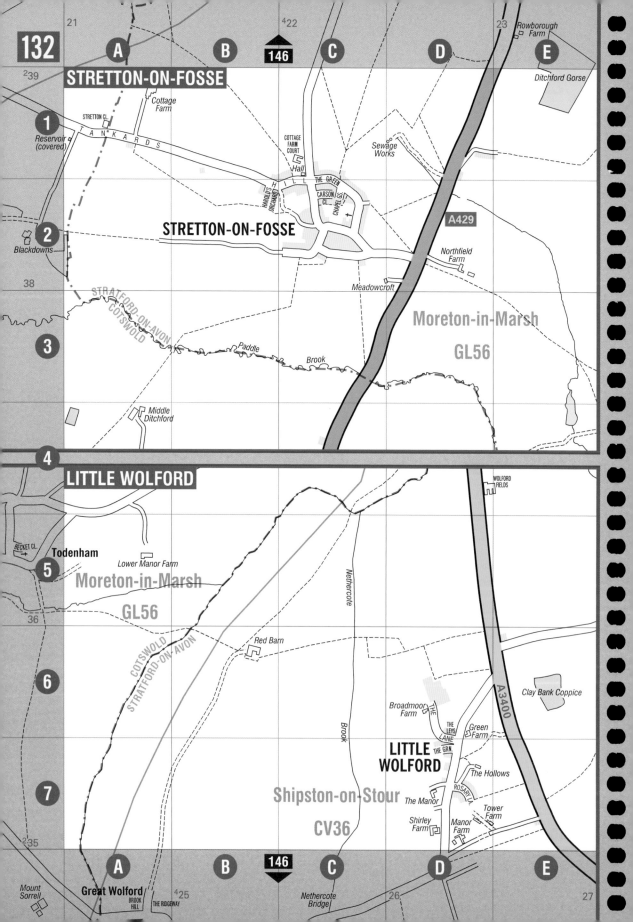

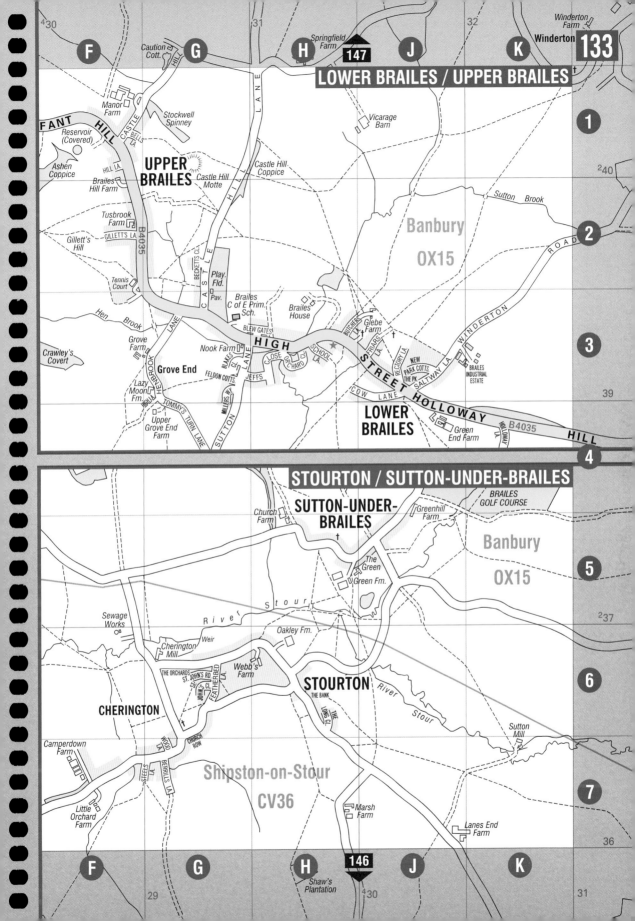

LOWER BRAILES / UPPER BRAILES

STOURTON / SUTTON-UNDER-BRAILES

Winderton Farm

Winderton

Springfield Farm

147

Caution Cott.

Manor Farm

Stockwell Spinney

Vicarage Barn

Reservoir (Covered)

FANT HILL

Ashen Coppice

Brailes Hill Farm

UPPER BRAILES

Castle Hill Motte

Castle Hill Coppice

HILL LA.

Tusbrook Farm

Gillett's Hill

GILLETT'S LA.

B4035

Tennis Court

Play. Fld.

Pav.

Brailes C of E Prim. Sch.

Brailes House

Banbury

OX15

Sutton Brook

ROAD

Hen Brook

Grove Farm

Crawley's Covert

Nook Farm

BLEW GATES

BLAKES

CLOSE

ORCHARD

SCHOOL LA.

HIGH

Butchers

Glebe Farm

FRIARS LA.

RECTORY LA.

SALTWAY LA.

WINDERTON LA.

NEW PARK COTTS. THE PK.

BRAILES INDUSTRIAL ESTATE

Winderton

STREET

Grove End

Feldon Cotts.

JEFFS

MILLERS WY.

HOLLOWAY

COW LANE

LOWER BRAILES

Lazy Moon Fm.

TOMMY'S TURN LANE

HENBROOK LANE

SUTTON LANE

Upper Grove End Farm

Green End Farm

HOLLOWAY LA.

B4035

HILL

39

STOURTON / SUTTON-UNDER-BRAILES

BRAILES GOLF COURSE

Church Farm

SUTTON-UNDER-BRAILES

Greenhill Farm

The Green

Green Fm.

Banbury

OX15

Sewage Works

Stour

River

Weir

Oakley Fm.

Cherington Mill

THE ORCHARDS

ST. JOHN'S RD.

ST. JOHN'S CL.

FEATHERBED

Webb's Farm

STOURTON

River

Stour

THE BANK

THE LONG CL.

CHERINGTON

Camperdown Farm

WOOD

CHURCH ROW

BERRILS LA.

ST. JOHN'S

Sutton Mill

Shipston-on-Stour

CV36

Little Orchard Farm

Marsh Farm

Lanes End Farm

146

Shaw's Plantation

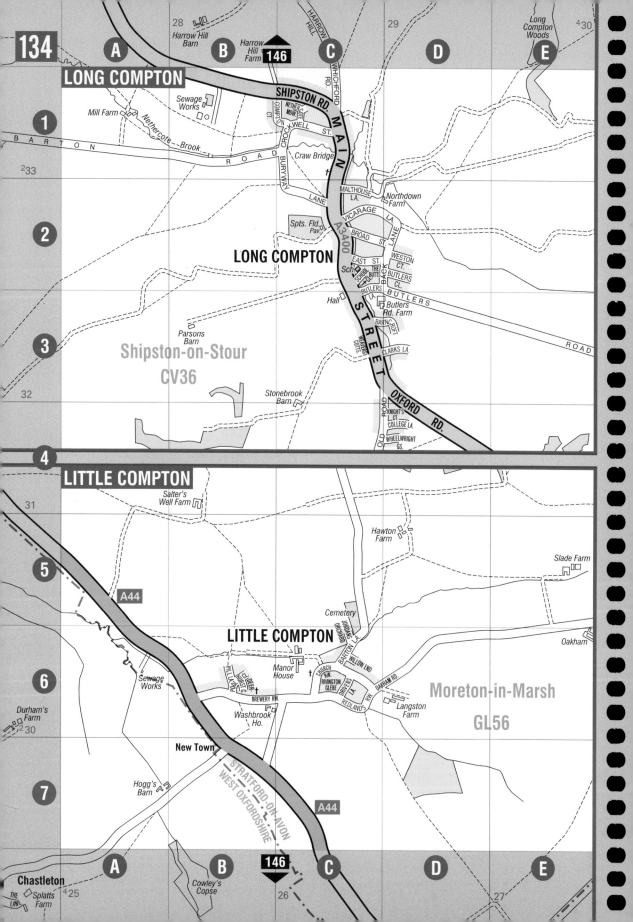

134

LONG COMPTON

28   29   30

Harrow Hill Barn

Harrow Hill Farm

HARROW HILL

WHICHFORD RD.

146

Long Compton Woods

A   **B**   **C**   **D**   **E**

SHIPSTON RD.

Mill Farm

Sewage Works

Nethercote Brook

BARTON ROAD

NETHER MDW.

COMPTON CT.

CROCKWELL ST.

Craw Bridge

BURYWAY LANE

MAIN

MALTHOUSE LA.

Northdown Farm

Spts. Fld. Pav.

VICARAGE LA.

WESTON CT.

LONG COMPTON

BROAD ST.

EAST ST.

Sch.

THE BUTTS

BUTLERS CL.

KNOB LA.

BUTLERS LA.

Hall

BUTLERS ROAD

Butlers Rd. Farm

BARNCROFT

WESTON COTS.

Parsons Barn

Shipston-on-Stour
CV36

33

32

STREET

CLARKS LA.

ROAD

Stonebrook Barn

OXFORD RD.

OLD ROAD

KNIGHT'S CT.

COLLEGE LA.

WHEELWRIGHT GS.

A3400

4

LITTLE COMPTON

Salter's Well Farm

Hawton Farm

Slade Farm

31

A44

Sewage Works

Cemetery

JORDANS ORCHARD

LITTLE COMPTON

BARTON LA.

Oakham

Manor House

CHURCH RW.

RIVINGTON GLEBE

WILLOW END

DRIVERS LA.

RW.

OAKHAM RD.

Moreton-in-Marsh
GL56

Durham's Farm

30

PILL RW.

POLE CT.

DEER WING CT.

BREWERY RW.

Washbrook Ho.

REDLANDS

Langston Farm

New Town

STRATFORD-ON-AVON

WEST OXFORDSHIRE

Hogg's Barn

A44

A   **B**   **C**   **D**   **E**

Chastleton

THE LANE

Splatts Farm

Cowley's Copse

146

25   26   27

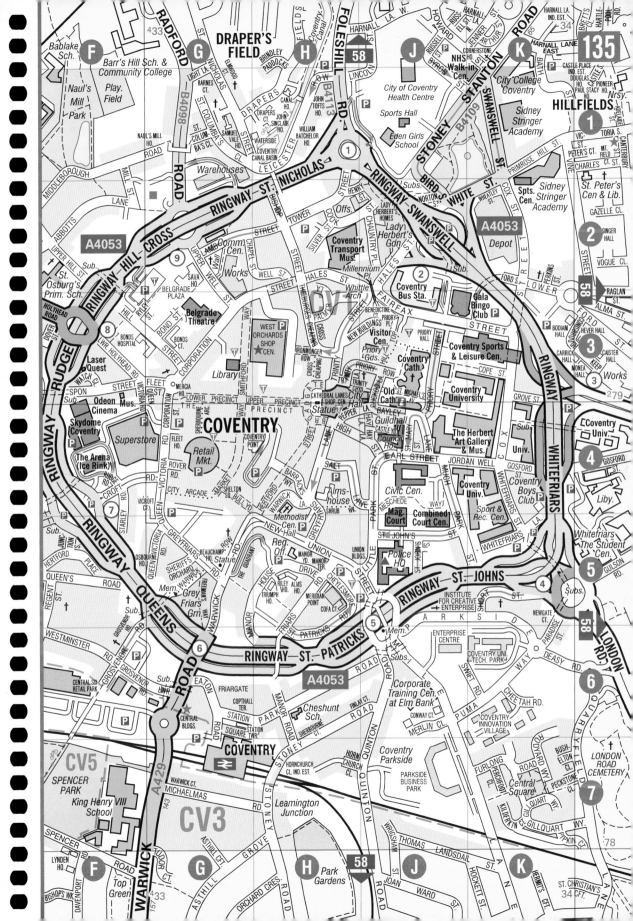

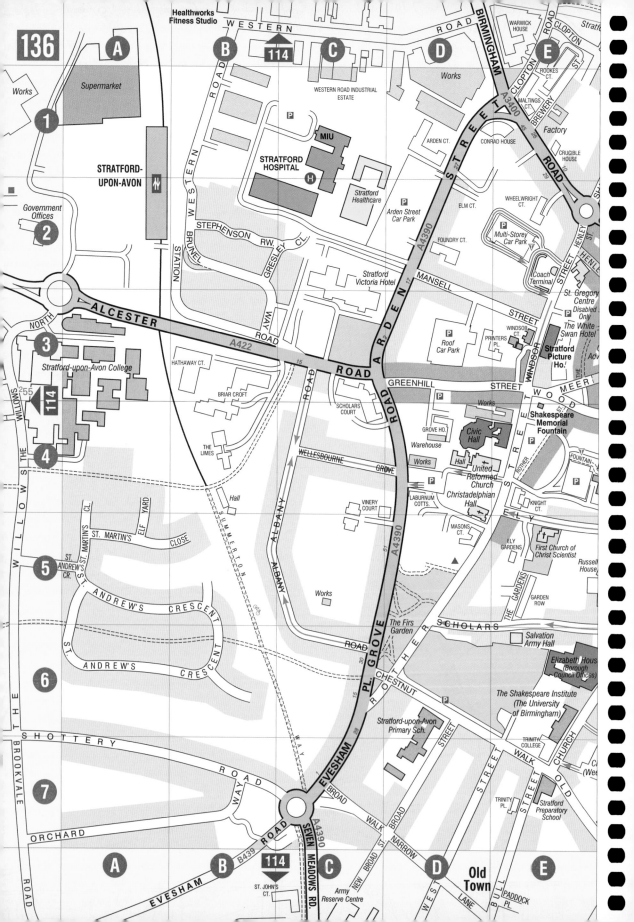

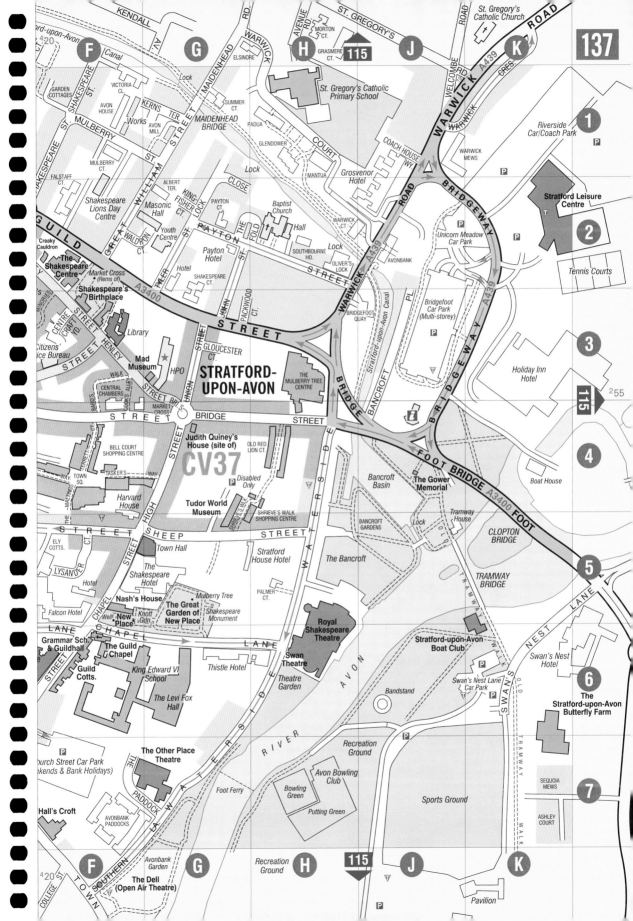

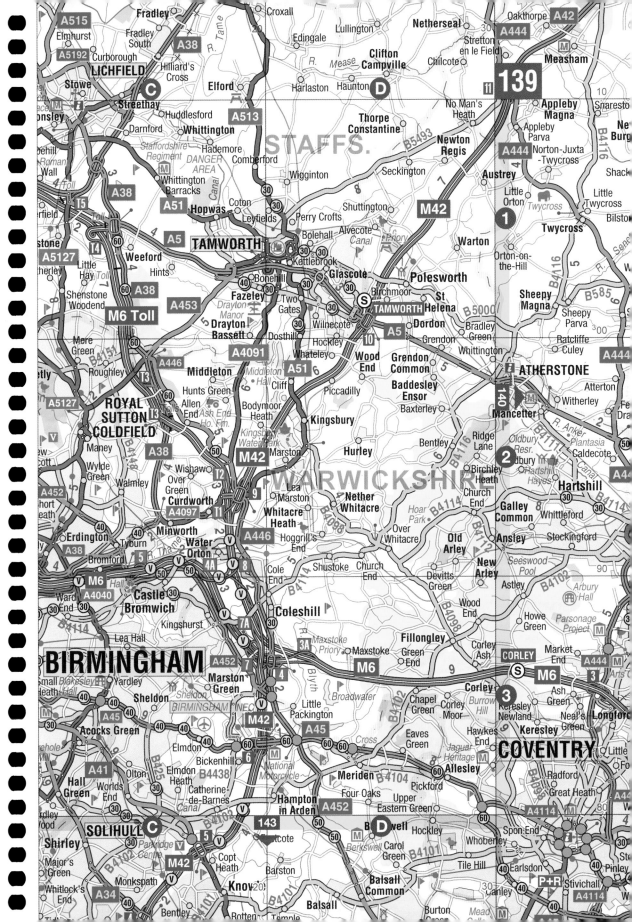

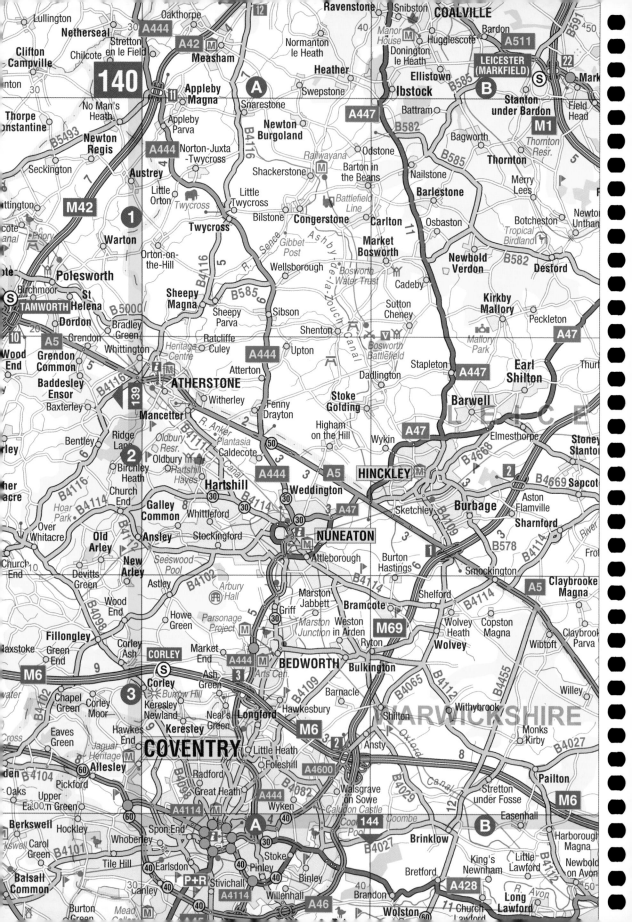

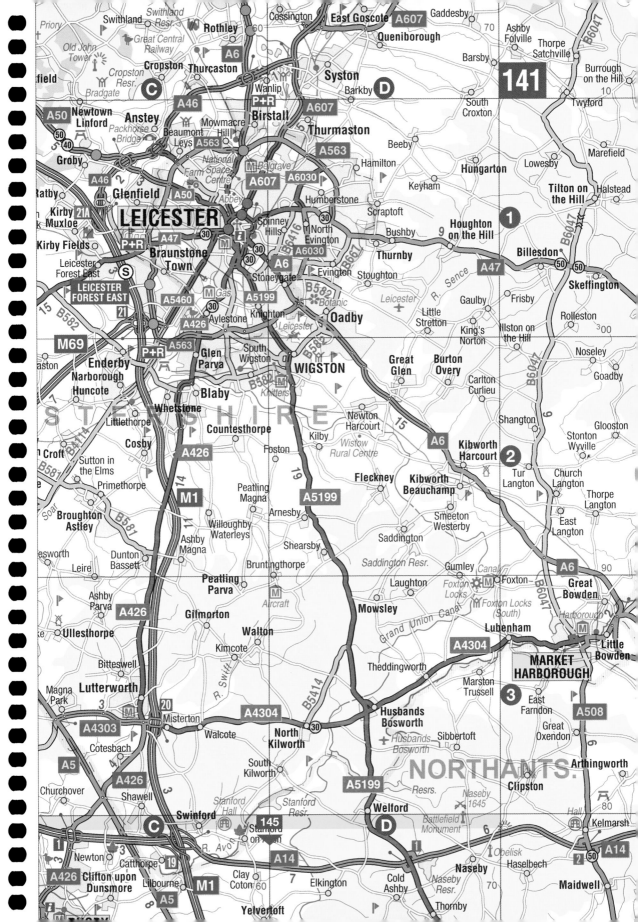

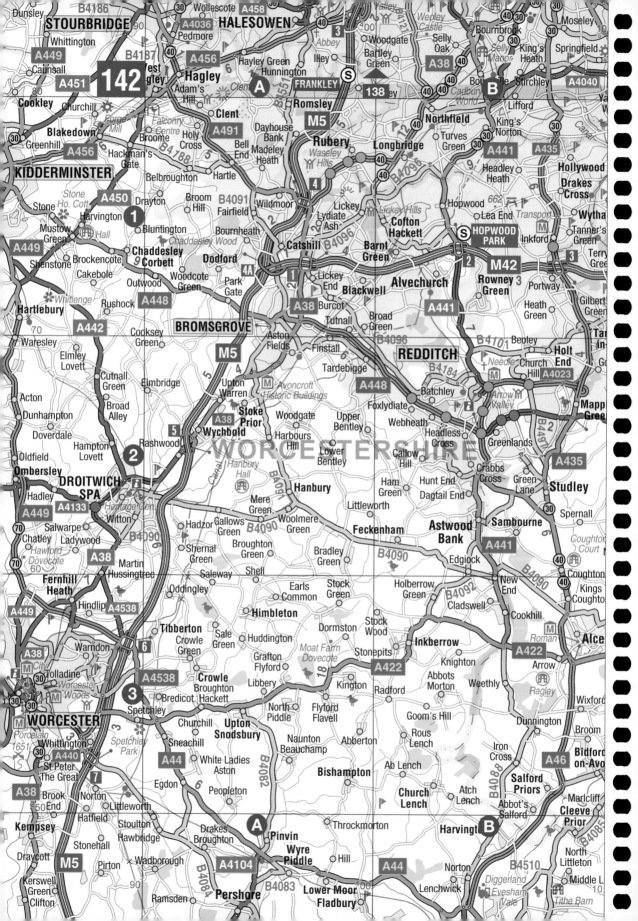

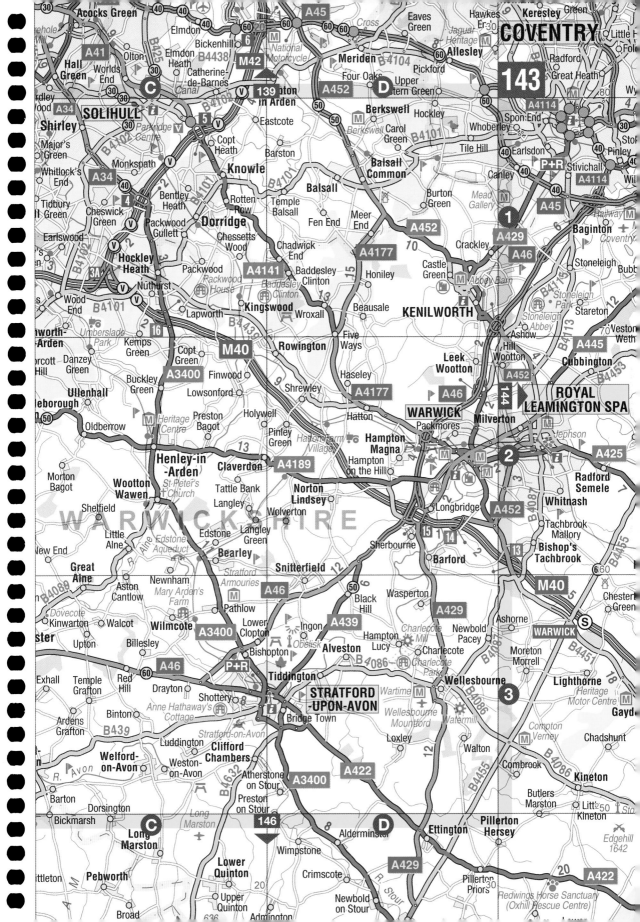

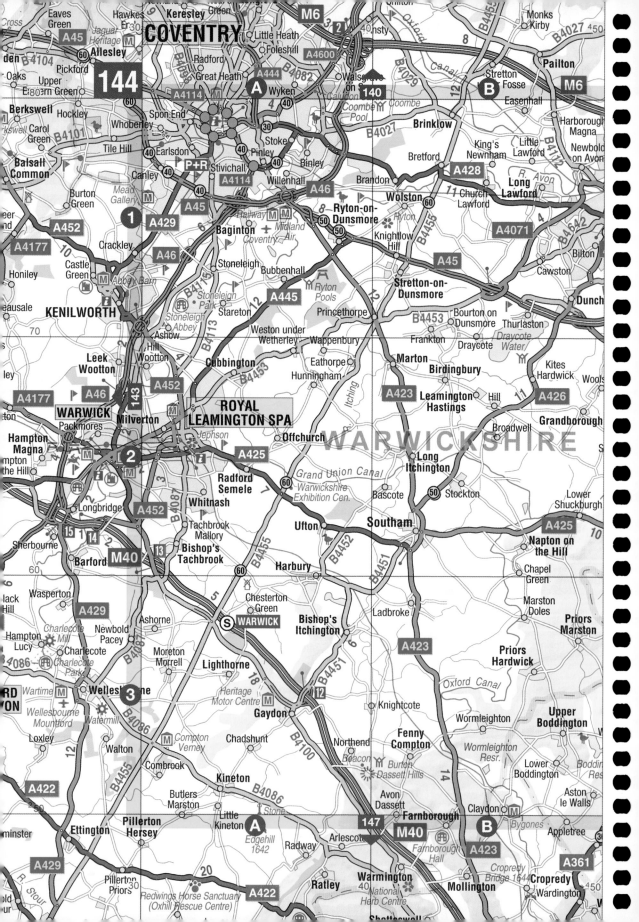

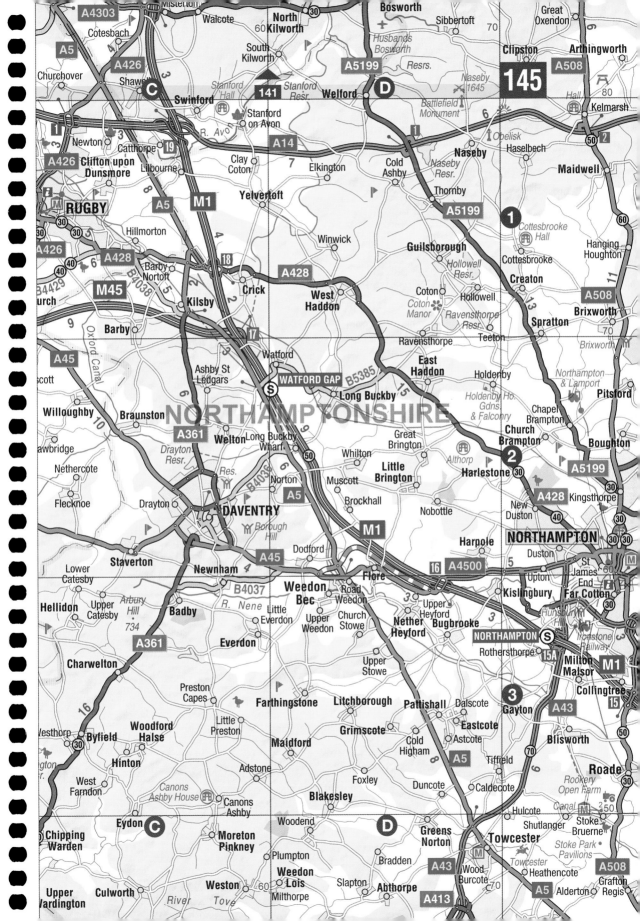

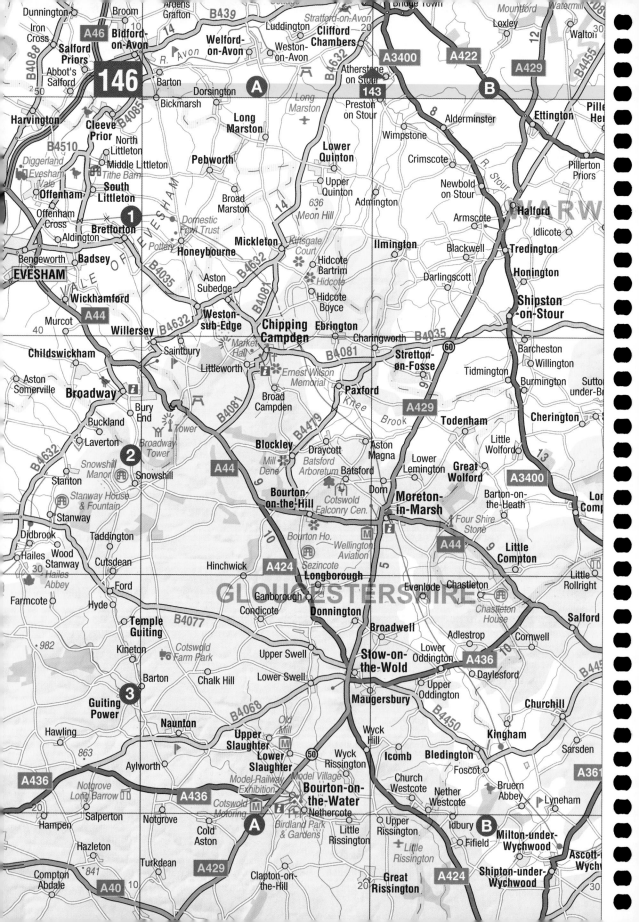

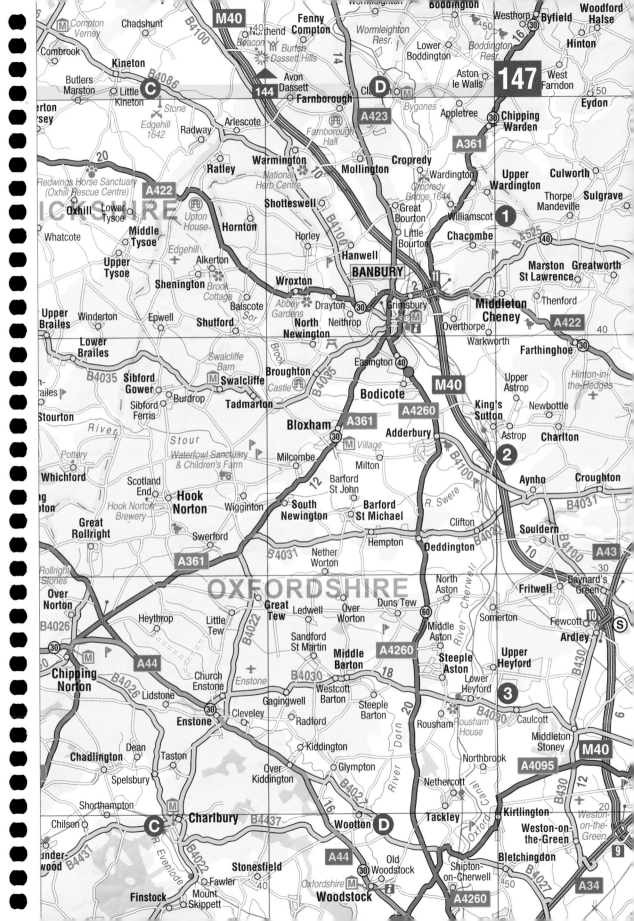

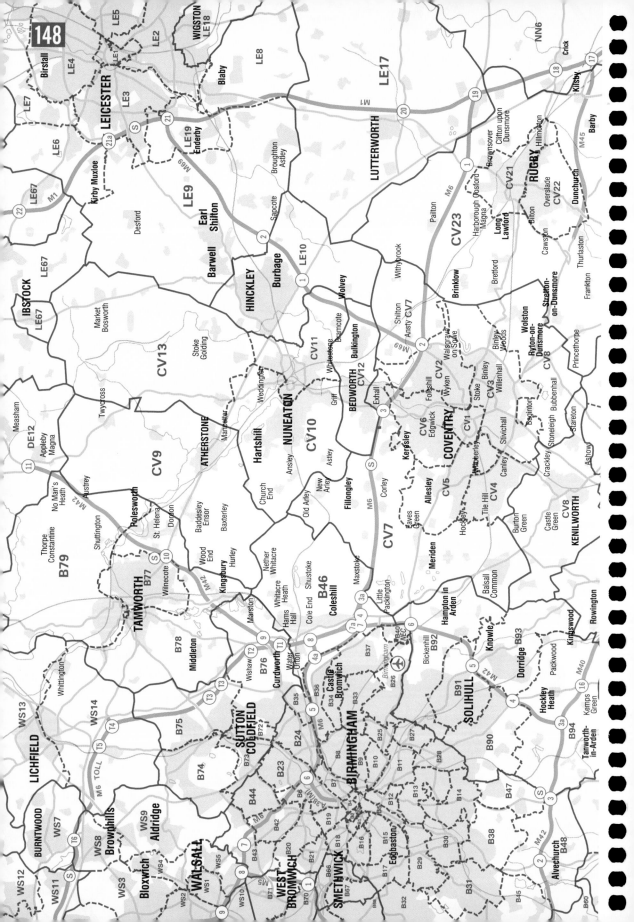

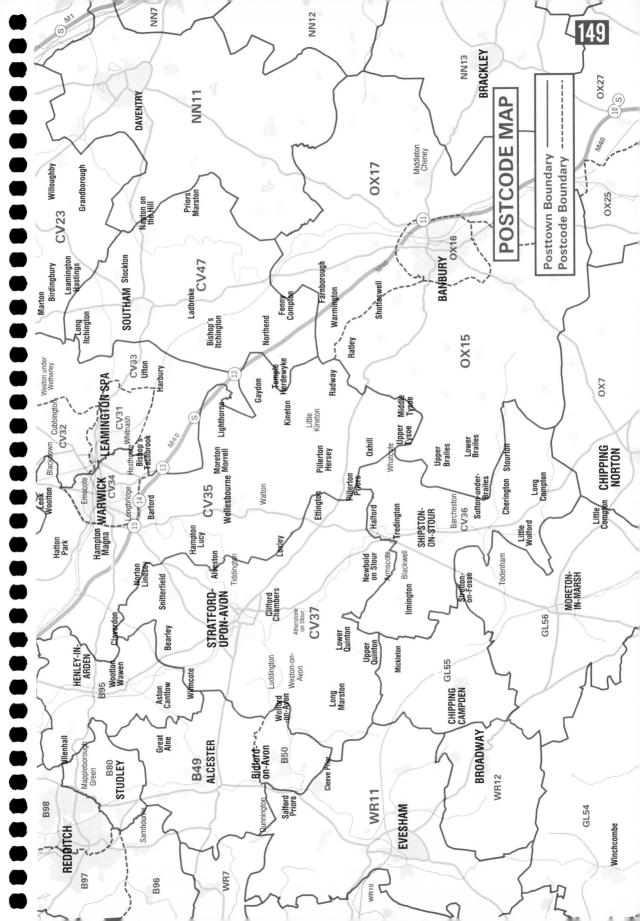

POSTCODE MAP

Posttown Boundary ———
Postcode Boundary - - - - - -

INDEX

Including Streets, Places & Areas, Industrial Estates,
Selected Flats & Walkways, Junction Names & Service Areas, Stations and Places of Interest.

HOW TO USE THIS INDEX

1. Each street name is followed by its Postcode District, then by its Locality abbreviation(s) and then by its map reference;
   e.g. **Abbey Hill** CV8 . . . .4D **78** is in the CV8 Postcode District and the Kenilworth Locality and is to be found in square 4D on page **78**. The page number is shown in bold type.

2. A strict alphabetical order is followed in which Av., Rd., St., etc. (though abbreviated) are read in full and as part of the street name;
   e.g. **Avoncliffe** appears after **Avon Cvn. Pk.** but before **Avon Cl.**

3. Streets and a selection of flats and walkways that cannot be shown on street map pages **6-134**, appear in the index with the thoroughfare to which they are connected shown in brackets; e.g. **Albion Ter.** B46: Wat O . . . .1B **24** (off St Pauls Ct.)

4. Addresses that are in more than one part are referred to as not continuous.

5. Places and areas are shown in the index in BLUE TYPE and the map reference is to the actual map square in which the town centre or area is located and not to the place name shown on the map. Map references for entries that appear on street map pages **6-134** are shown first, with references to road map pages **138-147** shown in brackets;
   e.g. **ALCESTER** 5B **112** (3B **142**)

6. An example of a selected place of interest is **Abbey Barn Mus.** 4C **78**

7. Examples of stations are:
   Atherstone Station (Rail) . . . . 3B **16**; **Atherstone Bus Station** . . . . 3C **16**; **Austin Drive (Park & Ride) (Coventry)** 7G **51**

8. Junction names and Service Areas are shown in the index in BOLD CAPITAL TYPE; e.g. **BELFRY JUNC.** 1C **18**

9. Map references for entries that appear on large scale pages **135-137** are shown first, with small scale map references shown in brackets;
   e.g. **Abbotts La.** CV1: Cov . . .2F **135** (4B **58**)

GENERAL ABBREVIATIONS

All. : Alley	**Cott.** : Cottage	**Ho's.** : Houses	**Pct.** : Precinct
App. : Approach	**Cotts.** : Cottages	**Ind.** : Industrial	**Ri.** : Rise
Arc. : Arcade	**Ct.** : Court	**Info.** : Information	**Rd.** : Road
Av. : Avenue	**Cres.** : Crescent	**Intl.** : International	**Rdbt.** : Roundabout
Blvd. : Boulevard	**Cft.** : Croft	**Junc.** : Junction	**Shop.** : Shopping
Bri. : Bridge	**Dr.** : Drive	**La.** : Lane	**Sth.** : South
Bldgs. : Buildings	**E.** : East	**Lit.** : Little	**Sq.** : Square
Bungs. : Bungalows	**Ent.** : Enterprise	**Lwr.** : Lower	**St.** : Street
Bus. : Business	**Est.** : Estate	**Mnr.** : Manor	**Ter.** : Terrace
Cvn. : Caravan	**Fld.** : Field	**Mans.** : Mansions	**Twr.** : Tower
C'way. : Causeway	**Flds.** : Fields	**Mdw.** : Meadow	**Trad.** : Trading
Cen. : Centre	**Gdn.** : Garden	**Mdws.** : Meadows	**Up.** : Upper
Chu. : Church	**Gdns.** : Gardens	**M.** : Mews	**Va.** : Vale
Chyd. : Churchyard	**Gth.** : Garth	**Mt.** : Mount	**Vw.** : View
Circ. : Circle	**Ga.** : Gate	**Mus.** : Museum	**Vs.** : Villas
Cir. : Circus	**Gt.** : Great	**Nth.** : North	**Vis.** : Visitors
Cl. : Close	**Grn.** : Green	**Pde.** : Parade	**Wlk.** : Walk
Coll. : College	**Gro.** : Grove	**Pk.** : Park	**W.** : West
Comn. : Common	**Hgts.** : Heights	**Pas.** : Passage	**Yd.** : Yard
Cnr. : Corner	**Ho.** : House	**Pl.** : Place	

LOCALITY ABBREVIATIONS

Alison Sq.—Ashwood Rd.

Alison Sq. CV2: Ald G . . . 2H 51
ALKERTON . . . 1C 147
Allan Rd. CV6: Cov . . . 3K 57
Allans Cl. CV23: Clift D . . . 3C 76
Allans Dr. CV23: Clift D . . . 3C 76
Allans La. CV23: Clift D . . . 3C 76
Allard Ho. CV3: W'hall . . . 2H 69
Allard Way CV3: Bin, Cov . . . 1G 69
Allen Cl. B80: Stud . . . 5D 92
Allendale Av. B80: Stud . . . 4D 92
Allendale Ct. B80: Stud . . . 4D 92
Allendale Cres. B80: Stud . . . 4D 92
ALLEN END . . . 2C 139
Allens Cl. CV9: Bad E . . . 3F 15
Allens Ct. CV2: Cov . . . 4F 59
Allerton Cl. CV2: Cov . . . 5A 60
Allerton Rd. CV23: Brow . . . 6K 65
ALLESLEY . . . 1F 57 (3D 139)
Allesley By-Pass CV5: Alle, Cov . . . 1F 57
Allesley Ct. CV5: Alle . . . 1E 56
Allesley Cft. CV5: Alle . . . 1E 56
Allesley Hall Dr. CV5: Alle, Cov . . . 2G 57
Allesley Old Rd. CV5: Cov . . . 2G 57
Allesley Pk. Pitch & Putt Course . . . 2G 57
Allesley Rd. CV21: N'bld A . . . 2F 75
Alliance Cl. CV11: Nun . . . 1B 32
Alliance Trad. Est. CV4: Tile H . . . 6E 56
Alliance Way CV2: Cov . . . 2G 59
Allibone Cl. CV31: W'nsh . . . 4E 102
Allied Cl. CV6: Cov . . . 4D 50
Allimore La. B49: Alc . . . 4A 112
Allitt Gro. CV8: Ken . . . 4F 79
All Oaks La. CV23: Brin . . . 4D 62
All Saints Cl. CV7: Withy . . . 1D 54
All Saint's La. *CV1: Cov . . . 4E 58*
(off Lwr. Ford St.)
All Saints La. CV1: Cov . . . 4E 58
All Saints Rd. CV12: Bed . . . 4F 41
CV34: Warw . . . 6J 97
All Saints Sq. CV12: Bed . . . 2H 41
Allwoods Cl. B49: Alc . . . 4A 112
Alma Ct. CV11: Bram . . . 6H 33
Alma St. CV1: Cov . . . 3K 135 (4E 58)
Almond Av. CV10: Nun . . . 5H 21
CV32: Lea S . . . 4D 98
Almond Cl. CV23: Barby . . . 7E 88
Almond Gro. CV21: N'bld A . . . 1E 74
CV34: Warw . . . 6J 97
Almond Tree Av. CV2: Cov . . . 4H 51
Almshouses CV12: Bed . . . 2J 41
CV34: Warw . . . 2G 101
(off Castle Hill)
Alne Bank Rd. B49: Alc . . . 4D 112
Alne Cl. B95: Hen A . . . 2H 93
ALNE END . . . 3F 113
Alpha Bus. Pk. CV2: Cov . . . 5K 51
Alpha Ho. CV2: Cov . . . 3G 59
Alpine Ct. CV8: Ken . . . 3E 78
Alpine Ri. CV3: Cov . . . 3A 68
Alspath La. CV5: East G . . . 3D 56
Alspath Rd. CV7: Mer . . . 5E 46
Althorpe Ind. Est. CV31: Lea S . . . 1E 102
Althorpe St. CV31: Lea S . . . 1E 102
Alton Cl. CV2: Cov . . . 4K 51
Alum Cl. CV6: Cov . . . 6D 50
ALVECHURCH . . . 1B 142
ALVECOTE . . . 3A 8 (1D 139)
Alvecote Cotts. B79: A'cte . . . 3A 8
Alvecote La. B79: A'cte . . . 3A 8
Alvecote Meadows . . . 3A 8
Alvecote Pools . . . 5B 8
Alvecote Pools Nature Reserve . . . 2A 8
Alvecote Priory (remains of) . . . 4B 8
Alverley Rd. CV6: Cov . . . 1C 58
Alverstone Rd. CV2: Cov . . . 3G 59
ALVESTON . . . 2B 116 (3D 143)
ALVESTON HILL . . . 6K 115
Alveston La. CV37: A'ton . . . 2A 116
Alveston Leys CV37: A'ton . . . 1B 116
Alveston Pl. CV32: Lea S . . . 6E 98
Alvin Cl. CV3: Bin . . . 6B 60
Alvis Ho. CV1: Cov . . . 5H 135
Alvis Retail Pk. CV5: Cov . . . 4A 58
Alvyn Smith Cl. CV2: Cov . . . 4H 51
Alwyn Freeman Ct. *CV7: Ker E . . . 7A 40*
(off Somers Rd.)
Alwyn Rd. CV22: Bil . . . 1C 86
Ambassador Ct. CV32: Lea S . . . 4D 98
Ambassador Rd. B26: Birm A . . . 2C 44
Amberley Av. CV12: Bulk . . . 2E 42
Ambien Rd. CV9: Ath . . . 4C 16
AMBLECOTE . . . 3A 138
Ambler Gro. CV2: Cov . . . 4J 59
Ambleside CV2: Walsg S . . . 4A 52
CV21: Brow . . . 1K 75
Ambleside Rd. CV12: Bed . . . 3G 41
Ambleside Way CV11: Nun . . . 5F 23
Ambrose Cl. CV21: Rugby . . . 2J 75
Amelia Cl. CV12: Bulk . . . 2E 42
Amelie Cres. CV3: Cov . . . 6J 59
Amersham Cl. CV5: Cov . . . 3F 57
Amey Way CV34: Warw . . . 7D 96
Amherst Bus. Cen.
CV34: Warw . . . 1D 100
Amherst Rd. CV8: Ken . . . 2C 78
Amis Way CV37: S Avon . . . 6H 115
Amos Av. CV10: Nun . . . 2H 31
Amos Jacques Rd. CV12: Bed . . . 1G 41
Amphion Bus. Pk. CV6: Ash G . . . 1E 50
Amroth M. CV31: Lea S . . . 2G 103
Amy Cl. CV6: Lford . . . 2F 51
Anchorway Rd. CV3: Finh . . . 4A 68
Anderson Av. CV22: Rugby . . . 1G 87
Anderson Dr. CV31: W'nsh . . . 6E 102
Anderton Cl. CV36: Ship S . . . 4H 131
Anderton Rd. CV6: Ald G . . . 1H 51
CV12: Bed . . . 4C 40
Andrews Cl. CV8: Bag . . . 6F 69
CV34: Warw . . . 6K 97
Anfield Ct. CV31: Lea S . . . 1F 103
Angela Av. CV2: Walsg S . . . 5A 52
Angelas Mdw. CV36: Ship S . . . 6J 131
Angel M. B46: Cole . . . 5F 25
Anglesey Av. B36: Cas B . . . 5B 24
Anglesey Cl. CV5: Alle . . . 7F 49
Angless Way CV8: Ken . . . 6D 78
Anglian Way CV3: Cov . . . 6G 59
(not continuous)
Angus Cl. CV5: East G . . . 3E 56
CV8: Ken . . . 3G 79
Anker Ct. CV11: Nun . . . 1B 32
Anker Dr. CV23: Long L . . . 3B 74
Ankerside B78: Pole . . . 6D 8
Anker St. CV11: Nun . . . 1K 31
Anker Vw. B78: Pole . . . 2D 10
Anley Way CV6: Cov . . . 1C 58
Anne Cres. CV3: W'hall . . . 3J 69
Anne Hathaway's Cottage . . . 5B 114
Anns La. CV23: Stret U . . . 6G 55
Ansell Ct. CV34: Warw . . . 1F 101
Ansell Dr. CV6: Lford . . . 1G 51
Ansell Way CV34: Warw . . . 1F 101
ANSLEY . . . 7A 20 (2D 139)
ANSLEY COMMON . . . 3D 20
Ansley Comn. CV10: Ans C . . . 3D 20
Ansley Hall CV10: Ans C . . . 4B 20
Ansley Hall Dr.
B78: Dord, Frly . . . 7A 10
Ansley La. CV7: Old A . . . 2D 28
CV10: Ansl . . . 6A 20, 2D 28
Ansley Rd. CV10: Nun . . . 1G 29
Anson Cl. CV22: Bil . . . 6C 74
CV35: Welle . . . 5G 117
Anson Way CV2: Walsg S . . . 6B 52
ANSTEY . . . 1C 141
Anstey Cft. B37: F'bri . . . 1A 34
ANSTY . . . 3F 53 (3A 140)
Ansty Golf Course . . . 3H 53
Ansty La. CV2: Ansty . . . 7K 53
Ansty Pk. CV7: Ansty . . . 6G 53
Ansty Rd. CV2: Cov, Walsg S . . . 3J 59
CV23: Brin, Stret U . . . 1A 62
Antelope Gdns. CV34: Warw . . . 7E 96
Antelope Ho. CV5: Cov . . . 5K 57
Anthony Way CV2: Cov . . . 5J 59
Antony Gardner Cres.
CV31: W'nsh . . . 4E 102
Antrim Cl. CV5: Alle . . . 7E 48
Apollo Cinema
Royal Leamington Spa . . . 7D 98
Apollo Ho. CV1: Cov . . . 5B 58
Apollo Way CV34: Warw . . . 3B 102
Appleby Hill CV9: Aus . . . 6G 7
APPLEBY MAGNA . . . 1A 140
APPLEBY PARVA . . . 2K 7 (1A 140)
Applecross Cl. CV4: Westw H . . . 2D 66
Appledore Dr. CV5: Alle . . . 2D 56
Apple Gro. CV22: Bil . . . 6B 74
Apple Pie La. CV10: Harts . . . 1G 21
APPLETREE . . . 1D 147
Apple Way CV4: Canly . . . 7G 57
Appleyard Cl. CV12: Bed . . . 3H 41
Approach, The CV31: Lea S . . . 2D 102
Aqua Pl. CV21: Rugby . . . 3J 75
Arabella Wlk. CV3: Cov . . . 6J 59
Aragon Dr. CV34: Warw . . . 2A 102
Arboretum, The CV4: Canly . . . 5H 67
Arborfields Cl. CV8: Ken . . . 1F 79
Arbor Way B37: Chel W . . . 4C 34
Arbour Cl. CV8: Ken . . . 6F 79
CV22: Rugby . . . 2D 86
Arbours, The CV22: Rugby . . . 6J 75
Arbury Av. CV6: Cov . . . 4E 50
CV12: Bed . . . 2G 41
Arbury Cl. CV32: Lill . . . 4E 98
Arbury Gth. CV10: Nun . . . 1C 30
Arbury Hall . . . 5D 30
Arbury Rd. CV10: Nun . . . 2D 30
Arcade, The CV9: Ath . . . 3C 16
Archer Cl. B80: Stud . . . 3C 92
Archer Rd. CV8: Ken . . . 6C 78
Archers Spinney
CV21: Hillm . . . 1D 88
Archery Flds. CV34: Warw . . . 2H 101
Archery Rd. CV7: Mer . . . 5D 46
CV31: Lea S . . . 7C 98
Arches Bus. Cen.
CV21: Rugby . . . 3J 75
Arches Ind. Est. CV1: Cov . . . 4A 58
CV21: Rugby . . . 4K 75
Arches La. CV21: Rugby . . . 3J 75
Arch Rd. CV2: Cov . . . 2A 60
Ard Cl. CV22: Caw . . . 7B 74
Arden Av. CV9: Ath . . . 3D 16
Arden Bus. Cen. B49: Alc . . . 2B 112
Arden Cl. B95: Hen A . . . 2H 93
CV7: Mer . . . 5E 46
CV22: Bil . . . 4D 86
CV31: Lea S . . . 3F 103
CV34: Warw . . . 6J 97
CV37: Wilm . . . 5J 113
Arden Ct. B49: Alc . . . 2B 112
B92: H Ard . . . 7G 45
CV3: Bin W . . . 1F 71
CV37: S Avon . . . 1D 136
Arden Cft. B46: Cole . . . 3F 25
Arden Forest Est. CV10: Ridge L . . . 1A 20
Arden Forest Ind. Est.
B49: Kinw . . . 2C 112
Arden Leys B94: Tan A . . . 3A 90
Arden M. B78: K'bry . . . 7E 12
CV37: Wilm . . . 5K 113
Arden Rd. B49: Alc . . . 3A 112
B95: Hen A . . . 3H 93
CV8: Ken . . . 6F 79
CV11: Nun . . . 3C 32
CV12: Bulk . . . 3E 42
ARDENS GRAFTON . . . 1K 123 (3C 143)
Arden St. CV5: Cov . . . 6K 57
CV9: Ath . . . 4D 16
CV37: S Avon . . . 3C 136 (4E 114)
Ardent Ct. B95: Hen A . . . 1H 93
Arderne De Gray Rd. CV8: Wols . . . 4K 71
Arderne Dr. B37: F'bri . . . 4A 34
ARDLEY . . . 3D 147
Arena Av. CV6: Cov . . . 4D 50
Arena Health & Fitness Club . . . *2E 50*
(within Ricoh Arena)
Arena, The (Ice Rink) . . . 4F 135 (5B 58)
Arena Retail Pk. CV6: Lford . . . 3F 51
Argent Ct. CV4: Canly . . . 2G 67
Argyle St. CV21: Rugby . . . 5J 75
(not continuous)
Argyle Way CV33: Bis T . . . 5C 108
Argyll St. CV2: Cov . . . 4G 59
Ariel Way CV22: Bil . . . 3D 86
Arkle Dr. CV2: Walsg S . . . 7B 52
Arklet Cl. CV10: Nun . . . 6H 21
ARLESCOTE . . . 5E 128 (1C 147)
Arlescote Cl. CV35: Hatt . . . 5A 96
Arley Dr. B78: Dord . . . 5B 10
Arley La. CV7: Fill . . . 6D 28
CV10: Ansl . . . 2G 29
Arley M. CV32: Lea S . . . 6C 98
Arley Sports Cen. . . . 2C 28
Arlidge Cres. CV8: Ken . . . 5G 79
Arlington Av. CV32: Lea S . . . 5D 98
Arlington Ct. CV32: Lea S . . . 5D 98
Arlington M. CV32: Lea S . . . 5D 98
Arlington Way CV11: Nun . . . 2B 32
Arlon Av. CV10: Nun . . . 4J 21
Armarna Dr. CV5: Milli W . . . 6K 47
Armfield St. CV6: Cov . . . 5G 51
Armorial Rd. CV3: Cov . . . 2B 68
Armour Ct. CV22: Caw . . . 7B 74
ARMSCOTE . . . 4G 127 (1B 146)
Armscote Gro. CV35: Hatt . . . 5A 96
Armscote Rd. CV36: Ilm . . . 6D 126
CV36: Tred . . . 6H 127
CV36: Wind . . . 6F 127
CV37: Arms, Wind . . . 6F 127
CV37: N'bld S . . . 3G 127
Armscott Rd. CV2: Cov . . . 1J 59
(not continuous)
Armson Rd. CV7: Exh . . . 5G 41
Armstrong Av. CV3: Cov . . . 6H 59
Armstrong Cl. CV22: Bil . . . 7E 74
CV31: W'nsh . . . 6E 102
Armstrong Dr. B36: Cas B . . . 3A 24
Arncliffe Cl. CV11: Nun . . . 2C 32
Arncliffe Way CV34: Warw . . . 6H 97
Arne Rd. CV2: Walsg S . . . 1C 60
ARNESBY . . . 2D 141
Arnhem Cnr. CV3: W'hall . . . 2K 69
Arnills Way CV23: Kils . . . 7J 89
Arno Ho. CV3: W'hall . . . 2H 69
Arnold Av. CV3: Cov . . . 3C 68
Arnold Cl. CV22: Rugby . . . 6G 75
Arnold Pl. CV34: Warw . . . 4E 100
Arnolds La. B46: Max . . . 1K 35
Arnold St. CV21: Rugby . . . 5H 75
Arnold Vs. CV21: Rugby . . . 5H 75
Arnside Cl. CV1: Cov . . . 3E 58
Arran Cl. CV10: Nun . . . 1F 31
Arran Way B36: Cas B . . . 5A 24
Arras Blvd. CV35: H Mag . . . 1C 100
ARROW . . . 6A 112 (3B 142)
Arrow Ct. B49: Alc . . . 3B 112
Arrow Cres. B49: Alc . . . 3B 112
Arrow Rd. CV10: Nun . . . 5A 22
ARROW RDBT. . . . 6A 112
Arrow Vw. B80: Stud . . . 2D 92
Artemis Dr. CV34: Warw . . . 3C 102
ARTHINGWORTH . . . 3D 141
Arthingworth Cl. CV3: Bin . . . 6A 60
Arthur Alford Ho. CV12: Bed . . . 4D 40
Arthur Rd. CV37: S Avon . . . 3E 114
Arthur Russell Ct. CV10: Nun . . . 1E 30
Arthur St. CV1: Cov . . . 1K 135 (3D 58)
CV8: Ken . . . 4E 78
Arthur Vick CV4: Canly . . . 4G 67
Artillery Rd. CV11: Bram . . . 6H 33
Arundel Cl. CV34: Warw . . . 7H 97
Arundel Rd. CV3: Cov . . . 2D 68
CV12: Bulk . . . 2E 42
Arundel Way CV22: Caw . . . 1A 86
Ascot Cl. CV3: W'hall . . . 2J 69
CV12: Bed . . . 1H 41
CV37: S Avon . . . 6C 114
Ascote Way CV47: Sou . . . 6J 107
Ascot Ride CV32: Lill . . . 4G 99
ASCOTT-UNDER-WYCHWOOD . . . 3C 147
Ashbourne Sq. CV9: Wood E . . . 2B 14
Ashbridge Rd. CV5: Cov . . . 3G 57
Ashbrook Ct. CV7: Ash G . . . 1B 50
Ashbrook Ri. CV10: Harts . . . 1G 21
Ashburton Rd. CV2: Cov . . . 6A 52
Ashbury Ct. B95: Hen A . . . 1H 93
Ashby Cl. CV3: Bin . . . 7B 60
Ashby Ct. CV11: Nun . . . 1K 31
ASHBY FOLVILLE . . . 1D 141
ASHBY MAGNA . . . 2C 141
ASHBY PARVA . . . 3C 141
Ashby Rd. CV23: Kils . . . 7J 89
CV31: Rad S . . . 3K 103
ASHBY ST LEDGARS . . . 2C 145
Ashcombe Dr. CV4: Tile H . . . 4D 56
Ash Ct. CV22: Rugby . . . 2E 86
Ash Cres. B37: K'hrst . . . 6A 24
Ashcroft Cl. CV2: Walsg S . . . 6C 52
Ashcroft Way CV2: Walsg S . . . 6D 52
Ashdale Cl. CV3: Bin W . . . 1G 71
Ashdene Gdns. CV8: Ken . . . 5F 79
Ashdown Cl. CV3: Bin . . . 7K 59
Ashdown Dr. CV10: Nun . . . 2F 31
Ash Dr. CV8: Ken . . . 5E 78
CV10: Harts . . . 3F 21
Ash End House Children's Farm
. . . 2C 139
Ashe Rd. CV10: Nun . . . 1B 30
Ashfield Av. CV4: Tile H . . . 6B 56
Ashfield La. B37: Mars G . . . 7B 34
Ashfield Rd. CV8: Ken . . . 6F 79
Ashford Dr. CV12: Bed . . . 2G 41
Ashford Gdns. CV31: W'nsh . . . 5D 102
Ashford Rd. CV31: W'nsh . . . 6D 102
ASH GREEN . . . 7C 40 (3A 140)
Ash Grn. La. CV7: Ash G . . . 7C 40
Ash Gro. B78: K'bry . . . 4E 12
CV7: Ash G . . . 6C 40
CV7: Old A . . . 2C 28
CV37: S Avon . . . 2D 114
CV47: Sou . . . 4H 107
Ashgrove CV36: Ship S . . . 6H 131
Ashgrove Pl. CV31: Lea S . . . 1E 102
Ashington Gro. CV3: Cov . . . 2G 69
Ashington Rd. CV12: Bed . . . 4C 40
Ash La. B79: No Hth . . . 2F 7
CV37: Bear . . . 7C 94
Ashlawn Railway Cutting Nature Reserve
. . . 1J 87
Ashlawn Rd. CV22: Hillm, Rugby . . . 4F 87
Ashlea B78: Dord . . . 5C 10
Ashleigh Cl. CV23: Barby . . . 7E 88
Ashleigh Dr. CV11: Nun . . . 3B 32
Ashley Ct.
CV37: S Avon . . . 7K 137 (5G 115)
Ashley Cres. CV34: Warw . . . 2K 101
Ashman Av. CV23: Long L . . . 3B 74
Ashmore Rd. CV6: Cov . . . 3B 58
ASHORNE . . . 3A 144
Ashorne Cl. CV2: Cov . . . 4J 51
(not continuous)
ASHOW . . . 7J 79 (1A 144)
Ashow Cl. CV8: Ken . . . 5F 79
Ash Pl. B50: Bidf A . . . 4G 123
Ash Priors Cl. CV4: Tile H . . . 6F 57
Ashridge Cl. CV11: Nun . . . 4B 32
Ashton Ct. CV32: Lill . . . 4G 99
Ash Tree Av. CV4: Tile H . . . 5E 56
Ash Tree Cl. CV35: Welle . . . 3J 117
Ash Tree Gro. CV7: Shilt . . . 7G 43
Ashurst Cl. CV6: Lford . . . 1H 51
ASHWOOD . . . 3A 138
Ashwood Av. CV6: Cov . . . 2K 57
Ashwood Ct. CV21: Rugby . . . 4F 75
Ashwood Dr. B37: Chel W . . . 2D 34
Ashwood Rd. CV10: Nun . . . 5K 21

Aspects Pk. Ga.—Barnes Ct.

Aspects Pk. Ga. CV11: Nun 4G 23
Aspen Cl. B49: Alc 3B 112
CV4: Tile H 6B 56
CV21: Brow 6J 65
Aspen Ct. *B95: Hen A* *1H 93*
(off Chestnut Wlk.)
Aspen Dr. B37: Chel W 5C 34
CV6: Lford 7J 41
Aspen Rd. CV21: Brow 6J 65
Aspens, The B78: K'bry 4D 12
Aspen Wlk. CV21: Brow 7J 65
Asplen Ct. CV8: Ken 5G 79
Aspley Ct. CV35: Hatt 4A 96
ASPLEY HEATH 3A 90
Aspley Heath La. B94: Tan A 3A 90
Assembly, The 1D 102
Assheton Cl. CV22: Bil 1C 86
ASTCOTE 3D 145
Aster Cl. CV11: Nun 3C 32
Aster Wlk. CV10: Nun 4G 31
Asthill Cft. CV3: Cov 7G 135 (7C 58)
Asthill Gro. CV3: Cov 7G 135 (7C 58)
ASTLEY 5J 29 (3A 140)
Astley Av. CV6: Cov 4E 50
Astley Castle 4J 29
Astley Cl. B98: Redd 1A 92
CV32: Lea S 5B 98
Astley La. CV7: Fill 2F 39
CV10: Asty, Nun 5J 29
CV12: Bed 5J 29
Astley Pl. CV21: Hillm 2D 88
Astley Wlk. CV47: Temp H 2B 120
ASTON 2B 138
ASTON CANTLOW 2K 113 (3C 143)
Aston Cantlow Rd.
B95: Aston C, Wilm 4F 113
CV37: Wilm 4F 113
ASTON FIELDS 2A 142
ASTON FLAMVILLE 2B 140
Aston Hill CV37: Wilm 5G 113
ASTON LE WALLS 3B 144
ASTON MAGNA 2A 146
Aston Pk. Ind. Est. CV11: Nun 5C 22
Aston Rd. CV5: Cov 6K 57
CV11: Nun 6C 22
ASTON SOMERVILLE 2A 146
ASTON SUBEDGE 1A 146
Astoria Dr. CV4: Tile H 3A 56
ASTROP 2D 147
ASTWOOD BANK 2B 142
Atcheson Cl. B80: Stud 3D 92
Atcheson Way CV36: Ship S 4F 131
ATCH LENCH 3B 142
Athena Ct. CV34: Warw 3B 102
Athena Dr. CV34: Warw 3B 102
Athena Gdns. CV6: Cov 5G 51
ATHERSTONE 3C 16 (2A 140)
Atherstone Bus Station 3C 16
Atherstone By-Pass CV9: Ath 2A 16
Atherstone Golf Course 5C 16
Atherstone La. CV9: Bax, Hur 7A 14
Atherstone Leisure Complex 3C 16
ATHERSTONE ON STOUR
....7D 124 (3D 143)
Atherstone Rd.
B46: Bntly, Over W 1F 27
CV9: Hur 7A 14
CV9: With 1E 16
CV10: Harts 7G 17, 1G 21
DE12: App M, A Par 1K 7
Atherstone Station (Rail) 3B 16
Atherston Pl. CV4: Canly 2H 67
Atholl Ct. CV10: Nun 2F 31
Atholl Cres. CV10: Nun 2E 30
Athol Rd. CV2: Walsg S 1C 60
Atkinson Ho. *CV34: H'cte* *5B 102*
(off Merlin Way)
Atkins Wlk. B78: Pole 2D 10
ATTERTON 2A 140
Atterton La. CV9: With 3G 17
CV13: Att 3G 17
Attleboro La. B46: Wat O 2A 24
ATTLEBOROUGH 2A 32 (2A 140)
Attleborough By-Pass CV11: Nun 2K 31
Attleborough Flds. Ind. Est.
CV11: Nun 1B 32
Attleborough Rd. CV11: Nun 1K 31
Attoxhall Rd. CV2: Cov 3A 60
Attwood Cres. CV2: Cov 7J 51
Atworth Cl. B98: Redd 2A 92
Auburndale Av. CV4: Tile H 4A 56
Auckland Dr. B36: Cas B 4A 24
Auden Cl. CV10: Gall C 7E 20
Augusta Pl. CV32: Lea S 7D 98
Augustine Av. B80: Stud 3C 92
Augustus Cl. B46: Cole 3F 25
Augustus Dr. B49: Alc 5B 112
Augustus Rd. CV1: Cov 3F 59
Austen Cl. CV10: Gall C 6E 20
Austen Ct. CV32: Cubb 2J 99
Austen Rd. CV37: S Avon 7H 115
Austin Cl. CV9: Ath 4C 16
Austin Dr. CV6: Cov 7G 51
Austin Drive (Park & Ride)
Coventry 7G 51
Austin Edwards Dr.
CV34: Warw 7K 97
Austin Ho. *B49: Gt Alne* *2G 113*
(off Woodland Dr.)
AUSTREY 7H 7 (1D 139)
Austrey La. B79: Newt R 5D 6
B79: No Hth 2F 7
CV9: Aus 3J 7
DE12: A Par 3J 7
Austrey Rd. B79: Wart 4H 9
Austwick Cl. CV34: Warw 6G 97
Autumn Cl. CV6: Cov 5F 51
Autumn Ho. B37: K'hrst 7B 24
Avebury Cl. CV11: Nun 2B 32
Aventine Way CV21: Rugby 1F 75
Avenue, The CV3: Cov 2G 69
CV35: Row 5H 91
CV37: B'ton 1C 114
Avenue Farm
CV37: S Avon 3D 114
Avenue Farm Ind. Est.
CV37: S Avon 3D 114
Avenue Flds. Ind. Est.
CV37: S Avon 3D 114
Avenue M CV8: S'lgh P 6A 80
Avenue Rd. CV8: Ken 3B 78
CV11: Nun 2J 31
CV21: Rugby 4E 74
CV31: Lea S 1C 102
CV37: S Avon 1H 137 (4F 115)
Avery Ct. CV34: Warw 2H 101
Aviemore Cl. CV10: Nun 2G 31
Avis Way CV31: W'nsh 6E 102
Avocet Cl. CV2: Ald G 3H 51
CV23: Brow 6J 65
Avon Av. CV35: Mid T 7C 130
Avonbank CV37: S Avon 2J 137
Avonbank Dr. CV37: S Avon 7B 114
Avonbank Paddocks
CV37: S Avon 7F 137
Avonbrook Cl. CV37: S Avon 3C 114
Avon Cvn. Pk. CV37: S Avon 2J 115
Avoncliffe CV37: Tidd 2A 116
Avon Cl. CV12: Bulk 6D 32
CV35: Barf 1C 108
CV37: Ett 2C 126
Avon Ct. CV21: Rugby 4G 75
CV32: Lea S 4D 98
Avon Cres. B49: Alc 3C 112
CV37: S Avon 6H 115
Avoncroft Ct. CV31: Lea S 1D 102
Avoncroft Ho. B37: Chel W 3A 34
Avondale Rd. CV5: Cov 7A 58
CV8: Bran 3H 71
CV32: Lill 3G 99
AVON DASSETT 3B 144
Avon Dassett Rd. CV47: Fen C 4F 121
Avon Dr. B36: Cas B 5A 24
Avon Flds. CV37: Ett 2C 126
Avonfields Cl. CV37: A'ton 2C 116
Avon Ho. CV37: S Avon 1F 137
Avonhurst CV37: Tidd 3J 115
Avon Ind. Est. CV21: Rugby 3J 75
CV37: S Avon 3E 114
Avonlea Ri. CV32: Lea S 5B 98
Avon Lodge CV11: Nun 6B 22
Avon Mdw. Cl. CV37: S Avon 6E 114
Avonmere CV21: N'bld A 1E 74
Avon Mill CV37: S Avon 1G 137
Avon Rd. CV4: Canly 2F 67
CV8: Ken 6C 78
CV31: W'nsh 5E 102
CV33: L Hth 2K 119
Avonside CV37: S Avon 6F 115
Avonside Cvn. Pk. CV37: Welf A 1A 124
Avon St. CV2: Cov 2H 59
CV21: Rugby 4G 75
CV23: Clift D 4A 76
CV34: Warw 1J 101
Avon Ter. CV8: Bubb 3J 81
Avonview CV37: S Avon 6G 115
Avon Vw. Pk. Homes
CV8: Rytn D 6A 70
Avon Way CV23: Long L 4B 74
CV35: Mid T 7D 130
Awson St. CV6: Cov 1F 59
Axholme Rd. CV2: Cov 3A 60
Axminster Cl. CV11: Nun 6F 23
Aylesbury Ct. *CV6: Cov* *7D 50*
(off Gressingham Gro.)
Aylesdene Ct. CV5: Cov 7K 57
Aylesford Dr. B37: Mars G 6A 34
Aylesford St. CV1: Cov 3E 58
CV31: Lea S 2E 102
AYLESTONE 1C 141
Aylstone Cl. CV37: Lwr Q 5H 125
AYLWORTH 3A 146
AYNHO 2D 147
Aynho Cl. CV5: East G 4E 56
Aysgarth Cl. CV11: Nun 2C 32
Azalea Rd. CV37: S Avon 7G 115

B

Babbacombe Rd. CV3: Cov 3D 68
Bablake Cl. CV6: Cov 6K 49
Bachelors Bench CV9: Ath 4C 16
Back La. B46: Shu 2B 26
B95: Hen A 1H 93
CV7: Mer 3A 56
CV23: Bird 5A 104
CV23: Harb M 4A 64
CV23: Long L 4A 74
CV34: Warw 2G 101
CV35: Mid T 6C 130
CV35: Oxh 1E 130
CV36: Long C 2D 134
CV37: Lwr Q 4J 125
OX17: Shotte 6G 129
Back St. CV11: Nun 6D 22
CV36: Ilm 7B 126
BACON'S END 1B 34
Bacons End B37: K'hrst 7B 24
Bacon's Yd. CV6: Cov 4F 51
Badbury Cl. B80: Stud 3C 92
Badbury Gdns. B80: Stud 3C 92
BADBY 3C 145
Badby Leys CV22: Rugby 2F 87
BADDESLEY CLINTON 1D 143
Baddesley Clinton 1C 143
Baddesley Cl. CV31: Lea S 3H 103
Baddesley Dr. B78: Dord 7C 10
BADDESLEY ENSOR 2F 15 (2D 139)
Baden W. Rd. CV35: Welle 4H 117
Badger Rd. CV3: Bin 7K 59
Badgers Cl. CV23: Long L 4K 73
CV37: Welf A 4A 124
Badgers Cres. CV36: Ship S 3H 131
Badgers La. CV35: Lwr T 4D 130
Badgers Retreat CV31: Lea S 4G 103
Badgers Way CV37: B'ton 1C 114
BADSEY 1A 146
Baffin Cl. CV22: Bil 7E 74
BAGINTON 6F 69 (1A 144)
Baginton Rd. CV3: Cov 2B 68
(not continuous)
Bagot Way CV34: H'cte 5C 102
Bagshaw Cl. CV8: Rytn D 7C 70
BAGWORTH 1B 140
Bailey Av. CV37: Lwr Q 5F 125
Bailey Cl. CV8: Wols 4K 71
Bailey Rd. CV23: Brow 6K 65
Bailey's La. CV23: Long L 3A 74
Bakehouse La. CV21: Rugby 5F 75
OX17: Shotte 6H 129
Baker Av. CV31: Lea S 2D 102
CV37: S Avon 4C 114
Baker Dr. CV35: Welle 3G 117
Baker Ho. CV22: Bil 1C 86
Bakers Ct. CV9: Ath 3C 16
Bakers Cft. CV9: Bad E 2F 15
Bakers La. CV5: Cov 4J 57
Baker St. CV6: Lford 7H 41
Bakewell Cl. CV3: Bin 7B 60
Balcombe Ct. CV22: Hillm 1A 88
Balcombe Rd. CV22: Hillm 1K 87
Baldwin Cft. CV6: Cov 5H 51
Baldwins La. CV35: Up Tys 7C 130
Balfour Pl. CV22: Hillm 7K 75
Ballantine Rd. CV6: Cov 1B 58
BALLARDS GREEN 1B 28
Ballards La. CV36: Ilm 6C 126
Ballard Wlk. B37: K'hrst 6A 24
Ballingham Cl. CV4: Tile H 5E 56
Ballin Rd. CV10: Nun 6A 22
Balliol Ho. B37: F'bri 3A 34
Balliol Rd. CV2: Cov 3H 59
Balmoral Cl. CV2: Cov 1B 60
Balmoral Ct. CV10: Nun 6K 21
Balmoral Rd. B36: Cas B 5A 24
Balmoral Way CV32: Cubb 1G 99
BALSALL 1D 143
BALSALL COMMON 1D 143
BALSCOTE 1C 147
Balthazar Cl. CV34: H'cte 4C 102
Bamburgh Gro. CV32: Lea S 4C 98
Ban Brook Copse WR11: Salf P 7C 122
Ban Brook Rd. WR11: Salf P 7B 122
BANBURY 1D 147
Banbury Rd. CV33: Bis T 5A 108
CV33: Gay, L Hth 4F 119
CV33: L Hth 1J 119
CV34: Warw 2H 101, 4A 108
CV35: Gay 4F 119, 1A 120
CV35: Kine 6D 120
CV35: Light 1J 119
CV35: Pill P 3D 126
CV37: Ett, Pill P 1A 126
(not continuous)
CV37: Gold, S Avon 5G 115
Banbury Rd.
CV47: Gay, Lit D, Temp H 1A 120
CV47: Ladb 3C 110
CV47: Sou 6H 107, 1C 110
(not continuous)
OX17: Warm 3H 129
Banbury Rd. Hill CV34: Warw 3J 101
Banbury St. CV35: Kine 6D 120
Bancroft Gdns.
CV37: S Avon 5J 137 (5F 115)
Bancroft Pl.
CV37: S Avon 4J 137 (4F 115)
Bangor Ho. B37: F'bri 1B 34
Banister Way CV36: Ship S 5H 131
Bank, The B50: Bidf A 6G 123
CV8: S'lgh 3C 80
CV35: Light 2G 119
CV36: Ilm 6C 126
CV36: Stourt 6H 133
Bank Cl. CV35: But M 7A 120
Bankcroft CV31: Lea S 3G 103
Bankfield Dr. CV32: Lea S 6A 98
Bank Rd. CV9: Ath 3D 16
Banks, The CV23: Kils 7J 89
Bankside Cl. CV3: Cov 2F 69
Bankside Rd. CV9: Wood E 2B 14
Banks Rd. CV6: Cov 2A 58
Bank St. CV21: Rugby 5G 75
Bank Vw. CV35: But M 7A 120
Banner La. CV4: Tile H 4B 56
Bannerlea Rd. B37: K'hrst 7A 24
BANNERS GATE 2B 138
Banning Cnr. CV37: Lwr Q 5H 125
Banquo App. CV34: H'cte 5D 102
Bantam Gro. CV6: Cov 3A 50
Bantock Rd. CV4: Tile H 5C 56
Baptist Cl. CV2: Ald G 2K 51
Barber Wlk. CV35: H Mag 1B 100
Barbican Ri. CV2: Cov 5A 60
Barbridge Cl. CV12: Bulk 3E 42
Barbridge Rd. CV12: Bulk 2D 42
BARBY 7E 88 (1C 145)
Barby La. CV22: Hillm 1B 88
CV23: Barby 4C 88
BARBY NORTOFT 3H 89 (1C 145)
Barby Rd. CV22: Rugby 6G 75
CV23: Barby, Kils 6G 89
Barby Sporting Club 5E 88
BARCHESTON 6K 131 (1B 146)
Barcheston Dr. CV35: Hatt 4A 96
Barcheston M. CV35: Hatt 4A 96
Bardley Dr. CV6: Cov 1C 58
BARDON 1B 140
Bardon Vw. Rd. B78: Dord 3D 10
Bard's Wlk.
CV37: S Avon 4F 137 (4F 115)
Bardswell Ct. CV37: S Avon 3E 114
BARFORD 2C 108 (2D 143)
Barford App. CV31: W'nsh 6F 103
Barford By-Pass
CV35: Barf, Sher, Wasp 1B 108
Barford Cl. CV3: Bin 1K 69
Barford Exchange CV35: Barf 3B 108
Barford Hill CV35: Barf 7G 101, 1D 108
Barford M. CV8: Ken 5F 79
Barford Rd. CV8: Ken 6F 79
CV34: Warw 7H 101
CV35: Sher 7C 100, 1A 108
BARFORD ST JOHN 2D 147
BARFORD ST MICHAEL 2D 147
BARKBY 1D 141
Barker's Butts La. CV6: Cov 2K 57
Barkus Cl. CV47: Sou 5J 107
Barle Gro. B36: Cas B 5A 24
BARLESTONE 1B 140
Barley Cl. B95: Hen A 2G 93
CV21: Hillm 1C 88
CV37: Snitt 5H 95
Barley Ct. CV32: Lea S 5D 98
Barley Flds. CV37: Long M 2G 125
Barley Lea, The CV3: Cov 7H 59
Barley Pl. *CV3: Cov* *7J 59*
(off The Barley Lea)
Barlichway B49: Alc 4D 112
Barling Way CV10: Nun 3H 31
Barlow Ct. B78: K'bry 5E 12
Barlow Rd. CV2: Ald G 3K 51
Barnaby Rd. CV21: Rugby 2G 75
Barnack Av. CV3: Cov 3B 68
Barnack Dr. CV34: Warw 6G 97
BARNACLE 7C 42 (3A 140)
Barnacle La. CV12: Bulk 4E 42
Barnard Cl. B37: Chel W 4D 34
CV32: Lill 4G 99
Barn Cl. B78: Dord 4C 10
CV5: Cov 2G 57
CV31: W'nsh 5F 103
CV37: Cliff C 5C 124
Barncroft CV36: Long C 3C 134
Barne Cl. CV11: Nun 5D 32
Barn End Rd. B79: Wart 6H 9
Barnes Ct. CV1: Cov 1G 135 (3C 58)

Barnes Wood La.—Bexfield Cl.

Barnes Wood La. B46: Neth W 5J 19
Barnfield Av. CV5: Alle 7E 48
Barn La. CV37: B'ton 1C 114
BARNMOOR GREEN 2A 94
Barnsley Cl. CV9: Ath 4C 16
Barns M., The B37: Mars G 7B 34
Barnstaple Cl. CV5: Alle 3D 56
BARNT GREEN 1B 142
Barnwell Cl. CV22: Dunc 5C 86
Baron Leigh Dr. CV4: Westw H 2B 66
Baron's Cft. CV3: Cov 1E 68
Barons Cft. CV10: Nun 7H 21
Baron's Fld. Rd. CV3: Cov 1D 68
Barpool Rd. CV10: Nun 7A 22
Barracks Grn. CV35: Lox 6C 116
Barrack St. CV34: Warw 1G 101
Barracks Way CV1: Cov 4H 135 (5C 58)
Barras Ct. CV2: Cov 3G 59
Barras Grn. CV2: Cov 3G 59
Barras Grn. Bungs. CV2: Cov 3G 59
Barras La. CV1: Cov 4B 58
Barrie Cl. CV37: S Avon 6H 115
Barrie Way CV2: Cov 1G 59
Barrington Rd. CV22: Bil 6C 74
Barr La. CV13: High H 1H 23
CV23: Brin 3C 62
Bar Rd. CV3: Cov 7E 58
Barrow Cl. CV2: Walsg S 1D 60
Barrowfield Ct. CV8: Ken 5D 78
Barrowfield La. CV8: Ken 5D 78
Barrow Rd. CV8: Ken 5D 78
BARSBY 1D 141
Barsby Cl. CV9: Ath 4C 16
BARSTON 1D 143
Barston Cl. CV6: Cov 3G 51
Barter Pl. CV21: Rugby 4J 75
Bartholomew Ct. CV3: Cov 2F 69
Bartlett Cl. CV6: Cov 4E 50
CV34: Warw 1H 101
BARTLEY GREEN 3B 138
Bartley Wlk. CV23: Long L 4B 74
BARTON
B50 7J 123 (3C 143)
GL54 3A 146
Barton Cres. CV31: Lea S 2G 103
Barton Flds. CV37: Welf A 3A 124
BARTON IN THE BEANS 1A 140
Barton La. GL56: Lit C 6C 134
Barton Mdw. CV37: Welf A 3A 124
Barton Moorings B50: Bart 7K 123
BARTON-ON-THE-HEATH 2B 146
Barton Rd. CV6: Cov 4F 51
CV10: Nun 3J 31
CV12: Bed 2G 41
CV22: Bil 1D 86
CV36: Long C 1A 134
CV37: Welf A 4A 124
Bartons Ct. CV2: Cov 3G 59
Barton's Mdw. CV2: Cov 1H 59
BARWELL 2B 140
Barwell Cl. CV32: Lea S 4D 98
Basant Cl. CV34: Warw 1J 101
BASCOTE 1F 107 (2B 144)
Bascote Chase CV47: Bas 1F 107
BASCOTE HEATH 1J 109
Bascote Ri. CV47: Sou 4G 107
Bascote Rd. CV33: Ufton 2H 109
CV47: Bas, Long I 4B 106, 1F 107
Baseley Way CV6: Lford 2D 50
Basford Brook Dr. CV6: Lford 1F 51
Basildon Wlk. CV2: Walsg S 7C 52
Baskerville Rd. CV11: Nun 5J 23
Basket Hall CV36: Ship S 3J 131
Bassett Rd. CV6: Cov 2A 58
Batchelor Cl. CV31: W'nsh 6E 102
Batchelors La. OX15: Ratl 6D 128
BATCHLEY 2B 142
Bateman Rd. B46: Cole 3F 25
Batemans Acre Sth. CV6: Cov 3A 58
Bates La. B94: Tan A 4C 90
Bates Rd. CV5: Cov 1J 67
Bath Pl. CV31: Lea S 1D 102
Bath Rd. CV9: Ath 4D 16
CV11: Nun 6D 22
Bath St. CV1: Cov 1K 135 (3D 58)
CV21: Rugby 5H 75
CV31: Lea S 1D 102
Bath St. M. CV21: Rugby 4H 75
Bathurst Cl. CV22: Bil 1E 86
Bathurst Rd. CV6: Cov 1A 58
Bathway Rd. CV3: Finh 4A 68
BATSFORD 2A 146
Batsford Cl. B98: Redd 2A 92
Batsford Flats CV36: Whatc 3A 130
Batsford Rd. CV6: Cov 2K 57
Battalion Ct. CV6: Cov 5A 50
Battle Ct. CV35: Kine 5D 120
Battle of Edgehill Commemoration Stone 3A 144
BATTRAM 1B 140
Bawnmore Ct. CV22: Bil 1D 86
Bawnmore Pk. CV22: Bil 2E 86
Bawnmore Rd. CV22: Bil 1D 86
Baxter Cl. CV4: Tile H 5E 56
CV9: Ath 4D 16
Baxter Ct. CV31: Lea S 1E 102
BAXTERLEY 5G 15 (2D 139)
Baychester Rd. CV4: Tile H 3A 56
Bayley La. CV1: Cov 4J 135 (5D 58)
Bayliss Av. CV6: Lford 2G 51
BAYNARD'S GREEN 3D 147
Bayton Ind. Est. CV7: Exh 6G 41
Bayton Rd. CV7: Exh 6G 41
Bayton Rd. Ind. Est. CV7: Exh 5H 41
Bayton Way CV7: Exh 6J 41
Baytree Cl. CV2: Cov 5K 51
Bazzard Rd. CV11: Bram 6H 33
CV12: Bulk 6H 33
Beacon Cl. B49: Alc 3C 112
Beacon Rd. CV6: Cov 3C 50
Beaconsfield Av. CV22: Rugby 7G 75
Beaconsfield Ct. CV11: Nun 6E 22
Beaconsfield Rd. CV2: Cov 5H 59
Beaconsfield St. CV31: Lea S 1F 103
Beaconsfield St. W.
CV31: Lea S 7F 99
Beake Av. CV6: Cov 5B 50
Beaker Pl. CV22: Caw 7B 74
Beale Cl. CV33: Bis T 5C 108
Beamish Cl. CV2: Walsg S 1C 60
Beanfield Av. CV3: Finh 4K 67
Bear Cl. B95: Hen A 1G 93
Bear La. B95: Hen A 1G 93
Bear La. Cl. B78: Pole 7D 8
BEARLEY 6D 94 (2C 143)
BEARLEY CROSS 6B 94
Bearley Grange CV37: Bear 6C 94
Bearley Grn. CV37: Bear 6D 94
Bearley Rd. B95: Aston C 2K 113
CV37: Snitt 5F 95
Bearley Station (Rail) 6B 94
Bear Rock Climbing Cen. 3G 67
BEARWOOD 3B 138
Beatty Dr. CV22: Bil 6D 74
Beaty's Gdns. CV32: Lill 3E 98
Beauchamp Av. CV32: Lea S 6D 98
Beauchamp Ct. B49: King C 2A 112
CV32: Lea S 6D 98
Beauchamp Gdns.
CV34: Warw 2K 101
Beauchamp Hill CV32: Lea S 6C 98
Beauchamp Ho. CV1: Cov 5G 135
Beauchamp M. CV32: Lea S 6D 98
Beauchamp Rd. B49: Alc 3C 112
CV8: Ken 7C 78
CV32: Lea S 6D 98
CV34: Warw 7K 97
Beaudesert Castle 1J 93
Beaudesert La. B95: Hen A 1H 93
Beaudesert Pl. B95: Hen A 2H 93
Beaudesert Rd. CV5: Cov 6A 58
Beaufell Cl. CV34: Warw 6G 97
Beaufort Av. CV32: Cubb 2G 99
Beaufort Cl. CV35: Welle 4G 117
Beaufort Dr. CV3: Bin 1B 70
Beaulieu Pk. CV31: Lea S 2H 103
Beaumaris Cl. CV5: Alle 2D 56
Beaumont Cl. CV47: Temp H 2B 120
Beaumont Ct. *CV6: Cov 3A 58*
(off Beaumont Cres.)
Beaumont Cres. CV6: Cov 3A 58
BEAUMONT LEYS 1C 141
Beaumont Pl. CV11: Nun 7A 22
Beaumont Rd. CV7: Ker E 7K 39
CV11: Nun 6A 22
Beaurevoir Way CV34: Warw 7J 97
BEAUSALE 1D 143
Beausale Cft. CV5: East G 4E 56
Beausale La. CV35: Beau, Hatt 3A 96
Beavers Brook Cl. CV31: Lea S 3G 103
Beavons Cl. B46: Wat O 1C 24
Beche Way CV5: Cov 2F 57
Beckbury Rd. CV2: Walsg S 7B 52
Becket Cl. GL56: Tod 5A 132
Beckett Rd. CV2: Cov 1H 59
Becketts Cl. OX15: Up Bra 2G 133
Beckfoot Cl. CV21: Brow 7K 65
Beckfoot Dr. CV2: Walsg S 5B 52
Beck's Cl. CV47: S'ton 6C 106
Becks Cft. B95: Hen A 2H 93
Becks Gro. CV7: Mer 1J 47
Beck's La. CV47: S'ton 6C 106
Becks La. CV7: Mer 1J 47
Bede Arc. CV12: Bed 2H 41
Bede Rd. CV6: Cov 1B 58
CV10: Nun 1D 30
CV12: Bed 1G 41
Bede Village CV12: Bed 5C 40
Bedford Ho. B36: Cas B 6B 24
Bedford Pl. CV32: Lea S 7D 98
Bedford St. CV1: Cov 5A 58
CV32: Lea S 7D 98
Bedlam La. CV6: Lford 4E 50
BEDWORTH 3H 41 (3A 140)
Bedworth Arts Cen. 3H 41
(off High St.)
Bedworth By-Pass CV7: Exh 5F 41
CV10: Griff 5F 41
CV12: Bed 5F 41
Bedworth Cl. CV12: Bulk 3D 42
BEDWORTH HEATH 3E 40
Bedworth Hill CV12: Bed 4J 41
Bedworth La. CV12: Bed 1C 40
Bedworth Leisure Cen. 4H 41
Bedworth Rd. CV6: Lford 1G 51
CV12: Bulk 3A 42
Bedworth Sloughs Nature Reserve 2F 41
Bedworth Station (Rail) 3J 41
Bedworth United FC 3H 41
BEDWORTH WOODLANDS 2E 40
BEEBY 1D 141
Beecham Rd. CV36: Ship S 3H 131
Beecham Wlk. CV37: S Avon 3B 114
Beech Av. B37: Chel W 4B 34
Beech Cliffe CV34: Warw 7H 97
Beech Cl. B49: Ove G 6D 112
B78: K'bry 4D 12
CV9: Hur 6K 13
CV10: Harts 3F 21
CV35: Row 6J 91
CV37: S Avon 5H 115
CV47: Sou 6G 107
Beech Ct. CV22: Hillm 1B 88
CV34: H'cte 6C 102
CV37: S Avon 5G 115
Beech Cft. CV47: Long I 2C 106
Beechcroft B95: Hen A 1H 93
CV12: Bed 4F 41
Beech Dr. CV8: Ken 4F 79
CV22: Bil 7C 74
CV23: Thurl 6K 85
Beecher's Keep CV8: Bran 3H 71
Beech Tree Pk. B50: Bidf A 4H 123
Beeches, The B78: Pole 2D 10
CV12: Bed 3E 40
CV23: Clift D 3B 76
CV33: Har 5G 109
Beeches Wlk. CV37: Tidd 3K 115
Beech Gro. B49: Gt Alne 2G 113
CV7: Old A 2C 28
CV34: Warw 6K 97
Beechmast Cl. CV22: Bil 1C 86
Beechnut Cl. CV4: Tile H 5B 56
Beech Rd. CV6: Cov 2B 58
CV35: Oxh 1E 130
Beech Tree Av. CV4: Tile H 5F 57
Beech Tree Pk. B50: Bidf A 4H 123
Beechwood Av. CV5: Cov 6J 57
Beechwood Ct. CV5: Cov 7K 57
CV21: Rugby 4F 75
Beechwood Cft. CV8: Ken 7D 78
BEECHWOOD GARDENS 7J 57
Beechwood Rd. CV10: Nun 5J 21
CV12: Bed 1J 41
Beehive Hill CV8: Ken 2B 78
Beehive La. B76: Curd 5C 18
Beeston Cl. CV3: Bin 7B 60
Beetle Dr. CV2: Cov 4J 51
BELBROUGHTON 1A 142
Beldesert Cl. B95: Hen A 2H 93
Belfry Golf Course, The 1B 18
BELFRY JUNC. 1C 18
Belgrade Plaza
CV1: Cov 2G 135 (4C 58)
Belgrade Theatre 3G 135 (4C 58)
Belgrave Dr. CV21: Brow 2K 75
Belgrave Rd. CV2: Cov 3K 59
Belgrave Sq. CV2: Cov 3A 60
Belgravia Ct. B37: K'hrst 7A 24
Bellairs Av. CV12: Bed 4E 40
Bellam Rd. CV35: H Mag 1B 100
Bellamy Cl. CV2: Cov 1H 59
Bell Brook CV37: Snitt 6G 95
Bellbrooke Cl. CV6: Cov 5H 51
Bell Cl. B36: Cas B 6B 24
Bell Ct. CV32: Lea S 5D 98
Bell Ct. Shop. Cen.
CV37: S Avon 4F 137 (5F 115)
Bell Dr. CV7: Ash G 6E 40
BELL END 1A 142
Bellerose Cl. CV4: Tile H 4A 56
Belle Vue CV10: Nun 1E 30
Bellfield B94: Tan A 3D 90
BELL GREEN 6H 51
Bell Grn. Rd. CV6: Cov 6G 51
Bellingham B77: Wiln 1A 10
Bell La. B80: Stud 3D 92
CV23: M Kirby 3J 55
CV37: Shot 5C 114
CV37: Snitt 6H 95
Bell Mead B80: Stud 3D 92
Bell Rd. CV21: Rugby 3H 75
Bells La. OX15: Up Bra 1F 133
Bell Twr. M.
CV32: Lea S 4D 98
Bellview Way CV6: Cov 5H 51
Bell Wlk. B37: F'bri 4A 34
CV5: Cov 6K 57
CV21: Hillm 1D 88
Belmont Ct. CV32: Lill 3E 98
Belmont Dr. CV32: Lill 3E 98
Belmont M. CV8: Ken 5D 78
CV32: Lill 3E 98
Belmont Rd. CV6: Cov 7F 51
(not continuous)
CV22: Rugby 1G 87
Belvedere Rd. CV5: Cov 7A 58
Benches Furlong CV23: Brow 6K 65
Benedictine Ct. CV1: Cov 3J 135
Benedictine Rd. CV3: Cov 1C 68
Benedict Sq. CV2: Cov 6J 51
BENGEWORTH 1A 146
Benjamins Yd. *CV36: Ship S 5H 131*
(off Old Rd.)
Bennett Ct. CV8: Wols 5H 71
Bennett Dr. CV34: Warw 1K 101
Bennett Pl. CV36: Ilm 6C 126
Bennett's Rd. CV7: Ker E 7K 39
Bennett's Rd. Nth.
CV7: Cor, Ker E 5H 39
Bennett's Rd. Sth. CV6: Cov 3K 49
CV7: Ker E 3K 49
Bennett St. CV21: Rugby 5F 75
Bennett Way CV37: S Avon 7H 115
Bennfield Rd. CV21: Rugby 5G 75
Benn Rd. CV12: Bulk 3D 42
Benn St. CV22: Rugby 6J 75
Benson Rd. CV6: Cov 5A 50
CV37: S Avon 3F 115
Benthall Rd. CV6: Cov 4F 51
BENTLEY
CV9 7H 15 (2D 139)
WS2 2A 138
Bentley Cl. CV32: Lill 4F 99
BENTLEY COMMON 6J 15
Bentley Ct. CV6: Cov 2C 50
BENTLEY HEATH 1C 143
Bentley La. B46: Max 3E 36
Bentley Rd. CV7: Exh 4G 41
CV11: Nun 7B 22
Bentree, The CV3: Cov 7H 59
BEOLEY 2B 142
Berenska Dr. CV32: Lea S 5E 98
Beresford Av. CV6: Cov 5D 50
Bericote Rd. CV32: B'dwn 1E 98
Berkeley Cl. CV11: Nun 1H 31
Berkeley Rd. CV8: Ken 3C 78
Berkeley Rd. Nth. CV5: Cov 6A 58
Berkeley Rd. Sth. CV5: Cov 7A 58
Berkett Rd. CV6: Cov 3B 50
Berkshire Cl. CV10: Nun 1E 30
BERKSWELL 1D 143
Berkswell Rd. CV6: Cov 4G 51
CV7: Mer 7E 46
BERMUDA 4G 31
Bermuda Bus. Pk. CV10: Griff 5G 31
(not continuous)
Bermuda Ind. Est. CV10: Nun 4H 31
Bermuda Innovation Cen.
CV10: Griff 6G 31
Bermuda Park Station (Rail) 4H 31
Bermuda Rd. CV10: Nun 2G 31
Bermuda Village CV10: Nun 3G 31
Berners Cl. CV4: Tile H 5C 56
Berrills La. CV36: Cher 7G 133
Berrington Rd. CV10: Nun 4H 21
CV31: Lea S 2F 103
Berry Av. CV36: Ship S 4G 131
Berrybanks CV22: Bil 7A 74
Berry Cl. CV36: Ship S 4G 131
Berryfields CV7: Fill 1C 38
Berry La. CV47: Sou 6G 107
Berry Mdw. CV47: Fen C 2G 121
Berry St. CV1: Cov 3E 58
Bertie Ct. CV8: Ken 5E 78
Bertie Rd. CV8: Ken 5D 78
Bertie Ter. CV32: Lea S 6C 98
Berwick Cl. CV5: East G 3F 57
CV34: Warw 5G 97
Berwicks La.
B37: Chel W, Mars G 4B 34
(not continuous)
Berwyn Av. CV6: Cov 5A 50
Berwyn Way CV10: Nun 7G 21
Best Av. CV8: Ken 3G 79
Beswick Gdns. CV22: Bil 2D 86
Betjeman Rd. CV37: S Avon 7H 115
Betony Rd. CV23: Newt 7K 65
Bettina Cl. CV10: Nun 6G 21
Bettman Cl. CV3: Cov 2E 68
Bettridge Pl. CV35: Welle 2H 117
Beverley Av. CV10: Nun 7G 21
Beverley Hill CV9: Wood E 2B 14
Beverley Rd. CV32: Lea S 6B 98
Beverly Dr. CV4: Canly 6H 67
Bevington Cres. CV6: Cov 2J 57
Bewick Cft. CV2: Cov 2G 59
Bexfield Cl. CV5: Alle 1E 56

154 A-Z Warwickshire Atlas

Biart Pl.—Boyce Way

Biart Pl. CV21: Rugby ... 4K 75
Bicester Rd. CV37: Lwr Q ... 6F 125
BICKENHILL ... 5D 44 (3C 139)
Bickenhill Grn. Ct. B92: Bick ... 5D 44
Bickenhill La. B37: Mars G ... 7C 34
(not continuous)
B40: Mars G ... 1D 44
B92: Cath B ... 7C 44
Bickenhill Parkway
B40: Nat E C ... 7D 34
Bickenhill Rd. B37: Mars G ... 6A 34
Bickenhill Trad. Est.
B37: Mars G ... 1D 44
BICKMARSH ... 3C 143
Bidavon Ind. Est.
B50: Bidf A ... 4H 123
Bideford Rd. CV2: Cov ... 7J 51
BIDFORD GRANGE ... 7K 123
Bidford Grange Golf Course ... 6K 123
BIDFORD-ON-AVON ... 6G 123 (3B 142)
Bidford Rd. B50: Broom ... 3F 123
Biffin Way CV31: W'nsh ... 6D 102
Big Apple, The
Rugby ... 2H 75
Bigbury Cl. CV3: Cov ... 3E 68
Biggin Hall Cres. CV3: Cov ... 5H 59
Biggin Hall La. CV23: Thurl ... 7J 85
Bilberry Rd. CV2: Cov ... 4K 51
BILBROOK ... 1A 138
Billesden Cl. CV3: Bin ... 7A 60
BILLESDON ... 1D 141
BILLESLEY ... 7F 113 (3C 143)
Billesley Rd. CV37: Wilm ... 7H 113
Billing Rd. CV5: Cov ... 4H 57
Billington Cl. CV2: Cov ... 5A 60
BILSTON ... 2A 138
BILSTONE ... 1A 140
BILTON ... 1C 86 (1B 144)
Bilton Flds. Farm La.
CV22: Rugby ... 3F 87
Bilton Ind. Est. CV3: Cov ... 6F 59
Bilton La. CV22: Bil, Long L ... 5B 74
CV22: Dunc ... 5D 86
CV23: Long L ... 5B 74
Bilton Rd. CV22: Bil, Rugby ... 1D 86
BINLEY ... 7A 60 (1A 144)
Binley Av. CV3: Bin ... 1B 70
Binley Bus. Pk. CV3: Bin ... 6C 60
(not continuous)
Binley Gro. CV3: Bin ... 1B 70
Binley Rd. CV3: Bin, Cov ... 4F 59
(not continuous)
BINLEY WOODS ... 1E 70
Binns Cl. CV4: Tile H ... 7C 56
Binswood Av. CV32: Lea S ... 5D 98
Binswood Cl. CV2: Cov ... 4K 51
Binswood End CV33: Har ... 5G 109
Binswood Hall CV32: Lea S ... 5D 98
Binswood Mans.
CV32: Lea S ... 5D 98
Binswood St. CV32: Lea S ... 6C 98
BINTON ... 3C 143
Binton Bridges Cvn. Pk.
CV37: Welf A ... 1A 124
Binton Rd. CV2: Cov ... 5K 51
CV37: Bint, Welf A ... 1A 124
Binton Vw. CV37: S Avon ... 3A 114
Birbeck Ho. B36: Cas B ... 6B 24
Birch Abbey B49: Alc ... 5B 112
Birch Cl. B78: K'bry ... 4E 12
CV5: Alle ... 1D 56
CV12: Bed ... 1K 41
Birch Coppice Bus. Pk.
B78: Dord ... 6B 10
Birch Ct. CV34: H'cte ... 6C 102
Birch Cft. B37: Chel W ... 4C 34
Birch Dr. CV22: Bil ... 6B 74
Birch End CV34: Warw ... 7K 97
Birches, The CV12: Bulk ... 1D 42
Birches La. CV8: Ken ... 6E 78
Birchfield Cl. CV9: Wood E ... 2K 13
Birchfield Gdns. CV6: Cov ... 6K 49
Birchfield Rd. CV6: Cov ... 7K 49
CV37: S Avon ... 2F 115
Birchgrave Cl. CV6: Cov ... 7G 51
Birch Gro. B78: B'moor ... 3A 10
CV35: Welle ... 3J 117
BIRCHLEY HEATH ... 2D 139
Birch Mdw. Cl. CV34: Warw ... 1F 101
BIRCHMOOR ... 3B 10 (1D 139)
Birchmoor Rd. B78: B'moor ... 2B 10
Birch Pl. B50: Bidf A ... 5G 123
Birch Tree Rd. CV10: Nun ... 5H 21
Birchway Cl. CV32: Lea S ... 6A 98
Birchwood Av. B78: Dord ... 3C 10
Birchwood Rd. CV3: Bin W ... 1E 70
BIRCHY CROSS ... 1E 90
Bird Gro. Ct. CV1: Cov ... 2D 58
Birdhaven Cl. CV35: L Hth ... 2K 119
Birdhope B77: Wiln ... 1A 10
Bird Ind. Pk. CV37: Long M ... 4G 125
BIRDINGBURY ... 5A 104 (2B 144)
Birdingbury Rd.
CV23: Hill, Lea H ... 5B 104
(not continuous)
CV23: Mart ... 2D 104
Bird Rd. CV33: L Hth ... 3K 119
CV34: H'cte ... 4A 102
Bird St. CV1: Cov ... 2J 135 (3D 58)
Birkdale Cl. CV6: Cov ... 2B 50
CV11: Nun ... 3C 32
BIRMINGHAM ... 3B 138
BIRMINGHAM AIRPORT
Cargo ... 2A 44
Passenger Terminals ... 2C 44
Birmingham Bus. Est.
B37: Mars G ... 5E 34
Birmingham International Station
(Rail) ... 2D 44
Birmingham Rd. B37: K'hrst ... 7B 24
B46: Cole ... 7C 24
B46: Neth W ... 4G 19
B46: Wat O ... 2A 24
B49: Alc ... 3A 112
B49: King C ... 1A 112
B76: Lea M ... 4G 19
B80: Map G, Stud ... 2D 92
B95: Hen A ... 1H 93
CV5: Alle, Milli W ... 6B 48
(not continuous)
CV7: Mer ... 6G 47
(Church La.)
CV7: Mer ... 3K 45
(Kenilworth Rd.)
CV8: Ken ... 1A 78
CV8: S'lgh ... 2B 80
CV10: Ansl ... 5A 20
CV34: Warw ... 7D 96
CV35: Bud, Hase, Hatt ... 5A 96
CV37: B'ton, Path, S Avon
... 1D 136 (1C 114)
CV37: Bear ... 6B 94
BIRSTALL ... 1C 141
Birstall Dr. CV21: Brow ... 2K 75
Birvell Ct. CV12: Bed ... 3J 41
BISHAMPTON ... 3A 142
Bishop Dr. B37: Chel W ... 2C 34
Bishopgate Bus. Pk. CV1: Cov ... 2C 58
Bishops Bowl Lakes ... 7K 109
Bishops Cleeve CV9: Aus ... 7G 7
Bishop's Cl. CV33: Bis T ... 5C 108
Bishops Cl. CV37: S Avon ... 3B 114
Bishop's Ct. B37: Mars G ... 5E 34
Bishops Ga. CV47: Bis I ... 5C 110
BISHOPSGATE GREEN ... 2D 58
Bishopsgate Ind. Est. CV1: Cov ... 2D 58
Bishops Hill CV35: Light ... 2G 119
BISHOP'S ITCHINGTON
... 6C 110 (3A 144)
BISHOP'S TACHBROOK
... 5C 108 (2A 144)
Bishop St. CV1: Cov ... 2H 135 (4C 58)
Bishop's Wlk. CV5: Cov ... 7F 135 (7B 58)
BISHOPTON ... 1C 114 (3C 143)
Bishopton Cl. CV5: East G ... 4F 57
Bishopton La. CV37: B'ton ... 3A 114
Bisset Cres. CV31: Lea S ... 2G 103
Bitham Rd. CV33: L Hth ... 1K 119
Bittern Wlk. CV2: Cov ... 4K 51
BITTESWELL ... 3C 141
Bixhill La. B46: Shu ... 2B 26
BLABY ... 2C 141
Black-a-Tree Ct. CV10: Nun ... 6A 22
Black-a-Tree Rd. CV10: Nun ... 7K 21
Blackbades Blvd. CV34: Warw ... 4D 100
BLACK BANK ... 4H 41
Black Bank CV7: Exh ... 4H 41
Blackberry Cl. CV23: Brow ... 7K 65
Blackberry La. CV2: Cov ... 1H 59
CV7: Ash G ... 1C 50
Blackbird Cft. B36: Cas B ... 5A 24
Blackburn Rd. CV6: Lford ... 3F 51
Blackcat Cl. B37: F'bri ... 2A 34
BLACKDOWN ... 2D 98
Blackdown Hall CV32: B'dwn ... 1D 98
Blackfirs La. B37: Mars G ... 6C 34
Blackford Cl. B95: Hen A ... 2H 93
Blackford Hill B95: Hen A ... 3J 93
Blackford Way CV35: Oxh ... 1E 130
Blackgreaves La. B76: Lea M ... 2F 19
Black Hall La. CV7: Fill ... 1A 38
BLACKHEATH ... 3A 138
BLACK HILL ... 7K 95 (3D 143)
Blackhill Ind. Est. CV37: Blk H ... 7K 95
Black Horse Rd. CV6: Lford ... 1H 51
CV7: Exh ... 7G 41
Black La. CV32: Lea S ... 5F 99
Blacklow Rd. CV34: Warw ... 6J 97
Blackman Way CV21: Rugby ... 4E 75
Black Pad CV6: Cov ... 6C 50
Black Prince Av. CV3: Cov ... 1D 68
Black Shale Dr. CV47: Sou ... 3H 107
Blackshaw Dr. CV2: Walsg S ... 1B 60
Blacksmith La. CV23: F'ton ... 7B 84
Blacksmiths La. CV47: N'end ... 1D 120
Blackthorn Cl. CV4: Canly ... 3H 67
CV21: Brow ... 7J 65
Blackthorn Ct. *B95: Hen A ... 1H 93*
(off Chestnut Wlk.)
Blackthorn Gro. CV11: Nun ... 2B 32
Blackthorn Rd. CV8: Ken ... 6E 78
CV37: S Avon ... 2F 115
Blackthorn Way B49: Alc ... 3B 112
Blackwatch Rd. CV6: Cov ... 6C 50
BLACKWELL
B60 ... 1A 142
CV36 ... 7F 127 (1B 146)
Blackwell Bus. Pk. CV36: Wind ... 7F 127
Blackwell La. CV35: Hatt ... 5B 96
Blackwell Rd. CV6: Cov ... 6E 50
CV36: Tred ... 7H 127
Blackwood Av. CV22: Bil ... 7C 74
Blacon Way CV37: S Avon ... 4B 114
Bladon Cl. CV11: Nun ... 3G 23
Bladon Wlk. CV31: Lea S ... 2G 103
Blair Dr. CV12: Bed ... 4D 40
Blair Gro. B37: Chel W ... 4D 34
Blake Cl. CV10: Gall C ... 6F 21
CV22: Bil ... 7C 74
BLAKEDOWN ... 1A 142
Blakelands Av. CV31: Lea S ... 2F 103
Blakes Cl. OX15: Lwr Bra ... 3G 133
BLAKESLEY ... 3D 145
Blanchfort Cl. CV4: Tile H ... 6D 56
Blandford Dr. CV2: Walsg S ... 2B 60
Blandford Rd. CV32: Lea S ... 6A 98
Blandford Way CV35: H Mag ... 1C 100
Bleaberry CV21: Brow ... 1J 75
Bleachfield St. B49: Alc ... 6B 112
BLEDINGTON ... 3B 146
Blenheim Av. CV6: Cov ... 4C 50
Blenheim Cl. B50: Bidf A ... 5G 123
CV11: Nun ... 2B 32
Blenheim Cres. CV31: Lea S ... 3G 103
Blenheim Rd. CV37: S Avon ... 6J 115
Blenheim Wlk. CV6: Cov ... 2B 50
CV35: Welle ... 5G 117
BLETCHINGDON ... 3D 147
Bletchley Dr. CV5: Cov ... 3F 57
Blew Gates OX15: Lwr Bra ... 3G 133
Blick Rd. CV34: H'cte ... 4A 102
Blind La. B94: Tan A ... 3A 90
CV8: Ken ... 7D 66
Blindpit La. B76: Wis ... 3A 18
Bliss Cl. CV4: Tile H ... 4C 56
BLISWORTH ... 3D 145
BLOCKLEY ... 2A 146
Blockley Rd. CV12: Bed ... 1J 41
Blondvil St. CV3: Cov ... 1C 68
Blossom Way CV22: Rugby ... 7J 75
Bloxam Gdns. CV22: Rugby ... 6F 75
BLOXHAM ... 2D 147
Bloxham Pl. CV21: Rugby ... 5G 75
Bloxham Way CV31: Rad S ... 3K 103
BLOXWICH ... 1B 138
Bluebell CV4: Canly ... 4G 67
Bluebell Cl. CV10: Harts ... 3F 21
CV23: Brow ... 7K 65
Bluebell Dr. B37: Chel W ... 3D 34
CV12: Bed ... 3E 40
Bluebell Rd. CV37: S Avon ... 7G 115
Bluebell Wlk. CV4: Tile H ... 6D 56
Bluebird Dr. CV6: Cov ... 5B 50
Blue Brick La. CV10: Nun ... 5J 21
Blue Cap Rd. CV37: S Avon ... 2F 115
Blue La. CV37: Lox ... 7C 116
Bluemel's Dr. CV8: Wols ... 4J 71
Blue Ribbon Pk. CV6: Cov ... 6E 50
Blundells, The CV8: Ken ... 4D 78
Blundells Cft. CV37: Welf A ... 2A 124
BLUNTINGTON ... 1A 142
BLUNT'S GREEN ... 4E 90
Blyth Cl. CV12: Bed ... 4C 40
CV22: Caw ... 1A 86
Blyth Ct. CV11: Nun ... 1J 31
Blythe Ct. B46: Cole ... 5G 25
BLYTHE END ... 2J 25
Blythe Rd. B46: Cole ... 5G 25
CV1: Cov ... 3E 58
Boar Cft. CV4: Tile H ... 5D 56
Boat La. CV37: Welf A ... 2A 124
Boatyard Dr. *B50: Bidf A ... 6G 123*
(off Holland Cl.)
Bockendon Rd. CV4: Westw H ... 4B 66
Boddington Cl. CV32: Cubb ... 2J 99
Bodiam Hall CV1: Cov ... 3K 135
BODICOTE ... 2D 147
Bodmin Rd. CV2: Cov ... 2B 60
Bodnant Way CV8: Ken ... 3G 79
BODYMOOR HEATH ... 7B 12 (2C 139)
Bodymoor Heath La.
B76: Bod H, Mars ... 5A 12, 1H 19
B78: Midd ... 5A 12
Bodymoor Heath Vis. Cen. ... 7B 12
Boehm Dr. B49: Kinw ... 3D 112
Bohun St. CV4: Tile H ... 6D 56
Boiler Ho. *CV1: Cov ... 2C 58*
(off Electric Wharf)
BOLEHALL ... 1D 139
Boleyn Cl. CV34: Warw ... 2A 102
Bolingbroke Dr. CV34: H'cte ... 5C 102
Bolingbroke Rd. CV3: Cov ... 6G 59
Bolton Cl. CV3: Cov ... 3E 68
Bolus La. B46: Max ... 1D 36
Bolyfant Cres. CV31: W'nsh ... 6E 102
Bond End CV23: M Kirby ... 3J 55
Bond Ga. CV11: Nun ... 7D 22
Bonds Ct. CV1: Cov ... 3G 135 (4C 58)
Bonds Hospital
CV1: Cov ... 3F 135 (4B 58)
Bond St. CV1: Cov ... 3G 135 (4C 58)
CV11: Nun ... 6D 22
CV21: Rugby ... 5F 75
Boneham Rd. CV31: W'nsh ... 6E 102
BONEHILL ... 1C 139
BONEY HAY ... 1B 138
Bonneville Cl. CV5: Milli W ... 6K 47
Bonniksen Cl. CV31: Lea S ... 3D 102
Bonnington Cl. CV21: Hillm ... 7D 76
Bonnington Dr. CV12: Bed ... 1G 41
Boot Hill CV9: Gren ... 1F 15
Booths Flds. CV6: Cov ... 4E 50
Border Ct. CV3: Cov ... 6G 59
Bordesley Ct. CV32: Lill ... 4E 98
Bordon Hill CV37: S Avon ... 6A 114
Bordon Pl. CV37: S Avon ... 6D 114
Borough Way CV11: Nun ... 7B 22
Borrowdale CV21: Brow ... 7J 65
Borrowdale Cl. CV6: Cov ... 6A 50
Borrowdale Dr. CV32: Lea S ... 5B 98
BORROWELL ... 6C 78
Borrowell La. CV8: Ken ... 5C 78
Borrowell Ter. CV8: Ken ... 5C 78
Bosley Cl. CV36: Ship S ... 6G 131
Boston Pl. CV6: Cov ... 6D 50
Boswell Dr. CV2: Walsg S ... 1C 60
Boswell Gro. CV34: Warw ... 6F 97
Boswell Rd. CV22: Rugby ... 2E 86
Bosworth Av. CV37: S Avon ... 6J 115
Bosworth Cl. CV8: Bag ... 5E 68
Bosworth Dr. B37: Chel W, F'bri ... 3A 34
BOTCHESTON ... 1B 140
Boteler Cl. B49: Alc ... 5B 112
Botoner Rd. CV1: Cov ... 5F 59
Bottom St. CV47: N'end ... 2D 120
Bottrill Ct. CV11: Nun ... 6C 22
Bottrill St. CV11: Nun ... 6C 22
Bott Rd. CV5: Cov ... 7H 57
Boucher Cl. CV37: Shot ... 6C 114
BOUGHTON ... 2D 145
Boughton Rd. CV21: Rugby ... 1H 75
Boulters La. CV9: Wood E ... 2K 13
Boundary La.
CV37: A'ton, S Avon ... 5K 115
Boundary Rd. CV21: Rugby ... 6K 75
Boundary Rd. Nth.
CV37: Long M ... 4H 125
Boundary Rd. W. CV37: Long M ... 5F 125
Bourchier Cl. CV4: Tile H ... 1A 66
BOURNBROOK ... 3B 138
Bourne Brook Cl. CV7: Fill ... 2B 38
Bournebrook Vw. CV7: Old A ... 3C 28
Bourne Cl. CV9: Ath ... 1D 16
Bourne End CV47: Sou ... 6G 107
BOURNHEATH ... 1A 142
BOURNVILLE ... 3B 138
Bourton Ct. CV31: Lea S ... 3F 103
Bourton Dr. CV31: Lea S ... 3F 103
BOURTON ON DUNSMORE
... 7C 84 (1B 144)
BOURTON-ON-THE-HILL ... 2A 146
BOURTON-ON-THE-WATER ... 3A 146
Bourton Rd. CV23: F'ton ... 7B 84
Boveney CV12: Bed ... 5C 40
Bowater Ct. CV3: Cov ... 2F 69
Bow Ct. CV5: Cov ... 7H 57
Bowden Way CV3: Bin ... 6B 60
Bowen Rd. CV22: Hillm ... 1K 87
Bowers Cft. CV32: Lill ... 3E 98
Bowet Cl. CV22: Caw ... 1K 85
Bow Fell CV21: Brow ... 1K 75
Bowfell Cl. CV5: East G ... 3E 56
Bow La. CV7: Withy ... 1D 54
CV23: M Kirby ... 1D 54
Bowler Cl. CV9: Ath ... 1B 16
Bowley Ho. CV21: Rugby ... 3G 75
Bowleys La. DE12: App M ... 1K 7
Bowling Grn. Cl. CV9: Bad E ... 2F 15
Bowling Grn. La. CV12: Bed ... 6E 40
Bowling Grn. St. CV34: Warw ... 2F 101
Bowls Ct. CV5: Cov ... 4K 57
Bowness Cl. CV6: Cov ... 6A 50
Box Bush Cotts. CV37: Long M ... 2G 125
Box Cl. CV31: W'nsh ... 5F 103
Boxhill, The CV3: Cov ... 6H 59
Box Rd. B37: Chel W ... 5C 34
Boxwood Dr. CV23: Kils ... 6J 89
Boyce Way CV23: Long L ... 3B 74

Boyd Cl. CV2: Walsg S 6B 52
Bracadale Cl. CV3: Bin ...4C 60
Bracebridge Rd. B78: K'bry ...5D 12
  CV9: Ath ...4B 16
Bracebridge St. CV11: Nun ...7C 22
Bracken Cl. CV22: Bil ...7E 74
Bracken Cft. B37: Chel W ...2C 34
Brackendale Dr. CV10: Nun ...2F 31
Bracken Dr. CV22: Bil ...7E 74
  LE10: Wlvy ...2H 33
Brackenhurst Rd. CV6: Cov ...7K 49
Brackley Cl. CV6: Cov ...7K 49
Brackley Cres. CV34: Warw ...5D 100
Bracknell Wlk.
  CV2: Walsg S ...7C 52
BRADDEN ...3D 145
Braddock Cl. CV3: Bin ...6C 60
Brade Dr. CV2: Walsg S ...7C 52
Bradestone Rd. CV11: Nun ...3K 31
Bradfield Cl. CV5: Cov ...2G 57
Bradford Cl. CV33: Bis T ...5B 108
Brading Rd. CV10: Nun ...5E 22
BRADLEY ...2A 138
BRADLEY GREEN
  B96 ...2A 142
  CV9 ...5J 11 (1D 139)
BRADMORE ...2A 138
Bradney Grn. CV4: Tile H ...1C 66
Bradnick Pl. CV4: Tile H ...6D 56
Bradshaw Cl. CV47: P Mars ...6G 111
Braemar Cl. CV2: Cov ...7A 52
Braemar Rd. CV32: Lill ...3F 99
Braemar Way CV10: Nun ...2G 31
Braeside Cft. B37: Chel W ...3D 34
Brafield Leys CV21: Rugby ...3G 87
Braids Cl. CV21: Rugby ...4K 75
Brailes Golf Course ...4K 133
Brailes Ind. Est. OX15: Lwr Bra ...3K 133
Brailes Rd. CV36: Ship S ...5J 131
Brailes Rd. Ind. Est.
  CV36: Ship S ...5J 131
Brakeley Cl. CV47: Long I ...2D 106
Brakesmead CV31: Lea S ...3D 102
Bramble Cl. B46: Cole ...5F 25
  CV11: Nun ...2B 32
Bramble St. CV1: Cov ...5E 58
Brambling Cl. CV23: Brow ...7J 65
BRAMCOTE ...6H 33 (3B 140)
Bramcote Cl. CV12: Bulk ...3F 43
BRAMCOTE MAINS ...2G 43
Bramcote Water Golf Course ...7K 33
Bramdene Av. CV10: Nun ...3D 22
Bramley Way B50: Bidf A ...5G 123
Brampton Way CV12: Bulk ...2D 42
Bramston Cres. CV4: Tile H ...6D 56
Bramwell Gdns. CV6: Lford ...1E 50
Brandfield Rd. CV6: Cov ...6K 49
BRANDON ...3H 71 (1B 144)
Brandon Castle ...4H 71
Brandon Ct. CV3: Bin ...1C 70
Brandon La. CV3: W'hall ...4K 69
  CV8: Bran ...3D 70
Brandon Marsh Nature Reserve ...4C 70
Brandon Marsh Nature Reserve Vis. Cen.
  ...4D 70
Brandon Pde. CV32: Lea S ...7E 98
Brandon Rd. CV3: Bin ...6B 60
  CV23: Bret ...2A 72
Brandon Wood Golf Course ...3E 70
Brand Rd. CV21: Rugby ...2H 75
Branksome Rd. CV6: Cov ...1J 57
Bransdale Av. CV6: Cov ...3D 50
Bransford Av. CV4: Canly ...3H 67
Branstree Dr. CV6: Cov ...4D 50
BRATCH, THE ...2A 138
Brathay Cl. CV3: Cov ...6B 60
BRAUNSTON ...2C 145
BRAUNSTON TOWN ...1C 141
Braunston Pl. CV22: Hillm ...1K 87
Bray Bank B46: Over W ...1F 27
Brayford Av. CV3: Cov ...2C 68
Brays Cl. CV23: Brin ...4C 62
Bray's La. CV2: Cov ...4G 59
Braytoft Cl. CV6: Cov ...4C 50
Brazil St. CV4: Tile H ...5C 56
Breach Brook Vw. CV12: Bed ...5D 40
Breach La. CV35: Clav ...2C 94
Breach Oak La. CV7: Cor ...2G 39
Bread and Meat Cl. CV34: Warw ...2F 101
Bream Cl. B37: Chel W ...3C 34
Breaside Wlk. B37: Chel W ...3C 34
BREDICOT ...3A 142
Bredon Av. CV3: Bin ...1B 70
Bree Cl. CV5: Alle ...7E 48
Breeden Dr. B76: Curd ...5B 18
Bremridge Cl. CV35: Barf ...3B 108
Brendan Cl. B46: Cole ...7G 25
Brendon Way CV10: Nun ...1A 30
Brentwood Av. CV3: Finh ...5C 68
Brentwood Gdns. CV3: Finh ...5C 68
Brese Av. CV34: Warw ...6H 97
BRETFORD ...1B 72 (1B 144)

Bretford Rd. CV2: Cov ...5J 51
  CV8: Bran ...2J 71
  CV23: Brin ...6C 62
BRETFORTON ...1A 146
Breton Ct. CV3: Cov ...7G 59
Bretts Cl. CV1: Cov ...1K 135 (3E 58)
Bretts Hall Est. CV10: Ans C ...4E 20
Brewer Rd. CV12: Bulk ...4F 43
Brewers Cl. CV3: Bin ...6C 60
Brewery Row GL56: Lit C ...6B 134
Brewery St.
  CV37: S Avon ...1E 136 (4E 114)
BREWOOD ...1A 138
Brewster Cl. CV2: Cov ...5A 60
Briar Cl. CV32: Lill ...5F 99
Briar Cft.
  CV37: S Avon ...3B 136 (5E 114)
Briardene Av. CV12: Bed ...3H 41
Briar Gdns. CV32: Lill ...5G 99
Briars, The B79: Wart ...6H 9
Briars Cl. CV2: Cov ...5J 59
  CV11: Nun ...6F 23
  CV23: Long L ...4B 74
Brickall, The CV37: Long M ...3G 125
Brickfield La. CV36: Ship S ...3G 131
Brickhill Cl. CV36: Ship S ...4G 131
Brickhill Dr. B37: F'bri ...3A 34
Brick Hill La. CV5: Alle ...6B 48
Brick Kiln Cl. CV35: N Lin ...2F 95
Brick Kiln La. CV9: Hur ...7J 13
Brick Kiln Way CV12: Bed ...2K 41
Brickyard Rd. CV47: Nap ...2F 111
Bridgeacre Gdns. CV3: Bin ...4B 60
Bridge Bus. Cen., The
  CV37: S Avon ...3C 114
Bridgecote CV3: W'hall ...2A 70
Bridge Ct. CV47: Sou ...6H 107
BRIDGE END ...3H 101
Bridge End CV34: Warw ...2H 101
  CV47: Sou ...5H 107
Bridge Foot
  CV37: S Avon ...3H 137 (4F 115)
Bridgefoot Quay
  CV37: S Avon ...3H 137 (4F 115)
Bridge House Theatre ...2J 101
Bridge La. CV9: With ...4G 17
  CV47: Ladb ...3C 110
Bridgeman Rd. CV6: Cov ...1J 57
Bridge Rd. CV35: But M ...7A 120
Bridge St. B78: Pole ...1D 10
  CV6: Cov ...7F 51
  CV8: Ken ...4D 78
  CV9: Hur ...7K 13
  CV11: Nun ...2J 31
  (Henry St.)
  CV11: Nun ...7D 22
  (Market Pl.)
  CV21: Rugby ...5J 75
  CV34: Warw ...7K 97
  CV35: Barf ...2B 108
  CV35: H Lucy ...2B 118
  CV35: Kine ...6C 120
  CV35: Welle ...3J 117
  CV37: S Avon ...4G 137 (4F 115)
  CV47: Fen C ...3C 110
BRIDGE TOWN ...6G 115 (3D 143)
Bridgetown Rd. CV37: S Avon ...6G 115
Bridget St. CV21: Rugby ...5F 75
Bridge Vw. B46: Cole ...5F 25
  CV8: Bag ...5D 68
Bridgeway
  CV37: S Avon ...2J 137 (4F 115)
Bridge Works Ind. Est. CV8: Ken ...5E 78
BRIDGTOWN ...1A 138
Bridle Brook La. CV5: Alle ...2D 48
Bridle Path, The CV5: Alle ...1F 57
Bridle Rd. CV21: Rugby ...5E 74
  CV35: L Hth ...2K 119
Bridleway, The CV10: Nun ...3G 31
Bridport Cl. CV2: Walsg S ...6B 52
Brierley Rd. CV2: Cov ...6J 51
Brightmere Rd. CV6: Cov ...3H 57
Brighton St. CV2: Cov ...4F 59
Bright Rd. CV6: Nun ...5H 21
Bright St. CV6: Cov ...1E 58
Brightwalton Rd. CV3: Cov ...1D 68
Brill Cl. CV4: Canly ...3G 67
Brimstone End CV31: Lea S ...4G 103
Brindle Av. CV3: Cov ...5J 59
Brindles All. CV36: Ship S ...4H 131
Brindley Paddocks
  CV1: Cov ...1H 135 (3C 58)
Brindley Rd. CV7: Exh ...6H 41
  CV21: Hillm ...7C 76
BRINKLOW ...4C 62 (1B 144)
Brinklow Castle ...3D 62
Brinklow Rd. CV3: Bin ...6B 60
  CV7: Ansty ...2G 53
  CV23: Brin, Eas ...4E 62

Brisbane Cl. CV3: Cov ...2E 68
Brisbane Ct. CV12: Bed ...3F 41
Briscoe Rd. CV6: Cov ...2C 50
Bristol Rd. CV5: Cov ...5K 57
Bristol Way CV35: Welle ...5G 117
Briton Rd. CV2: Cov ...3G 59
Britannia St. CV2: Cov ...4F 59
Brittain La. CV34: Warw ...2A 102
Britten Cl. CV11: Nun ...5C 32
Brittons La. CV35: N Lin ...1G 95
Brixham Cl. CV11: Nun ...6G 23
Brixham Dr. CV2: Cov ...1J 59
BRIXWORTH ...1D 145
Brixworth Cl. CV3: Bin ...7A 60
BROAD ALLEY ...2A 142
BROAD CAMPDEN ...2A 146
Broad Cl. CV33: Ufton ...3F 109
  CV37: Ett ...2C 126
Broadgate CV1: Cov ...4H 135 (5C 58)
BROAD GREEN ...1A 142
Broadhaven Cl. CV31: Lea S ...1G 103
Broadlands Cl. CV5: Cov ...5G 57
Broad La. B94: Tan A ...3A 90
  CV5: Cov, East G, Berk ...3B 56
  CV7: Berk ...3A 56
  CV7: Fill ...1J 37
Broad La. Trad. Est. CV4: Tile H ...3A 56
Broadlee B77: Wiln ...1A 10
BROAD MARSTON ...1A 146
Broadmead Ct. CV5: Cov ...5G 57
Broadmeadow La. CV37: B'ton ...3B 114
Broadmere Ri. CV5: East G ...5E 56
Broad Oak Ct. CV32: Lea S ...5E 98
Broad Pk. Rd. CV2: Cov ...7K 51
Broad St. CV6: Cov ...7E 50
  CV23: Brin ...4C 62
  CV34: Warw ...1H 101
  CV36: Long C ...2C 134
  CV37: S Avon ...7D 136 (5E 114)
Broad St. Jetty CV6: Cov ...7E 50
Broad Wlk.
  CV37: S Avon ...7C 136 (5E 114)
Broadwater CV5: Cov ...7A 58
BROADWAY ...2A 146
Broadway CV5: Cov ...7A 58
  CV32: Cubb ...2J 99
Broadway Mans. CV5: Cov ...6A 58
BROADWELL ...2D 145
  CV23 ...3B 144
  GL56 ...3B 146
Broadwells Ct. CV4: Westw H ...2D 66
Broadwells Cres. CV4: Westw H ...3D 66
BROCKENCOTE ...1A 142
Brockenhurst Way CV6: Lford ...7H 41
Brocket Pl. CV22: Caw ...1B 86
BROCKHALL ...2D 145
Brockhall Gro. B37: K'hrst ...7A 24
BROCKHURST ...3K 55
Brockhurst Dr. CV4: Tile H ...5B 56
Brockhurst La. CV23: M Kirby ...3K 55
BROCKMOOR ...3A 138
Brodick Way CV10: Nun ...1F 31
Brodie Cl. CV21: Rugby ...6J 75
Bromage Av. B78: K'bry ...5D 12
Brome Hall La. B94: Lapw ...4J 91
BROMFORD ...2C 139
Bromford Way CV37: S Avon ...3C 114
Bromhurst Way CV34: Warw ...4D 100
Bromleigh Dr. CV2: Cov ...5J 59
Bromleigh Vs. CV8: Bag ...6F 69
Bromley Cl. CV8: Ken ...3H 79
BROMSGROVE ...1A 142
Bromsgrove Rd. B80: Stud ...4B 92
Bromwich Cl. CV3: Bin ...7B 60
Bromwich Rd. B46: Cole ...2E 24
Bromwich Rd. CV21: Hillm ...7B 76
Bronte Cl. CV10: Gall C ...6B 20
  CV21: Rugby ...5J 75
Bronze Cl. CV11: Nun ...4A 32
Bronze Rd. CV2: Cov ...7B 74
Bronze Vw. CV4: Westw H ...1B 66
Brook Bus. Pk. CV35: Kine ...6B 120
Brook Cl. B37: K'bry ...6E 12
  CV1: Cov ...4E 58
Brook Cott. Cl. B46: Over W ...1F 27
Brook Cotts. CV36: W'gton ...7K 131
Brook Cft. B37: Mars G ...6B 34
Brookdale Rd. CV10: Nun ...4E 22
Brooke Cl. CV34: Warw ...3H 101
  CV37: S Avon ...6H 115
Brooke Cl. CV21: Rugby ...5F 75
  (off Lit. Pennington St.)
Brooke M. CV34: Warw ...2H 101
BROOK END ...3A 142
Brook End Cl. B95: Hen A ...2G 93
Brook End Dr. B95: Hen A ...2G 93
Brook Farm Wlk. B37: Chel W ...2D 34
Brookfield Ct. CV37: S Avon ...4B 114
Brookfield Dr. LE10: Wlvy ...2H 33
Brookfield Rd. CV32: Cubb ...2J 99

Brookford Av. CV6: Cov ...3A 50
Brookhampton Cl. CV35: Kine ...6A 120
Brookhampton La. CV35: Kine ...6B 120
Brook Hill CV36: Gt Wol ...7A 132
Brookhus Farm Rd. CV34: Lea S ...6B 98
Brooklands CV23: Clift D ...3C 76
Brooklands Way B37: Mars G ...5B 34
Brook La. CV10: Nun ...5D 22
  CV35: More M ...5C 118
Brooklea CV12: Bed ...3F 41
Brookline Dr. CV23: Brow ...7K 65
Brooklyn Rd. CV1: Cov ...1D 58
Brooks Cl. CV23: W'hby ...3H 105
Brookshaw Way CV2: Walsg S ...6B 52
Brookside B95: Woot W ...4J 93
  CV23: Stret D ...3H 83
  CV37: Snitt ...5G 95
Brookside Av. CV5: Cov ...4G 57
  CV8: Ken ...5C 78
  CV35: Welle ...3J 117
Brookside Cl. CV22: Rugby ...7G 75
  CV37: S Avon ...4C 114
Brookside Rd. CV37: S Avon ...4C 114
Brookstray Flats CV5: East G ...4F 57
Brook St. CV8: Wols ...5J 71
  CV12: Bed ...7H 31
  CV34: Warw ...2G 101
  CV47: Fen C ...3G 121
Brookvale Av. CV3: Bin ...6A 60
Brookvale Rd.
  CV37: S Avon ...7A 136 (5D 114)
Brook Vw. CV22: Dunc ...6B 86
Brook Wlk. CV9: Man ...5E 16
BROOM ...3F 123 (3B 142)
Broom Cl. CV22: Bil ...7E 74
Broomcroft Rd. B37: K'hrst ...7A 24
BROOME ...1A 142
Broome Cft. CV6: Cov ...3B 50
Broomey Croft Childrens Farm ...4B 12
Broomfield Pl. CV5: Cov ...5A 58
  (not continuous)
Broomfield Ri. CV10: Nun ...2F 31
Broomfield Rd. CV5: Cov ...6K 57
BROOM HILL ...1A 142
Broomybank CV8: Ken ...3F 79
BROUGHTON ...2D 147
BROUGHTON ASTLEY ...2C 141
BROUGHTON GREEN ...2A 142
BROUGHTON HACKETT ...3A 142
Browett Rd. CV6: Cov ...2A 58
BROWNHILLS ...1B 138
Browning Av. CV34: Warw ...3E 100
Browning Cl. CV10: Gall C ...6F 21
  CV37: S Avon ...7H 115
Browning Rd. CV2: Cov ...4J 59
  CV21: Hillm ...1D 88
Brownlow Dr. CV37: S Avon ...6D 114
BROWNLOW GREEN ...3A 96
Brownlow St. CV32: Lea S ...5E 98
Brown's Bri. Rd. CV47: Sou ...6H 107
BROWN'S GREEN ...2B 138
Brownshill Cl. CV6: Cov ...6K 49
BROWNSHILL GREEN ...5H 49
Brownshill Grn. Rd. CV5: Alle ...5H 49
  CV6: Cov ...5H 49
Brown's La. B78: Dord ...5C 10
  CV5: Alle ...5H 49
BROWNSOVER ...1K 75
Brownsover La. CV21: Brow ...1H 75
Brownsover Rd.
  CV21: N'bld A, Rugby ...1E 74
Broxell Cl. CV34: Warw ...7E 96
Bruce Rd. CV6: Cov ...6A 50
  CV7: Exh ...5F 41
Bruces Way CV37: S Avon ...4A 114
Bruce Williams Way
  CV22: Rugby ...6H 75
Brudenell Cl. CV22: Caw ...1A 86
BRUERN ABBEY ...3B 146
Brunel Cl. CV2: Cov ...4F 59
  CV31: W'nsh ...5F 103
Brunel Wlk. B78: Pole ...6D 8
Brunel Way
  CV37: S Avon ...2B 136 (4E 114)
Brunes Ct. CV21: Brow ...1K 75
Brunswick Cl. CV21: Rugby ...2J 75
Brunswick Ct. CV31: Lea S ...3E 102
Brunswick Ho. CV32: Lea S ...5D 98
  (off Lillington Av.)
Brunswick Rd. CV1: Cov ...5A 58
  CV31: Lea S ...3E 102
BRUNTINGTHORPE ...2D 141
Bruntingthorpe Way CV3: Bin ...7A 60
Brunton Cl. CV3: Bin ...2C 60
Brutus Dr. B46: Cole ...3E 24
Bryan M. B50: Bidf A ...6H 123
Bryanston Cl. CV2: Walsg S ...3C 60
Bryant Rd. CV7: Exh ...6G 41
  CV23: Brow ...6J 65
Brympton Rd. CV3: Cov ...5J 59

Bryn Jones Cl.—Castle Combe

Bryn Jones Cl. CV3: Bin 7B **60**
Bryn Rd. CV6: Cov 7F **51**
Bryony Cl. CV12: Bed 4E **40**
BUBBENHALL 4J **81** (1A **144**)
Bubbenhall Rd. CV8: Bag, Bubb 7F **69**
Buccleuch Cl. CV22: Dunc 5C **86**
Buchanan Cl. CV4: Tile H 4A **56**
Buchanan Rd. CV22: Bil, Rugby 7E **74**
Buchan Cl. CV10: Gall C 7E **20**
CV37: S Avon 7H **115**
Buckden Cl. CV34: Warw 6H **97**
Buckfast Cl. CV3: Cov 3E **68**
Buckhold Dr. CV5: Cov 2F **57**
Buckingham Cl. CV10: Nun 3H **31**
Buckingham Ri. CV5: Cov 3F **57**
Buckingham Rd. B36: Cas B 5A **24**
BUCKLAND 2A **146**
Buckland Rd. CV6: Cov 4B **50**
BUCKLEY GREEN 2C **143**
Buckley Rd. CV32: Lill 5F **99**
Bucknill Cres. CV21: Hillm 1D **88**
Bucksey Cl. CV6: Cov 4G **51**
Bucks Hill CV10: Nun 4G **21**
Buckwell La. CV23: Clift D 3C **76**
BUDBROOKE 1B **100**
Budbrooke Cl. CV2: Cov 4K **51**
Budbrooke Ind. Est.
CV34: Warw 1E **100**
Budbrooke Rd. CV34: Warw 1D **100**
BUGBROOKE 3D **145**
BULKINGTON 3E **42** (3A **140**)
Bulkington La. CV11: Nun 4C **32**
Bulkington Rd. CV7: Shilt 6G **43**
CV12: Bed 3J **41**
LE10: Wlvy 2G **33**
Bullfield Av. CV4: Tile H 6C **56**
Bullimore Gro. CV8: Ken 7E **78**
Bull Ring CV10: Nun 2H **31**
Bull Ring, The CV33: Har 6H **109**
Bull Ring Farm Rd. CV33: Har 5H **109**
Bull's Head La. CV3: Cov 5H **59**
Bulls Head Yd. B49: Alc 5B **112**
Bull St. CV11: Nun 2K **31**
CV37: S Avon 7E **136** (6E **114**)
CV47: Sou 5H **107**
Bull St. M. *CV47: Sou 5H* ***107***
(off Bull St.)
Bull Yd. CV1: Cov 4G **135** (5C **58**)
Bull Yd., The CV47: Sou 5H **107**
Bulwer Rd. CV6: Cov 7A **50**
Bulwick Cl. CV3: Bin 6D **60**
Bungalows, The CV37: Welf A 2B **124**
Bunkers Hill CV35: Pill H 1C **128**
Bunkers Hill La.
CV23: Bret, Chu L 3B **72**
BURBAGE 2B **140**
Burbage Av. CV37: S Avon 1E **114**
Burbages La. CV6: Lford 1D **50**
Burbury Cl. CV12: Bed 1J **41**
CV32: Lill 5G **99**
Burbury Ct. CV34: Warw 7K **97**
BURCOT 1A **142**
BURDROP 2C **147**
Burford M. CV31: Lea S 2G **103**
Burford Rd. CV37: S Avon 5J **115**
Burgage Pl. CV11: Nun 7D **22**
Burgage Wlk. CV11: Nun 7D **22**
(Corporation St.)
CV11: Nun 6C **22**
(Friary St.)
Burges, The CV1: Cov 2H **135** (4C **58**)
Burges Gro. CV34: Warw 6H **97**
Burghley Cl. CV11: Nun 2B **32**
Burgundy Gdns. CV31: Lea S 4G **103**
Burhill Way B37: F'bri 7B **24**
Burlington Rd. CV2: Cov 3F **59**
(not continuous)
CV10: Nun 5H **31**
Burlywood Cl. CV5: Alle 6F **49**
Burman Cl. CV32: Lill 3E **98**
Burman Dr. B46: Cole 7F **25**
BURMINGTON 2B **146**
Burnaby Cl. CV10: Nun 6G **21**
Burnaby Rd. CV6: Cov 5B **50**
Burnell Cl. B50: Bidf A 5F **123**
Burnett Rd. CV33: L Hth 3K **119**
Burnham Ri. CV11: Nun 5H **23**
Burnham Rd. CV3: Cov 2G **69**
Burnsall Cl. B37: F'bri 3A **34**
Burnsall Gro. CV5: Cov 7H **57**
Burnsall Rd. CV5: Cov 7G **57**
Burnsall Rd. Ind. Est. CV5: Cov 7G **57**
Burns Av. CV34: Warw 3E **100**
Burns Cl. CV37: S Avon 7H **115**
Burnside CV3: Bin 5C **60**
CV22: Rugby 6E **74**
CV37: Shot 5B **114**
Burns Rd. CV2: Cov 4J **59**
CV32: Lill 3F **99**
Burns Wlk. CV12: Bed 4J **41**
Burnthurst La. CV23: Prin 6C **82**
BURNTWOOD 1B **138**
BURNTWOOD GREEN 1B **138**
BURROUGH ON THE HILL 1D **141**
Burroughs Cl. CV2: Cov 1H **59**
Burrow Hill Hill Fort 6G **39**
Burrow Hill La. CV7: Cor 6G **39**
Burrows, The CV37: N'bld S 1G **127**
Burrows Cl. CV31: W'nsh 5F **103**
Burton Cl. CV5: Alle 4G **49**
BURTON DASSETT 4E **120**
Burton Dassett Hills Country Pk.
. . . . .2E **120**
BURTON GREEN 4A **66** (1D **143**)
BURTON HASTINGS 4H **33** (3B **140**)
Burton La. CV11: Burt H 5H **33**
BURTON OVERY 2D **141**
Burtons Pk. Rd. B36: Cas B 4A **24**
Burtons Way B36: Cas B 5A **24**
Bury, The *CV36: Ship S 4H* ***131***
(off Sheep St.)
Bury Ct. La. OX17: Shotte 6H **129**
BURY END 2A **146**
Bury Rd. CV31: Lea S 1C **102**
Bury Way La. CV36: Long C 1C **134**
Busby Cl. CV3: Bin 1B **70**
Busbys Piece CV23: M Kirby 3K **55**
Bushbery Av. CV4: Tile H 6D **56**
BUSHBURY 1A **138**
Bushbury Cft. B37: Chel W 2C **34**
BUSHBY 1D **141**
Bush Cl. CV4: Tile H 4D **56**
Bushelton Cl. CV1: Cov . . .7K **135** (6D **58**)
Bush Heath La. CV33: Har 6G **109**
Bush Heath Rd. CV33: Har 7H **109**
Bushley Cl. B98: Redd 1A **92**
Busby End CV34: H'cte 4C **102**
Butcher's Cl. CV23: Brin 4D **62**
Butchers Cl. CV47: Bis I 6B **110**
Butchers La. CV5: Alle 1G **57**
OX15: Lwr Bra 3H **133**
Butchers Rd. B92: H Ard 7G **45**
Butler Cl. CV8: Ken 2G **79**
CV31: W'nsh 6D **102**
Butler Cres. CV7: Exh 4G **41**
Butlers Cl. CV36: Long C 2D **134**
Butlers La. CV9: Gren 1F **15**
CV36: Long C 2C **134**
Butlers Leap CV21: Rugby 3J **75**
BUTLERS MARSTON 7A **120** (3A **144**)
Butlers Rd. CV36: Long C 3D **134**
Butlin Rd. CV6: Cov 2C **50**
CV21: Rugby 5K **75**
Buttercup Wlk. CV3: Cov 5J **59**
Buttercup Way CV12: Bed 3D **40**
CV37: S Avon 7G **115**
Butterfly Wlk. CV2: Cov 6J **51**
Buttermere CV21: Brow 1K **75**
Buttermere Av. CV11: Nun 5H **23**
Buttermere Cl. CV3: Bin 1B **70**
Butter St. B49: Alc 5C **112**
Butterworth Dr. CV4: Westw H 2E **66**
Butt Hill CV47: Nap 1J **111**
Butt La. CV5: Alle 7E **48**
CV33: Har 6J **109**
Butts CV1: Cov 5B **58**
Butts, The CV34: Warw 1G **101**
CV36: Long C 2C **134**
CV47: Nap 2H **111**
Butts Arena, The 5A **58**
Butts Cl. CV9: Aus 6G **7**
Butts La. B94: Tan A 3D **90**
Butts Rd. CV1: Cov 5A **58**
BYFIELD 3C **145**
Byfield Rd. CV6: Cov 2J **57**
CV47: P Mars 6H **111**
Byford Ct. CV10: Nun 7A **22**
Byford Dr. B78: Pole 2E **10**
Byford St. CV10: Nun 7A **22**
Byford Way B37: Mars G 5B **34**
Byron Av. CV12: Bed 3K **41**
CV34: Warw 4E **100**
Byron Rd. CV37: S Avon 6G **115**
Byron St. CV1: Cov 1J **135** (3D **58**)
Byron Wlk. CV47: Temp H 2A **120**
Bywater Cl. CV3: Cov 4B **68**

C

Cadbold Cl. CV35: Pill P 3B **128**
Cadden Dr. CV4: Tile H 5F **57**
CADEBY 1B **140**
Cadet Cl. CV3: Cov 6G **59**
Cadman Cl. CV12: Bed 2J **41**
Caen Cl. CV35: H Mag 1C **100**
Caernarfon Dr. CV11: Nun 1K **31**
Caesar Rd. CV8: Ken 6C **78**
Caesar Way B46: Cole 3F **25**
Caffrey Gro. B46: Cole 7G **25**
Caister Hall CV1: Cov 3K **135**
Caithness Cl. CV5: East G 3E **56**
CAKEBOLE 1A **142**
Calcott Ho. CV3: W'hall 2H **69**
Calcutt Mdw. CV47: Sou 5K **107**
CALDECOTE
CV10 . . . . .1B **22** (2A **140**)
NN12 .3D **145**
Caldecote Cl. CV10: Nun 4D **22**
Caldecote Hall Dr. CV10: Cald 1A **22**
Caldecote La. CV10: Cald 2A **22**
Caldecote Rd. CV6: Cov 2C **58**
Caldecott Ct. CV21: Rugby 4H **75**
Caldecott Pl. CV21: Rugby 6J **75**
Caldecott St. CV21: Rugby 6J **75**
Calder Cl. CV3: Cov 1E **68**
CV12: Bulk 3D **42**
Calder Wlk. CV31: Lea S 2G **103**
Caldwell Cvn. Pk. CV11: Nun 4K **31**
Caldwell Ct. CV11: Nun 3K **31**
Caldwell Rd. CV11: Nun 2J **31**
CALF HEATH 1A **138**
Calgary Cl. CV3: Bin 5C **60**
Caliban M. CV34: H'cte 5C **102**
Calico Way CV6: Cov 7D **50**
Callaways Rd. CV36: Ship S 6H **131**
Callendar Cl. CV11: Nun 4H **23**
Callier Cl. CV22: Caw 1B **86**
CALLOW HILL 2B **142**
Calmere Cl. CV2: Walsg S 6B **52**
Calpurnia Av. CV34: H'cte 6C **102**
Caludon Castle 2A **60**
Caludon Pk. Av. CV2: Cov 2A **60**
Caludon Rd. CV2: Cov 3G **59**
Caludon Ter. CV2: Cov 3A **60**
Calverly Ct. CV3: Cov 7G **59**
Calvert Cl. CV3: Cov 2D **68**
CV21: Brow 1A **76**
Calvestone Pl. CV22: Caw 2A **86**
Calvestone Rd. CV22: Caw 2A **86**
Calvestone Sq. CV22: Caw 1A **86**
Camberley Way CV37: Lwr Q 6F **125**
Camberwell Ter. CV31: Lea S 1E **102**
Camborne Dr. CV11: Nun 6G **23**
Cambridge Dr. B37: Mars G 5A **34**
CV10: Nun 1E **30**
Cambridge Gdns. CV32: Lea S 6E **98**
Cambridge St. CV1: Cov 2E **58**
CV21: Rugby 5J **75**
Camden St. CV2: Cov 3G **59**
Camel Cl. CV34: Warw 2A **102**
Camelia Rd. CV2: Cov 4H **51**
Camellia Ct. *CV9: Ath 3D* ***16***
(off Long St.)
Camelot Gro. CV8: Ken 4G **79**
Cameron Cl. CV5: Alle 7E **48**
CV32: Lill 3E **98**
Campbell Cl. CV10: Gall C 7F **21**
CV37: Shot 5C **114**
Campbell St. CV21: Rugby 5E **74**
Campden Gro. CV35: Hatt 5A **96**
Campden Hill CV36: Ilm 7A **126**
Campden Rd. CV36: Ship S 5F **131**
CV37: Cliff C 7A **124**
CV37: Lwr Q, Up Qui 7F **125**
CAMP HILL 5K **21**
Camp Hill Dr. CV10: Nun 4J **21**
Camp Hill Rd. CV10: Nun 4G **21**
Campion Cl. CV3: Cov 2D **68**
CV12: Bed 3D **40**
Campion Ct. CV32: Lea S 5E **98**
Campion Grn. CV32: Lea S 5E **98**
Campion Rd. CV32: Lea S 5E **98**
Campion Ter. CV32: Lea S 6E **98**
Campion Way CV23: Brow 7K **65**
Camp La.
OX17: Arles, Warm . . .5D **128**, 2F **129**
Camplea Cft. B37: F'bri 3A **34**
Campling Cl. CV12: Bulk 3D **42**
Campriano Dr. CV34: Warw 7J **97**
Campville Gro. B37: K'hrst 7A **24**
Camville CV3: Bin 5C **60**
Canada La. CV35: N Lin 3G **95**
Canal Ho. CV1: Cov 1H **135**
Canal Rd. CV6: Cov 6F **51**
Canalside B94: Lapw 3J **91**
CV6: Lford 7H **41**
Canalside Cotts. B76: Bod H 4B **12**
Canal Vw. CV1: Cov 3C **58**
Canberra Cl. CV35: Welle 5G **117**
Canberra Ct. CV12: Bed 3F **41**
Canberra M. CV32: B'dwn 3D **98**
Canberra Rd. CV2: Ald G 2J **51**
Canford Cl. CV3: Finh 5C **68**
CANLEY 2G **67** (1A **144**)
Canley Crematorium CV4: Canly 2H **67**
Canley Ford CV5: Cov 1J **67**
(not continuous)
Canley Rd. CV5: Cov 1H **67**
(not continuous)
Canley Station (Rail) 6H **57**
Canley Woodlands Local Nature Reserve
. . . . .1C **66**
Cannas Ct. CV4: Canly 2H **67**
Canners Way CV37: S Avon 3D **114**
CANNOCK 1A **138**
Cannocks La. CV4: Canly 2H **67**
CANNOCK WOOD 1B **138**
Cannon Cl. CV4: Cov 2J **67**
Cannon Hill Rd. CV4: Canly 3H **67**
Cannon Pk. Rd. CV4: Canly 3J **67**
Cannon Pk. Shop. Cen.
CV4: Canly 2G **67**
Canon Dr. CV7: Ash G 7D **40**
Canon Hudson Cl. CV3: W'hall 2J **69**
Canon Price Rd. CV35: Barf 2B **108**
CANONS ASHBY 3C **145**
Canon Young Rd. CV31: W'nsh 4F **103**
Canterbury Cl. B80: Stud 3B **92**
CV8: Ken 6G **79**
Canterbury Dr. B37: Mars G 6A **34**
Canterbury St.
CV1: Cov 1K **135** (3E **58**)
Canterbury Way CV11: Nun 3H **23**
Cantlow Cl. CV5: East G 4E **56**
Canton La. B46: Cole 6G **19**
CAPE, THE 7F **97**
Cape Ct. CV34: Warw 7F **97**
Cape Ind. Est. CV34: Warw 1G **101**
Cape Rd. CV34: Warw 7F **97**
Capmartin Rd. CV6: Cov 7B **50**
Captain's Hill B49: Alc 3D **112**
Capulet Cl. CV3: W'hall 2J **69**
CV22: Bil 3E **86**
Capulet Dr. CV34: H'cte 5B **102**
Carabiniers, The CV3: Cov 6G **59**
Caradoc Cl. CV2: Cov 7K **51**
Cardale Cft. CV3: Bin 6B **60**
Cardiff Cl. CV3: W'hall 3K **69**
Cardiff Gro. B37: Mars G 4A **34**
Cardigan Rd. CV12: Bed 4B **40**
Carding Cl. CV5: East G 3D **56**
Carew Cl. CV37: S Avon 2D **114**
Carew Wlk. CV22: Bil 7C **74**
Carey St. CV6: Cov 5H **51**
Cargill Cl. CV6: Lford 1F **51**
Carisbrooke Av. B37: Chel W 3C **34**
Carisbrook Rd. CV10: Nun 5E **22**
CARLTON 1A **140**
Carlton Cl. CV12: Bulk 2D **42**
Carlton Ct. CV5: Cov 4K **57**
CV23: Clift D 3B **76**
CARLTON CURLIEU 2D **141**
Carlton Gdns. CV5: Cov 7A **58**
Carlton Ho. CV32: Lea S 7D **98**
Carlton Rd. CV6: Cov 5F **51**
CV22: Bil 7D **74**
Carlyle Cl. CV10: Gall C 6E **20**
Carlyon Rd. CV9: Ath 2D **16**
Carlyon Rd. Ind. Est. CV9: Ath 2E **16**
(not continuous)
Carmelite Rd. CV1: Cov 5E **58**
Carnation Way CV10: Nun 4G **31**
Carnbroe Av. CV3: Bin 1B **70**
Carnegie Cl. CV3: W'hall 3H **69**
Carnoustie Cl. CV11: Nun 4E **32**
CAROL GREEN 1D **143**
Caroline Cl. CV11: Nun 5B **32**
Caroline Pl. CV12: Bulk 3E **42**
Carolyn La. Ct. *CV21: Rugby 4F* ***75***
(off Blackman Way)
Carpenter Rd. CV2: Cov 1H **59**
Carra Cl. CV10: Nun 6B **22**
Carr Cl. CV36: Ship S 4F **131**
Carriage Wheel La. CV36: Ilm 7B **126**
Carrick Hall CV1: Cov 3K **135**
Carroll Cl. CV37: S Avon 7H **115**
Carroll Cres. CV2: Cov 1G **59**
Carroll Dr. CV34: Warw 4D **100**
Carsal Cl. CV7: Ash G 1D **50**
Carson Cl. GL56: Stret O 2C **132**
Carter Dr. CV35: Barf 2B **108**
Carter Rd. CV3: Cov 7G **59**
Carters Cl. B37: Mars G 6A **34**
Carters La. CV37: Tidd 2K **115**
Carters Vw. CV37: Lwr Q 5G **125**
Carthusian Cl. CV8: Wols 4K **71**
Carthusian Rd. CV3: Cov 7C **58**
Cartmel Cl. CV5: East G 3E **56**
Cart's La. CV9: Gren 1F **15**
Carvell Cl. CV5: Alle 5F **49**
Carver Cl. CV2: Cov 5A **60**
Cascade Cl. CV3: Cov 2E **68**
Cashmore Av. CV31: Lea S 3D **102**
Cashmore Rd. CV8: Ken 5G **79**
CV12: Bed 4E **40**
Cash's Bus. Cen. CV1: Cov 2D **58**
Cash's La. CV1: Cov 1D **58**
Casita Gro. CV8: Ken 5G **79**
Caspian Way CV2: Walsg S 6C **52**
Cassandra Cl. CV4: Canly 5H **67**
Cassandra Gro. CV34: H'cte 4B **102**
CASTLE BROMWICH 3C **139**
Castle Cl. B95: Hen A 2J **93**
CV3: Cov 2D **68**
CV7: Fill 3C **38**
CV34: Warw 2F **101**
Castle Combe CV21: Rugby 2H **75**

Castle Ct.—Chestnut Cl.

Castle Ct. CV8: Ken 3E **78**
CV34: Warw 2G **101**
Castle Cres. CV35: Kine 5C **120**
Castle Dr. B46: Cole 7F **25**
CV10: Asty 5J **29**
CASTLE END 6E **78**
Castle Farm Recreation Cen. 5C **78**
Castle Ga. M. CV34: Warw 1H **101**
CASTLE GREEN 4B **78** (1D **143**)
Castle Grn. CV8: Ken 4B **78**
Castle Gro. CV8: Ken 5C **78**
Castle Hill CV8: Ken 4C **78**
CV34: Warw 2G **101**
OX15: Up Bra 1F **133**
Castle Hill La. OX15: Up Bra 3G **133**
Castle La. B46: Max, Shu 2A **26**
CV23: Wool 4H **105**
CV34: Warw 2G **101**
Castle M. CV21: Rugby 5H **75**
Castle Mound CV23: Barby 7E **88**
Castle Mound Way CV23: Brow 5K **65**
Castle Pl. Ind. Est.
CV1: Cov 1K **135** (3E **58**)
Castle Rd. B49: Alc 3B **112**
B80: Stud 3D **92**
B95: Hen A 2J **93**
CV8: Ken 4C **78**
CV10: Harts 2G **21**
CV10: Nun 4D **22**
CV35: Kine 5C **120**
Castle St. CV1: Cov 1K **135** (3E **58**)
CV21: Rugby 5H **75**
CV34: Warw 2G **101**
Castle Vw. CV10: Harts 2G **21**
Castle Yd. CV1: Cov 4J **135**
Caswell Rd. CV31: Lea S 2F **103**
Catesby Ho. B37: K'hrst 7A **24**
Catesby La. B94: Lapw 4G **91**
Catesby Rd. CV6: Cov 6B **50**
CV22: Rugby 7K **75**
Cathedral Lanes Shop. Cen.
CV1: Cov 3H **135** (4C **58**)
CATHERINE-DE-BARNES 3C **139**
Catherine de Barnes La.
B92: Bick, Cath B 7C **44**
Catherine St. CV2: Cov 4F **59**
Catherine Ward Hall *CV12: Bed 7H **31***
(off Mill Ter.)
CATHIRON 6K **63**
Cathiron La.
CV23: Brin, Cath, Harb M, Lit L
4D **62**
CATSHILL 1A **142**
Cattell Rd. CV34: Warw 1G **101**
Cattell Way CV12: Bed 4D **40**
CATTHORPE 1C **145**
Caudlewell Dr. CV36: Ship S 3J **131**
CAULCOTT 3D **147**
CAUNSALL 3A **138**
Cavalier Cl. CV11: Nun 2A **32**
Cavans Cl. CV3: Bin 7C **60**
Cavans Way CV3: Bin 7C **60**
Cave Cl. CV22: Caw 1A **86**
Cavell Ct. CV21: Rugby 5K **75**
Cavendish Cl. CV22: Caw 7A **74**
Cavendish Rd. CV4: Tile H 5C **56**
Cavendish Wlk. CV11: Nun 4E **32**
Caversham Cl. CV11: Nun 4G **23**
Cawnpore Rd. CV6: Cov 4B **50**
CAWSTON 2A **86** (1B **144**)
Cawston Grange Dr. CV22: Caw 1A **86**
Cawston La. CV22: Caw, Dunc 2A **86**
Cawston Way CV22: Bil 1C **86**
Cawthorne Cl. CV1: Cov 3E **58**
Cayzer Pl. CV35: Welle 3G **117**
Cecil Ct. CV31: Lea S 7E **98**
Cecil Leonard Knox Cres.
CV11: Bram 6H **33**
Cecily Rd. CV3: Cov 1D **68**
Cedar Av. CV8: Rytn D 7D **70**
Cedar Cl. CV32: Lill 3E **98**
CV37: S Avon 3G **115**
Cedar Ct. CV5: Alle 1E **56**
Cedar Cres. B78: K'bry 5E **12**
Cedar Dr. CV37: Snitt 5H **95**
Cedar Gro. CV34: Warw 6J **97**
Cedar Rd. CV10: Nun 5J **21**
Cedars, The CV7: Exh 5G **41**
CV32: Lea S 4E **98**
(Arbury Cl.)
CV32: Lea S 7B **98**
(The Oaks)
Cedars Av. CV6: Cov 2J **57**
Cedars M., The *CV32: Lea S 7B **98***
(off Cross Rd.)
Cedars Rd. CV7: Exh 4H **41**
Cedar Wlk. *B37: Chel W 3B **34***
(within Chelmsley Wood Shop. Cen.)
Cedar Way CV31: W'nsh 6G **103**
Cedric Cl. CV3: W'hall 3J **69**
Celandine CV23: Brow 7K **65**
Celandine Rd. CV2: Cov 4K **51**
Celandine Way CV12: Bed 3E **40**
Celilo Wlk. CV6: Ker E 2A **50**
Celtic Way NN6: Crick 3K **89**
Cemetery La. CV10: Harts 2G **21**
Centaur Rd. CV5: Cov 5K **57**
Centenary Bus. Cen.
CV11: Nun 1A **32**
Centenary Dr. CV7: Mer 5F **47**
Centenary Rd. CV4: Canly 1H **67**
Centora Wlk. CV4: Tile H 3A **56**
Central Av. CV2: Cov 5G **59**
CV11: Nun 6C **22**
CV31: Lea S 2D **102**
Central Blvd. CV2: Ansty 6E **52**
CV6: Ash G, Ker E 1K **49**
CV7: Ansty 6E **52**
CV7: Ash G 1K **49**
CV7: Ker E 1K **49**
Central Bldgs.
CV3: Cov 6G **135** (6C **58**)
Central Chambers CV37: S Avon 3F **137**
Central City Ind. Est. CV6: Cov 2F **59**
Central Dr. CV47: Bis I 6C **110**
Central Pk. Dr. CV23: Brow 5J **65**
Central Pk. Local Cen.
CV23: Brow 6J **65**
Central Six Retail Pk.
CV3: Cov 6F **135** (6B **58**)
Centre Craft Yd. CV37: S Avon 3F **137**
Centrovell Ind. Est. CV11: Nun 2J **31**
Centurion Cl. B46: Cole 3F **25**
Century Pk. B37: Mars G 7C **34**
Ceolmund Cres. B37: Chel W 2B **34**
Chace Av. CV3: W'hall 3H **69**
Chaceley Cl. CV2: Walsg S 6C **52**
CHACOMBE 1D **147**
CHADDESLEY CORBETT 1A **142**
CHADLINGTON 3C **147**
CHADSHUNT 3A **144**
CHAD VALLEY 3B **138**
Chadwick Cl. CV5: East G 4F **57**
CHADWICK END 1D **143**
Chadwick M. B98: Redd 1A **92**
Chaffinch Dr. B36: Cas B 5B **24**
Chalfont Cl. CV5: Cov 3F **57**
CV12: Bed 1G **41**
CHALK HILL 3A **146**
Chalk Hill Pl. CV31: Lea S 4G **103**
Challenge Bus. Pk. CV1: Cov 2D **58**
Challenge Cl. CV1: Cov 3D **58**
Chaloner Cl. CV2: Cov 4H **51**
Chamberlain Cl. CV32: Cubb 2H **99**
Chamberlaine St. CV12: Bed 2H **41**
Chamberlain Rd. CV21: Hillm 1D **88**
Chamberlains Grn. CV6: Cov 7K **49**
Chamberlain Wlk. *B46: Cole 5F **25***
(off Parkfield Rd.)
Chance Flds. CV31: Rad S 2K **103**
Chancellors Cl. CV4: Canly 4H **67**
Chancery Ct. CV10: Harts 4F **21**
Chancery La. CV10: Harts 4G **21**
Chanders Rd. CV34: Warw 6F **97**
Chandler Ct. CV5: Cov 7B **58**
Chandlers Rd. CV31: W'nsh 5E **102**
Chandley Row CV34: Warw 6F **97**
Chandley Wharf CV34: Warw 7F **97**
Chandos St. CV2: Cov 4G **59**
CV11: Nun 7C **22**
CV32: Lea S 6D **98**
Changebrook Cl. CV11: Nun 3G **23**
Channel Way CV6: Lford 7H **41**
Chantries, The CV1: Cov 2E **58**
Chantry, The CV34: Warw 6J **97**
Chantry Cres. B49: Alc 5B **112**
Chantry Heath La. CV8: S'lgh 4E **80**
Chantry Ind. Est. B76: Curd 4B **18**
CHAPEL BRAMPTON 2D **145**
Chapel Cl. B50: Bidf A 6G **123**
CV37: Welf A 3B **124**
Chapel Ct. *CV32: Lea S 7D **98***
(off Windsor St.)
CV32: Lea S 7E **98**
(Wood St.)
Chapel Cross *CV31: Lea S 1E **102***
(off Chapel St.)
CHAPEL END 4G **21**
Chapel Farm Cl. CV3: W'hall 2J **69**
CHAPEL FIELDS 5K **57**
Chapel Gdns. *B50: Bidf A 6G **123***
(off Salford Rd.)
GL56: Stret O 2C **132**
CHAPEL GREEN
CV47 4H **111** (2B **144**)
CV7 6A **38** (3D **139**)
Chapelhouse Rd. B37: F'bri 4A **34**
Chapel La. *B50: Bidf A 6G **123***
(off High St.)
B95: Aston C 1K **113**
B95: Ullen 5C **90**
CV7: Barn 7D **42**
CV8: Rytn D 6C **70**
CV9: With 3G **17**
Chapel La. CV23: Lilb 2J **77**
CV35: Pill P 3B **128**
CV37: N'bld S 1G **127**
CV37: S Avon 6F **137** (5F **115**)
CV47: Nap 2H **111**
OX15: Ratl 7D **128**
OX17: Shotte 6H **129**
Chapel M. CV21: Hillm 1C **88**
Chapel Row CV34: Warw 1G **101**
CV37: Welf A 3B **124**
Chapelry La. CV23: Long L 4B **74**
Chapel St. CV1: Cov 2G **135** (4C **58**)
CV11: Nun 7D **22**
CV12: Bed 2H **41**
(not continuous)
CV21: Rugby 5G **75**
CV23: Kils 7J **89**
CV23: Long L 4A **74**
CV31: Lea S 1E **102**
CV33: Har 6H **109**
CV34: Warw 1G **101**
CV35: Welle 3H **117**
CV37: S Avon 5F **137** (5F **115**)
CV37: Welf A 3A **124**
CV47: Bis I 6B **110**
OX17: Warm 2J **129**
Chapel Wlk. *B50: Bidf A 6G **123***
(off Chapel Cl.)
Chapman Cl. CV31: Rad S 3J **103**
Chapman Ct. CV34: Warw 7A **98**
Chapman Way B49: Alc 3C **112**
Chapple Hyam Av. CV47: Bis I 6B **110**
Chard Rd. CV3: Bin 7K **59**
CHARINGWORTH 2A **146**
Charingworth Dr. CV35: Hatt 5A **96**
Chariot Way CV21: Rugby 1G **75**
Charity Ho's., The CV23: C'over 1J **65**
Charity Rd. CV7: Ker E 6A **40**
CHARLBURY 3C **147**
Charlbury M. CV31: Lea S 2G **103**
CHARLECOTE 3C **118** (3D **143**)
Charlecote Cl. CV37: Tidd 4K **115**
Charlecote Flds. CV35: Welle 2H **117**
Charlecote Gdns. CV31: Lea S 3H **103**
Charlecote Mill 2B **118**
Charlecote Pk. 4B **118**
Charlecote Rd. CV6: Cov 4A **50**
CV35: Char 2B **118**
CV35: Welle 2H **117**
Charlecote Wlk. CV11: Nun 4B **32**
Charles Ct. CV34: Warw 7K **97**
Charles Eaton Ct. CV12: Bed 2E **40**
Charles Eaton Rd. CV12: Bed 2F **41**
Charlesfield Rd. CV22: Rugby 1G **87**
Charles Gardner Rd.
CV31: Lea S 2D **102**
Charles Lakin Cl. CV7: Shilt 1E **52**
Charles Rd. CV9: Man 4E **16**
Charles St. CV1: Cov 1K **135** (3E **58**)
CV7: New A 4E **28**
CV9: Hur 6K **13**
CV11: Nun 6B **22**
CV21: Rugby 5F **75**
CV34: Warw 7J **97**
Charles Warren Cl.
CV21: Rugby 5H **75**
Charles Watson Ct. CV32: Lill 5E **98**
Charlewood Rd. CV6: Cov 4B **50**
Charlotte Cl. CV10: Nun 5H **21**
Charlotte St. CV21: Rugby 5H **75**
CV31: Lea S 2D **102**
Charlotte Way CV9: Ath 4D **16**
CHARLTON 2D **147**
Charminster Dr. CV3: Cov 4D **68**
Charnwood Av. CV10: Nun 2D **30**
Charnwood Dr. CV10: Harts 1F **21**
Charnwood Way CV32: Lill 4G **99**
Charolais Cl. CV21: Rugby 4J **75**
Charter App. CV34: Warw 3F **101**
Charter Av. CV4: Tile H, Canly 1B **66**
Charterhouse Rd. CV1: Cov 5E **58**
Charter Rd. CV22: Hillm 1A **88**
Chartwell Cl. CV11: Nun 3B **32**
CHARWELTON 3C **145**
Charwelton Dr. CV21: Brow 2A **76**
Chase Cl. CV11: Nun 5E **22**
Chase La. CV8: Ken 2A **78**
Chase Mdw. Sq. *CV34: Warw 4D **100***
(off The Marish)
CHASE TERRACE 1B **138**
CHASETOWN 1B **138**
Chassieur Wlk. B46: Cole 4F **25**
CHASTLETON 7A **134** (3B **146**)
Chaters Orchard CV47: Long I 2C **106**
Chatham Cl. CV3: Cov 7J **59**
Chatham Rd. CV37: Lwr Q 6F **125**
Chatillon Cl. CV34: H'cte 5C **102**
CHATLEY 2A **142**
Chatsworth Dr. CV11: Nun 2B **32**
Chatsworth Gdns. CV31: Lea S 2H **103**
Chatsworth Gro. CV8: Ken 4G **79**
Chatsworth Ri. CV3: Cov 3E **68**
CHATTLE HILL 2D **24**
Chattle Hill B46: Cole 2E **24**
Chaucer Cl. CV37: S Avon 7J **115**
Chaucer Dr. CV10: Gall C 6F **21**
Chaucer Rd. CV22: Rugby 3F **87**
Chauntry Pl.
CV1: Cov 2J **135** (4D **58**)
Chaytor Dr. CV10: Nun 4F **21**
Chaytor Rd. B78: Pole 2D **10**
Cheadle Cl. CV2: Ald G 2G **51**
Cheam Cl. CV6: Cov 5G **51**
Chebsey Ct. CV47: Ladb 3C **110**
Chedham Rd. CV35: Welle 4H **117**
Cheeky Chimps
Warwick 7G **97**
Cheetah Rd. CV1: Cov 6K **135** (6D **58**)
Chelmar Cl. B36: Cas B 4A **24**
Chelmarsh CV6: Cov 1C **58**
Chelmsley Av. B46: Cole 6F **25**
Chelmsley Circ. B37: Chel W 3B **34**
Chelmsley La. B37: Mars G 5A **34**
Chelmsley Rd. B37: Chel W, F'bri 2A **34**
CHELMSLEY WOOD 3B **34**
Chelmsley Wood Ind. Est.
B37: F'bri 1B **34**
Chelmsley Wood Shop. Cen.
B37: Chel W 3B **34**
Chelney Wlk. CV3: Bin 6C **60**
Chelsea Cl. CV11: Nun 4G **23**
Chelsey Rd. CV2: Cov 6A **52**
Cheltenham Cl. CV12: Bed 1H **41**
Cheltenham Cft. CV2: Walsg S 7B **52**
Chelveston Rd. CV6: Cov 2J **57**
Chelwood Gro. CV2: Walsg S 6B **52**
Chenies Cl. CV5: Cov 4F **57**
Chepstow Cl. CV3: W'hall 3J **69**
CV37: S Avon 6D **114**
Chequer St. CV12: Bulk 3E **42**
CHERINGTON 6G **133** (2B **146**)
Cheriton Cl. CV5: Cov 3H **57**
Cherry Blossom Gro.
CV31: W'nsh 6F **103**
Cherrybrook Way CV2: Cov 5J **51**
Cherryburn Wlk. *CV22: Bil 6E **74***
(off Stourhead Rd.)
Cherry Cl. CV6: Cov 4D **50**
CV9: Hur 7K **13**
CV37: Ett 2B **126**
Cherryfield Cl. CV10: Harts 1G **21**
Cherry Gro. CV22: Bil 1E **86**
Cherry La. CV35: H Mag 2B **100**
CV37: Bear 7D **94**
Cherry Orchard B95: Hen A 1G **93**
CV8: Ken 4E **78**
CV35: Welle 2H **117**
CV36: Ship S 5H **131**
CV37: S Avon 6D **114**
Cherry St. CV34: Warw 1H **101**
CV37: S Avon 6E **114**
Cherry Tree Av. CV10: Nun 5K **21**
Cherry Tree Cres. WR11: Salf P 7B **122**
Cherry Tree Dr. CV4: Canly 7G **57**
Cherry Tree La. CV23: Bour D 7C **84**
Cherry Tree Wlk. CV47: Sou 4H **107**
Cherry Way CV8: Ken 4E **78**
Cherrywood Gro. CV5: Alle 2D **56**
Cherwell Dr. B36: Cas B 4A **24**
Cherwell Way CV23: Long L 4B **74**
Cheryton Cl. CV8: Wols 4K **71**
Chesford Cres. CV6: Cov 4H **51**
CV34: Warw 6K **97**
Chesford Gro. CV37: S Avon 3C **114**
Chesham St. CV31: Lea S 1F **103**
Cheshire Cl. CV3: Cov 6G **59**
CV22: Bil 1C **86**
Chesholme Rd. CV6: Cov 3B **50**
Chesils, The CV3: Cov 3C **68**
CHESLYN HAY 1A **138**
CHESSETTS WOOD 1C **143**
Chessetts Wood Rd. B94: Lapw 1H **91**
Chester Cl. B37: F'bri 3A **34**
Chester Ct. *B37: Chel W 3D **34***
(off Hedingham Gro.)
CHESTERFIELD 1C **139**
Chester Rd. B36: Cas B 6A **24**
B37: Chel W, F'bri 7B **24**
B46: Cole 6F **35**
CV7: Lit P 1G **45**
Chester St. CV1: Cov 4B **58**
CV21: Rugby 4J **75**
Chesterton Dr. CV10: Gall C 6E **20**
CV31: Lea S 3G **103**
CV37: S Avon 7H **115**
CHESTERTON GREEN 3A **144**
Chesterton Rd. CV6: Cov 7A **50**
CV33: Har 6F **109**
CV35: Light 2H **119**
Chesterton Windmill 3A **144**
Chestnut Av. CV8: Ken 6D **78**
Chestnut Cl. B78: K'bry 5E **12**
CV35: L Hth 2K **119**
CV37: Ett 2C **126**

158 A-Z Warwickshire Atlas

Chestnut Ct.—Close, The

Chestnut Ct. B49: Alc .5C **112**
B96: Sam .4A **92**
CV34: H'cte .6C **102**
Chestnut Cres. CV10: Nun .5K **21**
Chestnut Dr. CV11: Nun .1A **32**
Chestnut Fld. CV21: Rugby .5G **75**
Chestnut Gro. B46: Cole .5G **25**
CV4: Tile H .5E **56**
CV8: Wols .5J **71**
Chestnut Ho. B37: Chel W .3B **34**
Chestnut Pl. CV47: Sou .4H **107**
Chestnut Rd. CV12: Bed .1K **41**
Chestnuts, The CV3: Cov .7G **59**
CV12: Bed .3E **40**
Chestnut Sq. CV32: Lill .5F **99**
CV35: Welle .3H **117**
Chestnut Tree Av. CV4: Tile H .5E **56**
Chestnut Wlk. *B37: Chel W .3B 34*
(within Chelmsley Wood Shop. Cen.)
B95: Hen A .1G **93**
CV37: S Avon .6D **136** (5E **114**)
Chestnut Way B50: Bidf A .5G **123**
Cheswick Cl. CV6: Cov .7G **51**
CHESWICK GREEN .1C **143**
Chetton Av. CV6: Cov .2C **58**
Chetwode Cl. CV5: Cov .3F **57**
Chetwynd Av. B78: Pole .2D **10**
Chetwynd Dr. CV9: Gren .7G **11**
CV11: Nun .5D **32**
Cheveral Av. CV6: Cov .1B **58**
Cheveral Rd. CV12: Bed .2G **41**
Cheverel Pl. CV11: Nun .2H **31**
Cheverel St. CV11: Nun .1H **31**
Cheviot B77: Wiln .7A **8**
Cheviot, The CV4: Canly .2H **67**
Cheviot Cl. CV10: Nun .1B **30**
Cheviot Ri. CV32: Lill .4G **99**
Cheviot Wlk. CV23: Long L .4A **74**
CHEYLESMORE .7D **58**
Cheylesmore CV1: Cov .5H **135** (5C **58**)
Cheylesmore Shop. Pde.
CV3: Cov .1D **68**
Chichester Cl. CV11: Nun .4H **23**
Chichester Gro. B37: Chel W .4A **34**
(not continuous)
Chichester La. CV35: H Mag .2B **100**
Chickabiddy La. *CV47: Sou .5H 107*
(off Market Hill)
Chicory Dr. CV23: Brow .7K **65**
Chideock Hill CV3: Cov .2A **68**
Chiel Cl. CV5: East G .3D **56**
CHILCOTE .1D **139**
Childs Cl. CV37: S Avon .2D **114**
CHILDSWICKHAM .2A **146**
Chilham Dr. B37: Chel W .3C **34**
Chillaton Rd. CV6: Cov .4B **50**
CHILSON .3C **147**
Chiltern Ct. CV6: Cov .2A **58**
Chiltern Leys CV6: Cov .3A **58**
Chiltern Rd. B77: Wiln .1A **10**
Chilterns, The CV5: Cov .3F **57**
CHILVERS COTON .1H **31**
Chilvers Coton Heritage Cen. .2J **31**
Chilvers Ct. CV11: Nun .7D **22**
Chilvers Ri. CV10: Nun .2J **31**
CV11: Nun .2J **31**
Chilworth Cl. CV11: Nun .4A **32**
Chimes Ct. CV21: Rugby .2G **75**
Chimes La. CV31: W'nsh .6E **102**
Chines, The CV10: Nun .4E **22**
Chingford Rd. CV6: Lford .2G **51**
Chingley Bank B95: Hen A .2J **93**
CHIPPING CAMPDEN .2A **146**
CHIPPING NORTON .3C **147**
CHIPPING WARDEN .1D **147**
Chiswick Wlk. B37: Chel W .3D **34**
CHORLEY .1B **138**
Chorley Way CV6: Cov .1C **58**
Choyce Cl. CV9: Ath .1C **16**
Christchurch Cl. CV10: Nun .3F **31**
Christchurch Rd. CV6: Cov .1K **57**
Christie Way CV37: S Avon .7H **115**
Christine Ledger Sq.
CV31: Lea S .2E **102**
Christopher Hooke Ho. CV6: Cov .5E **50**
Christopher Way B46: Wat O .2B **24**
Chudleigh Rd. CV2: Cov .7A **52**
Church Av. B46: Wat O .1B **24**
Church Bank CV37: Welf A .2A **124**
CHURCH BRAMPTON .2D **145**
Church Cl. B37: K'hrst .6A **24**
CV7: Old A .2C **28**
CV8: Rytn D .6C **70**
CV9: Wood E .2K **13**
CV10: Harts .3G **21**
CV23: Harb M .4B **64**
CV31: W'nsh .4F **103**
CV37: A'ton .2B **116**
CV37: Ludd .1E **124**
CV47: Bis I .6B **110**
LE10: Wlvy .2J **33**
Church Cotts. CV10: Asty .5J **29**
Church Ct. CV6: Cov .5K **49**
Churchdale Cl. CV10: Nun .7H **21**
Church Dr. CV8: Ken .4D **78**
CHURCH END
B46 .2E **26** (2D **139**)
CV10 .2D **139**
CV2 .4H **59**
Church End CV31: Rad S .2J **103**
CHURCH ENSTONE .3C **147**
Church Farm Ct. CV35: Mid T .6D **130**
Churchfield CV37: Welf A .2A **124**
Church Flds. B49: Wix .1E **122**
CHURCH HILL .2B **142**
Church Hill B46: Cole .5G **25**
B95: Ullen .6B **90**
CV23: Stret D .4H **83**
CV32: Cubb .2J **99**
CV32: Lea S .7C **98**
CV33: Bis T .5C **108**
LE10: Wlvy .1J **33**
OX17: Warm .2J **129**
Church Hill Cl. LE10: Wlvy .2H **33**
Church Hill Ct. CV35: Light .2G **119**
CHURCHILL
DY10 .1A **142**
OX7 .3B **146**
WR7 .3A **142**
Churchill Av. CV6: Cov .5D **50**
CV8: Ken .3E **78**
Churchill Cl. CV37: Ett .1B **126**
Churchill Rd. CV22: Rugby .7G **75**
Churchlands Bus. Pk. CV33: Har .5J **109**
Church La. B46: Max .3C **36**
B76: Curd .5B **18**
B76: Lea M .4G **19**
B76: Wis .2A **18**
B78: K'bry .6E **12**
B79: No Hth .2G **7**
B79: Seck .5A **6**
B79: Shut .2B **8**
B92: Bick .5D **44**
B95: Aston C .2K **113**
CV2: Cov .4H **59**
CV5: East G .2A **56**
CV7: Ash G .6E **40**
CV7: Cor .6D **38**
CV7: Fill .2C **38**
CV7: Mer .6F **47**
CV7: Old A .2C **28**
CV8: S'lgh .3C **80**
CV9: Aus .7H **7**
CV10: Nun .4D **22**
CV23: Thurl .7K **85**
CV31: Rad S .2J **103**
CV31: W'nsh .4F **103**
CV32: Cubb .1J **99**
CV32: Lill .4E **98**
CV35: Barf .2C **108**
CV35: Gay .7G **119**
CV35: Leek W .1H **97**
CV35: Light .2G **119**
CV35: Oxh .1E **130**
CV36: Whatc .3A **130**
CV37: A'ton .2B **116**
CV37: Bear .6D **94**
CV37: Ett .2B **126**
CV37: N'bld S .1G **127**
CV37: Shot .4B **114**
CV37: Snitt .5H **95**
CV37: Welf A .2A **124**
OX17: Shotte .7H **129**
CHURCH LANGTON .2D **141**
CHURCH LAWFORD .3G **73** (1B **144**)
Church Lawford Bus. Cen.
CV23: Chu L .3E **72**
Church Lees CV33: Bis T .5C **108**
CHURCH LENCH .3B **142**
Church M. CV35: Kine .5D **120**
CHURCHOVER .1J **65** (3C **141**)
Churchover La.
CV23: C'over, Harb M .3D **64**
Church Pk. Cl. CV6: Cov .5K **49**
Church Path CV35: H Mag .2B **100**
Church Rd. B46: Shu .2B **26**
B78: Dord .5D **10**
B79: Wart .6G **9**
B95: Ullen .7A **90**
CV7: Shilt .1G **53**
CV8: Bag .6E **68**
CV8: Bubb .3J **81**
CV8: Rytn D .6D **70**
CV9: With .3G **17**
CV10: Harts .3G **21**
CV10: Nun .1C **30**
CV23: Chu L .3G **73**
CV23: Gran .6H **105**
CV35: Clav .2D **94**
CV35: Gay .6G **119**
CV35: N Lin .2G **95**
CV35: Sher .1A **108**
CV37: N'bld S .1G **127**
CV37: Snitt .6H **95**
Church Rd. CV37: Wilm .5J **113**
CV47: Ladb .3B **110**
CV47: Long I .2B **106**
Church Row CV36: Cher .7G **133**
GL56: Lit C .6C **134**
Churchside Arc. *CV21: Rugby .5G 75*
(off Lit. Church St.)
CHURCH STOWE .3D **145**
Church St. B49: Alc .5C **112**
B50: Bidf A .6H **123**
B80: Stud .4D **92**
CV1: Cov .3D **58**
CV9: Ath .3C **16**
CV11: Nun .7D **22**
CV12: Bulk .3E **42**
CV21: Rugby .5G **75**
CV23: C'over .1H **65**
(not continuous)
CV23: Clift D .3C **76**
CV23: Mart .2D **104**
CV31: Lea S .1E **102**
CV33: Har .6H **109**
CV34: Warw .2G **101**
CV35: Barf .2B **108**
CV35: H Lucy .2A **118**
CV35: Welle .2H **117**
CV36: Ship S .4H **131**
CV37: S Avon .7E **136** (5E **114**)
CV37: Welf A .2A **124**
CV47: Fen C .3G **121**
CV47: S'ton .6C **106**
DE12: App M .1K **7**
Church Ter. CV31: Lea S .1E **102**
CV32: Cubb .2J **99**
CV33: Har .5H **109**
CV36: Half .2J **127**
CV37: N'bld S .1G **127**
Church Vw. B79: Wart .5H **9**
CV8: Rytn D .6C **70**
Church Wlk. B46: Cole .5G **25**
CV5: Alle .1G **57**
CV9: Ath, Man .3D **16**
CV11: Nun .2A **32**
CV12: Bed .3H **41**
CV21: Rugby .5H **75**
CV22: Bil .1D **86**
CV23: Barby .7E **88**
CV23: Kils .6J **89**
CV23: Thurl .6K **85**
CV31: Lea S .1D **102**
CV35: Gay .7G 119
(off Church La.)
CV35: Welle .3H **117**
Church Way CV12: Bed .3H **41**
CHURCH WESTCOTE .3B **146**
Chylds Ct. CV5: Cov .2E **56**
Cicero App. CV34: H'cte .6C **102**
Cicey La. CV11: Burt H .4J **33**
Cinder La. CV9: Aus .1J **9**
Cineworld Cinema
Birmingham NEC .3E **44**
Rugby .2H **75**
Circle, The CV10: Nun .7K **21**
Circus Av. B37: Chel W .3C **34**
City Arc. CV1: Cov .4G **135** (5C **58**)
CLADSWELL .3B **142**
Clapham Sq. CV31: Lea S .1F **103**
Clapham St. CV31: Lea S .2F **103**
Clapham Ter. CV31: Lea S .1F **103**
CLAPTON-ON-THE-HILL .3A **146**
Clara St. CV2: Cov .5G **59**
Clare Cl. CV32: Lill .5G **99**
Clare Ct. CV21: Rugby .5F **75**
Clare Ho. B36: Cas B .5A **24**
Clare McManus Way CV2: Cov .5J **51**
Claremont Cl. CV12: Bulk .1D **42**
Claremont Rd. CV21: Rugby .5J **75**
CV31: Lea S .2D **102**
Claremont Wlk. CV5: Alle .1G **57**
Clarence Mans. *CV32: Lea S .6D 98*
(off Warwick St.)
Clarence Rd. CV21: Rugby .5E **74**
CV37: S Avon .4C **114**
Clarence St. CV1: Cov .3E **58**
CV11: Nun .7B **22**
CV31: Lea S .2E **102**
Clarence Ter. *CV32: Lea S .6D 98*
(off Warwick St.)
Clarendon Av. CV32: Lea S .6D **98**
Clarendon Cres. CV32: Lea S .6C **98**
Clarendon M. CV5: Cov .6K **57**
Clarendon Pl. CV32: Lea S .6C **98**
Clarendon Rd. CV8: Ken .6E **78**
Clarendon Sq. CV32: Lea S .6C **98**
(not continuous)
Clarendon St. CV5: Cov .6K **57**
CV32: Lea S .6E **98**
Clark Cl. CV36: Ship S .5H **131**
Clarke's Av. CV8: Ken .6E **78**
Clarksland Gro. B37: Mars G .5A **34**
Clarks La. CV36: Long C .3D **134**
Clarkson Cl. CV11: Nun .7E **22**
Clarkson Dr. CV31: W'nsh .4E **102**
Clark St. CV6: Cov .5G **51**
Clark Wlk. CV37: Ett .2C **126**
Classic Dr. CV6: Lford .3E **50**
CLAVERDON .2D **94** (2C **143**)
Claverdon Ho. CV34: Warw .7K **97**
Claverdon Rd. CV5: East G .4F **57**
Clay Av. CV11: Nun .4G **23**
Claybrook Dr. B98: Redd .1D **92**
CLAYBROOKE MAGNA .3B **140**
CLAYBROOKE PARVA .3B **140**
Claybrookes La. CV3: Bin .6C **60**
CLAY COTON .1C **145**
Claycroft CV4: Canly .3G **67**
CLAYDON .3B **144**
Claydon Gro. CV35: Hatt .4A **96**
CLAYHANGER .1B **138**
Clay Hill La. CV23: Lit L, Long L .2K **73**
Claylands CV35: Gay .6G **119**
Clay La. CV2: Cov .3G **59**
CV5: Alle .2C **48**
Claypitts Blvd. CV34: Warw .5D **100**
Claypool La. CV10: Nun .5H **21**
Clayton Rd. CV6: Cov .2J **57**
Cleaver Gdns. CV10: Nun .5D **22**
CLEEVE PRIOR .3B **142**
Cleeve Rd. B50: Marlc .7G **123**
Cleeves Av. CV34: Warw .2A **102**
Clematis Way CV10: Nun .4G **31**
Clemens St. CV31: Lea S .1E **102**
Clementine Wlk. CV3: Cov .5J **59**
Clements Cl. CV8: Ken .4E **78**
Clements St. CV2: Cov .4G **59**
Clement St. CV11: Nun .1H **31**
Clement Way CV22: Caw .1A **86**
Clennon Ri. CV2: Cov .6K **51**
CLENT .1A **142**
Clent Dr. CV10: Nun .1B **30**
Cleopatra Gro. CV34: H'cte .4C **102**
Cleveland Ct. CV32: Lea S .5D **98**
Cleveland Rd. CV2: Cov .3G **59**
CV12: Bulk .2D **42**
CLEVELEY .3C **147**
Cleveley Dr. CV10: Nun .4J **21**
Clifden Gro. CV8: Ken .3G **79**
CLIFF .2D **12** (2D **139**)
Cliffe Ct. CV32: Lea S .6B **98**
Cliffe Rd. CV32: Lea S .6B **98**
Cliffe Way CV34: Warw .7H **97**
Cliff Hall La. B78: Cliff .2C **12**
Clifford Bri. Rd. CV2: Walsg S .2B **60**
CV3: Bin .5B **60**
CLIFFORD CHAMBERS
.5C **124** (3C **143**)
Clifford Rd.
CV37: Cliff C, S Avon
.7F **115**, 4C **124**
Cliff Pool Nature Reserve .3B **12**
CLIFTON .2D **147**
CLIFTON CAMPVILLE .1D **139**
Clifton La. Cotts. B79: Thor C .1A **6**
Clifton New Wharf CV23: Clift D .3A **76**
Clifton Rd. B79: No Hth .1E **6**
CV10: Nun .7A **22**
CV21: Rugby .5H **75**
DE12: No Hth .1E **6**
Clifton St. CV1: Cov .3E **58**
Clifton Ter. CV8: Ken .3E **78**
CLIFTON UPON DUNSMORE
.3C **76** (1C **145**)
Clifton Wharf CV23: Clift D .3A **76**
Clinic Dr. CV11: Nun .1J **31**
Clinton Av. CV8: Ken .3B **78**
CV35: H Mag .1C **100**
Clinton La. CV8: Ken .2B **78**
Clinton Rd. B46: Cole .6F **25**
CV6: Cov .4F **51**
Clinton St. CV31: Lea S .1E **102**
CLIPSTON .3D **141**
Clipstone Rd. CV6: Cov .1J **57**
Cliveden Wlk. CV11: Nun .4A **32**
Clock La. B92: Bick .4D **44**
Clock Towers Shop. Cen.
CV21: Rugby .5G **75**
Cloister Cft. CV2: Walsg S .1B **60**
Cloister Crofts CV32: Lea S .4D **98**
Cloisters, The B80: Stud .3C **92**
CV32: Lea S .4D **98**
CV47: Sou .5J **107**
Cloister Way CV32: Lea S .4D **98**
CLOPTON .2F **115**
Clopton Cl. CV37: S Avon .2E **114**
Clopton Ct.
CV37: S Avon .1E **136** (4E **114**)
Clopton Cres. B37: F'bri .1B **34**
Clopton M. CV37: S Avon .2E **114**
Clopton Rd.
CV37: S Avon .1E **136** (4E **114**)
Close, The CV8: Bran .3H **71**
CV8: Ken .3E **78**
CV31: Lea S .2E **102**
CV35: H Lucy .2A **118**

Enright Cl.—Flavel Ct.

Enright Cl. CV32: Lea S 5C 98
Ensign Bus. Cen. CV4: Westw H 2D 66
Ensign Cl. CV4: Tile H 6B 56
Ensor Cl. CV11: Nun 6H 23
Ensor Dr. B78: Pole 1C 10
ENSTONE 3C 147
Enterprise Cen.
CV1: Cov 6J 135 (6D 58)
Enville Cl. B37: Mars G 4B 34
Epperston Ct. CV31: Lea S 1D 102
Epping Way CV32: Lill 3G 99
Epsom Cl. CV12: Bed 1H 41
Epsom Dr. CV3: W'hall 2J 69
Epsom Rd. CV22: Bil 7D 74
CV32: Lill 3G 99
EPWELL .1C 147
Epwell Rd. CV35: Up Tys 7C 130
ERDINGTON 2C 139
Erdington Rd. CV9: Ath 4C 16
Erica Av. CV12: Bed 3F 41
Erica Dr. CV31: W'nsh 6F 103
Eric Grey Cl. CV2: Cov 2G 59
Eric Inott Ho. CV3: Cov 2E 68
Erithway Rd. CV3: Finh 4B 68
Ernesford Grange Leisure Cen. 7K 59
Ernest Richards Rd. CV12: Bed 1H 41
Ernsford Av. CV3: Cov 6H 59
Esher Dr. CV3: Cov 1E 68
Eskdale CV21: Brow 7J 65
Eskdale Wlk. CV3: W'hall 1K 69
Esme Cl. CV3: Cov 5J 59
Essen La. CV23: Kils 6H 89
Essex Cl. CV5: East G 4F 57
CV8: Ken 7C 78
Essex Ct. CV34: Warw 7G 97
Essex Grn. CV47: Temp H 2A 120
Essex St. CV21: Rugby 4G 75
ESSINGTON 1A 138
Esterton Cl. CV6: Cov 4C 50
Etchills Wood Railway 6B 12
Ethelfield Rd. CV2: Cov 4H 59
Etone Ct. CV11: Nun 6C 22
Etone Sports Cen. 6E 22
Eton Rd. CV37: S Avon 6H 115
Ettingley Cl. B98: Redd 2A 92
ETTINGTON 2B 126 (1B 146)
Ettington Cl. CV35: Welle 4H 117
Ettington Rd. CV5: East G 4E 56
CV35: Welle 4H 117
(not continuous)
Europa Way CV34: Warw 7K 101
Eustace Rd. CV12: Bulk 4F 43
Euston Cres. CV3: W'hall 1J 69
Euston Pl. CV32: Lea S 7D 98
Evans Bus. Village CV11: Nun 2K 31
Evans Cl. CV12: Bed 2J 41
CV37: Shot 6C 114
Evans Gro. CV31: W'nsh 6E 102
Evans Rd. CV22: Bil 6C 74
Evelyn Av. CV6: Cov 4E 50
EVENLODE 3B 146
Evenlode Cl. CV37: S Avon 6H 115
Evenlode Cres. CV6: Cov 2K 57
Everard Cl. CV23: Clift D 3C 76
Everard Ct. CV11: Nun 2A 32
EVERDON 3C 145
Everdon Cl. CV22: Hillm 1K 87
Everdon Rd. CV6: Cov 4C 50
(not continuous)
Everest Rd. CV22: Rugby 1E 86
Everglade Rd. CV9: Wood E 1J 13
Evergreen Cl. CV5: Alle 5F 49
Evergreens, The CV10: Nun 5A 22
Eversleigh Rd. CV6: Cov 7J 49
Evesham Pl.
CV37: S Avon 7C 136 (5E 114)
Evesham Rd.
CV37: Bint, D'wll, S Avon
. . . . .6A 114, 1A 124
CV37: S Avon 7A 136 (6C 114)
WR11: Abb S, Salf P 7B 122
Evesham St. B49: Alc, Arr 6A 112
Evesham Wlk. CV4: Canly 3H 67
EVINGTON 1D 141
Evreux Way CV21: Rugby 5G 75
Ewart Pl. CV22: Caw 7B 74
Exbury Way CV11: Nun 4A 32
Excelsior Rd. CV4: Canly 7G 57
Exeter Cl. CV3: Bin 7K 59
Exeter Dr. B37: Mars G 5A 34
EXHALL
B49 . . . . .1G 123 (3C 143)
CV7 . . . . .6G 41
Exhall Basin CV6: Lford 1H 51
Exhall Cl. CV37: S Avon 6J 115
Exhall Grn. CV7: Exh 6F 41
EXHALL HALL GREEN 6F 41
Exhall Mobile Homes CV7: Ash G . . .6B 40
Exhall Rd. B49: Wix 1F 123
CV7: Ker E 7K 39
Exham Cl. CV34: Warw 6G 97
Exhibition Way B40: Nat E C 2D 44
Exis Ct. CV11: Nun 2A 32
Exminster Rd. CV3: Cov 3E 68
Exmoor Dr. CV32: Lill 3G 99
Exmouth Cl. CV2: Cov 7J 51
Expectations Dr. CV21: Rugby 3G 75
Exton Cl. CV7: Ash G 6C 40
EYDON .3C 145
Eydon Cl. CV21: Brow 2A 76
Eyffler Cl. CV34: Warw 1F 101

F

Fabian Cl. CV3: W'hall 1K 69
Fairbanks Cl. CV2: Walsg S 7C 52
Fairbourne Way CV6: Cov 6J 49
Fair Cl. CV23: F'ton 7A 84
Faircroft CV8: Ken 6D 78
Fairfax Cl. CV35: Barf 2B 108
Fairfax Ct. CV34: Warw 1H 101
Fairfax St. CV1: Cov 3J 135 (4D 58)
FAIRFIELD 1A 142
Fairfield CV7: Exh 4G 41
Fairfield Ct. CV3: Cov 1G 69
Fairfield Ri. CV7: Mer 5E 46
Fairfields Hill B78: Pole 2C 10
Fairfields Wlk. CV37: S Avon 4C 114
Fairhurst Dr. CV32: Lea S 4C 98
Fair Isle Dr. CV10: Nun 1F 31
Fairlands Pk. CV4: Canly 3J 67
Fairlawn Cl. CV32: Lea S 6B 98
Fairmile Cl. CV3: Bin 7J 59
Fairview Ind. Est. B76: Curd 4B 18
Fairview M. B46: Cole 5F 25
Fairview Wlk. CV6: Lford 4E 50
Fairwater Cres. B49: Alc 4D 112
Fairway CV11: Nun 3D 32
Fairway Ct. CV21: Rugby 4K 75
Fairway Ri. CV8: Ken 3G 79
Fairways, The CV32: Lea S 5B 98
Fairways Cl. CV5: Alle 1E 56
Falcon Av. CV3: Bin 7B 60
Falcon Cl. CV11: Nun 4D 32
Falcon Ct. *CV47: Sou* *5H 107*
(off Bull St.)
Falcon Cres. B50: Bidf A 5H 123
Falcon Way B26: Birm A 3A 44
Falkener Ho. CV6: Cov 7E 50
Falkland Cl. CV4: Tile H 1B 66
Falkland Pl. CV47: Temp H 2B 120
Falkland Way B36: Cas B 7B 24
Fallow Fld. Cl. CV22: Caw 7B 74
Fallowfields CV6: Cov 2B 50
Fallow Hill CV31: Lea S 2G 103
Falmouth Cl. CV11: Nun 6H 23
Falstaff Cl. CV11: Nun 3C 32
(not continuous)
Falstaff Ct.
CV37: S Avon 1F 137 (4F 115)
Falstaff Dr. CV22: Bil 4D 86
Falstaff Gro. CV34: H'cte 5C 102
Falstaff Rd. CV4: Tile H 5C 56
Fancott Dr. CV8: Ken 3D 78
Fant Hill OX15: Up Bra 1F 133
Faraday Av. B46: Cole, Curd 6E 18
B76: Curd 6E 18
Faraday Rd. CV22: Rugby 7J 75
Faraday Way CV21: Rugby 6K 75
Farber Rd. CV2: Walsg S 1C 60
FAR COTTON 3D 145
Farcroft Av. CV5: East G 3B 56
Fareham Av. CV22: Hillm 1A 88
FAREWELL 1B 138
Far Gosford St. CV1: Cov 5E 58
Fargo Village CV1: Cov 5F 59
Farley Av. CV33: Har 6G 109
Farley St. CV31: Lea S 1F 103
Farlow Cl. CV6: Cov 1G 59
Farman Rd. CV5: Cov 5K 57
Farm Cl. CV6: Cov 3B 50
CV33: Har 6G 109
CV36: Ship S 4G 131
CV37: B'ton 1C 114
FARMCOTE 3A 146
Farmcote Lodge *CV2: Ald G* *2H 51*
(off Farmcote Rd.)
Farmcote Rd. CV2: Ald G 2H 51
Farmers Ct. *CV21: Rugby* *4J 75*
(off Gavel Dr.)
Farmer Ward Rd. CV8: Ken 5E 78
Farm Gro. CV22: Rugby 7J 75
Farm La. CV9: Gren 3J 11
CV23: Eas 3J 63
Farm Pl. CV3: Cov 7J 59
Farm Rd. CV8: Ken 7C 78
CV32: Lill 4F 99
Farmside CV3: W'hall 3K 69
Farmstead, The CV3: Cov 7H 59
Farm St. CV33: Har 5G 109
Farm Wlk. CV33: Bis T 4C 108
FARNBOROUGH 6H 121 (1D 147)
Farnborough Av. CV22: Rugby 6E 74
Farnborough Hall 7G 121
Farnborough Rd. CV35: Rad 5B 128
OX17: Farnb, Moll 7J 121
Farndale Av. CV6: Cov 3D 50
Farndon Av. B37: Mars G 6B 34
Farndon Cl. CV12: Bulk 2D 42
Farnell Dr. CV37: S Avon 4C 114
Far Pool Mdw. CV35: Clav 2C 94
Farr Dr. CV4: Tile H 5F 57
Farren Rd. CV2: Cov 3K 59
Farriers, The B50: Broom 3E 122
Farriers Ct. CV23: Stret U 7F 55
Farriers Way CV11: Nun 2B 32
Farriers Yd. *CV32: Lea S* *6E 98*
(off Swan St.)
CV37: Ett 2C 126
Farrington Cl. CV35: Welle 4G 117
Farrington Ct. *CV35: Welle* *4H 117*
(off Farrington Cl.)
Farther Sand Cl. CV35: H Lucy 2A 118
Farthing Ct. CV21: Hillm 1D 88
FARTHINGHOE 2D 147
Farthing La. B76: Curd 5C 18
FARTHINGSTONE 3D 145
Farthing Wlk. CV4: Westw H 2B 66
Farzens Av. CV34: Warw 5D 100
Faseman Av. CV4: Tile H 4D 56
Faulconbridge Av. CV5: East G 3C 56
Faulconbridge Way CV34: H'cte . . .5C 102
Faulkes Rd. CV6: Cov 5B 50
Faultlands Cl. CV11: Nun 4B 32
(not continuous)
FAWLER 3C 147
Fawley Cl. CV3: W'hall 2K 69
Fawsley Leys CV22: Rugby 2G 87
Faygate Cl. CV3: Bin 4C 60
FAZELEY 1C 139
Featherbed La. CV4: Westw H 3E 66
CV7: Withy 1D 54
CV21: Hillm 1C 88
CV36: Cher 6G 133
CV36: Ilm 7C 126
CV37: Path, Wilm 5K 113
CV47: Bas H 1J 109
Feather La. CV10: Nun 4G 31
FEATHERSTONE 1A 138
Featherstone Cl. CV10: Nun 2J 31
FECKENHAM 2B 142
Fein Bank CV4: Tile H 5A 56
Feldon Cotts. OX15: Lwr Bra 3G 133
Feldon Edge CV36: Half 3K 127
Feldon Vw. CV37: N'bld S 1G 127
Feldon Way CV37: S Avon 7J 115
Fell Gro. CV32: Lill 4G 99
Fell Mill La.
CV36: H'ton, Ship S 1K 131
Fellmore Gro. CV31: Lea S 1G 103
Fellows Way CV21: Hillm 2B 88
Fell's La. CV47: Nap 2J 111
Felton Cl. CV2: Walsg S 5A 52
Felton Pl. CV36: Ship S 5F 131
Fencote Av. B37: F'bri 1A 34
FEN END 1D 143
Fennel Cl. CV23: Newt 7K 65
Fennell Ho. *CV1: Cov* *5B 58*
(off Meadow St.)
FENNY COMPTON 3G 121 (3B 144)
FENNY DRAYTON 2A 140
Fennyland La. CV8: Ken 2F 79
Fenside Av. CV3: Cov 4D 68
Fentham Ct. B92: H Ard 7H 45
Fentham Grn. B92: H Ard 7G 45
Fentham Rd. B92: H Ard 7G 45
Fenton Rd. CV5: Alle 6F 49
Fenwick Cl. B49: Alc 3D 112
CV6: Cov 5E 50
Fenwick Dr. CV21: Hillm 1C 88
Ferguson Cl. CV4: Tile H 4A 56
CV37: Ett 2C 126
Fern Cl. CV2: Cov 4J 51
CV23: Brow 7K 65
Ferndale Cl. CV9: Hur 7K 13
CV11: Nun 6F 23
Ferndale Ct. B46: Cole 7G 25
Ferndale Dr. CV8: Ken 7E 78
Ferndale M. B46: Cole 7G 25
Ferndale Rd. B46: Cole 7G 25
CV3: Bin W 1F 71
Ferndown Cl. CV4: Tile H 4D 56
Ferndown Ct. CV22: Bil 7E 74
Ferndown Rd. CV22: Bil 7E 74
Ferndown Ter. CV22: Bil 7E 74
Fern Gro. CV12: Bed 3E 40
Fernhill Cl. CV8: Ken 3C 78
Fernhill Dr. CV32: Lea S 6F 99
FERNHILL HEATH 3A 142
Fernhill Way LE10: Wlvy 2H 33
Fernwood Cl. B98: Redd 2A 92
Ferrers Cl. CV4: Tile H 5D 56
Ferriby Rd. CV22: Caw 1B 86
Ferrieres Cl. CV22: Dunc 6C 86
Ferry La. CV37: A'ton 2C 116
Fetherston Ct. CV31: Lea S 2D 102
Fetherston Cres. CV8: Rytn D 7D 70
FEWCOTT 3D 147
Fiddlers Grn. B92: H Ard 7G 45
Fld. Barn Rd. CV35: H Mag 1B 100
Field Cl. CV8: Ken 4F 79
CV33: Ufton 3F 109
CV34: Warw 1K 101
LE10: Wlvy 2H 33
Field Ct. CV2: Cov 7J 51
Fieldfare Cl. CV23: Brow 7J 65
Fieldfare Cft. B36: Cas B 4A 24
Field Ga. La. CV47: Fen C 2H 121
Fieldgate La. CV8: Ken 3C 78
CV31: W'nsh 6F 103
Fieldgate Lawn CV8: Ken 3D 78
FIELD HEAD 1B 140
Fieldhead La. CV34: Warw 2K 101
Fieldhouse Cl. B95: Hen A 2H 93
Fielding Cl. CV2: Walsg S 1C 60
CV9: Ath 1C 16
Fielding Way CV10: Gall C 6F 21
Field March CV3: W'hall 3A 70
Field M. CV22: Dunc 3A 86
Fields Ct. CV34: Warw 7H 97
Flds. Farm La. CV23: Mart 4C 104
Fieldside La. CV3: Bin 4B 60
Fields Pk. Dr. B49: Alc 4D 112
Field Vw. CV22: Caw 1B 86
Field Vw. Cl. CV7: Exh 5G 41
Fife Rd. CV5: Cov 5K 57
Fife St. CV11: Nun 7B 22
FIFIELD .3B 146
Fifield Cl. CV11: Nun 2K 31
Fighting Cl. CV35: Kine 5D 120
Fillingham Cl. B37: Chel W 4D 34
FILLONGLEY 2C 38 (3D 139)
Fillongley Rd. B46: Max 7C 26
CV7: Fill 7C 26
CV7: Mer 5E 46
Finbarr Cl. CV6: Cov 2E 58
Finch Cl. CV6: Cov 4C 50
Finch Way CV11: Nun 7H 23
Findley Cl. CV9: Man 5E 16
Findon Cl. CV12: Bulk 2E 42
Fineacre La. CV8: Rytn D 4E 82
CV23: Rytn D, Stret D 4E 82
Fingal Cl. CV3: W'hall 2J 69
Fingest Cl. CV5: Cov 3F 57
FINHAM 5C 68
Finham Ct. CV8: Ken 6D 78
Finham Cres. CV8: Ken 3F 79
Finham Flats CV8: Ken 3F 79
Finham Grn. Rd. CV3: Finh 5B 68
Finham Gro. CV3: Finh 5C 68
Finham Pk. CV3: Finh 6C 68
Finham Rd. CV8: Ken 3F 79
Finings Ct. CV32: Lea S 5D 98
Finlay Ct. CV1: Cov 6H 135 (6D 58)
Finmere CV21: Brow 2K 75
Finnemore Cl. CV3: Cov 3B 68
FINSTALL 1A 142
FINSTOCK 3C 147
FINWOOD 2C 143
Finwood Rd. CV35: Row 7G 91
Fircroft B78: K'bry 4D 12
Fircroft Ho. B37: Chel W 3A 34
Firedrake Cft. CV1: Cov 5F 59
Fire Station Rd. B26: Birm A 1A 44
Firethorn Cres. CV31: W'nsh 6E 102
Fir Gro. CV4: Tile H 5E 56
Firleigh Dr. CV12: Bulk 2F 43
(not continuous)
Firs, The B78: K'bry 4E 12
CV5: Cov 7A 58
CV7: Mer 5D 46
CV12: Bed 3E 40
CV37: Lwr Q 5J 125
Firs Dr. CV22: Rugby 6F 75
Firs Est. CV3: Cov 7B 58
Fir Tree Av. CV4: Tile H 5E 56
Fir Tree Gro. CV11: Nun 3K 31
Fir Tree La. CV7: New A 4E 28
Fisher Av. CV22: Hillm 1A 88
Fisher Rd. B49: Kinw 3D 112
CV6: Cov 6E 50
CV47: Bis I 6B 110
Fishers Cl. CV23: Kils 7H 89
Fishers Ct. CV34: Warw 4F 101
Fishers Wlk. CV9: Ath 4C 16
Fishery La. B46: Cole, Neth W 7H 19
Fishpond La. CV7: Lit P 7H 35
Fishponds Rd. CV8: Ken 6C 78
Fitton St. CV11: Nun 1H 31
Fitzalan Cl. CV23: Chu L 2F 73
Fitzroy Cl. CV2: Walsg S 1D 60
Fivefield Rd. CV7: Ker E 1H 49
FIVE WAYS 1D 143
FLADBURY 3A 142
Flamborough Cl. CV3: Bin 7B 60
Flaunden Cl. CV5: Cov 3F 57
Flavel Ct. CV9: Aus 7G 7

Genting International Casino—Greenlands Rd.

Genting International Casino
Birmingham NEC 3E 44
Gentlemans La. B95: Ullen 4A 90
GENTLESHAW 1B 138
Geoffrey Cl. CV2: Cov 2H 59
George, The *CV31: Lea S* *1E 102*
(off George St.)
George Birch Cl. CV23: Brin 4C 62
George Eliot Av. CV12: Bed 3K 41
George Eliot Bldgs.
CV11: Nun *7D 22*
(off Mill St.)
George Eliot Rd. CV1: Cov 2D 58
George Eliot St. CV11: Nun 2J 31
George Hodgkinson Cl.
CV4: Tile H 4D 56
George Marston Rd. CV3: Bin 6A 60
George Pk. Cl. CV2: Cov 5J 51
George Poole Ho. *CV1: Cov* *5B 58*
(off Windsor St.)
George Rd. B46: Wat O 1C 24
CV34: Warw 7J 97
George Robertson Cl.
CV3: Bin 1A 70
George Row CV23: Kils 6J 89
George's Elm La. B50: Bidf A 3G 123
George St. CV1: Cov 2D 58
CV7: New A 4E 28
CV11: Nun 2A 32
CV12: Bed 2H 41
CV21: Rugby 5F 75
CV31: Lea S 1E 102
CV47: S'ton 6C 106
George St. Ringway CV12: Bed 2H 41
Georgian Cl. B49: Alc 4B 112
Gerard Av. CV4: Canly 7F 57
Gerard Ct. CV22: Caw 1A 86
Gerard Pl. CV22: Caw 1A 86
Gerard Rd. B49: Alc 3D 112
CV22: Caw 1A 86
Gerard Row CV22: Caw 1A 86
Gerards Way B46: Cole 7G 25
Gerrards Rd. CV36: Ship S 5H 131
Gerrard St. CV34: Warw 2G 101
GIBBET HILL 6H 67
Gibbet Hill Rd. CV4: Canly 3F 67
Gibbons Cl. CV4: Tile H 5D 56
Gibbs Cl. CV2: Walsg S 1D 60
Gibraltar Cl. CV3: Cov 6F 59
Gibson Cres. CV12: Bed 4G 41
Gibson Dr. CV21: Hillm 7C 76
Gielgud Way CV2: Walsg S 6D 52
Giffard Wlk. *CV22: Caw* *1A 86*
(off Frewen Rd.)
Giffard Way CV34: Warw 6G 97
Gifford Rd. CV33: L Hth 1K 119
Gifford Wlk. CV37: S Avon 3B 114
GIGGETTY 2A 138
Gigg La. B76: Wis 1B 18
Gilbert Av. CV22: Bil 6D 74
Gilbert Cl. CV1: Cov 4E 58
CV12: Bed 4H 41
CV37: S Avon 1E 114
Gilbert Horal Cl. CV4: Tile H 7D 56
GILBERT'S GREEN 2B 90 (1C 143)
Giles Cl. CV6: Cov 4C 50
Gilfil Rd. CV10: Nun 3H 31
Gilkes La. CV35: Oxh 1E 130
Gillett Cl. CV11: Nun 1H 31
Gillett's La. OX15: Up Bra 2F 133
Gillian's Wlk. CV2: Walsg S 6C 52
Gillquart Way CV1: Cov ... 7K 135 (6D 58)
GILMORTON 3C 141
GILSON 3D 24
Gilson Dr. B46: Cole 5D 24
Gilson Rd. B46: Cole 3D 24
Gilson Way B37: K'hrst 7A 24
Gingles Ct. CV21: Hillm 1C 88
Ginkgo Wlk. CV31: Lea S 3D 102
Gipsy La. CV10: Nun 6J 31
CV11: Nun 6J 31
Girdlers Cl. CV3: Cov 3B 68
Girtin Cl. CV12: Bed 1G 41
Girton Ho. B36: Cas B 4A 24
Girvan Gro. CV32: Cubb 2G 99
Gisburn Cl. CV34: Warw 6H 97
Givens Ho. *CV1: Cov* *5B 58*
(off Meadow St.)
Glade, The CV5: East G 4D 56
Gladiator Way CV21: Rugby 1F 75
Gladstone Ct. CV32: Lea S 6D 98
Gladstone St. CV21: Rugby 4F 75
Glaisdale Av. CV6: Cov 3E 50
Glamorgan Cl. CV3: W'hall 3K 69
Glaramara Cl. CV21: Brow 1K 75
GLASCOTE 1D 139
Glascote Rd. B77: Glas, Tam, Wiln ... 7A 8
Glasshouse La. CV8: Ken 4G 79
Gleave Rd. CV31: W'nsh 5E 102
Glebe, The B95: Woot W 5H 93
CV7: Cor 6G 39
Glebe Av. CV12: Bed 4E 40
Glebe Cl. B50: Bidf A 6G 123
CV4: Tile H 1E 66
CV47: S'ton 6C 106
Glebe Cres. CV8: Ken 6E 78
CV21: Rugby 5E 74
Glebe Est. CV37: Wilm 5H 113
Glebefarm Gro. CV3: Bin 4B 60
Glebe Farm Ind. Est.
CV21: Rugby 1F 75
Glebe Farm Rd. CV21: Rugby 1F 75
Glebe Flds. B76: Curd 5B 18
Glebe La. CV11: Nun 5G 23
Glebe Pl. CV31: Lea S 1F 103
Glebe Ri. CV9: Aus 7H 7
Glebe Rd. B49: Kinw 3D 112
CV11: Nun 7E 22
CV35: Clav 2D 94
CV37: S Avon 3B 114
CV47: Sou 4G 107
Gleeson Dr. CV34: Warw 6G 97
Glen Cl. CV36: Ship S 4H 131
Glencoe Rd. CV3: Cov 5H 59
Glendale Av. CV8: Ken 3E 78
Glendale Way CV4: Tile H 5A 56
Glendon Gdns. CV12: Bulk 2E 42
Glendower CV37: S Avon 1H 137
Glendower App. CV34: H'cte 5C 102
Glendower Av. CV5: Cov 5H 57
Gleneagles Cl. CV11: Nun 3E 32
Gleneagles Rd. CV2: Cov 1A 60
Glenfern Gdns. CV8: Rytn D 6A 70
GLENFIELD 1C 141
Glenfield Av. CV10: Nun 4D 22
Glenhurst Rd. B95: Hen A 3G 93
Glenmore Dr. CV6: Lford 1F 51
Glenmount Av. CV6: Lford 1F 51
Glenn St. CV6: Cov 3D 50
GLEN PARVA 2C 141
Glenridding Cl. CV6: Lford 1F 51
Glenrosa Wlk. CV4: Tile H 1E 66
Glenroy Cl. CV2: Cov 1A 60
Glentworth Av. CV6: Cov 4A 50
Glenville Av. CV9: Wood E 2K 13
Glenwood Gdns. CV12: Bed 1G 41
Globe Ct. B49: Alc 5B 112
GLOOSTON 2D 141
Gloster Dr. CV8: Ken 3D 78
Gloster Gdns. CV35: Welle 5G 117
Glosters Grn. CV35: Kine 5D 120
Gloucester Cl. CV11: Nun 4H 23
Gloucester Ct.
CV37: S Avon 3G 137 (4F 115)
Gloucester St. CV1: Cov 4B 58
CV31: Lea S 1E 102
Gloucester Way B37: Mars G 4A 34
Glover Cl. CV34: Warw 4D 100
Glovers Cl. CV7: Mer 5E 46
CV9: Man 4E 16
Glovers Cft. B37: F'bri 2A 34
Glover St. CV3: Cov 7D 58
GLYMPTON 3D 147
GOADBY 2D 141
Goals Soccer Cen. AT7
Coventry 7G 51
Godfrey Cl. CV31: Rad S 3J 103
Godiva Lodge CV2: Cov 2G 59
Godiva Pl. CV1: Cov 4E 58
Godiva Trad. Est. CV6: Cov 6F 51
Godsons La. CV47: Nap 2J 111
Goggbridge La. CV34: Warw 5D 100
Goldacre Cl. CV31: W'nsh 4D 102
Gold Av. CV22: Caw 1B 86
Gold Cl. CV11: Nun 4A 32
Goldcrest Cft. B36: Cas B 4A 24
Golden Acres La. CV3: Bin 1B 70
Golden Eagle Cl. CV7: Ker E 6K 39
Goldicote Rd. CV35: Lox 7C 116
Goldrick Rd. CV6: Cov 1E 58
Goldsmith Av. CV22: Rugby 2F 87
CV34: Warw 3E 100
Goldsmith Way CV10: Nun 3G 31
Goldthorn Cl. CV5: East G 3B 56
Golf Cen., The 3B 92
Golf Dr. CV11: Nun 4C 32
Golf La. CV31: W'nsh 5F 103
Gooch's Way CV31: W'nsh 4E 102
Goodacre Cl. CV23: Clift D 3C 76
Goode Cl. CV34: Warw 1E 100
Goode Cft. CV4: Tile H 5D 56
Goodere Av. B78: Pole 2D 10
Goodere Dr. B78: Pole 7D 8
Goodfellow St. CV32: Lea S 6A 98
Goodman Way CV4: Tile H 6A 56
Goodway Ho. CV32: Lea S 7B 98
Goodwood Cl. CV3: W'hall 2J 69
CV37: S Avon 6C 114
GOODYERS END 5C 40
Goodyers End La. CV12: Bed 5C 40
GOOM'S HILL 3B 142
Goose La. CV37: Lwr Q, Up Qui .. 6H 125
GORCOTT HILL 2B 142
Gordon Cl. CV12: Bed 1H 41
Gordon Pas. CV31: Lea S 1E 102
Gordon St. CV1: Cov 6A 58
CV31: Lea S 1E 102
Goring Rd. CV2: Cov 3G 59
GORNALWOOD 2A 138
Gorse Cl. CV22: Bil 7E 74
Gorse Farm Rd. CV11: Nun 4D 32
Gorse La. B95: Woot W 4G 93
Gorse Lea CV47: Sou 4G 107
Gorseway CV5: Cov 4G 57
Gorsey Grn. La. CV7: Fill 4H 37
Gorsey La. B46: Cole 2E 24
Gorsey Way B46: Cole 2E 24
Gorsy Way CV10: Nun 6J 21
GOSFORD GREEN 5F 59
Gosford Ind. Est. CV1: Cov 5F 59
Gosford St.
CV1: Cov 4K 135 (5D 58)
GOSPEL END 2A 138
Gospel Oak La. CV37: Snitt 7F 95
Gospel Oak Rd. CV6: Cov 2B 50
Gosport Rd. CV6: Cov 6E 50
Gossett La. CV8: Bran 1G 71
Gould Rd. CV35: H Mag 1C 100
Governor's Ct. CV34: Warw 7F 97
Gower Memorial, The ... 4J 137 (5F 115)
Grace Rd. CV5: Milli W 6J 47
Grafton Cl. B98: Redd 1A 92
CV8: Ken 6E 78
Grafton Ct. CV4: Canly 1F 67
GRAFTON FLYFORD 3A 142
Grafton La. B50: Bidf A 5J 123
GRAFTON REGIS 3D 145
Grafton Rd. B49: Ard G, Wix 1F 123
B50: Ard G 1F 123
Grafton St. CV1: Cov 5E 58
Graham Cl. CV6: Cov 5H 51
Graham Rd. CV21: Rugby 4J 75
Graham St. CV11: Nun 6D 22
Gramer Ct. CV9: Man 5E 16
Gramercy Pk. CV4: Tile H 4A 56
Grammar School & Guildhall 6F 137
Granary Pl. B78: K'bry 7E 12
Granborough Cl. CV3: Bin 7B 60
Granborough Ct. CV32: Lill 4E 98
Granby Rd. CV10: Nun 1F 31
CV36: H'ton 1K 131
GRANDBOROUGH 6H 105 (2B 144)
Grandborough Flds. Rd.
CV23: Gran, Gran F 7F 105
Grand Depot Rd. CV11: Bram 6H 33
Grandsire Dr. CV21: Hillm 1C 88
Grandys Cft. B37: F'bri 2A 34
Grange, The CV32: Cubb 2K 99
CV32: Lea S 6F 99
CV34: Warw 1K 101
Grange Av. CV3: Bin 1B 70
CV3: Finh 5C 68
CV8: Ken 2C 78
Grange Cl. CV10: Nun 4H 21
CV22: Bil 1C 86
CV34: Warw 7A 98
CV47: Sou 4H 107
OX15: Ratl 6C 128
Grange Farm Dr. CV47: S'ton 6C 106
Grange Gdns. CV35: Welle 3H 117
Grange M., The CV32: Lea S 6B 98
Grangemouth Rd. CV6: Cov 1B 58
Grange Pk. CV37: S Avon 3F 115
Grange Rd. B50: Bidf A 6H 123
CV6: Lford 2G 51
CV10: Harts 1G 21
CV21: N'bld A 2E 74
CV32: Lill 4E 98
CV37: Bear 6C 94
Grange Wlk. CV6: Lford 1H 51
Granleigh Ct. CV32: Cubb 2J 99
Granoe Cl. CV3: Bin 7A 60
Grantham Rd. CV35: Welle 4H 117
Grantham St. CV2: Cov 4F 59
Grantley Dr. B37: F'bri 2B 34
Grant Rd. CV3: Cov 5H 59
CV7: Exh 5G 41
Grants Cl. CV47: Fen C 3G 121
Granville Ct. *CV36: Ship S* *4H 131*
(off West St.)
Granville Rd. CV35: Welle 3G 117
Granville St. CV32: Lea S 5E 98
Grapes Cl. CV6: Cov 2B 58
Grasmere Av. CV3: Cov 2K 67
Grasmere Cl. CV21: Brow 2K 75
Grasmere Ct. CV37: S Avon 1H 137
Grasmere Cres. CV11: Nun 4G 23
Grasmere Rd. CV12: Bed 3H 41
Grasscroft Dr. CV3: Cov 2E 68
Grassington Av. CV34: Warw 6H 97
Grassington Dr. B37: F'bri 4A 34
CV11: Nun 2C 32
Gratton Ct. CV3: Cov 2K 67
Gravel, The B76: Wis 1B 18
Gravel Hill CV4: Tile H 6C 56
GRAVELLY HILL 2C 139
Gravel Nth., The *B76: Wis* *1B 18*
(off Lichfield Rd.)
Graylands, The CV3: Finh 4C 68
Grayling Cres. CV31: Lea S 4G 103
Grayling Wlk. B37: Chel W 2C 34
Grays Orchard CV23: Thurl 7K 85
Grayswood Av. CV5: Cov 3H 57
GREAT ALNE 3F 113 (3C 143)
Great Balance CV23: Brin 4B 62
GREAT BARR 2B 138
Great Borne CV21: Brow 7J 65
GREAT BOURTON 1D 147
GREAT BOWDEN 3D 141
GREAT BRINGTON 2D 145
Gt. Central Way
CV21: Rugby 4K 75
Gt. Central Way Ind. Est.
CV21: Rugby 3K 75
Great Fld. Dr. CV34: Warw 5D 100
Great Garden of New Place, The
.... 5G 137
GREAT GLEN 2D 141
GREAT HEATH 1E 58 (3A 140)
Greatheed Rd. CV32: Lea S 6C 98
Gt. Orme Cl. CV22: Caw 7B 74
GREAT OXENDON 3D 141
GREAT RISSINGTON 3A 146
GREAT ROLLRIGHT 2C 147
GREAT SAREDON 1A 138
GREAT TEW 3C 147
Gt. William St.
CV37: S Avon 2F 137 (4F 115)
GREAT WOLFORD 7A 132 (2B 146)
Gt. Wood Cl. CV6: Cov 5B 50
GREATWORTH 1D 147
GREAT WYRLEY 1A 138
Greaves Cl. CV34: Warw 1A 102
Greaves Way, The CV47: Bis I 6C 110
GREEN, THE 6G 95
Green, The B46: Shu 2B 26
B76: Lea M 4G 19
B78: K'bry 5D 12
B79: Seck 5A 6
B94: Tan A 3D 90
B96: Sam 7B 92
CV7: Mer 5D 46
CV8: S'lgh 3C 80
CV9: Aus 7H 7
CV9: Man 5F 17
CV10: Harts 1G 21
CV11: Nun 2A 32
CV22: Bil 1C 86
CV22: Dunc 6C 86
CV23: Barby 7E 88
CV23: C'over 1H 65
CV23: Harb M 4B 64
CV23: Lilb 2J 77
CV23: Long L 4A 74
CV35: Clav 1D 94
CV35: Light 2G 119
CV35: Lit K 7C 120
CV35: Mid T 6C 130
CV35: Rad 5A 128
CV36: Lit Wol 7D 132
CV37: A'ton 1C 116
CV37: Snitt 7F 95
CV37: Wilm 5J 113
CV47: Long I 2C 106
CV47: N'end 1D 120
CV47: P Mars 6G 111
GL56: Stret O 2C 132
OX17: Warm 2J 129
Green Cl. B80: Stud 4D 92
CV23: Long L 4K 73
CV31: W'nsh 4F 103
Green Ct. CV21: Rugby 4K 75
Greendale Cl. CV9: Ath 4D 16
Greendale Rd. CV5: Cov 4H 57
CV9: Ath 4D 16
CV11: Nun 4H 23
GREEN END 4H 37 (3D 139)
Green End CV47: Long I 2C 106
Grn. End Rd. CV7: Fill 3E 36
Grn. Farm Cl. CV23: Lilb 2J 77
Grn. Farm End CV35: Kine 5D 120
Greenfield, The CV3: Cov 7H 59
Greenfield Cl. CV9: Gren 7G 11
Greenfields Cl. CV36: Ship S 5H 131
Greenfinch Cl. B36: Cas B 5A 24
Greenfinch Ct. CV2: Cov 6J 51
Greenfinch Rd. B36: Cas B 4A 24
Greengates B95: Hen A 1H 93
GREEN HEATH 1A 138
GREENHILL 1A 142
Greenhill Rd. CV22: Bil 7F 75
CV31: W'nsh 4F 103
Greenhill St.
CV37: S Avon 3D 136 (4E 114)
Greenland Av. CV5: Alle 2D 56
Greenland Ct. CV5: Alle 2D 56
GREENLANDS 2B 142
Greenlands Rd. B37: Chel W 3B 34

Green Lane—Hardingwood La.

GREEN LANE
B98 1B 92 (2B 142)
CV3 4B 68
Green La. B46: Cole 7F 25
(Castle Dr., not continuous)
B46: Cole 4B 24
(Collector Rd.)
B46: Cole 1D 34
(Drake Cft.)
B77: Wiln 3A 10
(not continuous)
B78: B'moor 3A 10
B80: Stud 2A 92
CV3: Cov, Finh 2A 68
CV7: Cor 7B 38
CV7: Fill 2D 38
CV8: Bran 1H 71
CV9: Gren 5J 11
CV10: Nun 5H 21
CV23: Brin 3B 62
CV23: Chu L 3G 73
CV34: Warw 7H 97
CV35: Oxh 1D 130
CV36: Ship S 5H 131
Green La. Cl. CV36: Ship S 5H 131
GREEN LANES 7D 90
Greenleaf Cl. CV5: East G 4E 56
Greenmoor Rd. CV10: Nun 7B 22
Greenodd Dr. CV6: Lford 1F 51
Greens Cl. CV23: C'over 1J 65
Greenside Cl. CV11: Nun 3E 32
Greensleeves Cl. CV6: Cov 4B 50
GREENS NORTON 3D 145
Green's Rd. CV6: Cov 5A 50
Greensward, The CV3: Bin 5C 60
Greensward Cl. CV8: Ken 3F 79
Greenswood CV37: Bear 6D 94
Greens Yd. CV12: Bed 2H 41
Greenway B78: Pole 6D 8
CV11: Nun 4D 32
CV34: Warw 6G 97
Greenway, The B37: Mars G 7A 34
Greenway Cl. CV36: Ship S 4G 131
Greenway Rd. CV36: Ship S 4G 131
Greenways CV4: Tile H 5A 56
Greenways, The CV32: Lill 4F 99
Greenways Ct. CV36: Ship S 4G 131
Greenwood Cl. CV23: Long L 3A 74
Greenwood Ct. CV11: Nun 1B 32
CV32: Lea S 6F 99
Greenwood Pl. CV6: Cov 5B 50
Greenwood Sq. *B37: Chel W 3B 34*
(within Chelmsley Wood Shop. Cen.)
Greenwood Way *B37: Chel W 3B 34*
(within Chelmsley Wood Shop. Cen.)
Gregory Av. CV3: Cov 2A 68
Gregory Hood Rd. CV3: Cov 3D 68
Greig, The 4C 112
Grenadier Dr. CV3: Cov 7F 59
GRENDON
CV9, Baddesley Ensor
7G 11 (2D 139)
CV9, Bradley Green 4J 11
Grendon Cl. CV4: Tile H 6A 56
GRENDON COMMON 1F 15 (2D 139)
Grendon Dr. CV21: Brow 1A 76
Grendon Rd. B78: Pole 1D 10
CV9: Gren, Pin 4J 11
Grenfell Cl. CV31: Lea S 2H 103
Grenville Av. CV2: Cov 4H 59
Grenville Cl. CV22: Bil 7C 74
Gresham Av. CV32: Lill 5F 99
Gresham Pl. CV32: Lill 5F 99
Gresham Rd. CV10: Nun 4H 31
Gresham St. CV2: Cov 5G 59
Gresley Cl.
CV37: S Avon 2B 136 (4E 114)
Gresley Rd. CV2: Cov 7K 51
Gressingham Gro. CV6: Cov 7D 50
Greswold Cl. CV4: Tile H 6D 56
Greswoldes, The CV31: Rad S 2K 103
Gretna Rd. CV3: Finh 4K 67
Greville Ho. *CV34: Warw 1H 101*
(off Yeomanry Cl.)
Greville Rd. B49: Alc 3A 112
CV8: Ken 5D 78
CV34: Warw 6K 97
Greville Smith Av. CV31: W'nsh 4F 103
Greycoat Rd. CV6: Cov 4A 50
Greyfriars Ct. CV6: Cov 7A 50
Greyfriars La. CV1: Cov 5H 135 (5C 58)
Greyfriars Rd. CV1: Cov 5G 135 (5C 58)
Greyhound Rd. CV6: Cov 4D 50
Grey Mill La. B95: Woot W 7G 93
Greys Rd. B80: Stud 4D 92
Gribble Dr. CV34: Warw 7D 96
GRIFF 6G 31 (3A 140)
Griff Cvn. Site CV10: Nun 5J 31
Griff Clara Ind. Est. CV10: Griff 5F 31
GRIFF HOLLOW 5J 31
Griffin Cen., The 5H 75
Griffin Cl. B46: Cole 7G 25
Griffin Rd. CV34: Warw 1A 102
Griffith Cl. CV37: B'ton 2C 114
Griffiths Ho. *CV21: Brow 1J 75*
(off Dovedale Cl.)
Griff La. CV10: Griff 5F 31
(not continuous)
Griff Way CV10: Nun 5H 31
GRIMSBURY 1D 147
GRIMSCOTE 3D 145
Grimshaw Hill B95: Ullen 7C 90
Grimstock Av. B46: Cole 3E 24
Grimstock Hill B46: Cole 3E 24
Grimston Cl. CV3: Bin 5C 60
Grindal Pl. CV22: Caw 1K 85
Grindle Rd. CV6: Lford 2F 51
Grindley Ho. *CV1: Cov 5B 58*
(off Windsor St.)
Grinham Av. B78: Pole 2E 10
Grizebeck Dr. CV5: Alle 2E 56
Grizedale CV21: Brow 1J 75
GROBY 1C 141
Grosvenor Casino
Coventry *3E 50*
(off Phoenix Way)
Grosvenor Ct. CV32: Lea S 6D 98
Grosvenor Ho. CV1: Cov 6F 135 (5B 58)
Grosvenor Lwr. Rd.
CV1: Cov 6F 135 (6B 58)
Grosvenor Rd. CV1: Cov 6F 135 (6B 58)
CV21: Rugby 5H 75
CV31: Lea S 3E 102
Grounds Farm La. CV8: Ken 5B 78
Grouse Cl. CV37: B'ton 2B 114
Grove, The B46: Cole 1F 35
B80: Stud 4C 92
(not continuous)
B92: H Ard 5G 45
CV12: Bed 2H 41
Grove Ct. CV5: Cov 7B 58
Grove Cft. CV35: H Hill 3A 100
GROVE END 3G 133
Grove Farm La. CV7: Ker E 3H 49
Grove Flds. CV10: Nun 3D 22
Grove Ho.
CV37: S Avon 4D 136 (5E 114)
Grovehurst Pk. CV8: S'lgh P 7B 80
Grovelands Ind. Est. CV7: Exh 7G 41
Grove La. B76: Wis 1A 18, 2A 18
B94: Lapw 1F 91
CV7: Ker E 6K 39
Grove Pk. CV35: H Hill 3A 100
Grove Pl. CV10: Nun 1D 30
CV31: Lea S 2E 102
(not continuous)
Grove Rd. CV7: Ansty 3E 52
CV9: Ath 4C 16
CV10: Nun 1D 30
CV37: S Avon 6C 136 (5E 114)
Grove Sports & Social Club 3C 16
Grove St. CV1: Cov 3K 135 (4D 58)
CV32: Lea S 7C 98
Grump St. CV36: Ilm 7B 126
Guardhouse Rd. CV6: Cov 6B 50
Guernsey Dr. B36: Cas B 6B 24
Guild Chapel, The 6F 137
Guild Cottages 6F 137
Guild Cotts., The
CV34: Warw 2G 101
(off Bowling Grn. St.)
Guildford Ct. CV6: Cov 7D 50
Guildford Cft. B37: Mars G 5A 34
Guild Rd. B95: Aston C 2K 113
CV6: Cov 7D 50
Guild St. CV37: S Avon 2F 137 (4F 115)
Guillemard Ct. B37: Chel W 4B 34
GUILSBOROUGH 1D 145
Guilsborough Rd. CV3: Bin 7A 60
Guinea Cres. CV4: Westw H 2B 66
GUITING POWER 3A 146
Gulistan Ct. CV32: Lea S 6C 98
Gulistan Rd. CV32: Lea S 6C 98
Gullet, The B78: Pole 1C 10
Gulliman's Way CV31: Lea S 2H 103
Gulson Rd. CV1: Cov 5K 135 (5E 58)
GUMLEY 2D 141
Gundry Cl. CV31: Lea S 1E 102
Gundulf Rd. CV37: Lwr Q 6F 125
GUN HILL 5D 28
Gun Hill CV7: New A 4E 28
Gun La. CV2: Cov 2G 59
Gunn Ct. B49: Gt Alne 2G 113
Gunn End CV36: Ship S 3H 131
Gunners La. B80: Stud 3D 92
Gunnery Ter. CV32: Lea S 6B 98
Gunnings Rd. B49: Alc 4C 112
GUNSTONE 1A 138
Gunton Av. CV3: W'hall 2J 69
Guphill Av. CV5: Cov 4H 57
Gurney Cl. CV4: Tile H 4C 56
Gutteridge Av. CV6: Cov 4A 50
Guy Pl. E. CV32: Lea S 6D 98
Guy Pl. W. CV32: Lea S 6D 98
Guy Rd. CV8: Ken 7D 78
GUY'S CLIFFE 4J 97
Guy's Cliffe Av. CV32: Lea S 5A 98
Guy's Cliffe Rd. CV32: Lea S 6B 98
Guy's Cliffe Ter. CV34: Warw 1H 101
Guys Cl. CV34: Warw 7H 97
Guys Comn. CV22: Dunc 6D 86
Guys Cross Pk. Rd.
CV34: Warw 7H 97
Guy St. CV32: Lea S 6D 98
CV34: Warw 1H 101
Gwendolyn Dr. CV3: Cov 5J 59
Gypsy La. B46: Wat O 2D 24
B78: Dord 6D 10
CV8: Ken 7D 78
CV9: Ath 1C 16

H

HACKMAN'S GATE 1A 142
Hackwell St. CV47: Nap 2H 111
Haddon End CV3: Cov 2E 68
Haddon Rd. CV32: Lill 5F 99
Haddon St. CV6: Cov 6G 51
HADEMORE 1C 139
Hadfield Cl. CV23: Clift D 3C 76
Hadfield Way B37: F'bri 1A 34
Hadleigh Rd. CV3: Finh 5C 68
HADLEY 2A 142
Hadley M. CV11: Nun 3K 31
Hadleys Cft. B78: K'bry 6E 12
Hadrian Cl. CV32: Lill 3F 99
Hadrian Dr. B46: Cole 3E 24
Hadrians Wlk. B49: Alc 5A 112
Hadrians Way CV21: Rugby 1F 75
HADZOR 2A 142
HAGLEY 3A 138
Haig Ct. CV22: Bil 7E 74
HAILES 2A 146
Hales Cl. CV37: Snitt 5G 95
Hales Ind. Pk. CV6: Lford 2E 50
HALESOWEN 3A 138
Hales St. CV1: Cov 2H 135 (4C 58)
(not continuous)
HALFORD 2J 127 (1B 146)
Halford Gro. CV35: Hatt 5A 96
Halford La. CV6: Cov 5A 50
Halford Lodge CV6: Cov 4A 50
Halford Rd. CV37: Arms 4G 127
CV37: Ett 2B 126
CV37: S Avon 6D 114
Halfway La. CV22: Dunc 6B 86
Halifax Cl. CV5: Alle 7E 48
CV35: Welle 5F 117
Hallam Rd. CV6: Cov 3B 50
Hallam's Cl. CV8: Bran 3H 71
Hallaton Cl. CV22: Caw 7A 74
Hallbrook Rd. CV6: Cov 3A 50
Hall Cl. CV8: S'lgh 3B 80
CV23: Kils 6J 89
Hall Cl., The CV22: Dunc 7C 86
Hall Ct. B78: Pole 1D 10
Hall Dr. B37: Mars G 6A 34
CV8: Bag 5E 68
HALL END 5B 10
HALLEND 6E 90
Hall End CV11: Nun 2K 31
Hall End Dr. B78: Dord 5B 10
Hall End Pl. CV11: Nun 2K 31
Hallfields CV31: Rad S 3J 103
Hall Gdns. CV9: With 3F 17
HALL GREEN
B28 3C 139
CV6 4H 51
Hall Grn. Rd. CV6: Cov 4H 51
Hall Gro. CV23: Brin 3C 62
Hall La. CV2: Walsg S 1B 60
CV9: With 3G 17
CV33: Har 5H 109
LE10: Wlvy 2H 33
Hall Rd. CV32: Lea S 6D 98
LE10: Wlvy 2H 33
Hall's Cl. CV31: W'nsh 5F 103
Hall's Croft 7F 137 (5F 115)
Halls Dr. CV2: Walsg S 7D 52
Hall Wlk. B46: Cole 7E 24
(Birmingham Rd.)
B46: Cole 1F 35
(The Grove)
Hallway Dr. CV7: Shilt 7G 43
HALSTEAD 1D 141
Hamar Way B37: Mars G 4B 34
Hambledon Cl. CV22: Caw 7A 74
Hambridge Rd. CV47: Bis I 6C 110
Hames La. B79: Newt R 4D 6
HAM GREEN 2B 142
HAMILTON 1D 141
Hamilton Cl. CV10: Nun 7J 21
CV12: Bed 4C 40
Hamilton Ct. CV10: Nun 7J 21
Hamilton Dr. B80: Stud 4C 92
Hamilton Rd. CV2: Cov 4G 59
CV31: Rad S 3J 103
CV37: Tidd 4K 115
Hamilton Ter. CV32: Lea S 7D 98
Hamilton Way CV10: Griff 5H 31
Hamlet, The CV35: Leek W 1J 97
Hamlet Cl. CV11: Nun 3C 32
CV22: Bil 3D 86
Hamlet Way CV37: S Avon 3D 114
Hammersley St. CV12: Bed 4E 40
Hammerton Way CV35: Welle 5G 117
HAMMERWICH 1B 138
Hammond Bus. Cen.
CV11: Nun 1A 32
Hammond Cl. CV11: Nun 1A 32
Hammond Grn. CV35: Welle 2H 117
Hammond Rd. CV2: Cov 3F 59
Hammonds Ter. CV8: Ken 4B 78
Hampden Ct. CV47: Temp H 2B 120
Hampden Way CV22: Bil 2C 86
Hampden Way CV35: Welle 4G 117
HAMPEN 3A 146
Hampshire Cl. CV3: Bin 7B 60
Hampton Av. CV10: Nun 7G 21
Hampton Cl. B98: Redd 1A 92
CV6: Cov 1F 59
Hampton Ct. B92: H Ard 7H 45
Hampton Cft. CV35: H Hill 3A 100
Hampton Grange CV7: Mer 5D 46
Hampton Gro. CV32: Lea S 6F 99
HAMPTON IN ARDEN 7G 45 (3D 139)
Hampton in Arden Station (Rail) 7H 45
Hampton La. CV7: Mer 6A 46
HAMPTON LOVETT 2A 142
HAMPTON LUCY 2B 118 (3D 143)
HAMPTON MAGNA 1B 100 (2D 143)
HAMPTON ON THE HILL
3A 100 (2D 143)
Hampton Rd. CV6: Cov 1F 59
CV34: Warw 3B 100
CV35: H Hill 3A 100
Hampton St. CV34: Warw 2F 101
HAMS HALL 7H 19
Hams Hall Distribution Pk.
B46: Cole 6F 19
Hams Hall National Distribution Pk.
B46: Cole 7H 19
Hams La. B46: Lea M 6F 19
B76: Lea M 6F 19
HAMSTEAD 2B 138
HANBURY 2A 142
Hanbury Cl. CV35: Kine 5D 120
Hanbury Pl. CV6: Cov 4G 51
Hanbury Rd. CV12: Bed 1J 41
Hancock Grn. CV4: Tile H 7D 56
Hancock Ho. *CV34: H'cte 5B 102*
(off Merlin Way)
Handcross Gro. CV3: Finh 3A 68
Handley Gro. CV34: Warw 6F 97
Handleys Cl. CV8: Rytn D 7C 70
Hands Paddock CV37: N'bld S 1G 127
HANDSWORTH 2B 138
Handsworth Cres. CV5: East G 3C 56
Hanford Cl. CV6: Cov 1E 58
Hanford Cl. Ind. Est. CV6: Cov 1E 58
Hangar Rd. B26: Birm A 3A 44
HANGING HOUGHTON 1D 145
Hangman's La. B79: Seck 4A 6
Hankinson M. CV34: Warw 6F 97
Hankinson Rd. CV34: Warw 7F 97
Hanover Gdns. CV21: Rugby 4H 75
CV32: Lea S 6E 98
Hanover Glebe CV11: Nun 2J 31
Hans Cl. CV2: Cov 3F 59
Hanson Av. CV36: Ship S 5G 131
Hanson Way CV6: Lford 2G 51
HANWELL 1D 147
Hanwood Cl. CV5: East G 3A 56
Hanworth Cl. CV32: Lill 4G 99
Hanworth Rd. CV34: Warw 7F 97
Harbet Dr. B40: Nat E C 2E 44
HARBORNE 3B 138
Harborough Cotts. B94: Lapw 3H 91
HARBOROUGH MAGNA 4B 64 (1B 144)
HARBOROUGH PARVA 5B 64
Harborough Rd. CV6: Cov 4B 50
CV23: Harb M 7C 64
Harbour Cl. B50: Bidf A 6F 123
Harbourne Cl. CV8: Ken 4E 78
HARBOURS HILL 2A 142
HARBURY 6H 109 (2A 144)
Harbury Ct. *CV32: Lea S 5D 98*
(off Lillington Av.)
Harbury La. CV33: Bis T, Ches 6D 102
CV34: H'cte 4A 102
Harbury Rd. CV47: Ladb 2A 110
Harbury Spoilbank Nature Reserve
5K 109
Harby Cl. B37: Mars G 5B 34
Harcourt CV3: W'hall 3A 70
Harcourt Gdns. CV11: Nun 1J 31
Hardingwood La. CV7: Fill 3G 37

Hardwick—Hermitage Rd.

HARDWICK . . . 2B 138
Hardwick Cl. CV5: East G . . . 3E 56
Hardwick Fld. La. CV34: Warw . . . 5D 100
Hardwick Rd. CV47: P Mars . . . 7F 111
Hardwyn Cl. CV3: Bin . . . 6D 60
Hardy Cl. CV10: Gall C . . . 7F 21
CV22: Bil . . . 6C 74
Hardy Rd. CV6: Cov . . . 7A 50
Hare & Hounds La. CV10: Nun . . . 2G 31
Harebell Wlk. B37: Chel W . . . 3D 34
Harebell Way CV23: Brow . . . 7K 65
Harefield Ho. CV2: Cov . . . 4H 59
Harefield La. CV10: Arb, Nun . . . 4F 31
Harefield Rd. CV2: Cov . . . 4H 59
CV11: Nun . . . 7D 22
Hares Leap CV37: B'ton . . . 1C 114
Hareway La. CV35: Barf . . . 7A 108
Harewood Rd. CV5: Cov . . . 4G 57
Harger Ct. CV8: Ken . . . 5D 78
Harger M. CV8: Ken . . . 5D 78
Hargrave Cl. B46: Wat O . . . 1B 24
CV3: Bin . . . 6C 60
CV23: Gran . . . 6H 105
Harington Rd. CV6: Cov . . . 2A 58
HARLASTON . . . 1D 139
Harlech Cl. CV8: Ken . . . 4G 79
HARLESTONE . . . 2D 145
Harley St. CV2: Cov . . . 4G 59
Harlow Wlk. CV2: Walsg S . . . 7C 52
Harmar Cl. CV34: Warw . . . 6F 97
Harmer Cl. CV2: Walsg S . . . 7C 52
Harmony Ct. CV10: Nun . . . 2H 31
Harnall La. CV1: Cov . . . 1K 135 (3D 58)
Harnall La. E. CV1: Cov . . . 1K 135 (3D 58)
Harnall La. Ind. Est.
CV1: Cov . . . 1K 135 (3D 58)
Harnall La. W.
CV1: Cov . . . 1H 135 (3D 58)
Harnall Row CV1: Cov . . . 4E 58
Harold Cox Pl. CV22: Bil . . . 3E 86
Harold Raffety Cl. CV6: Cov . . . 1E 58
Harold Rd. CV2: Cov . . . 5K 59
Harold's Orchard GL56: Stret O . . . 2B 132
Harold St. CV11: Nun . . . 1J 31
Harpenden Dr. CV5: Alle . . . 2E 56
Harper Rd. CV1: Cov . . . 5E 58
Harper's La. CV9: Man . . . 5F 17
Harpers Yd. CV23: Harb M . . . 4B 64
HARPOLE . . . 2D 145
Harrington Way CV10: Griff . . . 5G 31
Harriott Dr. CV34: H'cte . . . 4B 102
Harris Cl. B95: Hen A . . . 2H 93
CV35: Kine . . . 5D 120
CV36: Ship S . . . 5F 131
Harris Dr. CV22: Rugby . . . 1F 87
Harris M. B95: Hen A . . . 2H 93
Harrison Cl. CV21: Hillm . . . 1D 88
Harrison Cres. CV12: Bed . . . 3G 41
Harrison Way CV31: Lea S . . . 3D 102
Harris Rd. CV3: Cov . . . 5H 59
CV34: Warw . . . 7E 96
Harrow Cl. CV6: Lford . . . 2G 51
Harrow Hill CV36: Long C . . . 1C 134
Harrow Rd. CV31: W'nsh . . . 5F 103
Harry Caplan Ho. CV5: Alle . . . 1F 57
Harry Edwards Ho. CV2: Cov . . . 6K 51
Harry Rose Rd. CV2: Cov . . . 4A 60
Harry Salt Ho. *CV1: Cov . . . 4E 58*
(off Canterbury St.)
Harry Stanley Ho.
CV6: Cov . . . 6G 51
Harry Truslove Cl. CV6: Cov . . . 7A 50
Harry Weston Rd. CV3: Bin . . . 6B 60
Hart Cl. CV21: Hillm . . . 6K 75
Hartington Cres. CV5: Cov . . . 6J 57
Hartland Av. CV2: Cov . . . 1H 59
HARTLE . . . 1A 142
HARTLEBURY . . . 1A 142
Hartlepool Rd.
CV1: Cov . . . 1K 135 (3E 58)
Hartley Cl. CV6: Cov . . . 4F 51
Hartley Gdns. CV47: Sou . . . 6G 107
Harton Cl. CV4: Tile H . . . 6E 56
Hartridge Wlk. CV5: Cov . . . 3F 57
HARTSHILL . . . 3F 21 (2A 140)
Hartshill Hayes Country Pk. . . . 2F 21
Hartshill Hayes Country Pk. Vis. Cen.
. . . 2E 20
Hartshorne Rd. CV47: Bis I . . . 7B 110
Harvard Cl. CV35: Welle . . . 5G 117
Harvesters Cl. CV3: Bin . . . 5C 60
Harvest Hill Cl. CV31: Lea S . . . 2G 103
Harvest Hill La. CV5: Alle . . . 2J 47
CV7: Mer . . . 2J 47
Harvey Cl. CV5: Alle . . . 7E 48
HARVINGTON
DY10 . . . 1A 142
WR11 . . . 3B 142
Harvon Gth. CV21: Rugby . . . 4J 75
HASELBECH . . . 1D 145
Haselbech Rd. CV3: Bin . . . 6B 60
Haselbury Cnr. CV10: Nun . . . 3F 31
HASELEY . . . 2D 143
Haseley Cl. CV31: Lea S . . . 3F 103
Haseley Ct. CV37: Lwr Q . . . 5H 125
Haseley Rd. CV2: Cov . . . 5J 51
Haselor Cl. B49: Alc . . . 4D 112
Haselour Rd. B37: K'hrst . . . 7A 24
Hasilwood Sq. CV3: Cov . . . 5H 59
Hassall Cl. CV33: Bis T . . . 5C 108
Hastang Flds. CV31: Lea S . . . 3G 103
Hastings Rd. CV2: Cov . . . 3G 59
CV9: Gren . . . 6G 11
CV35: Welle . . . 2H 117
Haswell Cl. CV22: Rugby . . . 6J 75
Hatchford Wlk. B37: Chel W . . . 4B 34
HATFIELD . . . 3A 142
Hathaway Ct.
CV37: S Avon . . . 3B 136 (4E 114)
Hathaway Dr. CV11: Nun . . . 3C 32
CV34: Warw . . . 5F 97
Hathaway Grn. La.
CV37: S Avon . . . 4A 114
Hathaway Hamlet CV37: Shot . . . 4B 114
Hathaway La. CV37: Shot . . . 5C 114
Hathaway Rd. CV4: Tile H . . . 6B 56
Hatherell Rd. CV31: Rad S . . . 3J 103
HATHERTON . . . 1A 138
Hatteras Row CV10: Nun . . . 3G 31
Hatters Ct. CV12: Bed . . . 3J 41
Hatters Dr. CV9: Ath . . . 1C 16
HATTON . . . 2D 143
Hatton Cl. CV35: Hatt . . . 5A 96
Hatton Farm Village . . . 2D 143
HATTON PARK . . . 4A 96
Hatton Rd. CV35: N Lin . . . 1F 95
Hatton Ter. CV35: Hatt . . . 5A 96
Hauley Gro. CV31: W'nsh . . . 4E 102
Haunch La. B76: Lea M . . . 3G 19
Haunchwood Pk. Dr.
CV10: Gall C . . . 7D 20
Haunchwood Pk. Ind. Est.
CV10: Gall C . . . 7E 20
Haunchwood Rd. CV10: Nun . . . 7J 21
HAUNTON . . . 1D 139
Haven Cvn. Pk. B92: Bick . . . 4C 44
Haven Ct. CV22: Rugby . . . 5E 74
Havendale Cl. CV6: Cov . . . 2B 58
HAWBRIDGE . . . 3A 142
Haweswater Gro. CV11: Nun . . . 5J 23
Hawk Cl. CV11: Nun . . . 4D 32
Hawker Cl. CV3: Cov . . . 6H 59
HAWKESBURY . . . 7H 41 (3A 140)
Hawkes Dr. CV34: H'cte . . . 4B 102
HAWKES END . . . 4G 49 (3D 139)
Hawkeshead CV21: Brow . . . 1K 75
Hawkes Mill Cl. CV35: N Lin . . . 2G 95
Hawkes Mill La. CV5: Alle . . . 4E 48
Hawkeswell La. B46: Cole . . . 2G 35
Hawkesworth Dr. CV8: Ken . . . 3E 78
Hawkins Cl. CV22: Bil . . . 7E 74
Hawkins Rd. CV5: Cov . . . 5A 58
Hawksworth Cres. B37: Chel W . . . 2D 34
Hawksworth Dr. CV1: Cov . . . 4A 58
Hawlands CV21: Brow . . . 2J 75
HAWLING . . . 3A 146
Hawthorn Av. CV9: Hur . . . 6K 13
Hawthorn Cl. B49: Alc . . . 3B 112
CV21: Brow . . . 7H 65
Hawthorn Ct. CV4: Tile H . . . 5C 56
Hawthorne Av. CV7: New A . . . 4F 29
Hawthorne Cl. CV8: Wols . . . 4J 71
Hawthorne Ter. CV10: Nun . . . 6K 21
Hawthorn La. CV4: Tile H . . . 4C 56
(Delius St.)
CV4: Tile H . . . 5C 56
(Roosevelt Dr.)
Hawthorn Rd. CV31: Lea S . . . 2D 102
Hawthorns, The B78: K'bry . . . 4D 12
Hawthorn Ter. CV23: Harb M . . . 4B 64
Hawthorn Way CV10: Harts . . . 3F 21
CV22: Bil . . . 7B 74
CV36: Ship S . . . 6H 131
Haydock Cl. CV6: Ald G . . . 2H 51
CV37: S Avon . . . 6C 114
Haydon Cl. B80: Stud . . . 3D 92
Haydon Way B49: Cou . . . 6E 92
Hayes, The CV35: Leek W . . . 2H 97
Hayes Cl. CV21: Brow . . . 1K 75
Hayes Grn. Rd. CV12: Bed . . . 4F 41
Hayes La. CV7: Exh . . . 5F 41
Hayes Rd. CV10: Harts . . . 3F 21
Hay La. CV1: Cov . . . 4J 135 (5D 58)
Hayle Av. CV34: Warw . . . 6H 97
Hayle Cl. CV11: Nun . . . 6H 23
HAYLEY GREEN . . . 3A 138
Hay Mdw. CV36: Ship S . . . 4G 131
Haynestone Rd. CV6: Cov . . . 1J 57
Haynes Way CV21: Rugby . . . 7F 65
Hay Pool OX17: Farnb . . . 5J 121
Hayton Grn. CV4: Tile H . . . 7D 56
(not continuous)
Haytor Ri. CV2: Cov . . . 7J 51
Hayward Cl. CV35: H Mag . . . 2B 100
Haywards Grn. CV6: Cov . . . 7A 50
Haywood La. CV35: Row . . . 4K 91
Haywood Rd. CV34: Warw . . . 6D 96
(not continuous)
Hazel Cl. CV10: Harts . . . 4F 21
CV21: Brow . . . 7H 65
CV32: Lea S . . . 5E 98
Hazel Cft. B37: Chel W . . . 4B 34
Hazelcroft B78: K'bry . . . 4D 12
Hazelcroft Way CV12: Bed . . . 2K 41
Hazel Gro. CV12: Bed . . . 2K 41
Hazell Way CV10: Nun . . . 3G 31
Hazell Way Ind. Est. CV10: Nun . . . 3G 31
Hazel Rd. CV6: Cov . . . 5H 51
CV10: Nun . . . 6J 21
HAZELSLADE . . . 1B 138
Hazelwood Cl. CV22: Dunc . . . 6B 86
Hazlemere Cl. CV5: Cov . . . 3F 57
HAZLETON . . . 3A 146
Hazlewood Cl. B49: Alc . . . 5A 112
Headborough Rd. CV2: Cov . . . 2G 59
Headington Av. CV6: Cov . . . 4A 50
Headland Cl. CV37: Welf A . . . 3A 124
Headland Ri. CV37: Welf A . . . 3A 124
Headland Rd. CV37: Welf A . . . 2A 124
Headlands, The CV5: Cov . . . 3H 57
HEADLESS CROSS . . . 2B 142
HEADLEY HEATH . . . 1B 142
Healey Cl. CV21: Brow . . . 1J 75
Healey Ct. CV34: Warw . . . 1H 101
Health Cen. Rd. CV4: Canly . . . 4G 67
Healthworks Fitness Studio
. . . 1B 136 (3D 114)
Heanley La. CV9: Hur . . . 4A 14
Hearsall Comn. CV5: Cov . . . 5J 57
Hearsall Ct. CV4: Cov . . . 5H 57
Hearsall La. CV5: Cov . . . 5K 57
Hearth Ho. *CV21: Rugby . . . 2G 75*
(off Signalman Ct.)
Heart of England Crematorium
CV11: Nun . . . 1C 32
Heart of England Way CV11: Nun . . . 1B 32
Heart Pk. . . . 6K 37
HEATH . . . 5C 86
Heath, The CV22: Dunc . . . 6C 86
Heath Av. CV12: Bed . . . 4E 40
Heath Bus. Pk. CV8: Wols . . . 7B 72
HEATHCOTE . . . 5C 102
Heathcote Ind. Est. CV34: H'cte . . . 3A 102
Heathcote La. CV34: H'cte . . . 4A 102
Heathcote Pk. CV34: H'cte . . . 6C 102
Heathcote Rd. CV31: W'nsh . . . 5D 102
Heathcote St. CV6: Cov . . . 1A 58
Heathcote Way CV34: H'cte . . . 4B 102
Heath Cres. CV2: Cov . . . 1G 59
HEATHENCOTE . . . 3D 145
HEATH END
CV10 . . . 2E 30
WS3 . . . 1B 138
Heath End Rd. CV10: Nun . . . 2E 30
Heath End Trad. Est. CV10: Nun . . . 2F 31
HEATHER . . . 1A 140
Heather Cl. B36: Cas B . . . 4A 24
CV10: Nun . . . 1F 31
CV22: Bil . . . 7E 74
CV37: S Avon . . . 4C 114
CV47: Sou . . . 4H 107
Heather Ct. CV9: Ath . . . 2C 16
Heather Dr. CV12: Bed . . . 3E 40
Heather Rd. CV2: Cov . . . 4H 51
CV3: Bin W . . . 1E 70
Heath Farm La CV33: Light . . . 2H 119
Heath Farm La. CV35: Light . . . 2H 119
Heathfield Rd. CV5: Cov . . . 5G 57
HEATH GREEN . . . 1B 142
Heathgreen Cl. B37: Chel W . . . 2D 34
Heath Grn. Way CV4: Westw H . . . 2D 66
HEATH HAYES . . . 1B 138
Heathlands, The CV23: Clift D . . . 3C 76
Heath La. CV23: Brin . . . 7A 62
Heathmere Dr. B37: F'bri . . . 3A 34
Heath Rd. CV2: Cov . . . 3F 59
CV12: Bed . . . 4F 41
Heathside CV10: Nun . . . 2F 31
Heath Ter. CV32: Lea S . . . 6C 98
HEATH TOWN . . . 2A 138
Heath Way CV22: Hillm . . . 1K 87
Hebden Av. CV34: Warw . . . 6G 97
Hebden Way CV11: Nun . . . 2C 32
Heber Dr. CV33: Har . . . 6G 109
Hebe Way CV31: W'nsh . . . 6G 103
Heckley Rd. CV7: Exh . . . 6G 41
Heddle Gro. CV6: Cov . . . 6H 51
Hedgefield Way CV4: Tile H . . . 7D 56
Hedgehog Av. CV37: B'ton . . . 1C 114
Hedgerows, The CV10: Nun . . . 5A 22
Hedgerow Wlk. CV6: Cov . . . 2B 50
Hedges Cl. CV47: Ladb . . . 2C 110
WR11: Salf P . . . 7B 122
Hedgetree Cft. B37: Chel W . . . 3C 34
Hedge Way CV10: Nun . . . 4H 21
Hedingham Gro. B37: Chel W . . . 3D 34
HEDNESFORD . . . 1B 138
Heemstede La. CV32: Lea S . . . 5E 98
Heera Cl. CV6: Cov . . . 7D 50
Helena Cl. CV10: Nun . . . 1F 31
Helen St. CV6: Cov . . . 1F 59
Hele Rd. CV3: Cov . . . 2D 68
HELLIDON . . . 3C 145
Hellidon Cl. CV32: Lill . . . 5E 98
Hellidon Lakes Golf Course . . . 5K 111
Hellidon Rd. CV47: P Mars . . . 6G 111
Helmdon Cl. CV21: Brow . . . 2K 75
Helmsdale Rd. CV32: Lill . . . 3F 99
Helmswood Dr. B37: Chel W . . . 5C 34
Helston Cl. CV11: Nun . . . 6H 23
Helvellyn Way CV21: Brow . . . 1K 75
Hemdale CV11: Nun . . . 7H 23
Hemdale Bus. Pk. CV11: Nun . . . 7H 23
Hemingford Rd. CV2: Walsg S . . . 6C 52
Heming Rd. B98: Redd . . . 1D 92
Hemlingford Cft. B37: Mars G . . . 6A 34
Hemlingford Rd. B78: K'bry . . . 7E 12
Hemmings Cl. CV31: Rad S . . . 3J 103
Hemmings Mill CV35: Barf . . . 2B 108
Hempit La. B76: Wis . . . 4A 18
HEMPTON . . . 2D 147
Hemsby Cl. CV4: Canly . . . 1E 66
Hemsworth Dr. CV12: Bulk . . . 3D 42
Henbrook La. OX15: Up Bra . . . 3G 133
Henbury Dr. B37: Chel W . . . 1C 34
Henderson Cl. CV5: Alle . . . 7G 49
Henderson Rd. CV34: Warw . . . 7D 96
Hendre Cl. CV5: Cov . . . 5G 57
Henge Wlk. CV22: Caw . . . 7B 74
Hen La. CV6: Cov . . . 3C 50
Henley Cl. CV11: Nun . . . 3G 23
Henley Country Club Golf Course
. . . 1G 93
Henley Ct. B49: Alc . . . 4C 112
CV2: Cov . . . 7K 51
CV31: Lea S . . . 3F 103
HENLEY GREEN . . . 6K 51
HENLEY-IN-ARDEN . . . 1H 93 (2C 143)
Henley-in-Arden Heritage Cen. . . . 2H 93
Henley-in-Arden Station (Rail) . . . 2G 93
Henley Ind. Pk. CV2: Cov . . . 7A 52
Henley Mill La. CV2: Cov . . . 7H 51
Henley Rd. B49: Gt Alne . . . 3F 113
B95: Hen A, Ullen . . . 7D 90
B95: Ullen . . . 6B 90
CV2: Cov, Walsg S . . . 5H 51
CV31: Lea S . . . 3F 103
CV35: Clav . . . 1A 94
CV35: H Hill, N Lin . . . 1F 95, 4A 100
Henley St. B49: Alc . . . 4C 112
CV37: S Avon . . . 2E 136 (4E 114)
Henley Wlk. CV2: Cov . . . 6K 51
Henrietta St. CV6: Cov . . . 2E 58
Henry Boteler Rd. CV4: Canly . . . 1F 67
Henry St. CV1: Cov . . . 2H 135 (4C 58)
CV8: Ken . . . 4E 78
CV11: Nun . . . 2J 31
CV21: Rugby . . . 5G 75
Henry's Way *CV31: W'nsh . . . 4E 102*
(off Dobson La.)
Henry Tanday Ct. CV32: Lea S . . . 6C 98
Henson Rd. CV12: Bed . . . 4E 40
Henton Ct. CV6: Cov . . . 5F 51
Henwoods Ct. *CV36: Ship S . . . 3H 131*
(off Mayo Rd.)
Hepworth Rd. CV3: Bin . . . 5D 60
Herald Av. CV5: Cov . . . 6G 57
Herald Bus. Pk. CV3: Bin . . . 1B 70
Herald Rd. B26: Birm A . . . 2C 44
Heralds Ct. CV34: Warw . . . 7K 97
Herald Way CV3: Bin . . . 1C 70
Herbert Art Gallery & Mus., The
. . . 4J 135 (5D 58)
Herbert Bond Dr. CV8: Ken . . . 3B 78
Herberts La. CV8: Ken . . . 4E 78
Herbert St. CV10: Nun . . . 1E 30
Hercules La. CV35: Clav, Yarn C . . . 1B 94
Herders Way CV7: Ker E . . . 7K 39
Herdwick Ct. *CV21: Rugby . . . 4J 75*
(off Murray Rd.)
Herdwycke Cl. CV47: Sou . . . 5K 107
Hereburgh Way CV33: Har . . . 7H 109
Hereford Cl. CV10: Nun . . . 7K 21
Hereford Ct. CV21: Rugby . . . 4H 75
Hereford Rd. CV11: Bram . . . 6H 33
Hereford Wlk. B37: Mars G . . . 4A 34
Heritage Cl. CV22: Caw . . . 1A 86
Heritage Ct. CV4: Canly . . . 5H 67
Heritage Dr. CV6: Lford . . . 7J 41
Heritage Motor Cen. . . . 5F 119
Hermes Cl. CV34: Warw . . . 3C 102
Hermes Ct. CV34: Warw . . . 3C 102
Hermes Cres. CV2: Cov . . . 7K 51
Hermione Cl. CV34: H'cte . . . 5D 102
Hermitage Bus. Pk. B78: Pole . . . 1B 10
Hermitage Cl. B78: Pole . . . 1C 10
Hermitage La. B78: B'moor . . . 1B 10
Hermitage Rd. CV2: Cov . . . 3J 59

Hermitage Way—Hornchurch Cl.

Hermitage Way CV8: Ken 6E 78
Hermit's Cft. CV3: Cov 7K 135 (7D 58)
Heronbank CV4: Tile H 5A 56
Heron Cl. B49: Alc 3B 112
CV47: Sou 7G 107
Heron Ho. CV2: Cov 4H 59
Heron La. CV37: B'ton 2B 114
Heron Way CV34: H'cte 4B 102
CV37: N'bld S 1G 127
Herrick Rd. CV2: Cov 4K 59
Herring Rd. CV9: Ath 4D 16
Hertford Pl. CV1: Cov 5F 135 (5B 58)
Hertford Rd. B49: Alc 3C 112
CV37: S Avon 6E 114
Hertford St. CV1: Cov 4H 135 (5C 58)
Heslop Cl. CV3: Bin 7B 60
Hetton Cl. CV34: Warw 6H 97
Hever Hall CV1: Cov 3K 135
Hewitt Av. CV6: Cov 2B 58
Hexby Cl. CV2: Walsg S 1C 60
Hexworthy Av. CV3: Cov 3B 68
Heybrook Cl. CV2: Cov 7J 51
Heycroft CV4: Canly 4H 67
Heyford Cl. CV2: Ald G 3K 51
Heyford Leys CV22: Rugby 3F 87
Heynes Wlk. CV5: Alle 5F 49
HEYTHROP 3C 147
Heyville Cft. CV8: Ken 6G 79
Heywood Cl. CV6: Cov 7G 51
Hibberd Ct. CV8: Ken 5D 78
Hibbert Cl. CV22: Rugby 7F 75
Hickey La. B79: Newt R 5C 6
Hickman Rd. CV10: Gall C 7D 20
Hickmans Grn. Cl. CV34: Warw 5D 100
Hickory Cl. CV2: Walsg S 5B 52
Hicks Cl. CV34: Warw 5H 97
HIDCOTE BARTRIM 1A 146
HIDCOTE BOYCE 1A 146
Hidcote Cl. CV11: Nun 4B 32
CV22: Rugby 6E 74
CV31: Lea S 3G 103
Hidcote Gro. B37: Mars G 6A 34
Hidcote Ho. CV4: Tile H 1B 66
Hidcote Rd. CV8: Ken 3G 79
Higham La. CV11: Nun 6F 23
HIGHAM ON THE HILL 2A 140
High Ash Cl. CV7: Exh 6F 41
High Beech CV5: Alle 1E 56
High Brink Rd. B46: Cole 5F 25
Highbury Grn. CV10: Nun 4H 21
Highcroft CV35: Clav 2C 94
Highcroft Cres. CV32: Lea S 6A 98
Highdown Rd. CV31: Lea S 2F 103
Highfield CV7: Mer 5E 46
CV35: Hatt 4A 96
Highfield Cl. CV8: Ken 5C 78
CV37: Snitt 5G 95
Highfield La. CV7: Cor 4F 39
Highfield Rd. B80: Stud 3C 92
CV2: Cov 3F 59
CV11: Nun 2K 31
CV37: S Avon 2D 114
Highfield Ter. CV32: Lea S 6B 98
Highgrove CV4: Westw H 3D 66
CV22: Bil 2D 86
Highland Rd. CV5: Cov 6K 57
CV8: Ken 2F 79
CV32: Lill 3F 99
Highlands Cl. CV34: Warw 7H 97
High La. OX15: Up Bra 3G 133
Highley Dr. CV6: Cov 1C 58
High Lodge B46: Cole 2G 35
High Pk. Cl. CV5: East G 4D 56
High St. B46: Cole 4F 25
B49: Alc 5B 112
B50: Bidf A 6G 123
B50: Broom 3E 122
B78: Pole 7D 8
B80: Stud 3D 92
B92: H Ard 7G 45
B95: Hen A 2H 93
CV1: Cov 4H 135 (5C 58)
CV6: Cov 5K 49
CV8: Ken 4C 78
CV8: Rytn D 7D 70
CV9: Hur 6K 13
CV11: Nun 7C 22
CV12: Bed 3H 41
CV21: Hillm 1B 88
CV21: Rugby 5G 75
CV23: Mart 2D 104
CV31: Lea S 1D 102
CV32: Cubb 2J 99
CV33: Har 6H 109
CV34: Warw 2G 101
CV35: Barf 1C 108
CV36: Ship S 4H 131
CV37: S Avon 5G 137 (5F 115)
CV37: Welf A 2A 124
CV47: Bis I 6B 110
CV47: Fen C 3G 121
CV47: Nap 3H 111
High St. CV47: S'ton 6C 106
CV47: Sou 5H 107
OX15: Lwr Bra 3H 133
OX15: Ratl 7D 128
HIGH TOWN 1A 138
High Town CV23: Prin 7G 83
Highview CV9: Hur 7K 13
High Vw. Dr. CV7: Ash G 6C 40
High Vw. Rd. CV32: Cubb 2G 99
Highwayman's Cft. CV4: Canly 3H 67
Hiker Gro. B37: Chel W 3D 34
Hilary Rd. CV4: Canly 2H 67
CV10: Nun 6A 22
Hilditch Way CV11: Nun 2A 32
HILL
CV23 . . . . .7E 104 (2B 144)
WR10 . . . . .3A 142
Hill, The CV47: S'ton 5C 106
Hillary Rd. CV22: Rugby 1E 86
Hill Cl. CV32: Lill 4E 98
CV47: N'end 1D 120
Hill Close Gdns. 2F 101
Hill Cres. CV23: Stret D 3H 83
Hillcrest CV32: Cubb 2J 99
Hill Crest Farm Cl. B79: Wart 5H 9
Hillcrest Rd. B78: Dord 3D 10
CV10: Nun 5J 21
Hill Farm Av. CV11: Nun 3D 32
Hillfield Rd. CV22: Bil 7C 74
HILLFIELDS 1K 135 (3E 58)
Hillfields Ho. CV1: Cov 4E 58
Hillfort Cl. CV22: Caw 7A 74
Hillfray Dr. CV3: Cov 3G 69
Hilliard Cl. CV12: Bed 1G 41
HILLIARD'S CROSS 1C 139
Hill La. CV37: Up Qui 7H 125
OX15: Up Bra 1F 133
Hillman Way CV8: Rytn D 6A 70
CV37: Ett 2C 126
HILLMORTON 1C 88 (1C 145)
Hillmorton La. CV23: Clift D 6C 76
CV23: Lilb 3G 77
Hillmorton Rd. CV2: Cov 4J 51
CV22: Hillm, Rugby 6G 75
Hillmorton Wharf CV21: Hillm 2F 89
Hill Rd. CV7: Ker E 7K 39
CV23: Gran 6F 105
Hill Side B78: K'bry 7E 12
Hillside CV10: Harts 3F 21
CV33: Har 5G 109
CV47: Nap 1H 111
Hillside Cl. CV37: S Avon 3A 114
Hillside Cft. CV47: Nap 1H 111
Hillside Dr. B37: K'hrst 1A 34
CV10: Nun 4H 21
Hillside Gdns. B37: K'hrst 1A 34
Hillside Nth. CV2: Cov 1G 59
Hillside Rd. CV37: S Avon 3B 114
Hill St. CV1: Cov 3F 135 (4B 58)
CV10: Nun 7J 21
CV12: Bed 7H 31
CV21: Rugby 4F 75
CV32: Lea S 6E 98
CV34: Warw 7K 97
HILL TOP 3F 29
Hill Top CV1: Cov 3J 135 (4D 58)
CV9: Bad E 1E 14
CV35: Lox 6D 116
Hilltop Cl. CV47: Sou 4G 107
Hill Top Pk. CV23: Prin 7H 83
Hill Vw. CV37: S Avon 3A 114
CV47: Bis I 7B 110
Hill Vw. Rd. B50: Bidf A 5H 123
HILL WOOTTON 1A 98 (2A 144)
Hill Wootton Rd.
CV32: B'dwn, Hill W 1J 97
CV35: Hill W, Leek W 1J 97
Hillyard Rd. CV47: Sou 4G 107
HILTON .1B 138
Hilton Av. CV10: Nun 5G 21
Hilton Ct. CV5: Cov 5K 57
HIMBLETON 3A 142
Himbleton Dr. CV3: Bin 5C 60
HIMLEY .2A 138
Himley Rd. CV12: Bed 3D 40
HINCHWICK 2A 146
HINCKLEY 2B 140
Hinckley Rd. CV2: Walsg S 7C 52
CV7: Ansty 4E 52
CV11: Burt H 4J 33
CV11: Nun 6E 22
Hind Cl. CV34: Warw 5H 97
Hinde Cl. CV21: Brow 1J 75
HINDLIP .3A 142
HINKSFORD 3A 138
HINTON .3C 145
HINTS 1C 139
Hipsley La. CV9: Bax, Hur 4C 14
Hipswell Highway CV2: Cov 3K 59
Hiron, The CV3: Cov 7C 58
Hiron Cft. CV3: Cov 7C 58
Hiron Way CV34: Warw 1D 100
Hirsel Gdns. CV32: Lea S 5D 98
Hirst Cl. CV23: Long L 3A 74
Hitchman Ct. CV31: Lea S 3E 102
Hitchman M. CV31: Lea S 3E 102
Hitchman Rd. CV31: Lea S 2E 102
Hithersand Cl. CV35: H Lucy 2B 118
HMP Onley CV23: W'hby 7J 87
HMP Rye Hill CV23: W'hby 7K 87
Hoarestone Av. CV11: Nun 5C 32
Hoar Pk. 2D 139
Hobbins, The CV36: Ship S 5G 131
Hobgoblin La. CV7: Fill 3D 38
Hob La. CV8: Burt G 5A 66
Hobley Cl. CV22: Bil 2D 86
Hockett St. CV3: Cov 7K 135 (7D 58)
Hocking Rd. CV2: Cov 2K 59
HOCKLEY
B77 .1D 139
CV5 . . . . .3A 56 (1D 143)
Hockley Cl. CV23: Gran 6H 105
HOCKLEY HEATH 1C 143
Hockley La. CV5: East G 3A 56
CV37: Ett 2C 126
Hodgett's La. CV8: Burt G 3A 66
Hodgson Rd. CV37: S Avon 2E 114
Hodnell Dr. CV47: Sou 6J 107
Hodnet Cl. CV8: Ken 4F 79
Hogan Ho. CV22: Bil 1C 86
Hogarth Cl. CV12: Bed 1G 41
Hogarth Rd. CV37: Shot 6C 114
HOGGRILL'S END 7K 19 (2D 139)
Hoggrills End La. B46: Neth W 1B 26
Holbeche Cres. CV7: Fill 2C 38
Holbech Hill OX17: Farnb 5J 121
Holbein Cl. CV12: Bed 1G 41
HOLBERROW GREEN 3B 142
Holborn Av. CV6: Cov 4C 50
Holbrook Av. CV21: Rugby 4G 75
Holbrook Gro. B37: Mars G 4B 34
Holbrook La. CV6: Cov 3C 50
(not continuous)
Holbrook Pk. Est. CV6: Cov 6D 50
Holbrook Rd. CV23: Long L 3B 74
CV37: S Avon 4B 114
HOLBROOKS 3C 50
Holbrook Way CV6: Cov 5D 50
Holcot Leys CV22: Rugby 2G 87
HOLDENBY 2D 145
Holder Cl. B50: Bidf A 5G 123
Holioake Dr. CV34: Warw 2J 101
Holland Cl. B50: Bidf A 6G 123
Holland Cft. B76: Mars 1H 19
Holland Mdw. CV37: Welf A 4A 124
HOLLAND PARK 1B 138
Holland Rd. CV6: Cov 1A 58
Hollands Bldgs. CV9: Ath 3D 16
Hollands Mead CV9: Ath 4D 16
Holliars Gro. B37: K'hrst 7A 24
Hollick Cres. CV7: New A 4E 28
Hollick Way LE10: Wlvy 2H 33
Hollicombe Ter. CV2: Cov 6K 51
Hollies Rd. B78: Pole 2E 10
Hollinwell Cl. CV11: Nun 4E 32
Hollis La. CV8: Ken 7C 66
Hollis Rd. CV3: Cov 5G 59
Holloway CV47: Nap 2H 111
Holloway, The CV34: Warw 2F 101
CV47: P Mars 6G 111
Holloway Fld. CV6: Cov 1K 57
Holloway Hill OX15: Lwr Bra 4J 133
Holloway La. OX15: Lwr Bra 4K 133
Hollow Cres. CV6: Cov 2B 58
HOLLOWELL 1D 145
Hollowell Way CV21: Brow 1J 75
Hollows, The CV11: Nun 3B 32
Hollybank CV5: Cov 7A 58
Hollybank Est. CV9: Aus 6H 7
HOLLYBERRY END 1K 47
Hollybush Ho. *CV11: Nun 7D 22*
(off Bond Ga.)
Holly Bush La. CV47: P Mars 6G 111
Hollybush La. CV6: Lford 2G 51
Holly Dr. CV8: Rytn D 7D 70
CV9: Hur 7A 14
Hollyfast La. CV7: Cor 2F 49
Hollyfast Rd. CV6: Cov 7J 49
Holly Gro. CV4: Tile H 5F 57
CV23: Chu L 3F 73
Hollyhurst B46: Wat O 1C 24
CV12: Bed 4F 41
Hollyland B46: Shu 3B 26
Holly La. CV9: Ath 2A 16
(not continuous)
Holly La. Ind. Est. CV9: Ath 2B 16
Holly Lodge CV35: Welle 3H 117
Holly Lodge Wlk.
B37: F'bri 3A 34
Holly M. CV21: Brow 6J 65
Holly Orchard CV37: S Avon 3F 115
Holly Rd. CV36: Ship S 6H 131
Hollystitches Rd. CV10: Nun 5K 21
Holly St. CV32: Lea S 6E 98
Holly Wlk. CV8: Bag 6E 68
CV11: Nun 2B 32
CV32: Lea S 7D 98
CV37: S Avon 3B 114
HOLLYWOOD 1B 142
Holman Way CV11: Nun 1K 31
Holman Way Ind. Est. CV11: Nun . . .1K 31
Holmcroft CV2: Walsg S 6B 52
Holme Cl. CV21: Brow 2J 75
Holmes Ct. CV8: Ken 4D 78
Holmes Dr. CV5: East G 2B 56
Holmes Rd. CV31: W'nsh 5F 103
Holme Way CV23: Barby 7F 89
Holmewood Cl. CV8: Ken 4F 79
Holmfield Rd. CV2: Cov 4H 59
Holmsdale Rd. CV6: Cov 7E 50
Holroyd Ho. CV4: Tile H 5D 56
Holsworthy Cl. CV11: Nun 6F 23
Holt, The CV32: Lill 4F 99
Holt Av. CV33: Bis T 5B 108
HOLT END 2B 142
Holte Rd. CV9: Ath 2C 16
Holt Gdns. B80: Stud 5D 92
Holt Leys CV47: Sou 5J 107
Holtom St. CV37: S Avon 6E 114
Holt Rd. B80: Stud 5D 92
CV47: Sou 6K 107
HOLY CROSS 1A 142
Holy Cross Ct. CV2: Cov 3A 60
Holyhead Rd. CV1: Cov . . .3F 135 (2H 57)
CV5: Cov 2H 57
Holyoak Cl. CV12: Bed 4F 41
CV22: Bil 1C 86
Holyoke Gro. CV31: W'nsh 6F 103
Holyrood Ct. CV10: Nun 6K 21
Holy Trinity Church
(Shakespeare's Tomb) 6F 115
HOLYWELL 2C 143
Holywell Bus. Pk. CV47: Sou 6F 107
Holywell Cl. CV4: Tile H 6B 56
Holywell Rd. CV47: Sou 5G 107
Home Cl. CV8: Bubb 3J 81
Home Farm CV35: Leek W 1H 97
Home Farm Cl. CV9: With 3G 17
Home Farm Cres. CV31: W'nsh 4F 103
Home Farm La. CV9: Gren 3J 11
Homefield La. CV22: Dunc 5D 86
Home Furlong CV35: Welle 5G 117
Home Mdw. CV35: Clav 3D 94
Home Pk. Rd. CV11: Nun 1J 31
Homer Cl. CV34: Warw 3C 102
Homestalls Mdw. CV35: Pill P 3B 128
Homestead CV2: Cov 4J 51
Homeward Way CV3: Bin 6C 60
HONEYBOURNE 1A 146
Honeybourne Cl. CV5: East G 4F 57
Honeybourne Rd.
B50: Bickm, Bidf A 6G 123
Honeyfield Rd. CV1: Cov 2D 58
Honeysuckle Cl. CV12: Bed 3D 40
CV23: Brow 7K 65
Honeysuckle Dr. CV2: Cov 4H 51
Honeysuckle La. CV35: Welle 5H 117
HONILEY 1D 143
Honiley Way CV2: Cov 5K 51
HONINGTON 1J 131 (1B 146)
Honington Cl. CV35: Hatt 5B 96
Honiton Rd. CV2: Cov 2H 59
Honiwell Cl. CV33: Har 6G 109
Hood La. CV10: Ansl 1D 28
Hood St. CV1: Cov 4E 58
Hood St. Ind. Est. CV1: Cov 4E 58
Hood's Way CV22: Bil 6D 74
HOOK NORTON 2C 147
Hoo Wlk. B78: Pole 2E 10
Hope Aldridge Bus. Cen.
CV10: Nun 5D 22
Hope Cl. CV7: Ker E 6A 40
Hopedale Cl. CV2: Cov 4A 60
Hope St. CV1: Cov 5B 58
Hopkins Fld. CV37: Long M 2G 125
Hopkins Pct., The B49: Alc 4C 112
Hopkins Rd. CV6: Cov 3A 58
Hopkins Way CV35: Welle 1H 117
Hopper's La. CV35: Welle 2H 117
Hopps Lodge Dr. CV21: Rugby 5J 75
HOPSFORD 1A 54
Hopton Cl. CV5: East G 3E 56
Hopton Crofts CV32: Lea S 5A 98
HOPWAS 1C 139
Hopwas Gro. B37: K'hrst 7A 24
HOPWOOD 1B 142
HORESTON GRANGE 6H 23
Horeston Grange Shop. Cen.
CV11: Nun 6H 23
HORLEY 1D 147
Hornbeam Cl. CV10: Nun 5J 21
CV21: Brow 7H 65
Hornbeam Dr. CV4: Tile H 6B 56
Hornbeam Gro. CV31: Lea S 2G 103
Hornchurch Cl.
CV1: Cov 7H 135 (6C 58)

Lyttelton Rd.—Maxstoke Ct.

Lyttelton Rd. CV34: Warw 7G 97
Lyttelton Cl. CV3: Bin 6C 60

M

Macaulay La. CV35: Welle 4H 117
Macaulay Rd. CV2: Cov 3K 59
CV22: Rugby 2E 86
CV47: Bis I 7B 110
Macbeth App. CV34: H'cte 5B 102
Macbeth Cl. CV22: Bil 3E 86
Macdonald Rd. CV2: Cov 4K 59
McDonnell Dr. CV7: Exh 7F 41
Macefield Cl. CV2: Ald G 3K 51
Mackenzie Cl. CV5: Alle 7E 48
McKinnell Cres. CV21: Hillm 6A 76
Mackley Way CV33: Har 6G 109
McMahon Rd. CV12: Bed 5E 40
Madden Pl. CV22: Bil 6C 74
Madeira Cft. CV5: Cov 5J 57
MADELEY HEATH 1A 142
Madin Cl. CV4: Tile H 3A 56
Madison Cl. CV4: Tile H 4A 56
Mad Mus. 3G 137 (4F 115)
Madras Rd. CV37: Lwr Q 6F 125
Maffey Ct. CV22: Rugby 6G 75
Magdalen Cl. CV37: Lwr Q 5H 125
Magdalen Rd. CV23: W'hby 3J 105
Magistrates' Court
Coventry 4J 135 (5D 58)
Leamington Spa 7D 98
Nuneaton 7E 22
MAGNA PARK 3C 141
Magnet La. CV22: Bil 1C 86
Magnolia Av. CV21: Brow 7H 65
Magnolia Cl. CV3: Cov 3B 68
Magnolia Dr. CV31: W'nsh 6F 103
Magpie Ho. CV5: East G 2B 56
Maguire Ind. Est. CV4: Tile H 7D 56
Magyar Cres. CV11: Nun 5B 32
Maidavale Cres. CV3: Cov 3C 68
Maidenhair Dr. CV23: Brow 7K 65
Maidenhead Cl.
CV37: S Avon 3F 115
Maidenhead Rd.
CV37: S Avon 1G 137 (4F 115)
MAIDFORD 3D 145
MAIDWELL 1D 145
Main Rd. B79: Newt R, Shut 2B 8
CV7: Ansty 3F 53
CV7: Mer 5E 46
CV9: Aus 7H 7
CV9: Bax 4C 14
CV23: Kils 6H 89
CV37: Lwr Q 5H 125
Main St. CV7: Withy 1C 54
CV8: Bran, Wols 3H 71
CV21: N'bld A 1D 74
CV22: Bil 1C 86
CV23: Bird 5A 104
CV23: Bour D 7C 84
CV23: Clift D 3B 76
CV23: Eas 3J 63
CV23: F'ton 7B 84
CV23: Gran 6H 105
CV23: Harb M 4A 64
CV23: Long L 4A 74
CV23: M Kirby 3J 55
CV23: Stret U 7F 55
CV23: Thurl 7K 85
CV23: W'hby 3H 105
CV35: N Lin 2G 95
CV35: Oxh 1E 130
CV35: Up Tys, Mid T 7C 130
CV36: Long C 1C 134
CV37: A'ton, Tidd 3K 115
MAJOR'S GREEN 1C 143
Makepeace Av. CV34: Warw 6H 97
Makins Fishery 1K 43, 2G 33
Malam Cl. CV4: Tile H 6E 56
Maldale B77: Wiln 1A 10
Maldens, The CV36: Ship S 5H 131
Malham Cl. CV11: Nun 2C 32
Malham Rd. B77: Wiln 2A 10
CV34: Warw 6H 97
Malin Ct. B49: Alc 4B 112
Malins, The CV34: Warw 2K 101
Mallard Av. CV10: Nun 6H 21
Mallard Cl. CV37: B'ton 2B 114
CV47: Sou 7G 107
Mallard Ct. CV6: Cov 7D 50
(off Gressingham Gro.)
Mallard Rd. B80: Stud 3E 92
Mallerin Cft. CV10: Nun 6G 21
Malletts Cl. CV35: Mid T 7C 130
Mallory Dr. CV34: Warw 1F 101
Mallory Rd. CV33: Bis T 5A 108
CV33: L Hth 2K 119
Mallory Way CV6: Lford 1E 50
Mallow Cft. CV12: Bed 3E 40
Mallow Way CV23: Brow 7J 65
Malmesbury Rd. CV6: Cov 4A 50
Malt Ho. Cl. B50: Broom 3F 123
Malthouse Cl. CV10: Ansl 7A 20
CV47: N'end 2D 120
Malthouse Ct. CV34: Warw 1F 101
Malthouse La. CV8: Ken 2C 78
CV36: Long C 2C 134
CV47: N'end 2D 120
Malthouse Row
B37: Mars G 5A 34
Maltings, The B80: Stud 3C 92
CV11: Nun 6F 23
CV32: Lea S 5D 98
(not continuous)
CV37: S Avon 5F 137 (5F 115)
Maltings Ct. CV37: S Avon 1E 136
Malt Mill Cl. CV23: Kils 7J 89
Malt Mill Grn. CV23: Kils 7J 89
(off Main Rd.)
Malt Mill La. B49: Alc 5C 112
Malt Shovel Ct. CV47: Bis I 6B 110
(off Fisher Rd.)
Malvern Av. CV10: Nun 1B 30
CV22: Rugby 7K 75
Malvern Rd. CV5: Cov 3K 57
MANCETTER 5F 17 (2A 140)
Mancetter Rd. CV9: Man 4E 16
(not continuous)
CV10: Harts, Nun 7H 17, 1H 21
Mandale Cl. CV47: Bis I 7B 110
Mander Gro. CV34: Warw 4D 100
Manderley Cl. CV5: East G 2A 56
Manders Cft. CV47: Sou 5G 107
Mandrake Cl. CV6: Cov 2D 50
MANEY 2C 139
Manfield Av. CV2: Walsg S 7C 52
Manhattan Way CV4: Tile H 4A 56
Manning Wlk. CV21: Rugby 5G 75
(within Clock Towers Shop. Cen.)
Mann Pl. CV31: W'nsh 6E 102
Mann's Cl. CV8: Rytn D 1D 82
Manor Barns CV36: Ilm 6C 126
Manor Cl. CV9: Bad E 1E 14
Manor Ct. B49: Gt Alne 3F 113
CV8: Ken 3E 78
CV31: Lea S 1D 102
CV37: Ett 2B 126
CV47: Fen C 3G 121
Manor Ct. Av. CV11: Nun 6C 22
Manor Ct. Rd. CV11: Nun 7B 22
Manor Dr. B46: Cole 5D 24
CV23: Stret D 3H 83
CV37: Wilm 6K 113
Manor Est. CV8: Wols 5H 71
Mnr. Farm Cl. CV23: Barby 7F 89
Mnr. Farm Cotts.
CV37: Ludd 1E 124
Mnr. Farm Ct. CV35: Gay 6G 119
Mnr. Farm Rd. CV36: Tred 6J 127
Manor Grn. CV37: S Avon 5H 115
Manor Hall M. CV3: W'hall 2K 69
Manor Ho. CV31: Lea S 1D 102
Manor Ho. Cl. CV21: N'bld A 1D 74
Manor Ho. Dr.
CV1: Cov 6G 135 (5C 58)
Manor Ho. La. B46: Wat O 1B 24
Manor Ho. Way B46: Wat O 1B 24
Manor La. CV23: Clift D 2C 76
CV35: Kine 6D 120
CV35: Lox 6D 116
CV36: Ship S 4H 131
CV37: Ett 2B 126
Manor M. B80: Stud 3D 92
Manor Orchard CV33: Har 6G 109
Manor Pk. Rd. CV11: Nun 6B 22
Manor Rd. B80: Stud 3D 92
CV1: Cov 6H 135 (6C 58)
CV8: Ken 3D 78
CV9: Man 4D 16
CV21: Rugby 4H 75
CV23: Kils 6J 89
CV32: Lill 4F 99
CV33: Har 6H 109
CV35: Clav 1E 94
CV37: S Avon 5H 115
CV47: Bis I 6B 110
CV47: S'ton 6C 106
Manor Rd. Ind. Est. CV9: Man 4D 16
Manor Ter. CV1: Cov 5H 135 (5C 58)
Manor Vw. CV8: Wols 5H 71
Manor Yd. CV1: Cov 5H 135 (5C 58)
Mansard Ct. B46: Cole 5G 25
Manse Cl. CV7: Exh 4G 41
Manse Gdns. B80: Stud 3D 92
Mansell St.
CV37: S Avon 2D 136 (4E 114)
Mansel St. CV6: Cov 6E 50
Mansfield Ho. B37: Chel W 2C 34
Mansion Ho., The CV35: Lit K 6C 120
Mansions Cl. CV47: Bis I 6B 110
Mansley Bus. Cen., The
CV37: S Avon 3C 114
Manston Dr. CV35: Welle 4G 117
Mantilla Dr. CV3: Cov 3A 68
Mantua CV37: S Avon 1H 137
Manufacturing Technology Cen.
CV7: Ansty 6H 53
Maple Av. CV7: Exh 4H 41
Maplebeck Cl. CV5: Cov 4A 58
Maple Dr. B78: K'bry 4E 12
Maple Gdns. CV22: Rugby 7F 75
Maple Gro. B37: K'hrst 6A 24
CV21: Rugby 4G 75
CV34: Warw 6J 97
CV37: S Avon 2E 114
Maple Leaf Dr.
B37: Mars G 5B 34
CV9: Wood E 2B 14
Maple Rd. CV10: Nun 6K 21
CV31: Lea S 2D 102
Maples, The CV12: Bed 3E 40
Mapleton Rd. CV6: Cov 6K 49
Maple Wlk. B37: Chel W 3B 34
(within Chelmsley Wood Shop. Cen.)
CV6: Lford 1F 51
Maple Way CV35: Welle 5H 117
Maplin Cl. CV4: Canly 7G 57
Mapperley Cl.
CV2: Walsg S 6C 52
MAPPLEBOROUGH GREEN 2B 142
Marble All. B80: Stud 3D 92
Marbled Cl. CV31: Lea S 4G 103
March Ct. CV22: Rugby 7G 75
Marchfont Cl. CV11: Nun 2C 32
March Way CV3: Bin 1K 69
Marconi Cl. CV3: Cov 5J 59
Marconi Way B46: Cole 1F 25
Marcroft Pl. CV31: Lea S 2H 103
Mardol Cl. CV2: Cov 7K 51
MAREFIELD 1D 141
Margaret Av. CV12: Bed 2G 41
Margaret Cl. CV33: Har 6H 109
Margaret Ct. CV37: Tidd 3K 115
Margaret Rd. CV9: Ath 4D 16
Margeson Cl. CV2: Cov 5A 60
Margetts Cl. CV8: Ken 5D 78
Marie Brock Cl. CV4: Tile H 6F 57
Marie Cl. CV9: Man 4F 17
Marigold Rd. CV37: S Avon 7G 115
Marigold Wlk. CV10: Nun 4G 31
Marina Cl. CV4: Tile H 1C 66
Marion Rd. CV6: Cov 7D 50
Marish, The CV34: Warw 5D 100
Marjorie Way CV3: Cov 6J 59
Mark Antony Dr. CV34: H'cte 4B 102
MARKET BOSWORTH 1B 140
Market Cl. B95: Hen A 2H 93
Market Cnr. CV8: Bag 6F 69
CV31: Lea S 2D 102
Market Cross
CV37: S Avon 4G 137
MARKET END 3D 40 (3A 140)
Market End Cl. CV12: Bed 3D 40
Market Hall Mus. 2G 101
MARKET HARBOROUGH 3D 141
Market Harborough Rd.
CV23: Clift D, Newt 1C 76
Market Hill CV47: Sou 5H 107
Market Mall CV21: Rugby 5G 75
(within Clock Towers Shop. Cen.)
Market Pl. B49: Alc 5B 112
CV9: Ath 3C 16
(off Market St.)
CV11: Nun 7D 22
CV21: Rugby 5G 75
CV34: Warw 2G 101
CV36: Ship S 4H 131
CV47: Sou 5H 107
Market Sq. CV35: Kine 5D 120
Market St. B78: Pole 1D 10
CV9: Ath 3C 16
CV21: Rugby 4H 75
CV34: Warw 2F 101
Market Way B95: Hen A 2H 93
CV1: Cov 4G 135 (5C 58)
MARKFIELD 1B 140
Markham Dr. CV31: W'nsh 5F 103
Marks M. CV34: Warw 2G 101
Marlborough Dr. CV31: Lea S 2H 103
Marlborough M. B80: Stud 3D 92
Marlborough Rd. CV2: Cov 5G 59
CV11: Nun 7C 22
CV22: Bil 7E 74
MARLCLIFF 7G 123 (3B 142)
Marlcroft CV3: W'hall 2A 70
Marleigh Rd. B50: Bidf A 5G 123
Marlene Cft. B37: Chel W 4C 34
Marler Rd. CV4: Tile H 1D 66
Marloes Wlk. CV31: Lea S 2G 103
Marlow Cl. CV5: Cov 3F 57
Marlowe Cl. CV10: Gall C 6E 20
Marlowe Rd. CV37: S Avon 7H 115
Marlow Grn. CV47: Bis I 6B 110
Marlow Rd. CV9: Hur 6K 13
Marlston Wlk. CV5: Cov 3F 57
Marlwood Cl. CV6: Lford 2F 51
Marne Cl. CV34: Warw 7J 97
Marner Cres. CV6: Cov 1B 58
Marner Rd. CV10: Nun 3H 31
CV12: Bed 2G 41
Marnhull Cl. CV2: Walsg S 3B 60
Marram Ct. CV37: S Avon 3D 114
Marrick B77: Wiln 2A 10
Marriner's La. CV5: Cov 2F 57
Marriott Rd. CV6: Cov 3A 58
CV12: Bed 3D 40
Marsdale Dr. CV10: Nun 1E 30
Marsett B77: Wiln 2A 10
Marshall Av. CV36: Ship S 5H 131
Marshall Rd. CV7: Exh 5F 41
Marsham Cl. CV34: Warw 7K 97
Marshbrook Cl. CV2: Ald G 4K 51
Marshdale Av. CV6: Cov 3E 50
Marshfield Dr. CV4: Canly 6H 67
Marsh Ho. CV2: Walsg S 7C 52
Marsh La. B46: Wat O 1B 24
B76: Curd 6C 18
B92: H Ard 7G 45
(not continuous)
CV37: S Avon 2D 114
Marsh Rd. CV37: Wilm 5G 113
MARSTON
B76 ....1H 19 (2D 139)
CV8 ....3A 72
Marston Av. CV33: L Hth 2K 119
Marston Cl. CV32: Lill 5F 99
Marston Cft. B37: Mars G 6A 34
CV47: Sou 6K 107
MARSTON DOLES 3B 144
Marston Dr. B37: K'hrst 7A 24
Marston Fld. CV33: L Hth 2K 119
MARSTON GREEN 5A 34 (3C 139)
Marston Hall Ind. Est.
CV12: Bulk 7B 32
Marston Hill CV47: P Mars 5H 111
MARSTON JABBETT 7B 32 (3A 140)
Marston Lakes Golf Course, The ...2G 19
Marston La. B76: Curd 2E 18
CV11: Nun 2A 32
CV12: Bed, Bulk 1H 41
MARSTON ST LAWRENCE 1D 147
MARSTON TRUSSELL 3D 141
Marten Cl. CV35: H Mag 1C 100
Martin Cl. CV5: East G 3C 56
CV37: S Avon 2F 115
Martindale Rd. CV7: Exh 5J 41
MARTIN HUSSINGTREE 2A 142
Martinique Sq. CV34: Warw 2F 101
Martin La. CV22: Bil 2D 86
Martins Dr. CV9: Ath 1C 16
Martins Rd. CV12: Bed 4E 40
Martley Cl. CV3: Bin 5C 60
MARTON 2D 104 (2B 144)
Marton Ct. CV22: Dunc 2B 86
Marton Farm Cl. CV23: Mart 2D 104
Marton Rd. CV23: Bird 5A 104
CV47: Long I 1C 106
Martyrs Cl., The CV3: Cov 7D 58
Marwood Cl. CV11: Nun 5A 32
Mary Arden's Farm 5J 113
Mary Herbert St. CV3: Cov 1D 68
Mary Slessor St. CV3: W'hall 2J 69
Marystow Cl. CV5: Alle 6F 49
Masefield Av. CV34: Warw 4E 100
Masefield Rd. CV37: S Avon 6G 115
Mason Av. CV32: Lill 4G 99
Mason Cl. B50: Bidf A 5H 123
Mason Rd. CV6: Cov 5F 51
Masons Cl. CV37: Wilm 5J 113
Masons Ct. CV37: S Avon 5D 136
Masons Rd. CV37: S Avon 3C 114
Masons Rd. Ind. Est.
CV37: S Avon 3C 114
Masons Way CV37: S Avon 3C 114
Masser Rd. CV6: Cov 2C 50
Massey Cl. CV4: Tile H 4A 56
Masters Rd. CV31: W'nsh 3E 102
Master's Yd. CV23: Bird 5A 104
Mathecroft CV31: Lea S 3G 103
Matilda M. CV3: Cov 5J 59
Matlock Cl. CV21: Brow 1J 75
Matlock Rd. CV1: Cov 1D 58
Matterson Rd. CV6: Cov 2A 58
Matthews Cl. CV37: S Avon 3F 115
Maud Rd. B46: Wat O 1D 24
Maudslay Rd. CV5: Cov 5J 57
MAUGERSBURY 3A 146
Maureen Cl. CV4: Tile H 6A 56
Maurice Mead Ct. CV31: Lea S 2E 102
Mavor Dr. CV12: Bed 4D 40
Mawnan Cl. CV7: Exh 5H 41
Max Rd. CV6: Cov 2K 57
MAXSTOKE 3D 36 (3D 139)
Maxstoke Castle 5A 26
Maxstoke Cl. CV7: Mer 5D 46
Maxstoke Ct. B46: Cole 1G 35

Maxstoke Gdns.—Mitchell Av.

Maxstoke Gdns. CV31: Lea S 2D 102
Maxstoke La. B46: Cole 6G 25
CV7: Mer 5D 36
(not continuous)
Maxstoke Pk. Golf Course 6B 26
Maybird Cen., The
CV37: S Avon 3E 114
Maybrook Ind. Est.
CV37: S Avon 3E 114
Maybrook Rd. CV37: S Avon 3E 114
Maycock Rd. CV6: Cov 7D 50
Mayfair *B37: K'hrst* *7A 24*
(off Haselour Rd.)
Mayfair Dr. CV10: Gall C 7E 20
Mayfield B77: Wiln 2A 10
CV12: Bed 2H 41
Mayfield Av. CV37: S Avon 3F 115
Mayfield Cl. CV12: Bed 2H 41
CV31: Lea S 2G 103
Mayfield Ct. CV37: S Avon 4F 115
Mayfield Dr. B95: Hen A 1G 93
CV8: Ken 5G 79
Mayfield Rd. CV5: Cov 7A 58
CV11: Nun 2A 32
CV47: Sou 4H 107
Mayflower Dr. CV2: Cov 5K 59
May La. CV22: Bil 7D 74
Maynard Av. CV12: Bed 5D 40
CV34: Warw 1J 101
Mayne Cl. CV35: H Mag 2B 100
Mayo Dr. CV8: Ken 5E 78
Mayo Rd. CV36: Ship S 3H 131
Mayor's Cft. CV4: Canly 1F 67
Maypole La. CV9: Gren 2F 15
Maypole Rd. B79: Wart 5H 9
May St. CV6: Cov 6E 50
Mayswood Rd.
B95: Hen A, Woot W 3F 93
Maytree Cl. B37: F'bri 3A 34
Maywell Dr. B92: Sol 6A 44
Mead, The B78: K'bry 7E 12
Meadfoot Rd. CV3: W'hall 2K 69
Mead Gallery *4F 67*
(within Warwick Arts Cen.)
Meadowbank Dr. B46: Cole 3D 24
Meadow Cl. B78: K'bry 6E 12
CV7: Ansty 3F 53
CV23: Stret D 3J 83
CV32: Lill 3G 99
CV37: S Avon 4C 114
LE10: Wlvy 2H 33
Meadow Community Sports Cen.
..... 4G 79
Meadow Ct. CV11: Nun 7C 22
Meadow Cft. CV7: Old A 3C 28
Meadowcroft Cl. CV4: Tile H 7D 56
Meadow Crofts CV47: Bis I 5C 110
Meadow Dr. B92: H Ard 7H 45
Meadow Furlong CV23: Brow 6K 65
Meadow Gdns. CV9: Bad E 3F 15
Meadow Ho. CV1: Cov 4B 58
Meadow La. B94: Lapw 3J 91
Meadow Lea CV37: S Avon 4C 114
Meadow Pastures CV22: Caw 7B 74
Meadow Ri. B95: Ullen 6B 90
Meadow Rd. B49: Alc 3B 112
B95: Hen A 2H 93
CV6: Cov 2B 50
CV8: Wols 4J 71
CV9: Hur 6K 13
CV10: Harts 3F 21
CV21: N'bld A 2D 74
CV34: Warw 1J 101
CV47: Sou 4H 107
Meadows, The B50: Bidf A 5F 123
CV35: Leek W 1J 97
Meadowside CV11: Nun 3D 32
Meadow St. CV1: Cov 5B 58
CV9: Ath 4C 16
CV11: Nun 6C 22
Meadowsweet CV23: Brow 7J 65
Meadow Sweet Rd.
CV37: S Avon 2D 114
Meadow Vw. CV9: Wood E 2K 13
Meadow Vw. Cl. B49: Alc 4C 112
Meadow Vw. Ct. B80: Stud 4D 92
Meadow Way CV23: Harb M 4B 64
CV47: Fen C 2H 121
Meadway *CV2: Cov* *1H 59*
(off Beckett Rd.)
Meadway Nth. CV2: Cov 1H 59
Meakins Cl. CV34: Warw 4D 100
MEASHAM 1A 140
Medhurst Cl. CV22: Dunc 6C 86
Medina Rd. CV6: Cov 5E 50
Medland Av. CV3: Finh 3K 67
Medley Gro. CV31: W'nsh 5D 102
Medway Cft. B36: Cas B 5A 24
MEER END 1D 143
Meer St. CV37: S Avon ... 3E 136 (4F 115)
Meeting La. B49: Alc 4C 112
Melbourne Cl. CV11: Nun 4A 32
Melbourne Ct. CV12: Bed 3F 41
Melbourne Rd. CV5: Cov 5A 58
Meldrum Ct. CV47: Temp H 2A 120
Meldrum Rd. CV10: Nun 1D 30
Melford Ct. CV22: Bil 6E 74
Melfort Cl. CV3: Bin 5B 60
CV10: Nun 6H 21
Mellish Ct. CV22: Bil 7E 74
Mellish Rd. CV22: Bil 7E 74
Mellor Rd. CV21: Hillm 1D 88
Mellowdew Rd. CV2: Cov 3J 59
Mellowship Rd. CV5: East G 2A 56
Mellwaters B77: Wiln 2A 10
Melmerby B77: Wiln 2A 10
Melody Cl. CV2: Cov 5J 51
Melrose Av. CV12: Bed 5D 40
Melton Ct. CV22: Caw 1K 85
Melton Rd. CV32: Lill 3E 98
Melville Cl. CV7: Exh 5G 41
CV22: Bil 7E 74
Melville Rd. CV1: Cov 4A 58
Memorial Park (Park & Ride)
Coventry 1A 68
Memorial Rd. CV47: Fen C 3G 121
Menai Wlk. B37: F'bri 1B 34
Mendip Dr. CV10: Nun 1B 30
Mendip Way B77: Wiln 1A 10
Meon Cl. CV37: Up Qui 7H 125
MEON HILL 7K 125
MEON VALE 6F 125
Mercer Av. B46: Wat O 1A 24
CV2: Cov 2G 59
Mercer Ct. CV22: Hillm 1B 88
Mercers Mdw. CV7: Ker E 7A 40
Mercia Av. CV8: Ken 5C 78
Mercia Bus. Village
CV4: Westw H 2D 66
Mercia Ho.
CV1: Cov 3G 135 (4C 58)
Mercia Way CV34: Warw 1K 101
Mercot Cl. B98: Redd 1A 92
Mercury Dr. CV37: S Avon 7J 115
Meredith Rd. CV2: Cov 4K 59
MERE GREEN
B75 ..... 2C 139
WR9 ..... 2A 142
Merestone Cl. CV47: Sou 3H 107
Merevale Av. CV11: Nun 7B 22
Merevale Ct. CV11: Nun 7B 22
Merevale La. CV9: Ath 4H 15
Merevale Rd. CV9: Ath 2B 16
Merevale Vw. CV9: Ath 4B 16
MERIDEN 5E 46 (3D 139)
Meriden Bus. Pk. CV5: Alle 6K 47
Meriden Dr. B37: K'hrst 6A 24
Meriden Pk. Homes CV7: Mer 6E 46
Meriden Rd. B92: H Ard 7H 45
CV7: Fill 6J 37
CV7: Mer 7H 45
Meriden St. CV1: Cov 4B 58
Meridian Point CV1: Cov 5H 135
Merlin Av. CV10: Nun 5G 21
Merlin Cl. CV1: Cov 6J 135 (6D 58)
CV23: Brow 7J 65
Merlin Way CV34: H'cte 5B 102
Merrivale Rd. CV5: Cov 4J 57
Merryfields Way CV2: Walsg S 5B 52
MERRY LEES 1B 140
Mersey Rd. CV12: Bulk 3C 42
Merstone Cl. B37: Mars G 5C 34
Merton Ho. B37: F'bri 3A 34
Merttens Dr. CV22: Rugby 6F 75
Merynton Av. CV4: Canly 2J 67
Meschede Way
CV1: Cov 4J 135 (5D 58)
Meschines St. CV3: Cov 2D 68
Meto Lakha Cl. CV6: Cov 6F 51
Meulan La. CV10: Nun 3D 22
Mews, The B95: Woot W 5H 93
CV8: Ken 6C 78
CV9: Ath 3D 16
CV12: Bed 3H 41
CV21: Hillm 7C 76
Mews Rd. CV32: Lea S 7B 98
Mica Cl. CV21: Rugby 5J 75
Michaelmas Rd.
CV3: Cov 7G 135 (6C 58)
Michell Cl. CV3: Cov 7H 59
Mickle Mdw. B46: Wat O 1B 24
MICKLETON 1A 146
Mickleton Dr. CV35: Hatt 5A 96
Mickleton Rd. CV5: Cov 6A 58
CV36: Admi, Ilm 5A 126
Middelburg Cl. CV11: Nun 3C 32
MIDDLE ASTON 3D 147
MIDDLE BARTON 3D 147
Middle Bickenhill La. B92: Bick 1G 45
Middleborough Rd.
CV1: Cov 2F 135 (4B 58)
Middlecotes CV4: Tile H 6F 57
Middlefield Dr. CV3: Bin 6C 60
Middlefield La. CV37: N'bld S 1F 127
Middle La. B46: Neth W 5K 19
OX17: Shotte 6H 129
MIDDLE LITTLETON 3B 142
Middle Lock La. CV35: Hatt 5A 96
Middlemarch Bus. Pk.
CV3: W'hall 4J 69
(not continuous)
Middlemarch Rd. CV6: Cov 1B 58
CV10: Nun 3H 31
Middlemore Cl. B80: Stud 4C 92
Middle Ride CV3: W'hall 2K 69
Middle Rd. CV33: Har 5F 109
Middlesex Rd. CV3: Cov 6G 59
Middlesmoor B77: Wiln 2A 10
MIDDLE STOKE 4H 59
Middle St. CV23: Kils 6J 89
CV36: Ilm 6C 126
CV37: Arms 4F 127
MIDDLETON 2C 139
MIDDLETON CHENEY 1D 147
Middleton Cl. CV35: Up Tys 7C 130
Middleton Hall 2A 12
MIDDLETON STONEY 3D 147
MIDDLETOWN 6C 92
Middletown B80: Stud 6C 92
CV35: More M 4C 118
Middletown La. B80: Stud 7B 92
B96: Sam 7B 92
MIDDLE TYSOE 6C 130 (1C 147)
Midland Air Mus. 5H 69
Midland Rd. CV6: Cov 2E 58
CV11: Nun 6B 22
Midlands Hydroplane Club, The 7C 12
Midland Trad. Est.
CV21: Rugby 2G 75
Mid-Warwickshire Yacht Club 7F 99
Milby Ct. CV11: Nun 2J 31
Milby Dr. CV11: Nun 3G 23
Milby Hall CV10: Nun 2D 22
MILCOMBE 2D 147
Milcote Rd. CV37: Cliff C, Milc 5A 124
CV37: Welf A, W Avon 4B 124
Mildmay Cl. CV37: S Avon 7D 114
Mile End B94: Tan A 3D 90
Mile La. CV1: Cov 6J 135 (6D 58)
CV3: Cov 6J 135 (6D 58)
Miles Mdw. CV6: Cov 5H 51
CV37: N'bld S 1G 127
Milestone Dr. CV22: Rugby 1F 87
Milestone Ho. *CV1: Cov* *5B 58*
(off Windsor St.)
Milestone Rd. CV37: S Avon 7J 115
Mile Tree La. CV2: Ald G 6B 42
Milford Cl. CV5: Alle 1F 57
Milford St. CV10: Nun 2H 31
Milking La. B95: Hen A 2G 93
Mill, The B78: K'bry 7E 12
Millais Cl. CV12: Bed 1G 41
Mill Bank B46: Over W 1F 27
Millbank CV34: Warw 6J 97
Millbank M. CV8: Ken 3F 79
Millbeck CV21: Brow 1K 75
Millburn Hill Rd. CV4: Canly 3F 67
Mill Cl. B50: Broom 3E 122
CV2: Ald G 3H 51
CV8: Wols 5H 71
CV11: Nun 3B 32
CV35: N Lin 2F 95
CV47: Sou 4G 107
Mill Cotts. CV21: Rugby 2K 75
Mill Ct. CV36: Ship S 5H 131
Mill Cres. B78: K'bry 6E 12
CV35: Kine 5D 120
CV47: Sou 4G 107
MILL END 3F 79
Mill End CV8: Ken 3E 78
Millennium Way CV8: Wols 5H 71
Millers Bank B50: Broom 3E 122
Millers Cl. CV22: Dunc 5A 86
CV37: Welf A 3A 124
Millers Dale Cl. CV21: Brow 1J 75
Miller's La. CV23: M Kirby 3G 55
Millers Rd. CV34: Warw 7F 97
Millers Way OX15: Lwr Bra 3G 133
Millers Wharf B78: Pole 1C 10
Mill Farm Cl. CV22: Dunc 6C 86
Mill Farm Pk. CV12: Bulk 6D 32
Millfield CV31: Lea S 7E 98
Mill Fld. Cvn. Site CV37: Welf A 3A 124
Millfield Cl. CV37: Lwr Q 5H 125
Millfields Av. CV21: Hillm 1B 88
Mill Furlong CV23: Brow 6K 65
Mill Gdns. 7E 98
Mill Gdns. CV10: Nun 2H 31
Mill Hill CV8: Bag 4D 68
Millholme Cl. CV47: Sou 5J 107
Mill Ho. Cl. CV32: Lea S 7A 98
Mill Ho. Ct. CV6: Cov 7F 51
Mill Ho. Dr. CV32: Lea S 7A 98
Mill Ho. Ter. CV32: Lea S 7A 98
Milligan Ct. *CV34: H'cte* *5B 102*
(off Merlin Way)
Mill Ind. Pk., The B49: King C 1A 112
Milliners Ct. CV9: Ath 3C 16
MILLISON'S WOOD 6K 47
Mill La. B49: Aston C 4J 113
B49: Gt Alne 3G 113
B49: Ove G 6B 112
B50: Broom 3E 122
B94: Lapw 3H 91
B95: Aston C 4J 113
CV3: Bin 5B 60
CV7: Fill 7A 28
CV9: Man 5F 17
CV9: With 3F 17
CV11: Burt H 4H 33
CV12: Bulk 2C 42
CV23: Clift D 2A 76
CV32: Cubb 2K 99
CV33: Har 5H 109
CV35: Barf 2B 108
CV35: Kine 5D 120
CV35: Row 6H 91
CV36: Half 2J 127
CV36: Tred 6J 127
CV37: A'ton 1B 116
CV37: N'bld S 2H 127
CV37: S Avon 6F 115
CV37: Welf A 2A 124
CV47: Fen C 3G 121
LE10: Wlvy 1K 33
Mill M. B94: Lapw 3H 91
Mill Pk. CV6: Lford 2E 50
Mill Pleck B80: Stud 4D 92
Mill Pond Mdws. CV31: Lea S 3H 103
Mill Race La. CV6: Cov 3G 51
Mill Race Vw. CV9: Ath 1C 16
Mill Rd. CV21: Rugby 3J 75
CV31: Lea S 7E 98
CV47: Nap 2H 111
CV47: Sou 4G 107
Mill Row LE10: Wlvy 1K 33
Mill St. CV1: Cov 1F 135 (4B 58)
CV11: Nun 7D 22
CV12: Bed 2H 41
CV31: Lea S 1E 102
CV33: Har 5G 109
CV34: Warw 2H 101
CV35: Kine 5D 120
CV36: Ship S 5H 131
Mill Ter. CV12: Bed 7H 31
Mill Wlk. CV11: Nun 7D 22
Millway Dr. CV33: Bis T 4C 108
Millway Lodge *B49: Gt Alne* *2G 113*
(off Woodland Dr.)
Mill Yd. CV22: Dunc 6C 86
Mill Yd., The *CV2: Ald G* *3H 51*
(off Egret Wlk.)
Milner Cl. CV12: Bulk 3F 43
Milner Cres. CV2: Walsg S 5A 52
Milner Dr. B79: Shut 2B 8
Milrose Way CV4: Tile H 7D 56
MILTHORPE 3C 145
MILTON 2D 147
Milton Av. CV34: Warw 3E 100
Milton Cl. CV12: Bed 4K 41
MILTON MALSOR 3D 145
Milton Rd. CV37: S Avon 7H 115
Milton St. CV2: Cov 2G 59
MILTON-UNDER-WYCHWOOD 3B 146
MILVERTON 6A 98 (2A 144)
Milverton Ct. CV32: Lea S 7C 98
Milverton Cres. CV32: Lea S 6C 98
Milverton Cres. W. CV32: Lea S 6C 98
Milverton Hill CV32: Lea S 7C 98
Milverton Lodge *CV32: Lea S* *6C 98*
(off Milverton Cres. W.)
Milverton Rd. CV2: Cov 4J 51
Milverton Ter. CV32: Lea S 7C 98
Mimosa Cl. CV10: Nun 4G 31
Miners La. CV7: Ker E 6J 39
Miners Wlk. B78: Pole 1C 10
CV9: Wood E 2B 14
Minerva M. B49: Alc 4B 112
Minerva Mill Innovation Cen.
B49: Alc 4A 112
Minerva Mill Technology Cen.
B49: Alc *4B 112*
(off Station Rd.)
Minions Cl. CV9: Ath 3C 16
Minories, The
CV37: S Avon 3E 136 (4E 114)
Minster Cl. CV35: H Mag 2B 100
Minster Rd. CV1: Cov 4B 58
Minton Rd. CV2: Walsg S 6B 52
MINWORTH 2C 139
Minworth Rd. B46: Wat O 1A 24
Mira Dr. CV10: Cald 1D 22
Miranda Cl. CV3: W'hall 1K 69
Miranda Dr. CV34: H'cte 6C 102
Missing Oak Cl. CV12: Bed 2E 40
MISTERTON 3C 141
Mistyrose Cl. CV5: Alle 6F 49
Mitchell Av. CV4: Canly 1E 66

A-Z Warwickshire Atlas 175

N

Old Ho. La.—Park Lane

Old Ho. La. CV7: Cor ... 6E 38
Old Inn Ct. CV23: Lilb ... 1J 77
Old Kingsbury Rd. B76: Mars ... 1G 19
Old Leicester Rd. CV21: Rugby ... 1G 75
(not continuous)
Old Library, The CV31: Lea S ... 1D 102
Old Meeting Yd. CV12: Bed ... 2H 41
Old Mill Av. CV4: Canly ... 3H 67
Old Mill Ct. B46: Cole ... 5F 25
Old Mill Rd. B46: Cole ... 5F 25
OLD MILVERTON ... 4A 98
Old Milverton La. CV32: B'dwn ... 4A 98
Old Milverton Rd.
CV32: Lea S, Old M ... 4A 98
Old Orchard, The CV23: Bird ... 5A 104
CV35: Welle ... 4H 117
Old Penns La. *B46: Cole* ... *5F 25*
(off High St.)
Old Pound CV34: Warw ... 1G 101
Old Pound Cotts. CV36: Half ... 2K 127
Old Rectory Cl. CV23: C'over ... 1H 65
Old Rectory Gdn. B49: Alc ... 4B 112
Old Red Lion Ct.
CV37: S Avon ... 4H 137 (5F 115)
Old Rd. CV7: Mer ... 5G 47
CV36: Long C ... 4C 134
CV36: Ship S ... 5H 131
CV47: Bis I ... 6C 110
CV47: Sou ... 6H 107
OX15: Ratl ... 6C 128
Old School Ct. CV9: Gren ... 2G 15
CV10: Nun ... 1C 30
Old School La. CV35: H Hill ... 4A 100
CV35: Light ... 2H 119
CV37: Wilm ... 6J 113
Old School Mead B50: Bidf A ... 6F 123
Old School M. CV32: Lill ... 4F 99
Old Snitterfield Rd.
CV37: Bear ... 6D 94
Old Sq. CV34: Warw ... 2G 101
Old Sq., The CV37: Shot ... 5C 114
Old Station Rd. B92: H Ard ... 4F 45
Old Stone Yd. CV32: Lea S ... 6C 98
OLD TOWN ... 7D 136 (5E 114)
Old Town
CV37: S Avon ... 7E 136 (5E 114)
Old Town M. CV37: S Avon ... 6E 114
Old Town Sq. CV37: S Avon ... 6E 114
Old Tramway Wlk.
CV37: S Avon ... 5E 124
(Shipston Rd.)
CV37: S Avon ... 5J 137 (5G 115)
(Swan Nest La., not continuous)
Old Tree Cotts. *CV35: Up Tys* ... *7C 130*
(off Main St.)
Old Tree La. CV35: Up Tys ... 7C 130
Old Vicarage Dr. CV47: Long I ... 2C 106
Old Vicarage Gdns. B80: Stud ... 3D 92
Old Warwick Rd. B94: Lapw ... 3F 91
CV31: Lea S ... 1C 102
CV35: Row ... 3F 91, 4G 91
CV37: Ett ... 1B 126
Old Watling St. *CV9: Ath* ... *3B 16*
(off Long St.)
Old Winnings Rd. CV7: Ker E ... 7K 39
OLD WOODSTOCK ... 3D 147
Old Yd., The CV2: Walsg S ... 7B 52
Olive Av. CV2: Cov ... 2K 59
Oliver's Lock CV37: S Avon ... 2H 137
Oliver St. CV6: Cov ... 1F 59
CV21: Rugby ... 5F 75
Olivier Way CV2: Walsg S ... 6D 52
OLTON ... 3C 139
Olton Av. CV5: East G ... 3D 56
Olton Cl. CV11: Burt H ... 4J 33
Olton Pl. CV11: Nun ... 7A 22
Olympus Av. CV34: Warw ... 3B 102
Olympus Cl. CV5: Milli W ... 6K 47
Olympus Ct. CV34: Warw ... 3B 102
Omar Rd. CV2: Cov ... 5K 59
OMBERSLEY ... 2A 142
Ombersley Cl. B98: Redd ... 1A 92
Omega Pl. CV21: Rugby ... 4H 75
One O'Clock Ride CV3: Bin W ... 1G 71
Onley La. CV22: Rugby ... 3J 87
CV23: Barby ... 7D 88
Onley Ter. CV4: Canly ... 1G 67
Onslow Cft. CV32: Lea S ... 5D 98
Openfield Cft. B46: Wat O ... 2C 24
Ophelia Dr. CV34: H'cte ... 5C 102
CV37: S Avon ... 3D 114
Oratory Dr. CV3: W'hall ... 2J 69
Orchard, The B37: Mars G ... 5A 34
CV9: Bax ... 4F 15
(not continuous)
CV23: Mart ... 2D 104
CV34: Warw ... 3H 101
CV36: Whatc ... 3A 130
CV37: Lwr Q ... 5H 125
Orchard Blythe B46: Cole ... 6G 25
Orchard Bus. Pk.
CV21: Rugby ... 4G 75
Orchard Cl. B46: Cole ... 5F 25
B50: Bidf A ... 6G 123
B76: Curd ... 5B 18
B78: Pole ... 6D 8
CV9: Aus ... 6G 7
CV9: Hur ... 7K 13
CV9: With ... 3G 17
CV10: Harts ... 4G 21
CV35: Mid T ... 6C 130
CV36: Ship S ... 5H 131
CV37: Welf A ... 3B 124
CV47: Bis I ... 6C 110
LE10: Wlvy ... 2H 33
OX15: Lwr Bra ... 3H 133
Orchard Cotts. CV9: Ath ... 4D 16
Orchard Ct. CV3: Bin ... 6C 60
CV9: Ath ... 4C 16
CV32: Lea S ... 5D 98
CV37: Lwr Q ... 6H 125
Orchard Cres. CV3: Cov ... 7G 135 (7C 58)
Orchard Dr. B49: Alc ... 6B 112
CV5: East G ... 3A 56
Orchard Gro. CV47: S'ton ... 6C 106
Orchard La. CV8: Ken ... 6G 79
Orchard Pl. CV37: Cliff C ... 5B 124
Orchard Ri. B95: Hen A ... 1G 93
CV9: Gren ... 1F 15
Orchards, The CV36: Cher ... 6G 133
CV37: Wilm ... 5K 113
Orchard St. CV11: Nun ... 7E 22
CV12: Bed ... 7H 31
Orchard Way B80: Stud ... 5D 92
CV8: Bubb ... 4J 81
CV10: Nun ... 5H 21
CV22: Bil ... 1D 86
CV23: Stret D ... 3H 83
CV36: Ship S ... *5H 131*
(off Old Rd.)
CV37: S Avon ... 7A 136 (5D 114)
CV47: Long I ... 2B 106
CV47: Sou ... 4H 107
Orchid Cl. CV12: Bed ... 3E 40
Orchid Way CV23: Brow ... 7K 65
Ordnance Rd. CV6: Cov ... 2E 58
Orford Cl. CV35: Welle ... 3J 117
Orford Ri. CV10: Gall C ... 7D 20
Oriel Ho. B37: F'bri ... 2A 34
Orion Cres. CV2: Walsg S ... 4A 52
Orkney Cl. CV10: Nun ... 2F 31
Orkney Cft. B36: Cas B ... 5B 24
Orlando Cl. CV22: Bil ... 3D 86
Orlescote Rd. CV4: Canly ... 2H 67
Ormesby Cl. CV22: Bil ... 6E 74
Orpington Dr. CV6: Cov ... 2D 50
Orrian Cl. CV37: S Avon ... 2D 114
Orsino Cl. CV34: H'cte ... 6C 102
Orson Leys CV22: Rugby ... 2F 87
ORTON ... 2A 138
Orton Cl. B46: Wat O ... 1A 24
Orton La. CV9: Aus ... 7H 7
ORTON-ON-THE-HILL ... 1A 140
Orton Rd. B79: Wart ... 6G 9
CV6: Cov ... 3C 50
CV9: Wart, Ort H ... 6G 9
Orwell Cl. CV10: Gall C ... 6F 21
CV23: Clift D ... 3C 76
CV37: S Avon ... 7H 115
Orwell Rd. CV1: Cov ... 6F 59
OSBASTON ... 1B 140
Osbaston Cl. CV5: East G ... 3C 56
Osborne Ct. CV31: W'nsh ... 4E 102
Osborne Rd. CV5: Cov ... 7A 58
Osbourne Ho. CV1: Cov ... 5F 135
Osier Cl. CV21: Brow ... 7H 65
Oslo Gdns. CV2: Walsg S ... 7C 52
Osprey Cl. CV2: Walsg S ... 7D 52
CV11: Nun ... 4D 32
Osprey Ho. B80: Stud ... 3C 92
Ossetts Hole La.
CV35: Yarn C ... 1A 94
Oswald Rd. CV32: Lea S ... 7B 98
Oswald Way CV22: Rugby ... 5D 74
Oswin Gro. CV2: Cov ... 3J 59
Othello Av. CV34: H'cte ... 5D 102
Othello Cl. CV22: Bil ... 4D 86
Other Place Theatre, The
... 7G 137 (5F 115)
OTHERTON ... 1A 138
Otterbrook Ct. CV6: Cov ... 1B 58
Otters Holt CV37: B'ton ... 1C 114
Otters Rest CV31: Lea S ... 3H 103
Oulton Rd. CV21: Rugby ... 2H 75
Ousterne La. CV7: Fill ... 2B 38
Outermarch Rd. CV6: Cov ... 7C 50
Outram Av. CV23: Long L ... 4B 74
OUTWOOD ... 1A 142
OUTWOODS ... 7E 36
Outwoods Cl. CV9: Ath ... 4B 16
Oval, The ... 3H 41
Oval Rd. CV22: Hillm ... 1K 87
Overbare Cl. B94: Tan A ... 4D 90
Overbecks Cl. CV22: Bil ... 6E 74
Overberry Cl. CV2: Cov ... 4K 51
Overberry Orchard CV33: Bis T ... 5B 108
Overbrook Grange CV11: Nun ... 2H 23
Overdale Rd. CV5: Cov ... 4G 57
Overell Gro. CV32: Lea S ... 5B 98
OVER GREEN ... 2A 18 (2C 139)
Over Grn. Dr. B37: K'hrst ... 6A 24
OVER KIDDINGTON ... 3D 147
OVER NORTON ... 3C 147
OVERSLADE ... 7E 74
Overslade Cres. CV6: Cov ... 7J 49
Overslade La. CV22: Rugby ... 2D 86
Overslade Mnr. Dr. CV22: Rugby ... 1F 87
OVERSLEY GREEN ... 6C 112
Oversley Ho. B49: Alc ... 4C 112
Oversley Mill Pk.
B49: Ove G ... 6B 112
Overstone Rd. CV7: Withy ... 1C 54
Over St. CV6: Cov ... 6G 51
OVERTHORPE ... 1D 147
Overton Dr. B46: Wat O ... 1C 24
Overtons Cl. CV31: Rad S ... 3K 103
Over Vw. Way CV23: Cosf ... 5H 65
OVER WHITACRE ... 1G 27 (2D 139)
OVER WORTON ... 3D 147
Owenford Rd. CV6: Cov ... 6C 50
Owen Gro. CV31: W'nsh ... 6E 102
Owen Sq. *CV9: Ath* ... *3C 16*
(off Owen St.)
Owen St. CV9: Ath ... 3C 16
Owen Street Community Arts Cen.
... 3C 16
Owlets End B50: Bart ... 7J 123
Ox Cl. CV2: Cov ... 1G 59
Oxendon Way CV3: Bin ... 6A 60
Oxford Cl. CV11: Nun ... 3G 23
Oxford Gro. B37: Chel W ... 4A 34
Oxford Pl. CV32: Lea S ... 6D 98
Oxford Rd. CV8: Rytn D ... 6A 70
CV23: Mart, Prin ... 5F 83, 1D 104
CV36: Long C ... 3D 134
Oxford Row CV32: Lea S ... 6D 98
Oxford St. CV1: Cov ... 4E 58
CV21: Rugby ... 5J 75
CV32: Lea S ... 6D 98
CV47: Sou ... 5H 107
Oxford Way CV35: Welle ... 5F 117
OXHILL ... 1E 130 (1C 147)
Oxhill Bridle Rd. CV35: Pill H ... 1D 128
Oxhill Rd. CV35: Mid T ... 7C 130
OXLEY ... 1A 138
Oxley Dr. CV3: Finh ... 5C 68
Oxstalls Cotts. CV37: S Avon ... 1J 115
Oxway Cl. CV36: Ship S ... 4H 131

P

Packhorse Rd. CV37: S Avon ... 3A 114
Packington Av. CV5: Alle ... 1F 57
Packington La. B46: Cole ... 1G 35
B46: Max ... 3D 36
CV7: Lit P ... 1H 45
Packington Pk. ... 1B 46
Packington Pl. CV31: Lea S ... 1E 102
PACKMORES ... 7G 97 (2D 143)
Packmore St. CV34: Warw ... 7H 97
PACKWOOD ... 1C 143
Packwood Av. B94: Lapw ... 1G 91
CV21: Hillm ... 1D 88
Packwood Cl. CV11: Nun ... 4B 32
CV31: Lea S ... 3G 103
Packwood Ct.
CV37: S Avon ... 3G 137 (4F 115)
Packwood Grn. CV5: East G ... 4E 56
PACKWOOD GULLET ... 1C 143
Packwood House ... 1F 91
Packwood La. B94: Lapw ... 1F 91
Packwood M. CV34: Warw ... 7K 97
Packwood Rd. B94: Lapw ... 1F 91
Paddiford Pl. CV10: Nun ... 1C 30
Paddock, The B76: Curd ... 5C 18
CV37: S Avon ... 7F 137 (5F 115)
Paddock Cvn. Pk., The
B50: Bidf A ... 7G 123
Paddock Cl. B50: Bidf A ... 5F 123
CV47: Nap ... 2H 111
Paddock La. CV37: S Avon ... 6D 114
Paddock Pl.
CV37: S Avon ... 7E 136 (6E 114)
Paddocks, The CV12: Bulk ... 2D 42
CV23: Stret D ... 3H 83
CV34: Warw ... 1H 101
Paddocks Cl. B78: Pole ... 1C 10
CV8: Wols ... 5J 71
Paddox Cl. CV22: Hillm ... 1B 88
Paddox Ct. CV23: Kils ... 6J 89
Padmore Ct. CV31: Lea S ... 2F 103
Padstow Cl. CV11: Nun ... 6G 23
Padstow Rd. CV4: Tile H ... 7C 56
Padua CV37: S Avon ... 1H 137
Page Rd. CV4: Tile H ... 1C 66
Paget Ct. CV2: Ald G ... 3H 51
Paget's La. CV8: Bubb ... 4K 81
PAILTON ... 6K 55 (3B 140)
Pailton Cl. CV2: Cov ... 4J 51
Pailton Rd.
CV23: Harb M ... 7K 55, 1A 64
Paintball Coventry ... 4A 54
Pake's Cft. CV6: Cov ... 2A 58
Paladine Way CV3: Cov ... 7G 59
Palermo Av. CV3: Cov ... 2D 68
Pallett Dr. CV11: Nun ... 4G 23
Palmer Ct.
CV37: S Avon ... 5H 137
Palmer La.
CV1: Cov ... 3H 135 (4C 58)
Palmer Rd. CV31: W'nsh ... 4F 103
Palmer's Cl. CV21: Hillm ... 1D 88
PALMERS CROSS ... 1A 138
Palmers Leys CV35: Kine ... 5D 120
Palmerston Rd. CV5: Cov ... 7K 57
Palm Tree Av. CV2: Cov ... 4J 51
Pampas Cl. CV37: S Avon ... 2D 114
Panama Dr. CV9: Ath ... 1B 16
Pancras Cl. CV2: Walsg S ... 5A 52
Pandora Rd. CV2: Walsg S ... 6A 52
Pangbourne Cl. CV11: Nun ... 3G 23
Pangbourne Rd. CV2: Cov ... 6J 51
Pangfield Pk. CV5: Cov ... 3G 57
Pantolf Pl. CV21: N'bld A ... 1E 74
Papenham Grn. CV4: Tile H ... 7E 56
Parade CV32: Lea S ... 6D 98
Parade, The B37: K'hrst ... 6A 24
CV11: Nun ... 1J 31
Parade Ct. B80: Stud ... 3D 92
PARADISE ... 1F 59
Paradise St. CV1: Cov ... 6K 135 (6D 58)
CV21: Rugby ... 5J 75
CV34: Warw ... 7H 97
Paradise Way
CV2: Walsg S ... 5C 52
Paradise Works CV6: Cov ... 7F 51
Paragon Pk. CV6: Cov ... 1D 58
Paragon Way CV7: Exh ... 5H 41
Parbrook Cl. CV4: Tile H ... 7C 56
Parish End CV31: Lea S ... 4G 103
Park, The OX15: Lwr Bra ... 3J 133
Park & Ride
Austin Drive (Coventry) ... 7G 51
Memorial Park (Coventry) ... 1A 68
Stratford-upon-Avon ... 1C 114
Park Av. B46: Cole ... 6F 25
B78: Pole ... 2D 10
B80: Stud ... 4D 92
CV6: Cov ... 3C 50
CV11: Nun ... 1A 32
Park Cl. CV8: Ken ... 4F 79
CV35: Clav ... 2D 94
CV37: Wilm ... 6J 113
CV47: N'end ... 1D 120
Park Cotts. CV37: Snitt ... 5H 95
Park Ct. B46: Cole ... 5F 25
CV5: Alle ... 1F 57
CV21: Rugby ... *4H 75*
(off Park Rd.)
CV37: S Avon ... 3D 114
Park Dr. CV31: Lea S ... 1C 102
CV35: Clav ... 2D 94
Parkend CV21: Brow ... 1J 75
Parker Dr. CV31: W'nsh ... 6D 102
Parke Row CV35: Mid T ... 7C 130
Parkes Ct. CV34: Warw ... 1F 101
Parkes St. CV34: Warw ... 1F 101
Park Farm Cl. CV22: Bil ... 6D 74
Park Farm Ind. Est.
B98: Redd ... 1C 92
PARK FARM SOUTH ... 1C 92
Parkfield Ct. B46: Cole ... 5F 25
(Birmingham Rd.)
B46: Cole ... 6G 25
(Sumner Rd.)
Parkfield Dr. CV8: Ken ... 4F 79
Parkfield Rd. B46: Cole ... 5F 25
CV7: Ker E ... 7A 40
CV21: N'bld A, Rugby ... 2D 74
Parkfields CV47: Sou ... 5H 107
PARK GATE ... 1A 142
Parkgate Rd. CV6: Cov ... 3B 50
Park Gro. B46: Wat O ... 1C 24
Park Hall WR11: Salf P ... 6A 122
Park Hall M.
WR11: Salf P ... 6A 122
PARK HILL ... 4G 79
Park Hill CV8: Ken ... 4E 78
Parkhill Dr. CV5: Alle ... 3D 56
Park Hill La. CV5: Alle ... 1E 56
(not continuous)
Park Ho. CV37: Snitt ... 6H 95
Parkinson Dr. CV9: Ath ... 1D 16
Parkland Cl. CV6: Cov ... 3C 50
Parklands NN6: Crick ... 2K 89
Parklands Av. CV32: Lill ... 3G 99
PARK LANE ... 1A 138

Poplar Gro.—Ratley

Poplar Gro. CV8: Rytn D 7D 70
CV21: Rugby 4G 75
Poplar Ho. CV12: Bed 3K 41
Poplar Rd. CV5: Cov 6K 57
CV47: Bis I 6C 110
CV47: Nap 3G 111
Poplars, The B50: Bidf A 5G 123
CV10: Nun 1D 30
CV47: Nap 2G 111
Poplars Trad. Est. B80: Stud 1C 92
Poplar Ter. CV37: A'ton 1B 116
Poplar Way CV10: Harts 4F 21
CV31: W'nsh 6G 103
Poppleton Cl. CV1: Cov 6B 58
Poppy Cl. CV10: Nun 4G 31
CV23: Brin 4C 62
CV37: S Avon 7G 115
Poppy Ct. CV3: W'hall 2K 69
Poppy Dr. CV23: Brow 7K 65
Poppyfield Ct. CV4: Canly 5H 67
Porchester Cl. CV3: Bin 5C 60
Porlock Cl. CV3: Cov 3E 68
Porter Cl. CV4: Tile H 7C 56
Portia Cl. CV11: Nun 3C 32
Portia Rd. CV37: S Avon 3D 114
Portia Way CV34: H'cte 5C 102
Portland Ct. *CV32: Lea S 6D 98*
(off Portland St.)
Portland Dr. CV10: Nun 7G 21
Portland M. CV32: Lea S 7D 98
Portland Pl. CV21: Rugby 6K 75
Portland Pl. E. CV32: Lea S 7C 98
Portland Pl. W. CV32: Lea S 7C 98
Portland Rd. CV21: Rugby 6K 75
Portland Row CV32: Lea S 7C 98
Portland St. CV32: Lea S 7D 98
Portobello Way CV34: Warw 6K 97
Portreath Dr. CV11: Nun 6H 23
Portree Av. CV3: Bin 5B 60
Portsea Cl. CV3: Cov 2D 68
PORTWAY 1B 142
Portway Cl. CV4: Tile H 7C 56
CV31: Lea S 2H 103
Portwrinkle Av. CV6: Cov 1G 59
Poseidon Way CV34: Warw 4D 102
Postbridge Rd. CV3: Cov 3D 68
Post Ho. Gdns. CV23: Pail 6K 55
Postle Cl. CV23: Kils 7H 89
Post Office La. CV9: With 4G 17
CV35: Light 2G 119
CV47: S'ton 6C 106
Post Office Rd. CV9: Bad E 2F 15
Post Office Row CV10: Asty 5J 29
Post Office Yd. CV23: Brin 3D 62
Potlidgate Ct. CV12: Bed 3H 41
Potters Cl. CV23: Brin 4C 62
POTTER'S GREEN 5A 52
Potter's Grn. Rd. CV2: Walsg S 5A 52
Potters La. B78: Pole 2D 10
Potters Rd. CV12: Bed 4E 40
Potton Cl. CV3: W'hall 2A 70
Potts Cl. CV8: Ken 5G 79
Poultney Rd. CV6: Cov 1A 58
Pound, The CV33: Har 5J 109
Pound Cl. B94: Lapw 3G 91
CV36: Ship S 4H 131
Pound Fld. B95: Woot W 5G 93
Poundgate La. CV4: Westw H 2B 66
Pound La. B46: Cole 1G 35
CV32: Lill 4E 98
Pound Way CV47: Sou 5J 107
Powell Cl. CV33: Bis T 5C 108
Powell Rd. CV2: Cov 3G 59
Powell Way CV11: Nun 7D 22
Powerleague
Coventry 4B 56
Powers Ct. CV32: Lea S 6D 98
Powis Gro. CV8: Ken 4G 79
Poyser Rd. CV10: Nun 4J 31
Prebend, The CV47: N'end 1D 120
Precinct, The CV1: Cov 4G 135 (5C 58)
CV34: Warw 6J 97
CV35: Welle 3J 117
(off School La.)
Precision Way B49: Alc 2C 112
Prentice Cl. CV23: Long L 3B 74
Prentice M. CV37: B'ton 2C 114
Prescelly Ct. CV10: Nun 1B 30
PRESTON BAGOT 2C 143
PRESTON CAPES 3C 145
Preston Cl. CV4: Tile H 1D 66
PRESTON GREEN 3K 93
PRESTON ON STOUR 3D 143
Pretorian Way CV21: Rugby 1G 75
Priam Cir. CV34: H'cte 5D 102
Price Cl. E. CV34: Warw 4D 100
Price Cl. W. CV34: Warw 4D 100
Price Rd. CV32: Cubb 3J 99
Pridmore Rd. CV6: Cov 7D 50
Primary Wlk. CV22: Caw 1A 86
PRIMETHORPE 2C 141
Primrose Cl. CV23: Brow 7K 65
Primrose Ct. CV23: Harb M 4B 64
Primrose Dr. CV12: Bed 4E 40
Primrose Hill CV34: Warw 6E 96
Primrose Hill St.
CV1: Cov 1K 135 (3D 58)
Primrose La. B49: Ove G 6C 112
Primrose Way CV37: S Avon 7G 115
Prince Harry Rd. B95: Hen A 2H 93
Prince of Wales Rd. CV5: Cov 4J 57
Prince Regent Ct. CV31: Lea S 2D 102
Prince Rupert Cl. CV47: Temp H 3B 120
Princes Av. CV11: Nun 1H 31
Princes Cl. CV3: Cov 7H 59
Prince's Dr. CV31: Lea S 1B 102
CV32: Lea S 7B 98
Princes Dr. CV8: Ken 2F 79
Princes Dr. Ind. Est. CV8: Ken 1E 78
Prince's Rd. B78: Pole 7E 8
Princes Rd. CV9: Hur 6K 13
Princess Dr. CV6: Cov 5H 51
Princess Rd. CV9: Ath 2D 16
Princess St. CV6: Cov 7F 51
Prince's St. CV32: Lea S 6F 99
Princes St. CV11: Nun 1H 31
CV21: Rugby 4G 75
PRINCETHORPE 7G 83 (1B 144)
Prince Thorpe Ct. CV3: Bin 1A 70
Princethorpe Rd.
CV23: Bour D 6D 84
Princethorpe Way CV3: Bin 1K 69
Prince William Cl. CV6: Cov 1J 57
Printers Pl. CV37: S Avon 3D 136
Prior Deram Wlk. CV4: Canly 7F 57
Prior Pk. Rd. CV22: Bil 6D 74
Priors, The CV12: Bed 3J 41
Priorsfield Rd. CV6: Cov 3A 58
CV8: Ken 2B 78
Priorsfield Rd. Nth. CV6: Cov 3A 58
Priorsfield Rd. Sth. CV6: Cov 3A 58
Priors Grange WR11: Salf P 6B 122
Priors Gro. Cl. CV34: Warw 5D 100
PRIORS HARDWICK 3B 144
Priors Harnall CV1: Cov 3E 58
PRIORS MARSTON 5G 111 (3B 144)
Priors Mdw. CV47: Sou 5J 107
Priory Bungs. CV35: Pill P 3B 128
Priory Cl. B46: Cole 7G 25
B94: Lapw 1J 91
Priory Ct. B80: Stud 2D 92
CV5: Cov 6A 58
(off Albany Rd.)
CV11: Nun 7B 22
(not continuous)
Priory Cft. CV8: Ken 5D 78
Priory Hall CV1: Cov 3J 135 (4D 58)
Priory La. CV35: Pill P 3B 128
Priory M. CV34: Warw 1G 101
Priory Mill Wlk. CV6: Cov 2A 58
Priory Pk. 1G 101
Priory Pk. Karting Circuit 7A 8
Priory Pl. CV1: Cov 3J 135 (4D 58)
Priory Rd. B49: Alc 4B 112
CV8: Ken 4D 78
CV8: Wols 4K 71
CV34: Warw 1G 101
Priory Row
CV1: Cov 3J 135 (4D 58)
Priory Sq. B80: Stud 2D 92
Priory St. CV1: Cov 4J 135 (4D 58)
CV10: Nun 1C 30
CV31: Lea S 2D 102
Priory Ter. CV31: Lea S 1D 102
Priory Theatre 4D 78
Priory Tuery B49: Alc 5B 112
Priory Vis. Cen. 3J 135
Priory Wlk. CV9: Man 5E 16
CV34: Warw 1H 101
Privet Rd. CV2: Cov 4H 51
Proctor Way CV37: S Avon 3A 114
Proffitt Av. CV6: Cov 5G 51
Progress Cl. CV3: Bin 1C 70
Progress Way CV3: Bin 7C 60
Projects Dr. CV21: Rugby 2H 75
Prologis Pk. CV6: Ker E 1A 50
(not continuous)
Prospect Pk. CV21: Rugby 7G 65
Prospect Rd. CV31: Lea S 3F 103
Prospect Row CV35: Pill P 3C 128
PROSPECT VILLAGE 1B 138
Prospect Way CV21: Rugby 3J 75
Prospero Dr. CV34: H'cte 5C 102
Prossers Wlk. B46: Cole 5F 25
Providence St. CV5: Cov 7K 57
Ptarmigan Pl. CV11: Nun 1B 32
Puckerings La. CV34: Warw 2G 101
Pudding Bag La. CV23: Thurl 7K 85
Puma Way CV1: Cov 6J 135 (6D 58)
Pumphouse Cl. CV6: Lford 7H 41
Pumping Station Rd. CV3: Cov 6K 59
Pump La. B46: Shu 5G 27
CV7: Fill 3K 37
Purcell Av. CV11: Nun 5C 32
Purcell Cl. CV32: Lea S 7E 98
Purcell Rd. CV6: Cov 6H 51
Purefoy Rd. CV3: Cov 7D 58
Purley Chase Est.
CV10: Ans C 3C 20
Purley Chase Golf Course 1B 20
Purley Chase La.
CV9: Man 7B 16, 1A 20
Purley Vw. CV9: Man 5E 16
Purlieu La. CV8: Ken 4B 78
Purser Dr. CV34: Warw 4D 100
Purton Cl. B49: Alc 3C 112
Purton M. CV31: Lea S 2G 103
Putney Wlk. B37: F'bri 2B 34
Pye Ct. CV23: W'hby 2H 105
Pyree Sq. CV34: Warw 4D 100
Pytchley Rd. CV22: Rugby 7J 75
Pyt Pk. CV5: Cov 3H 57

Q

QE Community Sports Village 3E 16
Quadrant, The
CV1: Cov 5G 135 (5C 58)
CV11: Nun 1A 32
Quail Cl. CV37: B'ton 3B 114
Quantock Dr. CV10: Nun 1B 30
QUARRY BANK 3A 138
Quarry Cl. CV21: N'bld A 1F 75
CV35: Leek W 1H 97
Quarry Cotts. CV35: Leek W 1H 97
Quarryfield La.
CV1: Cov 6K 135 (6E 58)
CV3: Cov 6K 135 (6E 58)
Quarry Flds. CV35: Leek W 1H 97
Quarry La. CV9: Man 6D 16
CV11: Nun 3B 32
CV35: Row 5K 91
Quarry Rd. CV8: Ken 3C 78
CV9: Man 7D 16
CV47: Sou 3H 107
Quarry St. CV32: Lea S 7A 98
Quarrywood Gro. CV2: Cov 3G 59
Quarry Yd. CV10: Nun 7H 21
Quartz Point B46: Cole 6G 35
Quayside Ct. CV1: Cov 2C 58
Queen Elizabeth Rd.
CV10: Nun 5H 21
Queen Isabel's Av. CV3: Cov 7D 58
Queen Margaret's Rd. CV4: Canly 7F 57
Queen Mary's Rd. CV6: Cov 6D 50
CV12: Bed 7J 31
Queen Philippa St. CV3: Cov 2D 68
Queens Av. CV36: Ship S 4G 131
Queen's Cl. CV8: Ken 6D 78
Queens Cl. CV33: Har 6J 109
CV36: Ship S 5G 131
Queen's Ct. CV37: S Avon 6E 114
Queens Ct. CV11: Nun 7B 22
Queen's Dr. CV35: Row 5J 91
Queensferry Cl. CV22: Bil 1C 86
Queensland Av. CV5: Cov 5K 57
Queensland Gdns. CV12: Bed 3F 41
Queen's Pk. CV31: Lea S 2C 102
Queen's Rd. CV8: Ken 6D 78
CV9: Ath 3D 16
Queens Rd. CV1: Cov 5F 135 (5B 58)
CV11: Nun 7B 22
CV23: Bret 1C 72
CV36: Tred 6J 127
Queens Sq. CV34: Warw 2F 101
Queens St. CV36: Half 2J 127
Queen St. CV12: Bed 3J 41
CV32: Cubb 2H 99
CV32: Lea S 6E 98
Queens Way B78: Dord 4C 10
Queensway B50: Bidf A 5F 123
CV9: Hur 7K 13
CV10: Nun 5E 22
CV31: Lea S 2C 102
Queensway Trad. Est.
CV31: Lea S 2C 102
Queenswood Ct. CV7: Ker E 2H 49
Queen Victoria Rd.
CV1: Cov 3F 135 (4B 58)
(not continuous)
Queen Victoria St. CV21: Rugby 5J 75
QUENIBOROUGH 1D 141
Quernstone Cl. CV22: Caw 7B 74
Quilletts Cl. CV6: Cov 5G 51
Quiney's Leys CV37: Welf A 2A 124
Quiney's Rd. CV37: Shot 5C 114
Quinn Cl. CV3: Cov 1H 69
Quinneys Ct. B50: Bidf A 6H 123
Quinneys La. B50: Bidf A 6H 123
B98: Redd 1A 92
QUINTON 3A 138
Quinton Cl. CV35: Hatt 4A 96
Quinton Lodge CV3: Cov 1D 68
Quinton Pde. CV3: Cov 1D 68
Quinton Pk. CV3: Cov 1D 68
Quinton Rd. CV1: Cov 7J 135 (6D 58)
CV3: Cov 7J 135 (7D 58)
Quorn Way CV3: Bin 7A 60

R

Rabbit La. CV12: Bed 1C 40
Racemeadow Rd. CV9: Ath 2D 16
Radbourne Cl. CV47: Sou 6J 107
Radbourne La. CV47: Ladb 3E 110
Radbrook Way CV31: Lea S 2H 103
Radcliffe Gdns. CV31: Lea S 2E 102
Radcliffe Rd. CV5: Cov 7K 57
RADFORD
CV6 1B 58 (3A 140)
OX7 3D 147
WR7 3B 142
Radford Circ. CV6: Cov 3B 58
Radford Cl. CV9: Ath 1D 16
Radford Cotts. CV31: Lea S 1F 103
Radford Hall CV31: Rad S 2J 103
Radford Ho. CV6: Cov 7A 50
Radford Rd. CV1: Cov 1G 135 (1A 58)
CV6: Cov 7A 50
CV31: Lea S 1E 102
RADFORD SEMELE 3K 103 (2A 144)
Radley Dr. CV10: Nun 3G 31
Radlow Cres. B37: Mars G 5B 34
Radnor Ct. CV10: Nun 2E 30
Radnor Dr. CV10: Nun 2D 30
Radnor Wlk. CV2: Walsg S 6B 52
RADWAY 5B 128 (1C 147)
Raffles Pl. CV23: Long L 4B 74
Raglan Cl. CV11: Nun 7E 22
Raglan Ct. CV1: Cov 4E 58
Raglan Gro. CV8: Ken 4F 79
Raglan Ho. CV1: Cov 4E 58
Raglan St. CV1: Cov 3K 135 (4E 58)
Raglan Way B37: Chel W 4D 34
Ragley 3B 142
Ragley Mill La. B49: Alc 3B 112
Ragley Way CV11: Nun 2B 32
Railings, The CV21: Rugby 4H 75
Railport App. NN6: Crick 3K 89
Railway Cl. B80: Stud 3C 92
Railway Cres. CV36: Ship S 3H 131
Railway M. B49: Alc 4B 112
Railway St. CV23: Long L 4A 74
Railway Ter. CV9: Ath 3C 16
CV12: Bed 3J 41
CV21: Rugby 5H 75
Rainbow Flds. CV36: Ship S 4H 131
RAINSBROOK 3J 87
Rainsbrook Av. CV22: Hillm 1A 88
Rainsbrook Cl. CV47: Sou 5K 107
Rainsbrook Dr. CV11: Nun 3B 32
Rainsbrook Valley Railway 3J 87
Rainsford Cl. CV37: Cliff C 5C 124
Raison Av. CV11: Nun 3G 23
Raleigh Rd. CV2: Cov 4H 59
Ralph Cres. B78: K'bry 5D 12
Ralph Rd. CV6: Cov 2K 57
Rambures Cl. CV34: H'cte 5D 102
Ramp Rd. B26: Birm A 1C 44
Ramsay Cres. CV5: Alle 7F 49
Ramsay Grn. CV35: Welle 2H 117
RAMSDEN 3A 142
Ramsden Av. CV10: Nun 4H 21
Ramsden Ct. CV10: Nun 4H 21
Ramsden Rd. CV9: Man 4F 17
Ramsey Rd. CV31: Lea S 1F 103
Ramshill La. B95: Ullen 4C 90
Ranby Rd. CV2: Cov 3F 59
Randall Rd. CV8: Ken 6D 78
Randle Rd. CV10: Nun 7J 21
Randle St. CV6: Cov 2A 58
Randolph Cl. CV31: Lea S 2G 103
Ranelagh St. CV31: Lea S 2E 102
Ranelagh Ter. CV31: Lea S 2D 102
Range Mdw. Cl. CV32: Lea S 4A 98
Rangemoor CV3: W'hall 2K 69
Range Way B78: K'bry 6E 12
Rankine Cl. CV21: N'bld A 1D 74
Rannoch Dr. CV10: Nun 6H 21
Rannock Cl. CV3: Bin 5C 60
Ransome Rd. CV7: New A 4E 28
Ransom Rd. CV6: Cov 6E 50
Ranulf Cft. CV3: Cov 1C 68
Ranulf St. CV3: Cov 1C 68
Raphael Cl. CV5: Cov 4G 57
RASHWOOD 2A 142
RATBY 1C 141
Ratcliffe Ct. CV10: Nun 7H 21
RATCLIFFE CULEY 2A 140
Ratcliffe Rd. CV9: Ath 3D 16
Ratcliffe St. CV9: Ath 3C 16
Rathbone Cl. CV7: Ker E 7K 39
CV21: Hillm 1C 88
Rathbone Ct. CV6: Cov 1F 59
Rathlin Cft. B36: Cas B 6B 24
RATLEY 7D 128 (1C 147)

Ratliffe Rd.—Rounds Gdns.

Ratliffe Rd. CV22: Rugby 2F 87
Raveloe Dr. CV11: Nun 3K 31
Raven Cragg Rd. CV5: Cov 7J 57
Ravenglass CV21: Brow 1K 75
Ravensdale Av. CV32: Lea S 5A 98
Ravensdale Rd. CV2: Cov 4J 59
Ravensholst CV4: Canly 2H 67
RAVENSTHORPE 1D 145
Ravensthorpe Cl. CV3: Bin 7A 60
Ravenswood Hill B46: Cole 5F 25
Raven Way CV11: Nun 2B 32
Rawlinson Rd. CV32: Lill 5F 99
RAWNSLEY 1B 138
Rawnsley Dr. CV8: Ken 4F 79
Rawn Vw. CV9: Man 5E 16
Rayford Cvn. Pk. CV37: S Avon . . .3H 115
Raymond Cl. CV6: Lford 1F 51
Raynor Cres. CV12: Bed 4D 40
Raynsford Wlk. CV34: Warw 6F 97
Raywoods, The CV10: Nun 1F 31
Reading Av. CV11: Nun 3G 23
Reading Cl. CV2: Ald G 3H 51
Reading Ct. CV37: S Avon 3J 115
Readings, The CV47: Fen C 2G 121
Read St. CV1: Cov 4E 58
Read St. Ind. Est. CV1: Cov 4E 58
Reardon Ct. CV34: Warw 6G 97
Recreation Rd. CV6: Cov 3G 51
Rectory Cl. CV5: Alle 1G 57
CV7: Exh 4G 41
CV23: Barby 7E 88
CV31: W'nsh 4F 103
CV47: S'ton 6C 106
OX17: Warm 2J 129
Rectory Ct. *CV36: Ship S 5H 131*
(off Old Rd.)
Rectory Dr. CV7: Exh 4G 41
CV7: Old A 2C 28
Rectory La. CV5: Alle 1G 57
CV23: Barby 7E 88
CV36: Whatc 3A 130
OX15: Lwr Bra 3J 133
Rectory Rd. CV7: Old A 3C 28
Redcap Cft. CV6: Cov 2D 50
Redcar Cl. CV32: Lill 3F 99
Redcar Rd. CV1: Cov 2E 58
Red Deeps CV11: Nun 4K 31
REDDITCH 2B 142
Redditch Rd. B80: Stud 2C 92
B95: Oldb, Ullen 7A 90
Redditch Wlk. CV2: Walsg S 7C 52
Redesdale Av. CV6: Cov 3K 57
Redfern Av. CV8: Ken 3E 78
Redgrave Cl. CV2: Walsg S 6D 52
RED HILL
B49 .3C 143
CV7 . . . . .4E 38
Red Hill CV35: Welle 6H 117
Red Hill Cl. B80: Stud 1D 92
Redhill Cl. CV35: Welle 5G 117
Red Hill Furrows CV31: Lea S 3G 103
Redhill Rd. CV23: Long L 4B 74
Redhill Way CV35: Welle 5H 117
Red Horse Cnr. CV35: N Lin 2F 95
Redland Cl. CV2: Ald G 4A 52
Redland La. CV8: Rytn D 6C 70
Redland Rd. CV31: Lea S 3F 103
Redlands Cres. CV37: S Avon 4B 114
Redlands Row GL56: Lit C 6C 134
Red La. CV6: Cov 2E 58
CV8: Burt G 4A 66
CV10: Asty 5J 29
Red La. Ind. Est. CV6: Cov 1F 59
Red Lion Cl. CV47: Sou 4H 107
Red Lion Ct. CV35: Kine 6C 120
Red Lodge Dr. CV22: Bil 1E 86
Red Poll Rd. CV21: Rugby 4J 75
Red Rd. CV35: Lit K 7C 120
Redruth Cl. CV6: Cov 6G 51
CV11: Nun 7H 23
Redthorne Gro. CV8: Ken 1F 79
Redwing Cl. CV37: B'ton 2B 114
Redwings Horse Sanctuary
(Oxhill Rescue Cen.) 1C 147
Red Wing Wlk. B36: Cas B 4A 24
Redwood Cft. CV10: Nun 2G 31
Redwood Dr. B78: K'bry 4E 12
Redwood Ho. B37: K'hrst 7A 24
Redwood Pk. CV36: Ship S 5H 131
Redwood Rd. CV21: Brow 7H 65
Reeds Pk. CV33: Ufton 2F 109
Rees Dr. CV3: Finh 4C 68
Reeve Dr. CV8: Ken 5E 78
REEVES GREEN 7A 56
Regal Ct. CV9: Ath 3D 16
Regal Rd. CV37: S Avon 3E 114
Regency Arc. CV32: Lea S 7D 98
Regency Cl. CV10: Nun 5E 22
Regency Ct. CV5: Cov 7K 57
Regency Dr. B49: King C 2A 112
CV3: Finh 3K 67
CV8: Ken 6D 78
Regency Ho. CV32: Lea S 7E 98
Regency M. CV32: Lea S 7E 98
Regent Ct. Shop. Cen.
CV32: Lea S 7D 98
Regent Gro. CV32: Lea S 7D 98
Regent Pl. CV21: Rugby 4G 75
CV31: Lea S 1E 102
Regent St. CV1: Cov 5F 135 (6B 58)
CV11: Nun 6D 22
CV12: Bed 1J 41
CV21: Rugby 5G 75
CV32: Lea S 7C 98
Reg Hadden Ct. CV10: Nun 5E 22
Regiment Ct. CV6: Cov 5A 50
Regina Cres. CV2: Walsg S 7C 52
Regis Wlk. CV2: Walsg S 7B 52
Reignier Pl. CV34: H'cte 6D 102
Relay Bus. Pk. B77: Wiln 3A 10
Relay Dr. B77: Wiln 3A 10
Relton M. CV6: Cov 1F 59
Rembrandt Cl. CV5: Cov 4G 57
Remburn Gdns. CV34: Warw 7H 97
Remembrance Rd. CV3: W'hall 2K 69
Renfrew Wlk. CV4: Tile H 7E 56
Renison Rd. CV12: Bed 4E 40
Renolds Cl. CV4: Cov 5G 57
Renown Av. CV5: Cov 6G 57
(not continuous)
Renshaw Ind. Est. B80: Stud 3A 92
Repington Av. CV9: Ath 1C 16
Repton Dr. CV6: Cov 4H 51
Rescue Copse CV7: Gun H 4C 28
Reservoir Dr. B46: Shu 2B 26
Reservoir Rd. CV21: Rugby 2J 75
Resort World B40: Nat E C 3E 44
Retreat, The B95: Woot W 5H 93
Reuben Av. CV10: Nun 5G 21
Rex Cl. CV4: Tile H 7B 56
Reynolds Cl. CV21: Hillm 1D 88
Reynolds Rd. CV12: Bed 1G 41
Rhyl Rd. CV11: Bram 6H 33
Ribble Cl. CV12: Bulk 3D 42
Ribble Rd. CV3: Cov 5F 59
Ribble Wlk. B36: Cas B 4A 24
Ribbonbrook CV11: Nun 1K 31
Ribbonfields CV11: Nun 1K 31
Richard Joy Cl. CV6: Cov 4C 50
Richards Cl. CV8: Ken 4D 78
Richards Gro. CV31: Lea S 3E 102
Richardson Cl. CV34: Warw 6H 97
Richardson Way CV2: Walsg S 6D 52
Richborough Rd. CV37: Lwr Q 6F 125
Rich Cl. CV34: Warw 1J 101
Richmond Ho. B37: Chel W 4C 34
Richmond Rd. CV9: Ath 4C 16
CV11: Nun 1G 31
CV21: Rugby 6J 75
Richmond St. CV2: Cov 4G 59
Richmond Way B37: Chel W 2C 34
Rickyard, The CV23: Eas 3J 63
Rickyard Cl. B78: Pole 7D 8
Ricoh Arena 3E 50
Riddell Cl. B49: Alc 4D 112
Ridding Gdns. B78: Pole 2D 10
Riddings, The CV5: Cov 1H 67
CV9: Gren 1F 15
Riddings La. CV9: Gren 7F 11
Ridefort Cl. CV4: Tile H 6E 56
Rider Cl. CV10: Nun 3G 31
Rideswell Gro. CV31: W'nsh 7E 102
Ridge Ct. CV5: Alle 1E 56
Ridge Dr. CV21: Rugby 4K 75
RIDGE LANE 1A 20 (2D 139)
Ridge La. CV10: Ridge L 1A 20
Ridgeley Cl. CV34: Warw 5G 97
Ridgethorpe CV3: W'hall 3A 70
Ridgeway, The CV34: Warw 6J 97
CV36: Gt Wol 7A 132
CV37: Dray, S Avon, Wilm
. . . . .7H 113, 3A 114
Ridgeway Av. CV3: Cov 2C 68
Ridgeway Cl. B80: Stud 5D 92
Ridgewood Cl. CV32: Lea S 6A 98
Ridgley Rd. CV4: Tile H 6C 56
Ridgley Way CV33: Har 7H 109
Ridsdale Cl. WR11: Salf P 6B 122
Rigby Cl. CV34: H'cte 4B 102
Rigdale Cl. CV2: Cov 5A 60
Riley Cl. CV8: Ken 5G 79
Riley Ct. CV21: Rugby 5J 75
Riley Dr. B36: Cas B 3A 24
Riley Ho. CV1: Cov 5H 135 (5C 58)
Riley Sq. CV2: Cov 5H 51
Rimell Cl. CV37: N'bld S 1G 127
Ringway Hill Cross
CV1: Cov 3F 135 (4B 58)
Ringway Queens
CV1: Cov 5F 135 (5B 58)
Ringway Rudge
CV1: Cov 4F 135 (5B 58)
Ringway St Johns
CV1: Cov 5J 135 (5D 58)
Ringway St Nicholas
CV1: Cov 2G 135 (4C 58)
Ringway St Patrick's
CV1: Cov 6H 135 (6C 58)
Ringway Swanswell
CV1: Cov 2J 135 (4D 58)
Ringway Whitefriars
CV1: Cov 3K 135 (5D 58)
Ringwood Highway CV2: Walsg S . . .4A 52
Rinill Gro. CV31: Lea S 2H 103
Riplingham CV32: Lea S 5D 98
Ripon Cl. CV5: Alle 6E 48
Risborough Cl. CV5: Cov 4G 57
Risdale Cl. CV32: Lea S 5B 98
Rise, The B37: Mars G 6A 34
Rising La. B93: Bad C 1K 91
B94: Lapw 2G 91
River Arrow Nature Reserve 4B 112
Riverbank Gdns. CV37: S Avon . . .5G 115
River Cl. CV12: Bed 4F 41
CV32: Lea S 7A 98
River Ct. CV1: Cov 4B 58
River Dr. CV9: Ath 1C 16
Riverford Cft. CV4: Canly 4H 67
Riverhead Ct. *B50: Bidf A 6G 123*
(off Salford Rd.)
Rivermead CV11: Nun 7B 22
Rivermead Dr. CV37: Tidd 3K 115
Riversdale CV32: Lea S 7C 98
Riversdale Rd. CV9: Ath 3E 16
Riverside B49: Alc 4D 112
B80: Stud 3D 92
CV9: With 4G 17
CV32: Lea S 7C 98
CV37: S Avon 3H 115
Riverside Cvn. Pk. CV37: Tidd 3J 115
Riverside Cl. CV3: Cov 1F 69
Riverside Ct. *B46: Cole 5G 25*
(off Prossers Wlk.)
Riverside Dr. B95: Woot W 5J 93
Riverside Gdns. B95: Hen A 2H 93
Riverside Wlk. CV31: Lea S 1A 102
CV34: Warw 2H 101
Riverslea Rd. CV3: Cov 6J 59
Riversleigh Rd. CV32: Lea S 6A 98
Riversley Rd. CV11: Nun 1J 31
River Wlk. CV2: Cov 4J 51
River Way CV36: Ship S 3J 131
Rivington Glebe GL56: Lit C 6C 134
Roach Cl. B37: Chel W 2C 34
ROADE 3D 145
Roadway Cl. CV12: Bed 3H 41
ROAD WEEDON 3D 145
Roanne Ringway CV11: Nun 7C 22
Robbins Ct. CV22: Hillm 1A 88
Robbins Way CV32: Lill 5F 99
Robert Atchinson Way
CV7: Ker E 7K 39
(off Coopers Mdw.)
Robert Cl. CV3: W'hall 4J 69
Robert Cramb Av. CV4: Tile H 7D 56
Robert Hill Cl. CV21: Hillm 7C 76
Robert Mounford Way
CV4: Tile H 7D 56
Robert Rd. CV7: Exh 5F 41
Roberts Cl. CV23: Stret D 3H 83
Robertson Cl. CV23: Clift D 3C 76
Robey's La. B78: A'cte, B'moor 7A 8
Robin Cl. B36: Cas B 4A 24
Robin Hood Rd. CV3: W'hall 2J 69
Robinia Cl. CV32: Lill 6F 99
Robins Gro. CV34: Warw 4D 100
Robinson Rd. CV12: Bed 5D 40
ROBINSON'S END 1B 30
Robins Way CV10: Nun 1A 30
Robotham Cl. CV21: N'bld A 2F 75
Rocheberie Way CV22: Rugby 1F 87
Rochester Cl. CV11: Nun 1H 31
Rochester Rd. CV5: Cov 7J 57
Rochford Ct. CV31: Lea S 1C 102
Rock Cl. CV6: Cov 5H 51
CV10: Gall C 7E 20
Rocken End CV6: Cov 6D 50
Rock Farm La. CV8: Bag 1F 81
Rockingham Dr. CV11: Nun 5B 32
Rock La. CV7: Cor 6G 39
Rock Mill La. CV32: Lea S 6A 98
Rockwell Lodge *B49: Gt Alne 2G 113*
(off Woodland Dr.)
Rocky La. CV8: Ashow, Ken 6G 79
Rodhouse Cl. CV4: Tile H 6B 56
Rodney Cl. CV22: Bil 7C 74
Rodway Dr. CV5: East G 3B 56
Rodyard Way CV1: Cov . . .7K 135 (6D 58)
Roebuck Pk. B49: Alc 3A 112
Roebuck Rd. CV37: B'ton 1C 114
Roe Cl. CV34: Warw 7H 97
Roe Ho. La. CV9: App M, Aus 4J 7
Rofs Cft. B78: Pole 7D 8
Rogers La. CV37: Ett 3B 126
Rogers Way CV34: Warw 4D 100
Rohan Gdns. CV34: Warw 6J 97
Roisins Vineyard CV12: Bed 3D 40
Rokeby Ct. CV22: Rugby 2F 87
Rokeby St. CV21: Rugby 5K 75
Roland Av. CV6: Cov 3B 50
Roland Mt. CV6: Cov 3C 50
Rollason Cl. CV6: Cov 6C 50
Rollason Rd. CV6: Cov 6B 50
Rollasons Yd. CV6: Cov 3G 51
ROLLESTON 1D 141
Roman Alcester Mus. 5B 112
Roman Cl. B50: Bidf A 6H 123
Romani Cl. CV34: Warw 1F 101
Roman Pk. B46: Cole 3F 25
Roman Rd. CV2: Cov 4H 59
Roman Way B46: Cole 2E 24
B49: Alc 5B 112
B78: Dord 4D 10
CV3: Finh 5D 68
CV21: Rugby 1G 75
CV36: Half 3J 127
CV47: Sou 5J 107
Romeo Arbour CV34: H'cte 5C 102
Romford Rd. CV6: Cov 4B 50
Romney Pl. CV22: Rugby 2F 87
Romsey Av. CV10: Nun 3E 22
ROMSLEY 1A 142
Romsley Rd. CV6: Cov 1C 58
Romulus Wlk. CV4: Tile H 4A 56
Ro-Oak Rd. CV6: Cov 2K 57
Rookery, The *B49: Alc 5C 112*
(off Stratford Rd.)
CV10: Gall C 6D 20
CV37: A'ton 1B 116
Rookery La. CV6: Cov 2B 50
CV37: Ett 2B 126
CV37: N'bld S 1G 127
Rookes Ct. CV37: S Avon 1E 136
Rooks Nest CV23: Brin 4C 62
Roosevelt Dr. CV4: Tile H 5C 56
Rootes Halls CV4: Canly 4G 67
Roper Cl. CV21: Hillm 1C 88
Ropewalk B49: Alc 4B 112
Ropewalk Shop. Cen. CV11: Nun . . .7D 22
Rosary La. CV36: Lit Wol 7D 132
Rosaville Cres. CV5: Alle 1E 56
Rose Av. B95: Hen A 1H 93
CV6: Cov 2K 57
Roseberry Av. CV2: Cov 5H 51
Rose Cott. Flats CV5: East G 2B 56
Rose Cft. CV8: Ken 3C 78
Rosefield Pl. CV32: Lea S 7D 98
Rosefield St. CV32: Lea S 7D 98
Rosefield Wlk. *CV32: Lea S 7D 98*
(off Rosefield St.)
Rose Gdns. B95: Woot W 5J 93
Rosegreen Cl. CV3: Cov 2E 68
Rose Hill CV9: Ath 4E 16
Rosehip Dr. CV2: Cov 1H 59
Roseland Rd. CV8: Ken 6D 78
Roselands Av. CV2: Cov 6K 51
Rose La. CV11: Nun 1J 31
CV35: Welle 5H 117
CV47: Nap 3H 111
Rosemary Cl. CV4: Tile H 4C 56
Rosemary Hill CV8: Ken 4D 78
Rosemary M. CV8: Ken 4D 78
Rosemary Way CV10: Nun 4G 31
Rosemount Cl. CV2: Cov 7A 52
Rosemullion Cl. CV7: Exh 5H 41
Rose Rd. B46: Cole 4F 25
Rosewood CV11: Nun 3B 32
Rosewood Av. CV22: Rugby 1G 87
Rosewood Cres. CV32: Lill 5F 99
Ross Cl. CV5: East G 2E 56
Ross Ct. CV21: Rugby 5K 75
Rossendale Way CV10: Nun 2D 30
Rosslyn Av. CV6: Cov 1J 57
Ross Way CV11: Nun 5D 32
Rotherby Gro. B37: Mars G 6A 34
Rotherfield Cl. CV31: Lea S 1F 103
Rotherham Cl. CV22: Caw 1K 85
Rotherham Rd. CV6: Cov 4B 50
Rotherhams Hill CV9: Bad E 3F 15
ROTHERSTHORPE 3D 145
Rother St.
CV37: S Avon 6D 136 (5E 114)
Rothesay Av. CV4: Tile H 5F 57
Rothesay Cl. CV10: Nun 2G 31
ROTHLEY 1C 141
Rothley Dr. CV21: Brow 1A 76
Rothwell Rd. CV34: Warw 6E 96
ROTTEN ROW 1C 143
Rough Hill Wood (Nature Reserve)
. . . . .2A 92
Roughknowles Rd.
CV4: Westw H 2B 66
ROUGHLEY 2C 139
Rouncil La. CV8: Ken 7C 78
Round Av. CV23: Long L 3A 74
Roundhouse Dr. CV22: Caw 7A 74
Round Ho. Rd. CV3: Cov 7G 59
Rounds Gdns. CV21: Rugby 5F 75

Rounds Hill—St Osburg's Rd.

Rounds Hill CV8: Ken 7C 78
Round St. CV21: Rugby 5F 75
Rouse La. CV35: Oxh 1E 130
ROUSHAM 3D 147
ROUS LENCH 3B 142
Rover Dr. B36: Cas B 3A 24
Rover Rd. CV1: Cov 4G 135 (5C 58)
Row, The CV7: Ansty 3F 53
CV8: Bag 6F 69
Rowan Cen., The CV9: Ath 3D 16
Rowan Cl. B78: K'bry 5E 12
CV3: Bin W 1F 71
CV37: S Avon 2E 114
Rowan Dr. CV22: Bil 6B 74
CV34: Warw 7H 97
Rowan Gdns. B78: Pole 2E 10
Rowan Gro. CV2: Walsg S 4A 52
Rowan Ho. CV4: Westw H 2D 66
Rowan Pl. B50: Bidf A 4G 123
Rowans, The CV9: Ath 4E 16
CV12: Bed 3E 40
CV23: Gran 6H 105
Rowan Way B37: Chel W 4C 34
CV10: Harts 3E 20
Rowborough Cl. CV35: Hatt 5A 96
Rowcroft Rd. CV2: Walsg S 1C 60
Rowe Cl. CV21: Hillm 1E 88
ROWINGTON 7J 91 (2D 143)
Rowington Cl. CV6: Cov 2H 57
ROWINGTON GREEN 5H 91
Rowington Grn. CV35: Row 5H 91
Rowland Av. B78: Pole 6D 8
B80: Stud 4D 92
Rowland Ct. CV7: Old A 3C 28
Rowland St. CV21: Rugby 5F 75
Rowlands Way CV9: Ath 1B 16
CV36: Whatc 3B 130
Rowley Cres. CV37: S Avon 3F 115
Rowley Dr. CV3: W'hall 4H 69
Rowley La. CV3: W'hall 5K 69
ROWLEY REGIS 3A 138
Rowley Rd. CV3: W'hall 5F 69
CV8: Bag 5F 69
CV31: W'nsh 5E 102
ROWLEYS GREEN 2E 50
Rowley's Grn. CV6: Lford 2E 50
Rowleys Grn. Ind. Est.
CV6: Lford 2E 50
Rowley's Grn. La. CV6: Lford 2E 50
ROWNEY GREEN 1B 142
Rowse Cl. CV21: Brow 1J 75
Roxburgh Cft. CV32: Cubb 2F 99
Roxburgh Rd. CV11: Nun 3A 32
Royal Ct. CV21: Rugby 5F 75
Royal Cres. CV3: W'hall 3J 69
ROYAL LEAMINGTON SPA
. . . . .7D 98 (2A 144)
Royal Mdw. Dr. CV9: Ath 1D 16
Royal Oak La. CV7: Ash G 6C 40
CV12: Bed 6C 40
Royal Oak Yd. CV12: Bed 1H 41
Royal Priors Shop. Cen.
CV32: Lea S 7D 98
Royal Pump Rooms 7D 98
Royal Regiment of Fusiliers Mus., The
. . . . .1H 101
(off St John's Ct.)
Royal Shakespeare Theatre
. . . . .5H 137 (5F 115)
Royal Spa Cen., The 7E 98
ROYAL SUTTON COLDFIELD 2C 139
Royston Cl. CV3: Bin 4C 60
Rubens Cl. CV5: Cov 4G 57
RUBERY 1A 142
Rudgard Rd. CV6: Lford 2G 51
Rudge Rd. CV1: Cov 4F 135 (5B 58)
Rufford Cl. B49: Alc 3C 112
RUGBY 5G 75 (1C 145)
Rugby Art Gallery & Mus. 5G 75
Rugby Golf Course 4A 76
Rugby La. CV23: Stret D 3J 83
Rugby Rd. CV3: Bin W 7D 60
CV7: Withy 2C 54
CV8: Bran 7D 60
CV8: Wols 4A 72
CV12: Bulk 3F 43
CV22: Dunc 6D 86
CV23: Barby 7E 88
CV23: Brin 4D 62
CV23: Chu L 3G 73
CV23: Clift D 3B 76
CV23: Eas 4K 63
CV23: Harb M, Harb P 4B 64
CV23: Kils 3F 89
CV23: Lilb, Clift D 2G 77
CV23: Long L 4B 74
CV23: Pail 7K 55
CV23: Prin 7C 82
(Leamington Rd.)
CV23: Prin 7G 83
(Southam Rd.)
CV23: S Ash 2C 54
Rugby Rd. CV32: Cubb, W Weth 2G 99
CV32: Lea S 7A 98
CV33: Wapp, W Weth 2G 99
CV47: Sou, S'ton 3H 107
Rugby RUFC 6E 74
Rugby School Sports Cen. 6H 75
Rugby Station (Rail) 4J 75
Rugby Theatre 5G 75
Rugby Western Relief Rd.
CV21: N'bld A, Rugby 7A 74
CV23: Caw, Law H, Long L 2J 85
Rumer Cl. CV37: Long M 1G 125
Runcorn Cl. B37: F'bri 1C 34
Runcorn Wlk. CV2: Walsg S 1C 60
Runnymede Gdns. CV10: Nun 1F 31
Rupert Brooke Rd. CV22: Rugby 2E 86
Rupert Kettle Dr. CV47: Bis I 5C 110
Rupert Rd. CV6: Cov 6B 50
RUSHALL 1B 138
Rushall Path CV4: Canly 1F 67
RUSHBROOK 2A 90
Rushbrook La. B94: Tan A 1A 90
Rushbrook Rd. CV37: S Avon 7H 115
Rush La. B50: Bidf A 5E 122
B77: Dost, Hock 1D 12
Rushmoor Dr. CV5: Cov 4K 57
Rushmore St. CV31: Lea S 1F 103
Rushmore Ter. CV31: Lea S 1F 103
RUSHOCK 1A 142
Rushock Cl. B98: Redd 1B 92
Rusina Ct. CV31: Lea S 2D 102
Ruskin Cl. CV6: Cov 1H 57
CV10: Gall C 6F 21
CV22: Rugby 3F 87
Russell Av. CV22: Dunc 5D 86
Russell Cl. CV47: Long I 2C 106
Russell St. CV1: Cov 1J 135 (3D 58)
CV32: Lea S 6D 98
Russell St. Nth.
CV1: Cov 1J 135 (3D 58)
Russell Ter. CV31: Lea S 1E 102
Russelsheim Way CV22: Rugby 6G 75
Russet Gro. CV4: Canly 5H 67
Russet Way B50: Bidf A 5G 123
Rutherford Glen CV11: Nun 3B 32
Rutherglen Av. CV3: Cov 2G 69
Rutland Av. CV10: Nun 7A 22
Rutland Cl. CV21: Hillm 6A 76
Rutland Cft. CV3: Bin 7B 60
Rydal Av. CV11: Nun 5H 23
Rydal Cl. CV5: Alle 6F 49
CV21: Brow 2K 75
Ryde Av. CV10: Nun 5E 22
Ryder Cl. CV35: H Mag 2B 100
Ryder Row CV7: New A 4E 28
Ryders Hill Cres. CV10: Nun 4H 21
Rye Cl. CV22: Dunc 6C 86
CV37: S Avon 2D 114
Ryeclose Cft. B37: Chel W 2D 34
Ryefield La. B76: Wis 2B 18
Rye Flds. CV33: Bis T 5B 108
Rye Hill CV5: Alle 1E 56
Rye Hill Office Pk. CV5: Alle 7E 48
Ryelands, The CV23: Law H 2G 85
Rye Piece Ringway CV12: Bed 2H 41
Ryhope Cl. CV12: Bed 4C 40
Ryland Cl. CV31: Lea S 2G 103
Ryland Rd. CV35: Barf 1C 108
Ryland St. CV37: S Avon 6E 114
Ryley St. CV1: Cov 3F 135 (4C 58)
Rylston Av. CV6: Cov 5A 50
Rylstone Way CV34: Warw 6G 97
Ryon Hill CV37: Ing 1K 115
RYTON 3F 43 (3A 140)
Ryton Cl. CV4: Canly 7F 57
Ryton Gdns. CV12: Bulk 3F 43
RYTON-ON-DUNSMORE
. . . . .7D 70 (1A 144)
Ryton Pools Country Pk. 3A 82
Ryton Pools Country Pk. Vis. Cen.
. . . . .4A 82
Ryton Rd. CV8: Bubb 5H 81

S

Sabin Cl. CV47: Long I 2B 106
Sackville Cl. CV37: S Avon 3B 114
Sackville Ho. CV1: Cov 3E 58
(off Adelaide St.)
SADDINGTON 2D 141
Saddington Rd. CV3: Bin 7A 60
Saddledon St. CV35: Mid T 6D 130
Sadler Cl. CV37: S Avon 1E 114
Sadler Gdns. CV12: Bed 3J 41
Sadler Rd. CV6: Cov 5A 50
Sadlers Av. CV36: Ship S 4G 131
Sadlers Cl. CV36: Ship S 4G 131
Sadlers Mdw. B46: Over W 2J 27
Saffron Cl. CV23: Brow 7K 65
Saffron Ct. CV1: Cov 3E 58
Saffron Gdns. CV11: Nun 6C 22
Saffron Mdw. CV37: S Avon 6E 114
Saffron Wlk. CV37: S Avon 6E 114
St Agatha's Rd. CV2: Cov 4G 59
St Agnes Cl. B80: Stud 3B 92
St Agnes Way CV11: Nun 7G 23
St Albans Cl. CV32: Lea S 5A 98
St Andrews Ct. CV21: Rugby 4G 75
St Andrew's Cres.
CV37: S Avon 5A 136 (5D 114)
St Andrews Cres.
CV22: Rugby 1G 87
St Andrews Dr. CV11: Nun 3D 32
St Andrew's Rd. CV5: Cov 7K 57
CV32: Lill 2F 99
St Anne's Rd. CV22: Bil 7E 74
St Ann's Cl. CV31: Lea S 1G 103
St Ann's Rd. CV2: Cov 4G 59
St Asaphs Av. B80: Stud 3C 92
St Augustine's Wlk. CV6: Cov 7A 50
St Austell Cl. CV11: Nun 6H 23
St Austell Rd. CV2: Cov 4A 60
St Bartholomews Cl. CV3: Bin 5C 60
St Benedicts Cl. CV9: Ath 3C 16
St Bernards Wlk. CV3: W'hall 2K 69
St Blaise Av. B46: Wat O 2B 24
St Brides Cl. CV31: Lea S 2G 103
SAINTBURY 2A 146
St Buryan Cl. CV11: Nun 6H 23
Saintbury Cl. CV37: S Avon 6J 115
St Catherine's Cl. CV3: Cov 7H 59
St Catherine's Cres.
CV31: W'nsh 5D 102
St Catherines Lodge CV6: Cov 3A 58
St Chads M. B94: Lapw 3J 91
St Chads Rd. B80: Stud 3B 92
CV33: Bis T 5B 108
St Christian's Cft.
CV3: Cov 7K 135 (7D 58)
St Christian's Rd. CV3: Cov 7E 58
St Christopher's Cl. CV34: Warw 7F 97
St Clements Ct. CV2: Cov 6K 51
CV9: Ath 3D 16
(off South St.)
St Columba's Cl.
CV1: Cov 1G 135 (3C 58)
St Davids Cl. CV31: Lea S 1G 103
St Davids Orchard CV3: Bin 1B 70
St Davids Wlk. CV37: N'bld S 1G 127
St Davids Way CV10: Griff 6G 31
St Declan Cl. CV10: Nun 1C 30
St Edithas Rd. B78: Pole 2D 10
St Ediths Cl. CV23: M Kirby 3J 55
St Ediths Grn. CV34: Warw 7K 97
St Edmonds Rd. CV9: Hur 6K 13
St Elizabeth's Rd. CV6: Cov 7E 50
St Faith's Rd. B49: Alc 3B 112
St Fremund Way CV31: Lea S 3G 103
St Georges Av. CV22: Rugby 7G 75
St George's Bus. Pk. CV34: Warw . . .7F 97
St George's Cl. CV37: S Avon 3C 114
St George's Rd. CV1: Cov 5F 59
CV9: Ath 1C 16
St Georges Rd. CV31: Lea S 2D 102
St Georges Way CV10: Nun 3H 31
St Giles Rd. CV7: Ash G 7D 40
CV35: Gay 7G 119
St Govans Cl. CV31: Lea S 2G 103
St Gregory's Rd.
CV37: S Avon 1H 137 (4F 115)
ST HELENA 2D 10 (1D 139)
St Helena Rd. B78: Pole 2E 10
St Helens Rd. CV31: Lea S 3D 102
St Helen's Way CV5: Alle 6F 49
St Ives Rd. CV2: Cov 4K 59
St Ives Way CV11: Nun 6G 23
St James' Av. CV35: Welle 2H 117
St James Cl. CV37: A'ton 2C 116
St James Ct. CV3: W'hall 2A 70
CV47: Sou 5H 107
(off Market Hill)
St James Cres. CV47: Sou 4G 107
ST JAMES' END 2D 145
St James Gdns. CV12: Bulk 3E 42
St James La. CV3: W'hall 3J 69
St James Mdw. Rd. CV32: Lea S . . .5A 98
St James Rd. CV47: Sou 4H 107
ST JOHNS 7D 78
St Johns CV34: Warw 1H 101
St John's Av. CV8: Ken 6D 78
St Johns Av. CV22: Hillm 1A 88
St John's Cl. CV36: Cher 6G 133
CV37: S Avon 6E 114
St Johns Cl. B95: Hen A 2G 93
St John's Ct. CV34: Warw 1H 101
CV37: S Avon 7B 136 (6E 114)
St Johns Courtyard CV9: Ath 3C 16
St Johns Flats CV8: Ken 6E 78
St John's House Mus. 1H 101
St John's La. CV23: Long L 3A 74
St John's Rd. CV36: Cher 6G 133
St Johns Rd. CV10: Ans C 3D 20
CV31: Lea S 2E 102
St John's St. CV1: Cov 5J 135 (5D 58)
CV8: Ken 6E 78
St Johns Ter. CV31: Lea S 2E 102
St John St. CV21: Rugby 4G 75
St Josephs CV23: M Kirby 3K 55
St Judes Av. B80: Stud 3B 92
St Jude's Cres. CV3: W'hall 1K 69
St Just's Rd. CV2: Cov 3B 60
St Laurence Av. CV34: Warw 3F 101
St Laurence Cl. CV7: Mer 5F 47
CV35: Row 7J 91
St Laurence Way B50: Bidf A 5G 123
St Lawrence Cl. CV47: Nap 2J 111
St Lawrence Rd. CV10: Ansl 7A 20
St Lawrence's Rd. CV6: Cov 5F 51
St Leonard's Cl. B37: Mars G 6A 34
St Leonards Cl. B78: Dord 4D 10
CV47: P Mars 5G 111
St Leonards Vw. B78: Dord, Pole . . .2C 10
St Leonard's Wlk. CV8: Rytn D 7C 70
St Luke's Rd. CV6: Cov 3D 50
St Luke's Way CV10: Nun 7H 21
St Margaret Rd. CV1: Cov 5F 59
St Margarets Av. CV8: Wols 4J 71
St Margarets Ho. CV31: W'nsh 4F 103
St Margaret's Rd. CV31: Lea S 3F 103
St Mark's Av. CV22: Bil 2C 86
St Mark's Cl. B95: Ullen 5B 90
CV10: Nun 7H 21
CV35: Gay 7G 119
St Mark's Ct. CV22: Bil 1D 86
St Mark's La. CV32: Lea S 6C 98
St Mark's M. CV32: Lea S 6C 98
St Mark's Rd. CV32: Lea S 6B 98
St Martin's Av. B80: Stud 3C 92
St Martin's Cl.
CV37: S Avon 5A 136 (5D 114)
St Martin's Rd. CV3: Finh 4C 68
(not continuous)
St Marys Acre CV37: Bear 7D 94
St Mary's Cl. B95: Ullen 6B 90
CV47: Sou 4J 107
St Marys Cl. CV34: Warw 7F 97
St Mary's Ct. CV8: Ken 6D 78
CV11: Nun 6C 22
(off Up. Abbey St.)
St Marys Courtyard CV9: Ath 3C 16
(off Market St.)
St Mary's Cres. CV31: Lea S 1F 103
St Marys Gro. B79: Newt R 5D 6
St Mary's Guildhall 4J 135
(off Bayley La.)
St Marys Priory Rd. CV6: Cov 5B 50
St Mary's Rd. B49: Alc 4D 112
CV7: Fill 2C 38
CV9: Ath 3D 16
CV11: Nun 6C 22
CV31: Lea S 1F 103
CV37: S Avon 3F 115
St Mary's Ter. CV31: Lea S 1F 103
St Mary St. CV1: Cov 4J 135 (5D 58)
St Matthew's Cl. CV10: Nun 7H 21
St Matthews Cl. WR11: Salf P 6A 122
St Matthews St. CV21: Rugby 5G 75
St Michael's Av. CV1: Cov 3J 135
St Michael's Cl. CV7: Gun H 4D 28
CV33: Ufton 2F 109
CV35: Clav 2D 94
CV47: Bis I 6B 110
St Michaels Cl. CV9: Ath 2D 16
CV9: Wood E 2K 13
CV21: Brow 1H 75
St Michael's Cres. CV47: S'ton 6C 106
St Michael's Rd. CV2: Cov 4G 59
CV35: Clav 2D 94
St Michaels Rd. CV34: Warw 7E 96
St Michael's Way CV10: Nun 7H 21
St Nicholas Av. CV8: Ken 6D 78
St Nicholas Chu. St.
CV34: Warw 2H 101
St Nicholas Cl. B49: Alc 4C 112
CV1: Cov 2C 58
CV9: Aus 6H 7
St Nicholas Ct. CV6: Cov 1B 58
(Dugdale Rd.)
CV6: Cov 7F 51
(Torcastle Cl.)
CV34: Warw 2H 101
(off St Nicholas Chu. St.)
St Nicholas Est. CV9: Gren 1F 15
St Nicholas Pk. CV34: Warw 2H 101
St Nicholas Pk. Leisure Cen. 1J 101
St Nicholas Rd. B95: Hen A 2H 93
CV31: Rad S 3J 103
St Nicholas St.
CV1: Cov 1G 135 (2C 58)
St Nicholas Ter. CV31: Rad S 4J 103
St Nicholas Wlk. B76: Curd 5B 18
ST NICOLAS PARK 4G 23
St Nicolas Pk. Dr. CV11: Nun 4F 23
St Nicolas Rd. CV11: Nun 6E 22
St Osburg's Rd. CV2: Cov 4G 59

St Patricks Rd.—Sherbourne

St Patricks Rd.
CV1: Cov 6H 135 (5C 58)
St Paul's Cl. CV34: Warw 2F 101
St Pauls Ct. B46: Wat O 1B 24
St Paul's Cres. B46: Cole 5F 25
St Paul's Rd. CV6: Cov 1E 58
CV10: Nun 1C 30
St Pauls Sq. CV32: Lea S 6E 98
St Paul's Ter. CV34: Warw 2F 101
St Peter's Av. CV9: With 4G 17
St Peter's Cl. CV9: With 4G 17
St Peters Cl. B46: Wat O 2B 24
St Peter's Ct. CV1: Cov 1K 135
CV35: Kine 5D 120
St Peter's Dr. CV10: Gall C 7E 20
St Peters La. B92: Bick 5D 44
St Peter's Rd. CV21: Rugby 6J 75
CV32: Lea S 7D 98
CV35: Welle 2H 117
St Peters Rd. CV9: Man 4F 17
CV35: Kine 5D 120
St Peters Way
CV37: B'ton, S Avon 2C 114
ST PETER THE GREAT 3A 142
St Phillips Ct. B46: Cole 5G 25
Saints Way CV10: Nun 6E 22
St Swithin's Dr.
CV37: Lwr Q 5H 125
St Thomas' Ct. CV1: Cov 5B 58
St Thomas Ho. *CV1: Cov 5B 58*
(off Albany Rd.)
St Thomas Rd. CV6: Cov 3G 51
St Thomas's Cl. CV10: Nun 1C 30
St Vincents Ho. B46: Cole 7G 25
St Wilfreds Cotts. CV7: Old A 2C 28
St Wulstan Ct. CV47: Sou 5J 107
St Wulstan Way CV47: Sou 4J 107
Salcombe Cl. CV3: W'hall 2K 69
CV11: Nun 6G 23
SALE GREEN 3A 142
Salemorton Ct. CV22: Dunc 3B 86
SALEWAY 3A 142
SALFORD 3B 146
Salford Cl. B98: Redd 1A 92
CV2: Cov 2G 59
SALFORD PRIORS 7C 122 (3B 142)
Salford Rd. B50: Bidf A 7D 122
Salisbury Av. CV3: Cov 2C 68
Salisbury Cl. CV8: Wols 5H 71
Salisbury Dr. B46: Wat O 1C 24
CV10: Nun 4G 21
Salix Cl. CV4: Canly 7G 57
Sallieforth Pl. B50: Bidf A 6G 123
SALPERTON 3A 146
Salters La. B95: Woot W 6A 94
Saltisford CV34: Warw 1F 101
Saltisford Gdns. CV34: Warw 7F 97
Saltisford Office Pk.
CV34: Warw 1F 101
Salt La. CV1: Cov 4H 135 (5C 58)
Salt St. B79: App M, No Hth 2G 7
CV9: A Par, Aus 2G 7
Saltway La. OX15: Lwr Bra 3J 133
Salvia Way CV12: Bed 3D 40
SALWARPE 2A 142
Samantha Cl. CV37: Welf A 4A 124
SAMBOURNE 6A 92 (2B 142)
Sambourne La.
B96: A'wd B, Sam 6A 92
B96: Sam 7B 92
Sambourne Pk. B96: Sam 6A 92
Sam Gault Cl. CV3: Bin 1B 70
Sammons Way CV4: Tile H 6B 56
Sampson Cl. CV2: Cov 5J 51
Samuel Hayward Ho. *CV2: Cov 5H 51*
(off Roseberry Av.)
Samuel Rd. CV2: Cov 1H 59
Samuel Va. Ho.
CV1: Cov 1G 135 (3C 58)
Sanctus Ct. CV37: S Avon 6E 114
Sanctus Dr. CV37: S Avon 6E 114
Sanctus Rd. CV37: S Avon 6D 114
Sanctus St. CV37: S Avon 6E 114
Sanda Cft. B36: Cas B 6B 24
Sand Barn La. CV37: Blk H, Snitt . . .6K 95
Sandby Cl. CV12: Bed 1G 41
Sandel Cl. CV37: S Avon 4D 114
Sanders Cl. CV9: Ath 2D 16
Sanders Ct. CV34: Warw 7K 97
Sanders Rd. CV6: Lford 7H 41
WR11: Salf P 7C 122
Sandfield Ct. CV37: S Avon 6E 114
Sandfield La. CV37: N'bld S 1G 127
Sandfield Rd. CV37: S Avon 6E 114
Sandford Cl. CV2: Ald G 3K 51
SANDFORD ST MARTIN 3D 147
Sandford Way CV22: Dunc 6C 86
Sandgate Cres. CV2: Cov 5A 60
Sandhurst Gro. CV6: Cov 2B 58
Sandilands Cl. CV2: Cov 3A 60
Sandon Rd. CV11: Nun 6C 22
Sandown Av. CV6: Cov 4F 51
Sandown Cl. CV32: Lill 3G 99
CV37: S Avon 6C 114
Sandown Rd. CV21: Rugby 4J 75
Sandpiper Cl. CV23: Brow 6J 65
CV37: B'ton 2C 114
Sandpiper Rd. CV2: Ald G 3H 51
Sandpits, The CV12: Bulk 3E 42
Sandpits Cl. B76: Curd 5B 18
CV35: Mid T 6C 130
Sandpits La. CV6: Cov 4J 49
CV7: Ker E 4J 49
Sandpits Rd. CV35: Mid T 7C 130
Sandringham Cl. CV4: Westw H 2D 66
Sandringham Ct. CV10: Nun 5A 22
Sandwick Cl. CV3: Bin 7B 60
Sandy La. B46: Over W 1G 27
B79: Newt R 1D 6
CV1: Cov 2C 58
CV6: Cov 2C 58
CV7: Fill 2D 38
CV21: Rugby 5E 74
CV23: M Kirby 2J 55
CV23: Mart 3E 104
CV32: B'dwn 1C 98
Sandy La. Bus. Pk. CV1: Cov 2C 58
Sandythorpe CV3: W'hall 2A 70
Sandy Way CV35: Barf 3C 108
Sandy Way La. B78: Dord 3F 11
Santos Cl. CV3: Bin 7B 60
SAPCOTE 2B 140
Sapcote Gro. CV6: Ald G 2H 51
Sapper Cl. CV37: Lwr Q 6F 125
Sapphire Ct. CV2: Walsg S 5D 52
Sapphire Dr. CV31: Lea S 3D 102
Sapphire Ga. CV2: Cov 5J 59
Sarawak Pl. CV22: Caw 1B 86
Sargasso La. CV10: Nun 3G 31
Sargeaunt St. CV31: Lea S 1D 102
Sark Dr. B36: Cas B 6B 24
SARSDEN 3B 146
Satchwell Ct. CV32: Lea S 7D 98
Satchwell Pl. CV31: Lea S 1E 102
Satchwell Wlk. *CV32: Lea S 7D 98*
(off Park St.)
Saturn Way CV37: S Avon 7J 115
Saumur Way CV34: Warw 2A 102
Saunders Av. CV12: Bed 3H 41
Saunton Cl. CV5: Alle 5F 49
Saunton Pl. CV22: Bil 7F 75
Saunton Rd. CV22: Bil 7F 75
Savages Cl. CV33: Bis T 5D 108
Sava Ho. CV1: Cov 2G 135 (4C 58)
Savannah Cl. CV4: Tile H 4A 56
Saville Gro. CV8: Ken 3G 79
SAWBRIDGE 7K 105 (2C 145)
Sawbridge Rd. CV23: Gran 6H 105
Saxon Cl. B78: Pole 1C 10
B80: Stud 2D 92
CV3: Bin W 1F 71
CV22: Caw 1A 86
CV37: S Avon 5G 115
Saxon Ct. *B50: Bidf A 6G 123*
(off High St.)
CV32: Lea S 6B 98
Saxon Dr. NN6: Crick 3K 89
Saxonfields B50: Bidf A 6G 123
Saxon Mdws. CV32: Lea S 5A 98
Saxon Rd. CV2: Cov 3H 59
Saxon Sanctuary, The 5H 93
Saxon Way B37: K'hrst 2A 34
Sayer Dr. CV5: Alle 6F 49
Scafell CV21: Brow 1K 75
Scafell Cl. CV5: East G 3E 56
Scar Bank CV34: Warw 6G 97
Scarborough Way CV4: Tile H 1D 66
Scarman Rd. CV4: Canly 4E 66
Schofield Rd. B37: K'hrst 7A 24
Scholars Ct.
CV37: S Avon 4C 136 (5E 114)
Scholars Dr. CV22: Caw 1B 86
Scholars La.
CV37: S Avon 5D 136 (5E 114)
Scholfield Rd. CV7: Ker E 7A 40
School Av. WR11: Salf P 6B 122
School Bell M. CV8: S'lgh 3B 80
School Cl. B37: K'hrst 6A 24
CV3: Cov 5F 59
CV36: Long C 2C 134
Schoolfield Gro. CV21: Rugby 5F 75
School Gdns. CV21: Hillm 7C 76
School Hill CV10: Harts 4F 21
CV47: Nap 2H 111
School Ho. La. CV2: Walsg S 1C 60
School La. B76: Lea M 4G 19
B79: Shut 2C 8
CV7: Exh 6E 40
CV8: Ken 4D 78
CV10: Gall C 5D 20
CV23: Stret D 3H 83
CV31: Rad S 3J 103
CV37: Bear 6D 94
CV37: Ett 2B 126
School La. CV37: Tidd 2K 115
CV47: Ladb 3C 110
CV47: P Mars 5G 111
LE10: Wlvy 2J 33
OX15: Lwr Bra 3H 133
OX17: Warm 2H 129
School Rd. B49: Alc 4B 112
B95: Hen A 2G 93
CV12: Bulk 3D 42
CV35: Welle 3H 117
CV37: Snitt 6G 95
WR11: Salf P 5A 122
School St. CV8: Wols 5J 71
CV21: Hillm 7C 76
CV22: Dunc 6C 86
CV23: C'over 1J 65
CV23: Chu L 3F 73
CV23: Long L 4A 74
CV47: S'ton 6C 106
CV47: Sou 5J 107
School Wlk. CV11: Nun 2A 32
Scimitar Way CV3: Cov 2F 69
Scotchill, The CV6: Cov 5A 50
SCOTLAND END 2C 147
Scots Cl. CV22: Bil 2C 86
Scots La. CV6: Cov 1K 57
Scott Av. CV10: Nun 3E 22
Scott Cl. B50: Bidf A 5F 123
CV37: S Avon 6H 115
Scott Rd. CV8: Ken 7C 78
CV31: Lea S 2F 103
Scowcroft Dr. CV47: Bis I 7B 110
SCRAPTOFT 1D 141
Seabroke Av. CV22: Rugby 5F 75
Seaford Cl. CV6: Ald G 2H 51
Seagrave Rd. CV1: Cov 5E 58
Sealand Dr. CV12: Bed 2G 41
Seashell Cl. CV5: Alle 6F 49
Seathwaite CV21: Brow 1J 75
Seaton Cl. CV11: Nun 6G 23
Sebastian Cl. CV3: W'hall 3H 69
SECKINGTON 5A 6 (1D 139)
Seckington La. B79: Newt R 5C 6
Second Av. CV3: Cov 6J 59
Sedgemoor Cl. CV37: S Avon 6J 115
Sedgemoor Rd.
CV3: W'hall 3H 69
Sedge Rd. CV23: Newt 7K 65
SEDGLEY 2A 138
Sedlescombe Lodge
CV22: Rugby 1F 87
Sedlescombe Pk. CV22: Rugby 1F 87
Seedfield Cft. CV3: Cov 1D 68
Seekings, The
CV31: W'nsh 5F 103
Seekings Dr. CV8: Ken 5F 79
Seeney La. B76: Mars 1H 19
Seeswood Cl. CV10: Nun 2C 30
Sefton Rd. CV4: Canly 2J 67
Seggs La. B49: Alc 5B 112
Segrave Cl. CV35: Kine 5D 120
Selborne Rd. CV22: Bil 1D 86
Selby Way CV10: Nun 6G 21
SELLY OAK 3B 138
Selsey Cl. CV3: W'hall 4J 69
Selside CV21: Brow 1K 75
Selworthy Rd. CV6: Cov 3D 50
Selwyn Cl. CV35: Welle 2H 117
Selwyn Ho. B37: Chel W 2D 34
Semele Cl. CV31: Rad S 3J 103
Seneschal Rd. CV3: Cov 1E 68
Sennen Cl. CV11: Nun 6H 23
Sephton Dr. CV6: Lford 7J 41
Sequoia M.
CV37: S Avon 7K 137 (5G 115)
Serin Ho. CV6: Cov 3H 51
Servite Ho. B46: Cole 5G 25
CV8: Ken 6D 78
Sessile Oak Cl. CV21: Brow 6H 65
Sett, The CV35: Oxh 1D 130
Seven Acre Cl. CV33: Bis T 5B 108
Seven Foot La. CV10: Nun 5H 21
Seven Mdws. Rd.
CV37: S Avon 7C 136 (6E 114)
Seven Stars Ind. Est. CV3: Cov 1G 69
(not continuous)
Severn Cl. B36: Cas B 5A 24
CV32: Lill 4G 99
Severn Ct. B49: Kinw 2D 112
Severn Rd. CV1: Cov 6F 59
CV12: Bulk 2C 42
Sevilla Cl. CV3: Bin 5C 60
Sevincott Cl. CV37: S Avon 3B 114
Sewall Highway CV2: Cov 1H 59
CV6: Cov 6G 51
Sewell Pl. CV21: Hillm 7B 76
Seymour Cl. CV3: W'hall 3J 69
CV35: H Mag 2B 100
Seymour Gro. CV34: Warw 2B 102
Seymour Homes
B95: Woot W 5H 93
Seymour Pl. CV8: Ken 3C 78
Seymour Rd. B49: Alc 3C 112
CV11: Nun 1K 31
CV21: Rugby 2J 75
CV37: Shot 6C 114
SHACKERSTONE 1A 140
Shadowbrook La. B92: H Ard 6D 44
Shadowbrook Rd. CV6: Cov 2A 58
Shaftesbury Av. CV7: Ker E 6A 40
Shaftesbury Rd. CV5: Cov 7K 57
Shaft La. CV7: Mer 2H 47
Shakesfield Cl. CV36: Tred 6J 127
Shakespeare Av. CV12: Bed 3K 41
CV34: Warw 3E 100
Shakespeare Cen., The 2F 137
Shakespeare Ct.
CV37: S Avon 2G 137
Shakespeare Dr. CV11: Nun 3C 32
Shakespeare Gdns. CV22: Rugby . . .1E 86
Shakespeare Institute, The
The University of Birmingham
. . . . .6E 136 (5E 114)
Shakespeare Memorial Fountain
. . . . .4E 136
Shakespeare's Birthplace 2F 137
Shakespeare St. CV2: Cov 2H 59
CV37: S Avon 2E 136 (4F 115)
Shakleton Rd. CV5: Cov 5A 58
Shamble, The *CV36: Ship S 4H 131*
(off Market Pl.)
SHANGTON 2D 141
Shanklin Dr. CV10: Nun 5E 22
Shanklin Rd. CV3: W'hall 4H 69
Shapfell CV21: Brow 1K 75
SHARESHILL 1A 138
SHARNFORD 2B 140
Sharp Cl. CV6: Cov 4C 50
Sharpe Cl. CV34: Warw 7G 97
Sharpley Ct. CV2: Walsg S 6C 52
Sharratt Rd. CV12: Bed 3F 41
Shawbury La. B46: Shu 2E 26
CV7: Fill 6G 27
Shawbury School La. B46: Shu 5G 27
Shawbury Village B46: Shu 6G 27
Shaw Cl. CV37: Snitt 5G 95
Shawe Av. CV10: Nun 4D 22
SHAWELL 3C 141
SHEARSBY 2D 141
Shearwater Dr. CV23: Brow 6J 65
Sheelin Cres. CV10: Nun 6B 22
Sheepclose Dr. B37: F'bri 2A 34
Sheepcote Cl. CV32: Lea S 6E 98
Sheepcote Dr. CV23: Long L 4A 74
Sheep Dip La. CV23: Prin 6G 83
Sheep St. CV21: Rugby 5G 75
CV36: Ship S 4H 131
CV37: S Avon 5G 137 (5F 115)
SHEEPY MAGNA 1A 140
SHEEPY PARVA 1A 140
Sheepy Rd. CV9: Ath 1C 16
Shelbourne Rd. CV37: S Avon 3A 114
Shelby La. CV37: Snitt 5J 95
SHELDON 3C 139
Sheldon Gro. CV34: Warw 6H 97
Sheldons, The CV36: Ship S 3H 131
Sheldrake Cl. CV3: Bin 6C 60
SHELFIELD
B49 . . . . .2C 143
WS4 . . . . .1B 138
Shelfield Cl. CV5: East G 4F 57
SHELFORD 3B 140
SHELL 3A 142
Shelley Av. CV34: Warw 4E 100
Shelley Cl. CV12: Bed 4K 41
Shelley Ct. CV2: Cov 3J 59
Shelley Rd. CV2: Cov 4J 59
CV37: S Avon 6G 115
Shellon Cl. CV3: Bin 7B 60
Shelton Sq. CV1: Cov 4G 135 (5C 58)
SHENINGTON 1C 147
Shenington Rd. CV35: Up Tys 7D 130
SHENSTONE
DY10 .1A 142
WS14 .1C 139
Shenstone Av. CV22: Hillm 7A 76
SHENSTONE WOODEND 1C 139
SHENTON 1A 140
Shenton Wlk. B37: K'hrst 7A 24
Shepherd Cl. CV4: Tile H 4D 56
CV47: Long I 2D 106
Shepherd Pl. CV35: Kine 6C 120
Shepherds Hill CV47: Sou 5J 107
Shepherds La. CV7: Mer 3C 46
Shepherd St. CV23: Mart 2D 104
Shepperton Bus. Pk.
CV11: Nun 3J 31
Shepperton Ct. CV11: Nun 2J 31
Shepperton St. CV11: Nun 2J 31
Sheppey Dr. B36: Cas B 7B 24
Sherard Cft. B36: Cas B 6B 24
Sherborne Cl. B46: Cole 1G 35
SHERBOURNE
. . . . .7B 100, 1A 108 (2D 143)

Stratford Rd.—Thelsford

Stratford Rd. CV35: H Lucy 2A 118
CV35: Lox 4B 116
CV35: Sher 7A 100
CV35: Welle 2F 117
CV36: Ilm 4C 126
CV36: Ship S 4H 131
CV37: Ett 1B 126
CV37: N'bld S 1G 127
Stratford St. CV2: Cov 3G 59
CV11: Nun 7D 22
STRATFORD-UPON-AVON
. . . . .3F 137 (5F 115)
Stratford-upon-Avon Boat Club
. . . . .6J 137 (5F 115)
Stratford-upon-Avon Butterfly Farm, The
. . . . .6K 137 (5G 115)
Stratford-upon-Avon
(Park & Ride) 1C 114
Stratford-upon-Avon Racecourse
. . . . .7C 114
Stratford-upon-Avon Station
(Rail) 2A 136 (4D 114)
Strath Cl. CV21: Hillm 2C 88
Strathearn Rd. CV32: Lea S 6C 98
Strathmore Av. CV1: Cov 5E 58
Stratton St. CV9: Ath 3D 16
Strawberry Flds. CV7: Mer 5D 46
Strawberry Wlk. CV2: Cov 4K 51
Streamside Cl. CV5: Alle 6E 48
STREET ASHTON 5H 55
STREETHAY 1C 139
STREETLY 2B 138
STRETTON 1A 138
Stretton Av. CV3: W'hall 3J 69
Stretton Cl. GL56: Stret O 1A 132
Stretton Ct. CV21: Brow 1K 75
Stretton Cres. CV31: Lea S 3F 103
STRETTON EN LE FIELD 1A 140
Stretton Lodge CV3: W'hall 2J 69
STRETTON-ON-DUNSMORE
. . . . .3H 83 (1B 144)
STRETTON-ON-FOSSE . . .2C 132 (2B 146)
Stretton Rd. CV8: Wols 2J 83
CV10: Nun 1G 31
CV23: Wols 2J 83
STRETTON UNDER FOSSE
. . . . .7G 55 (3B 140)
Stroma Way CV10: Nun 2F 31
Stuart Cl. CV34: Warw 3F 101
Stuart Ct. CV6: Cov 6G 51
CV32: Lea S 6C 98
Stuart Gdns. CV47: Temp H 2A 120
Stubbs Cl. CV12: Bed 1G 41
Stubbs Gro. CV2: Cov 2H 59
Studland Av. CV21: Hillm 7B 76
Studland Grn. CV2: Walsg S 3C 60
STUDLEY 3D 92 (2B 142)
Studley Leisure Cen. 3D 92
Studley Point B80: Stud 2D 92
Studley Rd. B98: Redd 1B 92
Sturley Cl. CV8: Ken 3F 79
Sturminster Cl. CV2: Walsg S 3C 60
Stylers Way B95: Hen A 2H 93
Styles Cl. CV31: Lea S 1E 102
CV35: H Mag 1B 100
Styvechale Av. CV5: Cov 7K 57
SUCKLE GREEN 7F 11
Sudbury Cl. CV32: Lill 5G 99
Sudeley Rd. CV10: Nun 4J 31
Suffolk Cl. CV5: East G 4F 57
CV10: Nun 1E 30
CV12: Bed 2G 41
Suffolk St. CV32: Lea S 6E 98
SULGRAVE 1D 147
Sulgrave Cl. CV2: Cov 7A 52
Sullivan Ct. CV6: Cov 7H 51
Sullivan Rd. CV6: Cov 7H 51
Summer Ct. CV37: S Avon 1G 137
SUMMER HILL 2A 138
Summerhill Dr. CV11: Nun 5J 23
Summerhill La. CV4: Tile H 4A 56
Summerton Rd. CV31: W'nsh 5E 102
Summerton Way
CV37: S Avon 5B 136 (5E 114)
Sumner Cl. CV35: H Mag 2B 100
Sumner Rd. B46: Cole 6G 25
Sunart Way CV10: Nun 6H 21
Sunbeam Cl. B36: Cas B 3A 24
CV21: Rugby 5J 75
Sunbeam Way CV3: Cov 7G 59
Sunbridge Ter. CV21: Rugby 5J 75
Sunbury Rd. CV3: W'hall 3J 69
Suncliffe Dr. CV8: Ken 7D 78
Sunderland Pl. CV35: Welle 5G 117
Sundew St. CV2: Cov 4K 51
Sundorne Cl. CV5: East G 3E 56
Sunfields Cl. B78: Pole 2E 10
Sunflower Dr. CV10: Nun 4G 31
Sunningdale Av. CV6: Cov 4D 50
CV8: Ken 5F 79
Sunningdale Cl. CV11: Nun 3C 32
Sunnybank Av. CV3: W'hall 3H 69
Sunnyside B95: Aston C 1K 113
Sunnyside Cl. CV5: Cov 4K 57
Sunnyside Ct. CV10: Nun 1F 31
Sunset Cl. B78: Pole 2D 10
Sunshine Cl. CV8: Ken 7E 78
Sunshine Cotts.
CV37: Shot 5C 114
Sunshine Wlk. CV2: Cov 5J 51
Sun St. CV21: Rugby 5J 75
Sunway Gro. CV3: Cov 2B 68
Surrey Cl. CV10: Nun 1E 30
Surrey Ct. CV34: Warw 7G 97
Surrey Dr. CV3: Cov 6G 59
Sussex Cl. CV10: Nun 1E 30
Sussex Ct. CV34: Warw 7G 97
Sussex Rd. CV5: Cov 3K 57
Sutcliffe Dr. CV33: Har 6G 109
Sutherland Av. CV5: East G 3E 56
Sutherland Cl.
CV34: Warw 6G 97
Sutherland Dr. CV12: Bed 1G 41
Sutton Av. CV5: East G 2A 56
SUTTON CHENEY 1B 140
SUTTON COLDFIELD, ROYAL 2C 139
Sutton Ct. CV6: Lford 7J 41
Sutton Dr. CV31: W'nsh 6E 102
Sutton Ho. CV22: Bil 7C 74
SUTTON IN THE ELMS 2C 141
Sutton La. OX15: Lwr Bra 4G 133
Sutton Pk. CV10: Nun 4G 21
Sutton Stop CV6: Lford 1H 51
SUTTON-UNDER-BRAILES
. . . . .5H 133 (2C 147)
Swadling St. CV31: Lea S 2D 102
Swain Crofts CV31: Lea S 2F 103
SWALCLIFFE 2C 147
Swaledale CV4: Canly 2H 67
Swallow Av. B36: Cas B 4A 24
Swallow Cl. CV37: S Avon 2F 115
Swallow Ct. CV12: Bed 5C 40
Swallowdean Rd. CV6: Cov 6J 49
Swallow Dr. CV34: H'cte 4A 102
Swallowgate Bus. Pk. CV6: Cov 5C 50
Swallow Rd. CV6: Cov 5B 50
Swanage Grn. CV2: Walsg S 3C 60
Swan Bus. Pk., The
CV37: S Avon 3D 114
Swan Cl. CV10: Nun 4H 31
Swan Ct. CV37: S Avon 5G 115
Swancroft Rd. CV2: Cov 2F 59
Swanfold CV37: Wilm 5J 113
Swan La. CV2: Cov 3F 59
Swan Mdw. CV34: Warw 5D 100
Swans Cl. CV37: Wilm 5J 113
Swansnest Gro. CV10: Nun 4H 31
Swan's Nest La.
CV37: S Avon 6K 137 (5G 115)
Swan St. B49: Alc 5B 112
CV32: Lea S 6E 98
CV34: Warw 2G 101
Swanswell St.
CV1: Cov 1K 135 (3D 58)
Swanswood Gro. B37: Chel W 2C 34
Swan Theatre
Stratford-upon-Avon
. . . . .6H 137 (5F 115)
SWEPSTONE 1A 140
SWERFORD 2C 147
Swift Av. CV21: Brow 7H 65
Swift Cl. B36: Cas B 4A 24
CV8: Ken 7E 78
Swift Ct. CV10: Harts 3G 21
Swift Gdns. CV47: Sou 7H 107
Swift Pk. CV21: Rugby 1G 75
(not continuous)
Swift Point CV21: Rugby 6F 65
Swift Rd. CV1: Cov 6J 135 (6D 58)
CV37: S Avon 2F 115
Swift's Cnr. CV3: Cov 7E 58
Swift Valley Country Pk.
(Nature Reserve) 7G 65
Swift Valley Ind. Est.
CV21: Rugby 7F 65
Swillington Rd. CV6: Cov 2B 58
Swinburne Av. CV2: Cov 5K 59
Swinburne Cl. CV10: Gall C 6F 21
Swindale Cft. CV3: Bin 7B 60
SWINDON 2A 138
SWINFORD 1C 145
Swinnerton Heritage CV10: Nun 3D 22
SWITHLAND 1C 141
Sycamore Av. B78: Pole 2D 10
Sycamore Cl. CV35: Welle 3J 117
CV37: S Avon 2E 114
CV47: S'ton 6B 106
Sycamore Ct. CV5: Alle 7D 48
CV35: Lit K 7C 120
Sycamore Cres. B37: Mars G 5A 34
CV7: New A 4F 29
Sycamore Gro. CV21: Rugby 4G 75
CV34: Warw 6J 97
CV47: Sou 3H 107
Sycamore Rd. B78: K'bry 4D 12
CV2: Cov 4H 51
CV10: Nun 5J 21
Sycamores, The CV12: Bed 3E 40
SYDENHAM 1G 103
Sydenham Dr. CV31: Lea S 2F 103
Sydenham Ind. Est. CV31: Lea S . . .2F 103
(not continuous)
Sydenham Sports Cen. 3G 103
Sydnall Flds. CV6: Lford 2F 51
Sydnall Rd. CV6: Lford 2F 51
Sydney Ct. CV12: Bed 3F 41
Sylan Ct. OX17: Farnb 6J 121
Sylvan Dr. CV3: Cov 2K 67
Sylvia Bird Cl. CV3: Cov 6J 59
Symons Av. CV36: Ship S 5F 131
Synkere Cl. CV7: Ker E 7A 40
SYSTON 1D 141
Sywell Leys CV22: Rugby 3F 87

T

Tachbrook Cl. CV2: Cov 4J 51
Tachbrook Ct. CV31: Lea S 2D 102
TACHBROOK MALLORY
. . . . .7D 102 (2A 144)
Tachbrook Pk. CV34: Warw 3C 102
Tachbrook Pk. Dr. CV34: Warw 2B 102
Tachbrook Pk. Ind. Est.
CV34: Warw 3B 102
Tachbrook Rd.
CV31: Lea S, W'nsh 6D 102
Tachbrook St. CV31: Lea S 3D 102
(not continuous)
Tackford Rd. CV6: Cov 7G 51
TACKLEY 3D 147
TADDINGTON 2A 146
TADMARTON 2C 147
Tainter Cl. CV21: Rugby 3H 75
Tainters Hill CV8: Ken 3D 78
Tait Way CV35: Welle 5F 117
Talbot Cl. CV10: Nun 7J 21
Talbot Ct. CV32: Lea S 6E 98
CV35: Welle 3J 117
Talbot Rd. CV37: S Avon 3F 115
Talisman Cl. CV8: Ken 6D 78
Talisman Sq. CV8: Ken 5D 78
Talisman Theatre 6D 78
Talland Av. CV6: Cov 1G 59
Tallants Cl. CV6: Cov 6G 51
Tallants Rd. CV6: Cov 6F 51
Tamar Cl. CV12: Bulk 2D 42
CV23: Long L 3B 74
Tamar Dr. B36: Cas B 4A 24
Tamarisk Cl. CV12: Bed 1J 41
Tamar Rd. CV12: Bulk 3C 42
Tame Av. B36: Cas B 4A 24
Tame Bank B78: K'bry 5D 12
Tamora Cl. CV34: H'cte 5B 102
TAMWORTH 1D 139
Tamworth Municipal Golf Course . . .6A 8
Tamworth Rd.
B46: Neth W, Over W 1F 27
B46: Over W 3H 27
B76: Midd, Wis 1C 18
B77: Dost 2D 12
(not continuous)
B78: Cliff, K'bry 2D 12
B78: Pole 1A 10
CV6: Cov 4E 38
CV7: Cor, Ker E 4E 38
(not continuous)
CV7: Fill, Old A 3H 27
CV9: Wood E 2K 13
Tamworth Sailing Club 7C 12
TAMWORTH SERVICE AREA 3A 10
Tancred Cl. CV31: Lea S 3D 102
Tankards Hill GL56: Stret O 1A 132
TANNER'S GREEN 1B 142
Tanners Gro. CV6: Lford 2D 50
Tanner's La. CV4: Tile H 6A 56
CV7: Berk 6A 56
Tannery, The CV36: Ship S 4G 131
Tannery Cl. CV9: Ath 3D 16
Tannery Ct. CV8: Ken 5D 78
Tanser Ct. CV22: Dunc 6C 86
TANWORTH-IN-ARDEN . . .3D 90 (1C 143)
Tanyard, The B95: Hen A 1H 93
Tanyard Cl. CV4: Tile H 6B 56
Tapcon Way CV2: Cov 2B 60
Tappinger Gro. CV8: Ken 4G 79
Tapping Way CV34: Warw 5E 100
TARDEBIGGE 2B 142
Tarlington Rd. CV6: Cov 1J 57
Tarn Cl. CV12: Bed 3G 41
Tarquin Cl. CV3: W'hall 1K 69
Tarragon Cl. CV2: Cov 5K 51
Tarrant Wlk. CV2: Walsg S 2C 60
Tasker's Way
CV37: S Avon 4F 137 (5F 115)
TASTON 3C 147
Tatler Cl. CV34: Warw 6K 97
Tatnall Gro. CV34: Warw 7G 97
TATTLE BANK 4B 94 (2C 143)
Tattle Bank CV47: Sou 6H 107
Taunton Way CV6: Cov 4A 50
Taverners La. CV9: Ath 4C 16
Tavern La. CV37: Shot 5C 114
Tavistock St. CV32: Lea S 6D 98
Tavistock Wlk. CV2: Cov 7J 51
Tavistock Way CV11: Nun 6F 23
Tay Cft. B37: F'bri 1C 34
Taylor Av. CV32: Lill 5F 99
Taylor Cl. CV8: Ken 3F 79
Taylor Ct. CV34: Warw 1F 101
Taylors La. CV37: Up Qui 7F 125
Tay Rd. CV6: Cov 1B 58
Teachers Cl. CV6: Cov 2A 58
Tea Gdn., The CV12: Bed 5E 40
Teagles Gdns. CV7: Gun H 5D 28
Teal Cl. CV37: B'ton 2B 114
Teal Rd. B80: Stud 3D 92
Teal Way CV11: Nun 7H 23
Teasdale Pl. CV34: Warw 5E 100
Teasel Cl. CV23: Brow 7K 65
Technology Dr. CV21: Rugby 2G 75
Technology Retail Pk.
CV21: Rugby 3H 75
Ted Pitts La. CV5: Alle 4F 49
Teeswater Cl. CV23: Long L 4A 74
TEETON 1D 145
Tee Tong Rd. CV23: Long L 4B 74
Telegraph St. CV36: Ship S 4H 131
Telfer Rd. CV6: Cov 7B 50
Telford Av. CV32: Lill 2F 99
Telford Rd. CV7: Exh 5J 41
Templar Av. CV4: Tile H 6E 56
Templar Dr. CV10: Nun 3G 31
Templar Ind. Pk. CV4: Tile H 7F 57
Templars, The CV34: Warw 3H 101
Templars Flds. CV4: Canly 1F 67
TEMPLE BALSALL 1D 143
Temple Ct. B46: Cole 3F 25
Temple End CV33: Har 6F 109
TEMPLE GRAFTON 3C 143
Temple Gro. CV34: Warw 3F 101
TEMPLE GUITING 3A 146
TEMPLE HERDEWYKE 2A 120
Temple Hill LE10: Wlvy 1J 33
Templer Ct. CV11: Nun 1J 31
Temple St. CV21: Rugby 6J 75
Temple Way B46: Cole 3E 24
Ten Acres B49: Alc 4C 112
Tenby Cl. CV12: Bed 4C 40
Tene Cl. CV22: Caw 7A 74
Teneriffe Rd. CV6: Cov 5F 51
Tenlons Rd. CV10: Nun 2F 31
Tenlons Rd. Ind. Est. CV10: Nun 2F 31
Tennant Cl. CV21: Hillm 7A 76
Tennant St. CV11: Nun 1A 32
Tennyson Av. CV22: Rugby 2E 86
CV34: Warw 4E 100
Tennyson Cl. CV8: Ken 5G 79
Tennyson Rd. CV2: Cov 4J 59
CV37: S Avon 7G 115
Tenpin
Coventry 6D 52
Royal Leamington Spa 2C 102
Ten Shilling Dr. CV4: Westw H 2B 66
Tenter St. CV9: Ath 3C 16
Terminal Rd. B26: Birm A 3A 44
Terrace, The CV35: More M 5C 118
CV37: Snitt 6G 95
CV37: Welf A 3B 124
Terrace Rd. CV9: Ath 3C 16
Terracotta Dr. CV2: Cov 3G 59
Terrett Ct.
CV37: S Avon 4F 137 (5F 115)
Terry Av. CV32: Lea S 6A 98
Terry John Cl. CV22: Dunc 6C 86
Terry Rd. CV1: Cov 5F 59
CV3: Cov 6G 59
TERRY'S GREEN 1C 143
TETTENHALL 2A 138
Tewkesbury Dr. CV12: Bed 2J 41
Thackeray Cl. CV10: Gall C 7F 21
CV22: Rugby 2F 87
CV37: Lwr Q 5G 125
Thackeray Rd. CV2: Cov 1G 59
Thackhall St. CV2: Cov 3F 59
Thames Cl. CV12: Bulk 2C 42
Thamley Rd. CV6: Cov 3A 58
Thane Cl. B80: Stud 3D 92
Thatchings, The CV22: Dunc 6C 86
The . . . .
Names prefixed with 'The' for example 'The Abbey' are indexed under the main name such as 'Abbey, The'
Theatre St. CV34: Warw 2F 101
Thebes Cl. CV5: Milli W 6K 47
THEDDINGWORTH 3D 141
Theddingworth Cl. CV3: Bin 7A 60
THELSFORD 1E 118

Tysoe Rd.—Warwick Cl.

Tysoe Rd. CV35: Lit K 7C 120
CV35: Lwr T 4D 130
CV35: Oxh 2E 130, 5A 130
CV35: Rad 6A 128
Tythbarn Leys CV23: Brow 7K 65
Tything Pk. B49: Kinw 2D 112
Tything Rd. (East) B49: Kinw 2D 112
Tything Rd. (West) B49: Kinw 2C 112

U

Ubique Av. CV37: Lwr Q 6F 125
UFTON 2F 109 (2A 144)
Ufton Cft. CV5: East G 4E 56
Ufton Flds. CV33: Ufton 4F 109
Ufton Fields (Nature Reserve) . . .3G 109
Ufton Hill CV33: Ufton 2F 109
Ufton Rd. CV33: Har 5J 109
ULLENHALL 6B 90 (2C 143)
Ullenhall La. B95: Oldb, Ullen 5A 90
Ullenhall St. B95: Ullen 5B 90
ULLESTHORPE 3C 141
Ullswater Av. CV11: Nun 5G 23
CV32: Lea S 5A 98
Ullswater Rd. CV3: Bin 6A 60
CV12: Bed 3G 41
Ulverscroft Rd. CV3: Cov 1C 68
Ulverston CV21: Brow 1K 75
Umberslade Pk. 1C 143
Underhill Cl. CV3: Finh 5D 68
Underpass, The B40: Nat E C 2D 44
Unicorn Av. CV5: East G 3C 56
Unicorn La. CV5: East G 3D 56
(not continuous)
Union Bldgs. CV1: Cov 5H 135 (5C 58)
Union Ct. *CV31: Lea S 2E 102*
(off Ranelagh Ter.)
Union Pl. CV6: Lford 1F 51
Union Rd. CV32: Lea S 6C 98
Union St. CV22: Rugby 6G 75
CV37: S Avon 3G 137 (4F 115)
Union Wlk. CV31: Lea S 1E 102
University of Warwick
Central Campus 3G 67
Gibbet Hill Campus 5H 67
Westwood Campus 1G 67
University of Warwick Science Pk.
CV4: Canly 2F 67
University Rd. CV4: Canly 3F 67
Uplands CV2: Cov 2G 59
Up. Abbey St. CV11: Nun 6C 22
UPPER ASTROP 2D 147
UPPER BENTLEY 2A 142
UPPER BILLESLEY 7H 113
UPPER BODDINGTON 3B 144
UPPER BRAILES 1F 133 (2C 147)
Upper Cape CV34: Warw 7F 97
UPPER CATESBY 3C 145
UPPER EASTERN GREEN
. . . . .2B 56 (3D 139)
Up. Eastern Grn. La. CV5: East G . . .2A 56
Up. Farm Mdw. CV35: Gay 7G 119
Upperfield Way *CV3: Bin 6C 60*
(off Middlefield Dr.)
Upper Gro. St. CV32: Lea S 6C 98
UPPER HEYFORD
NN7 . . . . .3D 145
OX25 . . . . .3D 147
Up. Hill St. CV1: Cov 2F 135 (4B 58)
CV32: Lea S 6E 98
Up. Holly Wlk. CV32: Lea S 6E 98
Up. Ladyes Hill CV8: Ken 3E 78
UPPER LADYES HILLS 3F 79
Upper Mall *CV32: Lea S 7D 98*
(within Royal Priors Shop. Cen.)
UPPER ODDINGTON 3B 146
Upper Pk. CV3: W'hall 3K 69
Up. Precinct CV1: Cov 3G 135 (4C 58)
UPPER QUINTON 7H 125 (1A 146)
Upper Ride CV3: W'hall 3K 69
UPPER RISSINGTON 3B 146
Up. Rosemary Hill CV8: Ken 4D 78
UPPER SLAUGHTER 3A 146
Up. Spon St. CV1: Cov 4A 58
Up. Spring La. CV8: Ken 2D 78
UPPER STOKE 3G 59
UPPER STOWE 3D 145
UPPER SWELL 3A 146
UPPER TYSOE 7C 130 (1C 147)
UPPER WARDINGTON 1D 147
UPPER WEEDON 3D 145
Up. Well St. CV1: Cov 2G 135 (4C 58)
Up. York St. CV1: Cov 6B 58
UPTON
B49 .3C 143
CV13 . . . . .2A 140
NN5 .2D 145
Upton Dr. CV11: Nun 4B 32
Upton House & Gdns. 1C 147
Upton Rd. CV22: Rugby 5D 74
UPTON SNODSBURY 3A 142
UPTON WARREN 2A 142
Usk Way B36: Cas B 4A 24
Utrillo Cl. CV5: Cov 4G 57
Uxbridge Av. CV3: Cov 5J 59

V

Vale, The CV3: Cov 7H 59
CV10: Nun 7K 21
Vale Cl. CV21: Hillm 1C 88
Vale Ct. B80: Stud 3D 92
Valencia Rd. CV3: Bin 5C 60
Valenders La. CV36: Ilm 7C 126
Valentine Cl. CV37: S Avon 7D 114
Vale Vw. CV10: Nun 7K 21
Valiant Cl. CV33: L Hth 2K 119
Vallet Av. B49: Alc 3B 112
Valletta Way CV35: Welle 4G 117
Valley, The CV31: Rad S 4J 103
Valley Dr.
CV21: Cosf, Rugby 6F 65
Valley Rd. CV2: Cov 1G 59
CV10: Gall C 7D 20
CV31: Rad S 4J 103
CV32: Lill 4F 99
Van Dyke Cl. CV5: Cov 4G 57
Vanguard Av. CV5: Cov 6G 57
Vanguard Cen. CV4: Canly 2G 67
Vanguard Rd.
B26: Birm A 2C 44
Vantage Pk. CV6: Cov 6F 51
Vardon Dr. CV3: Finh 4D 68
Vauxhall Cl. CV1: Cov 4E 58
Vauxhall Cres. B36: Cas B 3A 24
Vauxhall St. CV1: Cov 4E 58
Veasey Cl. CV11: Nun 1A 32
Vecqueray St. CV1: Cov 5E 58
Ventnor Cl. CV2: Cov 4A 60
Ventnor St. CV10: Nun 5E 22
Verbena Cl. CV2: Cov 5H 51
Verden Av. CV34: Warw 4D 100
Verdon Pl. CV35: Barf 2C 108
Verdun Cl. CV31: W'nsh 6F 103
Vere Rd. CV21: Hillm 7B 76
Vermont Gro. CV31: Lea S 2H 103
Verney Cl. CV35: Light 2G 119
Verney Dr. CV37: S Avon 2E 114
Verney Gdns. CV37: S Avon 2E 114
Verney Ho's. CV35: Lit K 7C 120
Verney Rd. CV33: L Hth 1K 119
Vernon Av. CV22: Hillm 1A 88
Vernon Cl. CV1: Cov 4E 58
CV32: Lea S 4C 98
Vernon Ct. CV1: Cov 4E 58
Vernons Ct. CV10: Nun 7K 21
Vernons La. CV10: Nun 7K 21
CV11: Nun 7K 21
Vernons M. CV10: Nun 7A 22
Verona Cl. CV11: Nun 3C 32
Vesey Cl. B46: Wat O 2B 24
Viaduct Cl. CV21: Rugby 4K 75
Vicarage Cl. B78: Dord 5C 10
CV9: Ath 4D 16
Vicarage Fld. CV34: Warw 7K 97
Vicarage Gdns. CV8: Ken 7E 78
Vicarage Hill B94: Tan A 2B 90
CV23: Clift D 4A 76
Vicarage La. B46: Wat O 2B 24
CV7: Ash G 6C 40
CV22: Dunc 6D 86
CV33: Har 6H 109
CV35: Sher 7B 100, 1A 108
CV36: Long C 2C 134
CV47: P Mars 5G 111
Vicarage Ri. CV33: Bis T 5C 108
Vicarage Rd. CV8: S'lgh 3B 80
CV22: Rugby 5F 75
CV32: Lill 4F 99
CV47: Nap 2J 111
Vicarage St. CV11: Nun 7E 22
Vicroft Ct. CV1: Cov 4F 135 (5B 58)
Victor Hodges Ho.
CV47: Sou 5H 107
Victoria Av. CV21: Rugby 4F 75
Victoria Bus. Cen.
CV31: Lea S 1E 102
(off Neilston St.)
Victoria Bus. Pk. *CV31: Lea S 1E 102*
(off Neilston St.)
Victoria Cl.
CV37: S Avon 1F 137 (4F 115)
Victoria Colonnade
CV31: Lea S 1D 102
(off Victoria Ter.)
Victoria Ct. CV5: Cov 3H 57
Victoria M. CV3: Bin 5A 60
CV34: Warw 1F 101
Victoria Rd. B50: Bidf A 4F 123
CV9: Man 5E 16
CV10: Harts 3G 21
CV31: Lea S 7C 98
Victoria St. CV1: Cov 1K 135 (3E 58)
CV11: Nun 7D 22
CV21: Rugby 5E 74
CV31: Lea S 1C 102
CV34: Warw 1F 101
Victoria Ter. CV31: Lea S 1D 102
CV47: S'ton 6C 106
Victoria Way B46: Cole 7G 25
Victory Rd. CV6: Cov 6E 50
Viggen Way CV7: Ansty 6G 53
VIGO 1B 138
Villa Cl. CV12: Bulk 4D 42
Villa Cres. CV12: Bulk 4E 42
Village Hall Yd. CV47: Long I 2C 106
Village M. CV22: Bil 1D 86
Village Rd. OX17: Warm 2J 129
Villa Rd. CV6: Cov 1B 58
Villebon Way CV31: W'nsh 6E 102
Villiers Ct. CV5: Alle 6K 47
Villiers Rd. CV8: Ken 4F 79
Villiers St. CV2: Cov 4G 59
CV11: Nun 1H 31
CV32: Lea S 6E 98
Vincent Av. CV37: S Avon 3E 114
Vincent Ct. CV37: S Avon 3F 115
Vincent St. CV1: Cov 5B 58
CV32: Lea S 6E 98
Vincent Wyles Ho. CV2: Cov 4A 60
Vinecote Rd. CV6: Lford 3F 51
Vine Cotts. CV35: H Lucy 2B 118
Vine Ct. CV34: Warw 7H 97
Vine La. CV34: Warw 7G 97
Vinery Ct.
CV37: S Avon 4C 136 (5E 114)
Vine St. CV1: Cov 1K 135 (3E 58)
Violet Cl. CV2: Cov 3J 51
CV12: Bed 3E 40
CV23: Brow 7K 65
Virgin Active
Coventry 1F 69
Rugby .2H 75
Virginia Pl. CV10: Nun 1E 30
Virginia Rd. CV1: Cov 4E 58
Viscount Cen. CV4: Canly 2F 67
Viscount Cl. CV31: Lea S 2D 102
Viscount Ho. B26: Birm A 2C 44
Vittle Dr. CV34: Warw 1F 101
Vogue Cl. CV1: Cov 2K 135 (4E 58)
Voyage Rd. CV21: Rugby 2G 75
Vulcan Vw. CV35: Welle 5F 117
Vulcan Way CV33: L Hth 2K 119

W

Wackrill Dr. CV32: Lill 4G 99
WADBOROUGH 3A 142
Wade Av. CV3: Cov 3B 68
Wadebridge Dr. CV11: Nun 7F 23
Wade Gro. CV34: Warw 5G 97
Wade Ho. CV22: Bil 1C 86
Wade La. CV33: L Hth 2K 119
Wadham Ho. B37: Chel W 2C 34
Wadleys Cl. B50: Bidf A 5G 123
Waggestaff Dr. CV10: Nun 4F 21
Waggoners Cl. CV8: Bubb 4J 81
Wagstaffe Cl. CV33: Har 6G 109
Wagstaff Way B37: Mars G 5A 34
Wagtail Av. CV47: Sou 7G 107
Wainbody Av. Nth. CV3: Cov 3A 68
Wainbody Av. Sth. CV3: Finh 4K 67
Wain Cl. B49: Alc 3D 112
Wakefield Cl. CV3: Bin 1B 70
CV9: Hur 7J 13
Wakefield Gro. B46: Wat O 1B 24
Wakefield Way B49: Kinw 3D 112
Wakeford Cl. CV10: Ridge L 1A 20
Wake Gro. CV34: Warw 3D 100
Wakehurst Cl. CV11: Nun 4B 32
WALCOT 3C 143
WALCOTE 3C 141
Waldon Wlk. B36: Cas B 4A 24
Waldron Ct.
CV37: S Avon 2F 137 (4F 115)
Walford Gro. CV34: Warw 6H 97
Walford Pl. CV22: Hillm 1B 88
Walkers Orchard CV8: S'lgh 3B 80
Walkers Rd. CV37: S Avon 2F 115
Walker's Ter. CV23: Brin 2B 62
Walker's Way CV8: Ken 7D 78
Walkers Way B46: Cole 6G 25
CV12: Bed 4F 41
Walkley Av. CV36: Ship S 4F 131
WALL 1C 139
Wallace Ct. CV34: Warw 1F 101
Wallace Rd. CV6: Cov 6A 50
Wall Av. B46: Cole 7F 25
WALLBROOK 2A 138
Waller Cl. CV35: Leek W 1H 97
Waller St. CV32: Lea S 5E 98
WALL HEATH 3A 138
WALL HILL 2E 48
Wall Hill Ct. CV7: Cor 1D 48
Wall Hill Rd. CV5: Alle, Cor 2F 49
CV7: Cor 6A 38
Wallingford Av. CV11: Nun 4G 23
Wallsgrove Cl. CV32: Lill 4F 99
Wallwin Ct. *CV34: Warw 2F 101*
(off Friars St.)
Wallwin Pl. CV34: Warw 1F 101
Walmer Way B37: Chel W 2C 34
WALMLEY 2C 139
Walmsley Cl. CV5: Alle 5G 49
Walnut Cl. B37: Chel W 4B 34
CV10: Harts 3F 21
CV10: Nun 5K 21
Walnut Ct. CV31: W'nsh 4D 102
Walnut Cft. CV9: Bad E 3F 15
Walnut Dr. CV9: Man 4E 16
CV32: Lill 4F 99
Walnut St. CV2: Cov 4H 51
Walnut Tree Cl. CV8: Ken 6E 78
Walnut Way CV22: Bil 7B 74
WALSALL 2B 138
Walsall St. CV4: Canly 1E 66
WALSALL WOOD 1B 138
Walsgrave Gdns.
CV2: Walsg S 7C 52
WALSGRAVE ON SOWE . . .7C 52 (3A 140)
Walsgrave Retail Pk.
CV2: Walsg S 7D 52
Walsgrave Rd. CV2: Cov 4F 59
Walsgrave Triangle Bus. Pk.
CV2: Walsg S 5C 52
Walsh La. CV7: Mer 4G 47
Walsingham Dr. CV10: Griff 4G 31
Walter Scott Rd. CV12: Bed 4J 41
Waltham Cres. CV10: Nun 7G 21
WALTON
CV35 . . . . .7J 117 (3D 143)
LE17 . . . . .3C 141
Walton Cl. CV3: Bin 1A 70
CV11: Nun 5C 32
Walton Ct. *CV32: Lea S 5D 98*
(off Lillington Av.)
Walton Flds. CV35: Kine 6E 120
Walton La. CV35: Pill P 2B 128
Walton Rd. CV35: W'ton, Welle . . .4H 117
Walton Way CV35: Welle 4H 117
Wanley Rd. CV3: Cov 2D 68
WANLIP .1D 141
Wansfell Cl. CV4: Tile H 1E 66
Wantage Rd. B46: Cole 3E 24
WAPPENBURY 2A 144
Wappenbury Cl. CV2: Cov 4J 51
Wappenbury Rd. CV2: Cov 4K 51
WAPPING 2C 92
WARD END 3C 139
Warden Rd. CV6: Cov 1B 58
Wardens, The CV8: Ken 4G 79
Wardens Av., The CV5: Alle 1F 57
Ward Gro. CV34: Warw 1A 102
WARDINGTON 1D 147
Wardour Dr. B37: Chel W 3C 34
Ward's Hill CV35: N Lin 2G 95
Wards La. B50: Bidf A 5G 123
Wareham Grn. CV2: Walsg S 2C 60
Ware Orchard CV23: Barby 7E 88
Ware Rd. CV23: Barby 7E 88
WARESLEY 2A 142
Waringford Cl. CV34: Warw 5E 100
Waring Way CV22: Dunc 5D 86
WARKWORTH 1D 147
WARMINGTON 2J 129 (1D 147)
Warmington Cl. CV3: Bin 7A 60
Warmington Gro. CV34: Warw 7D 96
Warmwell Cl. CV2: Walsg S 3B 60
WARNDON 3A 142
Warneford M. CV31: Lea S 1E 102
Warner Cl. CV34: Warw 6F 97
Warner Ct. B50: Bidf A 6F 123
Warner Row CV6: Cov 7G 51
Warners Ct. *CV12: Bed 3G 41*
(off Newtown Rd.)
Warren Cl. CV8: Rytn D 7C 70
CV32: Lea S 4D 98
Warren Fld. CV8: Rytn D 7C 70
Warren Grn. CV4: Tile H 1D 66
Warren Rd. CV22: Hillm 7K 75
WARTON 5H 9 (1D 139)
Warton Cl. CV8: Ken 5G 79
Warton La. B79: Aus, Wart 4H 9
B79: Wart 7G 9
CV9: Aus 7F 7
CV9: Gren 7G 9
WARWICK 2G 101 (2D 143)
Warwick Arts Cen. 4F 67
Warwick Av. CV5: Cov 1A 68
Warwick By-Pass
CV35: Barf 7H 101
CV35: Bud, Guys C, H Mag, H Hill
. . . . .3C 100
Warwick Castle 2G 101
Warwick Cl. B80: Stud 4C 92

Warwick Ct.—Wharrage Rd.

Warwick Ct. B37: Chel W 3D 34
(off Hedingham Gro.)
CV3: Cov 7G 135
CV32: Lea S 6D 98
CV37: S Avon 1H 137 (4F 115)
(not continuous)
Warwick Cres.
CV37: S Avon 1J 137 (4G 115)
Warwick Dr. CV9: Ath 1C 16
Warwick Gdns. CV10: Nun 1E 30
Warwick Golf Course 2F 101
Warwick Grn. CV12: Bulk 4E 42
Warwick Ho. CV37: S Avon 1E 136
Warwick Ho. Bus. Pk.
CV47: Sou 7H 107
Warwick La. CV1: Cov 4H 135 (5C 58)
Warwick M.
CV37: S Avon 1K 137 (4G 115)
Warwick New Rd. CV32: Lea S 7A 98
Warwick Parkway Station
(Rail) 1C 100
Warwick Pl. CV32: Lea S 7B 98
CV36: Ship S 4G 131
CV47: Sou 5H 107
Warwick Racecourse 2E 100
Warwick Rd. B95: Hen A 2H 93
CV1: Cov 5G 135 (5C 58)
CV3: Cov 7F 135 (7B 58)
CV8: Ken 5D 78
CV8: S'lgh 2B 80
CV8: Wols 5H 71
CV35: Kine 5C 120
CV35: Leek W, Ken 7E 78, 1H 97
CV35: N Lin 2G 95
CV35: Welle 2H 117
CV37: Blk H, Up Ful 7K 95
CV37: Ing, S Avon 3H 137 (4F 115)
CV47: Sou 6G 107
Warwick Row CV1: Cov 5G 135 (5C 58)
Warwicks, The CV35: H Mag 2B 100
Warwickshire Exhibition Cen. 2A 144
Warwickshire Golf Course, The 2G 97
Warwickshire Justice Cen. 7E 22
Warwickshire Yeomanry Mus. 2G 101
Warwick Sq. CV21: Rugby 5J 75
Warwick Station (Rail) 1H 101
Warwick St. CV5: Cov 7K 57
CV21: Rugby 5G 75
CV32: Lea S 6C 98
CV47: Sou 5H 107
Warwick Technology Pk.
CV34: Warw 3K 101
Warwick Ter. CV32: Lea S 6C 98
Wasdale Cl. CV32: Lea S 6B 98
Washbourne Rd. CV31: W'nsh 5E 102
Washbrook La. CV5: Alle 4E 48
Washbrook Pl. CV36: Ilm 7C 126
Washford Dr. B98: Redd 1B 92
Washford Ind. Est. B98: Redd 1D 92
Washford Trade Pk. B98: Redd 1B 92
WASPERTON 3D 143
Wasperton Cl. CV3: Bin 7B 60
Wasperton La. CV35: Barf 3C 108
Waste La. CV6: Cov 5J 49
CV9: Ath, Gren 1H 15
Watch Cl. CV1: Cov 3F 135 (4B 58)
Watchmaker Ct. CV1: Cov 5B 58
Watcombe Rd. CV2: Cov 6A 52
Watercall Av. CV3: Cov 3C 68
Waterfall Cl. CV7: Mer 5E 46
Waterford Way CV3: Cov 6J 59
Waterfront, The CV7: Exh 4H 41
Watergall Cl. CV47: Sou 6J 107
Water Lily Way CV10: Nun 4G 31
Waterloo Av. B37: F'bri 1B 34
Waterloo Cl. CV35: Welle 4G 117
Waterloo Ct. CV34: Warw 7J 97
Waterloo Cres. B50: Bidf A 5H 123
Waterloo Dr. CV37: S Avon 6J 115
Waterloo Ind. Est. B37: F'bri 7B 24
B50: Bidf A 4H 123
Waterloo Pk. B50: Bidf A 4H 123
Waterloo Pl. CV32: Lea S 6D 98
Waterloo Ri. CV37: S Avon 7J 115
Waterloo Rd. B50: Bidf A 2F 123
Waterloo St. CV1: Cov 3E 58
CV31: Lea S 1F 103
Waterman Rd. CV6: Cov 2F 59
Watermill, The B78: K'bry 7E 12
WATER ORTON 1B 24 (2C 139)
Water Orton La. B76: Min 7A 18
Water Orton Station (Rail) 1A 24
Watersbridge Gdns. CV10: Nun 3J 31
Watersfield Gdns. CV31: Lea S 1G 103
Waterside B78: Pole 1D 10
CV1: Cov 1H 135 (3C 58)
CV6: Lford 7J 41
CV37: S Avon 7G 137 (5F 115)
Waterside Ct. CV31: Lea S 2E 102
Waterside Dr. CV21: Rugby 2J 75
Watersmeet Gro. CV2: Cov 1H 59
Watersmeet Rd. CV2: Cov 1H 59
Waterson Cft. B37: Chel W 2D 34
Water Twr. La. CV8: Ken 3D 78
Waterways, The CV37: S Avon 3D 114
Watery La. B46: Neth W 2J 25
B95: Ullen 6B 90
CV6: Cov, Ker E 2K 49
CV7: Cor 2C 48
CV7: Ker E 2K 49
CV8: Bubb 4G 81
CV9: Bad E 1D 14
CV35: Pill H 1D 128
CV35: Sher 7C 100
CV36: Ship S 4H 131
WATFORD 2D 145
Wathen Grange School CV9: Man 5E 16
Wathen Rd. CV32: Lea S 5E 98
CV34: Warw 7G 97
Watitune Av. CV10: Nun 3D 22
Watling Ct. CV11: Nun 1B 32
Watling Rd. CV8: Ken 3F 79
Watling St. B78: Dord, Gren 4A 10
CV9: Ath, Gren 7G 11
CV9: Man, With 4E 16
CV10: Cald, Harts, Nun
. . . . . 5G 17, 1D 22
CV11: Nun 1D 22
CV23: Clift D, Hillm, Kils 1F 77
CV23: Kils 6J 89
(not continuous)
Watson Cl. CV34: Warw 6G 97
Watson Rd. CV5: Cov 5H 57
Watton La. B46: Wat O 2C 24
Wattons La. CV47: Sou 5H 107
(not continuous)
Wattons Lodge CV47: Sou 5H 107
Watts La. CV21: Hillm 1D 88
Watts Rd. B80: Stud 5D 92
Waugh Cl. B37: Chel W 3B 34
Wavebeck Ct. CV23: Long L 3B 74
Waveley Rd. CV1: Cov 4A 58
Wavendon Cl. CV2: Walsg S 5B 52
Waveney Cft. B36: Cas B 4A 24
Wavere Ct. CV21: Brow 1K 75
Waverley Av. CV11: Nun 3A 32
Waverley Edge CV8: Bubb 5H 81
Waverley Rd. CV8: Ken 6E 78
CV21: Hillm 7C 76
CV31: Lea S 2E 102
Waverley Sq. CV11: Nun 4B 32
Wavers Marston B37: Mars G 5A 34
Waverton Av. B79: Wart 5H 9
Waverton M. CV31: Lea S 2G 103
Waver Way CV23: Cosf 5J 65
Wavytree Cl. CV34: Warw 1F 101
Wawensmere Rd. B95: Woot W 5F 93
Wayside B37: Mars G 5A 34
Weale Gro. CV34: Warw 6H 97
Weatheroak Rd. B49: Alc 4D 112
Weaver Dr. CV23: Long L 4C 74
Weaver Gdns. CV7: Exh 5G 41
Weavers Cl. CV12: Bulk 3C 42
CV36: Ship S 4H 131
Weavers Cotts. CV36: Long C 3C 134
Weavers Wlk. CV6: Cov 6H 51
Webb Dr. CV23: Brow 7K 65
Webb Ellis Bus. Pk.
CV21: Rugby 4H 75
Webb Ellis Road 6E 74
Webb Ellis Rd. CV22: Rugby 6E 74
Webb Ellis Rugby Mus., The 5G 75
Webb St. CV10: Nun 1C 30
WEBHEATH 2B 142
Webster Av. CV8: Ken 3F 79
Webster St. CV6: Cov 7E 50
WEDDINGTON 5D 22 (2A 140)
Weddington Ind. Est. CV10: Nun 6D 22
Weddington La. CV10: Cald, Nun 1C 22
Weddington Rd. CV10: Nun 2C 22
Weddington Ter. CV10: Nun 6D 22
Wedgewood Cl. CV2: Walsg S 6A 52
Wedgewood Ho. B37: F'bri 1B 34
Wedge Woods CV5: Cov 7K 57
Wedgnock Grn. CV34: Warw 7F 97
Wedgnock Ind. Est. CV34: Warw 6E 96
(not continuous)
Wedgnock La. CV34: Warw 6E 96
CV35: Beau, Leek W 1A 96
WEDNESBURY 2A 138
WEDNESFIELD 1A 138
Wedon Cl. CV4: Tile H 1C 66
WEEDON BEC 3D 145
WEEDON LOIS 3D 145
WEEFORD 1C 139
WEETHLY 3B 142
Weft Way CV11: Nun 5J 23
Weilerswist Dr. CV31: W'nsh 4D 102
Weir Way CV3: Cov 6J 59
Weland Cl. B46: Wat O 2B 24
Weland Ct. B46: Wat O 2B 24
Welchman Pl. CV35: Mid T 7D 130
Welcombe Cotts. CV37: S Avon 3F 115
Welcombe Ct. CV37: S Avon 3F 115
Welcombe Golf Course 1J 115
Welcombe Hills Obelisk 3D 143
Welcombe Rd.
CV37: S Avon 1J 137 (4F 115)
Welcome St. CV9: Ath 3D 16
WELFORD 3D 141
Welford Gro. CV35: Hatt 4A 96
WELFORD-ON-AVON 2A 124 (3C 143)
Welford Pl. CV6: Cov 7D 50
Welford Rd. B50: Bart 7H 123
CV21: Rugby 4J 75
CV37: Long M 3G 125
Welgarth Av. CV6: Cov 1J 57
Welland Cl. CV23: Long L 3B 74
Welland Rd. CV1: Cov 6F 59
WELLESBOURNE 3H 117 (3D 143)
Wellesbourne Distribution Pk.
CV35: Welle 4F 117
Wellesbourne Gro.
CV37: S Avon 4C 136 (5E 114)
Wellesbourne Ho.
CV35: Welle 4H 117
Wellesbourne Rd.
CV5: East G 4E 56
CV35: Barf, Wasp 2B 108
CV35: Char 2A 116
CV35: Light 4F 119
CV35: Lox, Welle 6D 116
CV37: A'ton, Char 2A 116
Wellesbourne Wartime Mus. 3D 143
Wellington Av. CV37: Lwr Q 6F 125
Wellington Cl. CV35: Welle 5G 117
Wellington Dr. CV37: S Avon 6J 115
Wellington Gdns. CV1: Cov 5B 58
Wellington Rd. B50: Bidf A 4H 123
CV32: Lill 4F 99
Wellington St. CV1: Cov 3E 58
Well La. B94: Tan A 4D 90
Wellmeadow Gro. B92: H Ard 7G 45
WELLSBOROUGH 1A 140
Wells Cl. CV10: Gall C 7E 20
Wells Ct. CV3: Cov 1F 69
Well Spring Cl. CV9: Ath 3E 16
Wells St. CV21: Rugby 5H 75
Wells Ter. CV5: Cov 5K 57
Well St. CV1: Cov 2H 135 (4C 58)
Wells Wlk. B37: Mars G 4A 34
Welsh Cl. CV34: Warw 5G 97
Welsh Rd. CV2: Cov 3H 59
CV32: Cubb 3J 99
CV33: Cubb, Off 3J 99
CV47: Bas 1J 109
Welsh Rd. E. CV47: Sou 5J 107
Welsh Rd. W. CV47: Sou 3F 107
WELTON 2C 145
Welton Pl. CV22: Hillm 1K 87
Welton Rd. CV34: Warw 6F 97
Wembrook Cl. CV11: Nun 2K 31
Wembrook Ho. CV11: Nun 2A 32
Wendiburgh St. CV4: Canly 1E 66
Wendover Ri. CV5: Cov 3G 57
Wenlock Way CV10: Nun 7G 21
Wentworth Av. CV47: Temp H 3B 120
Wentworth Dr. CV6: Cov 2B 50
CV11: Nun 3C 32
Wentworth Rd. CV22: Bil 7E 74
CV31: Lea S 2H 103
WERGS 1A 138
Wesley Rd. CV21: Hillm 1C 88
Wessex Cl. CV12: Bed 1G 41
Wessex Ct. B79: Shut 2C 8
Wessex M. CV22: Caw 1B 86
Wessons Rd. B50: Bidf A 5H 123
West Av. CV2: Cov 5G 59
CV6: Ker E 1A 50
CV12: Bed 3K 41
Westbourne Gro. CV22: Bil 7F 75
WEST BROMWICH 2A 138
Westbrook Ct.
CV5: East G 3E 56
Westbury Ct. CV34: Warw 1J 101
Westbury M. CV2: Cov 3G 59
Westbury Rd. CV5: Cov 2H 57
CV10: Nun 7J 21
Westcliff Dr. CV34: Warw 5G 97
Westcliffe Dr. CV3: Cov 3B 68
Westcotes CV4: Tile H 6F 57
WESTCOTT BARTON 3D 147
West Dr. B95: Woot W 4H 93
West End CV35: Rad 6A 128
W. End Ct. CV34: Warw 2F 101
(off Crompton St.)
Western Heights Rd.
CV37: Lwr Q 6F 125
Western Rd.
CV37: S Avon 1B 136 (4E 114)
Western Rd. Ind. Est.
CV37: S Avon 1C 136 (4E 114)
WEST FARNDON 3C 145
Westfield Cl. CV10: Nun 6E 22
CV37: S Avon 2E 114
Westfield Cres. CV35: Welle 3G 117
Westfield Ho. B36: Cas B 5A 24
Westfield Rd. CV22: Rugby 6F 75
CV47: Sou 6G 107
Westfields B78: B'moor 2C 10
(Dexter Way)
B78: B'moor 2A 10
(Green La.)
Westgate Cl. CV34: Warw 2F 101
Westgate Ho. CV34: Warw 2G 101
(off Market St.)
Westgate Rd. CV21: Hillm 7A 76
West Grn. Dr. CV37: S Avon 4A 114
Westgrove Ter. CV32: Lea S 7B 98
WEST HADDON 1D 145
WEST HAGLEY 3A 138
Westham Ho. B37: F'bri 1B 34
Westham La. CV35: Barf 3A 108
Westhill Rd. CV6: Cov 1K 57
CV32: B'dwn 1E 98
Westholme Ct. B50: Bidf A 6G 123
(off Westholme Rd.)
Westholme Rd. B50: Bidf A 5F 123
WESTHORP 3C 145
Westlea Rd. CV31: Lea S 2C 102
Westleigh Av. CV5: Cov 1K 67
W. Leyes CV21: Rugby 5G 75
West Mall B37: Chel W 3B 34
(within Chelmsley Wood Shop. Cen.)
Westmead Av. B80: Stud 3D 92
Westmede Cen. CV5: Cov 4G 57
W. Midlands Freeport
B26: Birm A 3A 44
Westminster Dr. CV10: Nun 5G 21
Westminster Rd.
CV1: Cov 6F 135 (6B 58)
Westmorland Av. CV10: Nun 7K 21
Westmorland Rd. CV2: Cov 3B 60
W. Oak Ho. CV4: Westw H 2C 66
W. of St Laurence CV35: Row 7J 91
WESTON 3C 145
Westonbirt Cl. CV8: Ken 3G 79
Weston Cl. CV22: Dunc 5C 86
CV31: Lea S 2G 103
CV34: Warw 1H 101
Weston Ct. CV21: Rugby 4J 75
CV36: Long C 2D 134
WESTON IN ARDEN 2D 42 (3A 140)
Weston La. CV8: Bubb 5H 81
CV12: Bulk 2D 42
CV33: W Weth 5H 81
Weston Lawns Fisheries 2A 42
WESTON-ON-AVON 3C 124 (3C 143)
WESTON-ON-THE-GREEN 3D 147
WESTON-SUB-EDGE 1A 146
WESTON UNDER WETHERLEY 2A 144
W. Orchards Shop. Cen.
CV1: Cov 3H 135 (4C 58)
West Pk. CV4: Tile H 7D 56
West Pk. Cl. CV37: S Avon 4A 114
W. Point Dr. B80: Stud 1C 92
West Ridge CV5: Cov 2E 56
West Rock CV34: Warw 1F 101
(off Theatre St.)
West St. CV1: Cov 4E 58
CV23: Long L 3A 74
CV31: Lea S 1E 102
CV34: Warw 3F 101
CV36: Ship S 4H 131
CV37: S Avon 7D 136 (6E 114)
West Vw. CV10: Ans C 3D 20
West Vw. Rd. CV22: Rugby 6D 74
CV32: Cubb 2G 99
Westway CV21: Rugby 5G 75
Westwood Bus. Pk.
CV4: Westw H 2E 66
Westwood Cl. CV10: Nun 1F 31
Westwood Cres. CV9: Ath 4C 16
Westwood Hall CV4: Canly 2F 67
WESTWOOD HEATH 2D 66
Westwood Heath Rd.
CV4: Westw H 2A 66
Westwood Rd. CV5: Cov 6A 58
CV9: Ath 3C 16
CV22: Hillm 2B 88
Westwood Way CV4: Westw H 2C 66
Wetherby Way CV37: S Avon 6D 114
Wetherell Way CV21: Brow 1J 75
Wexford Rd. CV2: Cov 5K 51
Weymouth Cl. CV3: W'hall 3K 69
Whaley's Cft. CV6: Cov 6B 50
Wharf, The CV23: Stret U 7E 54
CV36: Ship S 3H 131
CV47: Fen C 1K 121
Wharf Ct. CV34: Warw 7J 97
Wharf Gdns. CV10: Nun 2H 31
Wharf La. CV37: Wilm 5K 113
Wharf Rd. CV6: Cov 2F 59
CV37: S Avon 3E 114
CV47: Fen C 2J 121
Wharf St. CV34: Warw 1J 101
Wharrad Cl. B50: Bidf A 5H 123
Wharrage Rd. B49: Alc 4D 112

A-Z Warwickshire Atlas 189

Whatcote—Wolston

WHATCOTE 3A 130 (1B 146)
Whatcote Rd. CV35: Oxh 1D 130
WHATELEY 1G 13 (2D 139)
Whateley Ct. CV11: Nun 7C 22
Whateley La. B78: What 1G 13
Whateley's Dr. CV8: Ken 4E 78
Whateley Vs. CV9: Wood E 1H 13
Wheatcroft Dr. B37: Chel W 4C 34
Wheate Cft. CV4: Tile H 5D 56
Wheaten Cl. B37: Chel W 2D 34
Wheatfield Cl. B36: Cas B 5A 24
Wheatfield Rd. CV22: Bil 7C 74
Wheathill Cl. CV32: Lea S 5C 98
Wheatley Grange B46: Cole 6F 25
Wheatley St. CV1: Cov 2K 135
WHEATON ASTON 1A 138
WHEATSTONE PARK 1A 138
Wheat St. CV11: Nun 7D 22
Wheelbarrow La. CV35: Clav 2E 94
Wheeley Moor Rd.
B37: K'hrst 7A 24
Wheelhouse, The B78: K'bry 7E 12
Wheelwright Ct.
CV37: S Avon 2E 136
Wheelwright Gdns.
CV36: Long C 4D 134
Wheelwright La.
CV6: Ash G, Cov 2C 50
CV7: Ash G 2C 50
Wheelwright Way CV35: Welle 5F 117
Wheler Rd. CV3: Cov 7G 59
Whernside CV21: Brow 1J 75
WHETSTONE 2C 141
Whetstone Dr. CV21: Brow 1K 75
Whichcote Av. CV7: Mer 5E 46
WHICHFORD 2C 147
Whichford Pottery 2C 147
Whichford Rd. CV36: Long C 1C 134
Whiley Cl. CV23: Clift D 3B 76
WHILTON 2D 145
Whimbrel Cl. CV23: Brow 7J 65
Whimbrel Ho. CV6: Cov 3H 51
WHITACRE HEATH 5K 19 (2D 139)
Whitacre Heath (Nature Reserve)
5H 19
Whitacre Rd. CV11: Nun 7F 23
CV32: Lill 5E 98
Whitacre Rd. Ind. Est. CV11: Nun 7F 23
Whitaker Rd. CV5: Cov 4G 57
Whitburn Rd. CV12: Bed 3C 40
Whitchurch Way CV4: Tile H 7D 56
White Barn Cl. CV23: W'hby 3H 105
Whitebeam Cl. CV4: Tile H 6B 56
Whitebeam Rd. B37: Chel W 5C 34
Whitebeam Way CV10: Nun 4J 21
Whitefield Cl. CV4: Westw H 1B 66
Whitefields Flats CV4: Canly 4G 67
Whitefields Golf Course 5H 85
Whitefriars Dr. CV22: Caw 7A 74
Whitefriars La.
CV1: Cov 5K 135 (5D 58)
Whitefriars St.
CV1: Cov 4K 135 (5D 58)
Whitehall Chambers *CV11: Nun* *7D 22*
(off Vicarage St.)
Whitehall Cl. CV10: Harts 1F 21
Whitehall Rd. CV21: Rugby 6H 75
White Hart La. CV33: Ufton 2F 109
Whitehead Dr. CV8: Ken 2G 79
CV35: Welle 2J 117
Whiteheads Ct. CV32: Lea S 6D 98
Whitehorse Cl. CV6: Lford 7H 41
White Horse Hill CV37: Snitt 6H 95
White Ho., The B95: Hen A 2H 93
Whitehouse Cres. CV10: Nun 1D 30
Whitehouse Rd. B78: Dord 3C 10
WHITE LADIES ASTON 3A 142
Whitelaw Cres. CV5: Alle 1F 57
WHITEMOOR 4F 79
Whitemoor La. B96: Sam 7A 92
Whitemoor Rd. CV8: Ken 4E 78
White Pump La. B95: Ullen 4C 90
Whiteside Cl. CV3: Bin 7B 60
Whites Row CV8: Ken 7E 78
WHITE STITCH 2E 46
Whitestitch La. CV7: Mer 3D 46
WHITESTONE 4B 32
Whitestone Rd. CV11: Nun 4C 32
White St. CV1: Cov 2J 135 (4D 58)
Whitethorn Dr. CV32: Lill 5F 99
Whitfield Cl. CV37: Tidd 3K 115
WHITLEY 2G 69
Whitley Bus. Pk. CV3: Cov 3F 69
Whitley Ct. CV3: Cov 1F 69
Whitley Hill B95: Hen A 3K 93
Whitley Rd. B95: Hen A 2J 93
Whitley Village CV3: Cov 1F 69
WHITLOCK'S END 1C 143
Whitman Way CV34: Warw 4E 100
Whitmore Mnr. Cl. CV6: Cov 5B 50
WHITMORE PARK 5B 50
Whitmore Pk. Ind. Est. CV6: Cov 5C 50
Whitmore Pk. Rd. CV6: Cov 3C 50
Whitmore Rd. CV31: W'nsh 5E 102
WHITNASH 4E 102 (2A 144)
Whitnash Gro. CV2: Cov 2K 59
Whitnash Rd. CV31: W'nsh 4F 103
WHITTINGTON
CV9 7K 11, 1A 16 (2D 139)
DY7 3A 138
WR5 3A 142
WS14 1C 139
WHITTINGTON BARRACKS 1C 139
Whittington Cl. CV34: Warw 7K 97
Whittington La. CV9: Whitt 1K 15
Whittle Cl. CV3: Bin 7B 60
CV22: Bil 2D 86
Whittle Ct. CV32: Lea S 6F 99
WHITTLEFORD 7H 21 (2A 140)
Whittleford Rd. CV10: Nun 7H 21
Whitworth Av. CV3: Cov 6H 59
Whitworth Cl. CV35: Welle 4G 117
WHOBERLEY 5H 57 (1D 143)
Whoberley Av. CV5: Cov 4H 57
Whoberley Ct. CV5: Cov 4G 57
WIBTOFT 3B 140
Wickham Cl. CV6: Cov 4K 49
Wickham Ct. CV32: Lill 3F 99
WICKHAMFORD 1A 146
Wickham Rd. B80: Stud 3E 92
Wickmans Dr. CV4: Tile H 5A 56
Wiclif Way CV10: Nun 1B 30
Widdecombe Cl. CV2: Cov 6K 51
Widdrington Rd. CV1: Cov 2C 58
Wiggins Cl. CV21: Hillm 1D 88
Wiggins Hill Rd. B76: Min, Wis 5A 18
WIGGINTON
B79 1D 139
OX15 2C 147
Wight Cft. B36: Cas B 6B 24
WIGHTWICK 2A 138
WIGSTON 2D 141
Wigston Cl. CV8: Wols 4K 71
Wigston Hill CV9: Bax 6F 15
Wigston Rd. CV2: Walsg S 5B 52
CV21: Hillm 1C 88
Wike La. B96: Sam 7B 92
Wilcox Cl. CV8: Wols 4K 71
CV47: Bis I 7B 110
Wilcox Leys CV35: More M 5C 118
Wildcroft Rd. CV5: Cov 5G 57
Wilderness B95: Woot W 4J 93
Wildey Rd. CV12: Bed 3D 40
WILDMOOR 1A 142
Wildmoor Cl. CV2: Ald G 2H 51
Wilf Brown Cl. CV21: Brow 7J 65
Wilhelmina Cl. CV32: Lea S 7C 98
Wilkes Dr. CV31: Rad S 3K 103
Wilkes Way B50: Bidf A 5G 123
Wilkins Cl. CV35: Barf 2B 108
Wilkinson Way B46: Shu 2C 26
Wilkins Way CV36: Ilm 6D 126
Willans Pl. CV21: Rugby 4F 75
Willburton M. CV22: Caw 7B 74
Willday Dr. CV9: Ath 1C 16
WILLENHALL
CV3 2K 69 (1A 144)
WV13 2A 138
Willenhall La. CV3: Bin 2A 70
WILLERSEY 2A 146
Willes Rd. CV31: Lea S 6E 98
CV32: Lea S 6E 98
Willes Ter. CV31: Lea S 7F 99
Willett Gdns. CV35: Welle 2H 117
Willett Ho. *CV35: Welle* *2H 117*
(off Willett Gdns.)
WILLEY 3B 140
William Arnold Cl. CV2: Cov 3G 59
William Batchelor Ho.
CV1: Cov 1H 135
William Beesley Cres.
CV11: Bram 6G 33
William Bree Rd. CV5: East G 2A 56
William Bristow Rd. CV3: Cov 1E 68
William Cree Cl. CV8: Wols 5H 71
William Groubb Cl. CV3: Bin 1A 70
William James Way B95: Hen A 1H 93
William Kirby Cl. CV4: Tile H 6E 56
William McCool Cl. CV3: Bin 7B 60
William McKee Cl. CV3: Bin 1A 70
William Malcolm Ho. CV2: Cov 4A 60
Williamsbridge Rd. CV4: Tile H 4A 56
WILLIAMSCOT 1D 147
Williamson Ct. CV5: Cov 7K 57
Williams Rd. CV31: Rad S 4J 103
Williams St. CV11: Nun 1A 32
CV12: Bed 3K 41
CV21: Rugby 5H 75
CV32: Lea S 7E 98
William Tarver Cl. CV34: Warw 1J 101
William Thomson Ho. *CV1: Cov* *3E 58*
(off Clifton St.)
WILLINGTON 7K 131 (2B 146)
Willington St. CV11: Nun 6B 22
Willis Cft. B79: Wart 5H 9
Willis Gro. CV12: Bed 2J 41
WILLOUGHBY 3H 105 (2C 145)
Willoughby Av. CV8: Ken 6C 78
Willoughby Cl. B49: King C 1A 112
CV3: Bin 7A 60
Willoughby Ct. CV35: Lit K 6C 120
Willoughby Pl. CV22: Hillm 1K 87
Willoughby Rd. CV23: Barby, Kils 7J 89
WILLOUGHBY WATERLEYS 2C 141
Willow Bank CV37: Welf A 2A 124
Willowbank M. CV1: Cov 5E 58
Willowbrook CV4: Tile H 1E 66
Willowbrook Cotts.
CV37: S Avon 5D 114
Willow Brook Rd. CV8: Wols 4J 71
Willow Cl. B49: Alc 6B 112
B78: K'bry 5E 12
CV10: Harts 4F 21
CV12: Bed 7G 31
CV31: W'nsh 6F 103
Willow Ct. CV34: H'cte 6C 102
Willow Courtyard CV2: Cov 7K 51
Willowdene Home Pk.
CV37: Wilm 4H 113
Willow Dr. CV35: Welle 3H 117
Willow End GL56: Lit C 6C 134
Willowfields Rd. CV11: Nun 3C 32
Willowford Cl. CV23: Long L 4A 74
Willow Gdns. CV22: Rugby 6J 75
CV47: Sou 5H 107
Willow Gro. CV4: Tile H 5F 57
CV47: Long I 1C 106
Willowherb Cl. CV3: Bin 7B 60
Willow Ho. CV32: Lea S 7B 98
Willow La. CV7: Fill 7A 28
CV22: Rugby 6J 75
Willow Meer CV8: Ken 4F 79
Willow Ri. CV35: Oxh 1E 130
Willow Rd. CV10: Nun 6K 21
Willows, The CV9: Ath 1D 16
CV12: Bed 3E 40
CV37: S Avon 6A 136 (5D 114)
Willow Sheets Mdw. CV32: Cubb 1J 99
Willows La. CV9: Gren 7G 11
Willows Nth., The
CV37: S Avon 4A 136 (5D 114)
Willow Tree Gdns. CV21: Hillm 7C 76
Willow Wlk. CV7: Old A 3C 28
Willow Way B37: Chel W 3B 34
B80: Stud 5D 92
Wilman Cl. CV4: Tile H 6E 56
WILMCOTE 5J 113 (3C 143)
Wilmcote Grn. CV5: East G 4E 56
Wilmcote La.
B95: Aston C 2K 113, 4F 113
Wilmcote Station (Rail) 5K 113
Wilmhurst Rd. CV34: Warw 7E 96
Wilmot Av. B46: Cole 6F 25
WILNECOTE 1D 139
Wilnecote Gro. CV31: Lea S 3F 103
Wilson Av. B37: Chel W 2C 34
Wilson Cl. CV22: Bil 6C 74
Wilson Grn. CV3: Bin 6B 60
Wilson Gro. CV8: Ken 5G 79
Wilson Rd. CV37: S Avon 4D 114
Wilsons La. CV6: Lford 1F 51
CV7: Exh 7G 41
Wilton Ct. CV8: Ken 5D 78
Wilton Dr. CV34: Warw 5E 100
Wiltshire Cl. CV5: East G 4F 57
CV12: Bed 2G 41
WIMBLEBURY 1B 138
Wimborne Dr. CV2: Walsg S 3B 60
Wimbourne Cl. CV10: Nun 6G 21
WIMPSTONE 1B 146
Winceby Pl. CV4: Tile H 6B 56
Winchat Cl. CV3: Bin 6B 60
Winchcombe Rd. B49: Alc 4D 112
Winchester Av. CV10: Nun 4D 22
Winchester Ct. CV22: Dunc 5C 86
Winchester Dr. B37: Chel W 3A 34
Winchester St. CV1: Cov 4E 58
Wincote Cl. CV8: Ken 5E 78
Wincott Cl. CV37: S Avon 6H 115
Windermere Av. CV3: Bin 6A 60
CV5: East G 3C 56
CV11: Nun 4G 23
Windermere Cl. CV21: Brow 1J 75
Windermere Dr. CV32: Lea S 5B 98
WINDERTON 1K 133 (1C 147)
Winderton Av. CV35: Hatt 5A 96
Winderton Rd.
OX15: Lwr Bra, Wind 3K 133
Winding Ho. La.
CV6: Ash G, Lford 2C 50
Windmill Av. B46: Cole 5F 25
Windmill Cl. B79: Wart 6H 9
CV8: Ken 3E 78
CV21: Hillm 1D 88
CV36: Ilm *6C 126*
(off Elm Cl.)
Windmill Ct. CV6: Cov 3G 51
Windmill Cft. CV32: Cubb 2H 99
Windmill Hill CV32: Cubb 2H 99
Windmill Hill, The CV5: Alle 7E 48
Windmill Hill Community Nature Area
3K 21
Windmill Ind. Est. CV5: Alle 7D 48
Windmill La. CV7: Cor 7B 38
CV9: Aus 6G 7
CV9: Bax 5G 15
CV10: Asty 7J 29
CV22: Dunc 5A 86
CV47: Ladb, Sou 2C 110
(not continuous)
Windmill Rd. CV6: Cov 3F 51
CV7: Exh 5F 41
CV9: Ath 2C 16
CV10: Nun 4J 21
CV31: Lea S 3D 102
Windmill Village Golf Course 7D 48
Windmill Way CV35: Mid T 7C 130
CV47: Sou 4G 107
Windridge Cl. CV3: W'hall 2K 69
Windrush Way CV23: Long L 3B 74
Windsor Ct. CV4: Tile H 5F 57
CV10: Nun 5K 21
CV21: Rugby 5G 75
CV32: Lea S 7D 98
CV37: S Avon 3E 136 (4E 114)
Windsor Gdns. CV10: Nun 7K 21
Windsor Pl. CV32: Lea S 7D 98
Windsor Rd. B36: Cas B 5A 24
B78: Pole 6D 8
Windsor St. CV1: Cov 5B 58
CV11: Nun 7C 22
CV21: Rugby 5J 75
CV32: Lea S 7D 98
CV37: S Avon 3E 136 (4E 114)
Windward Way B36: Cas B 5A 24
WINDY ARBOUR 6F 79
Windy Arbour CV8: Ken 4F 79
Winfield Rd. CV11: Nun 6C 22
Winfield St. CV21: Rugby 4K 75
Wingfield Ho. B37: K'hrst 7A 24
Wingfield Rd. B46: Cole 7F 25
Wingfield Way CV6: Cov 4A 50
Wingrave Cl. CV5: Alle 1E 56
Winifred Av. CV5: Cov 6A 58
Winnallthorpe CV3: W'hall 2A 70
Winn Cl. CV8: Ken 3G 79
Winsford Av. CV5: Cov 3F 57
Winsford Ct. CV5: Cov 3G 57
Winsham Wlk. CV3: Finh 5C 68
Winslow Cl. CV5: Cov 4F 57
CV32: Lea S 6A 98
Winslow Ho. *CV1: Cov* *5B 58*
(off Meadow St.)
WINSON GREEN 3B 138
Winspear Cl. CV7: Mer 5E 46
Winster Cl. CV7: Ker E 6A 40
Winston Av. CV2: Cov 6K 51
Winston Cl. CV2: Cov 6K 51
CV37: Shot 6C 114
Winston Cres. CV32: Lill 4G 99
Winterborne Gdns. CV10: Nun 2F 31
Winterton Rd. CV12: Bulk 4E 42
WINWICK 1D 145
Winwick Pl. CV22: Bil 1C 86
Winyates Rd. CV33: L Hth 2K 119
Wise Gro. CV21: Hillm 6B 76
CV34: Warw 5G 97
Wise Mnr. *CV34: H'cte* *5B 102*
(off Merlin Way)
Wise St. CV31: Lea S 1D 102
Wise Ter. CV31: Lea S 1D 102
WISHAW 1B 18 (2C 139)
Wishaw La. B76: Curd 3A 18
Wisley Gro. CV8: Ken 4G 79
Wisteria Cl. CV2: Cov 4H 51
Wisteria Way CV10: Nun 4G 31
WITHERLEY 4G 17 (2A 140)
Witherley Rd. CV9: Ath 3D 16
Withy Bank CV31: Lea S 4G 103
WITHYBROOK 1D 54 (3B 140)
Withybrook Cl. CV2: Cov 4K 51
Withybrook La. CV7: Shilt, Withy 7H 43
Withybrook Rd. CV12: Bulk 3F 43
Witnell Rd. CV6: Cov 1C 58
WITTON 2A 142
WIXFORD 1E 122 (3B 142)
Wixford Rd. B50: Ard G 2K 123
Woburn Cl. CV31: Lea S 2H 103
Woburn Ct. CV1: Cov 6A 58
Woburn Dr. CV10: Nun 2G 31
Wolds La. LE10: Wlvy 2J 33
Wolfe Rd. CV4: Tile H 1D 66
Wolford Flds. CV36: Lit Wol 4E 132
WOLLASTON 3A 138
WOLLESCOTE 3A 138
Wolseley Cl. B36: Cas B 3A 24
Wolsey Rd. CV22: Bil 4D 86
WOLSTON 5J 71 (1B 144)

SAFETY CAMERA INFORMATION

PocketGPSWorld.com's CamerAlert is a self-contained speed and red light camera warning system for SatNavs and Android or Apple iOS smartphones/tablets. Visit www.cameralert.com to download.

Safety camera locations are publicised by the Safer Roads Partnership which operates them in order to encourage drivers to comply with speed limits at these sites. It is the driver's absolute responsibility to be aware of and to adhere to speed limits at all times.

By showing this safety camera information it is the intention of Geographers' A-Z Map Company Ltd. to encourage safe driving and greater awareness of speed limits and vehicle speed. Data accurate at time of printing.

Printed and bound in the United Kingdom by Polestar Wheatons Ltd., Exeter.

HOSPITALS, HOSPICES and selected HEALTHCARE FACILITIES covered by this atlas.

N.B. Where it is not possible to name these facilities on the map,
the reference given is for the road in which they are situated.

ALEXANDRA HOSPITAL 1B **92**
Woodrow Drive
REDDITCH
B98 7UB
Tel: 01527 503030

CALUDON CENTRE 1B **60**
Clifford Bridge Road
COVENTRY
CV2 2TE
Tel: 02476 968100

COVENTRY MYTON HOSPICE 2B **60**
University Hospital
Clifford Bridge Road
Walsgrave
COVENTRY
CV2 2DX
Tel: 02476 841900

ELLEN BADGER HOSPITAL 4H **131**
Stratford Road
SHIPSTON-ON-STOUR
CV36 4AX
Tel: 01608 661410

GEORGE ELIOT HOSPITAL 2H **31**
College Street
NUNEATON
CV10 7DJ
Tel: 02476 351351

HILL CREST MENTAL HEALTH UNIT 1B **92**
Alexandra Hospital
Quinneys Lane
REDDITCH
B98 7WG
Tel: 01527 500575

HOSPITAL OF ST CROSS 7H **75**
Barby Road
RUGBY
CV22 5PX
Tel: 01788 572831

MARY ANN EVANS HOSPICE 2G **31**
Eliot Way
George Eliot Hospital
NUNEATON
CV10 7QL
Tel: 02476 865440

MERIDEN BMI HOSPITAL 1C **60**
Clifford Bridge Road
University Hospital Coventry
COVENTRY
CV2 2LQ
Tel: 02476 647000

MINOR INJURIES UNIT (ELLEN BADGER HOSPITAL) 4H **131**
Stratford Road
SHIPSTON-ON-STOUR
CV36 4AX
Tel: 01608 661410

MINOR INJURIES UNIT (STRATFORD HOSPITAL) 1C **136** (4E **114**)
Arden Street
STRATFORD-UPON-AVON
CV37 6NX
Tel: 01789 205831

NHS WALK-IN CENTRE (CAMP HILL) 5J **21**
Ramsden Avenue
Camp Hill
NUNEATON
CV10 9EB
Tel: 02476 390008

NHS WALK-IN CENTRE (COVENTRY) .1J **135** (3D **58**)
Stoney Stanton Road
COVENTRY
CV1 4FH
Tel: 0300 200 0060

ROYAL LEAMINGTON SPA REHABILITATION HOSPITAL .4C **102**
Heathcote Lane
WARWICK
CV34 6SR
Tel: 01926 317700

RUGBY MYTON DAY HOSPICE 7H **75**
Barby Road
RUGBY
CV22 5PY
Tel: 01788 550085

ST MICHAEL'S HOSPITAL (WARWICK) 7F **97**
St Michael's Road
WARWICK
CV34 5QW
Tel: 01926 406789

SHAKESPEARE HOSPICE 4B **114**
Church Lane
Shottery
STRATFORD-UPON-AVON
CV37 9UL
Tel: 01789 266852

STRATFORD HOSPITAL 1C **136** (4E **114**)
Arden Street
STRATFORD-UPON-AVON
CV37 6NX
Tel: 01789 205831

UNIVERSITY HOSPITAL (COVENTRY) 1C **60**
Clifford Bridge Road
COVENTRY
CV2 2DX
Tel: 02476 964000

URGENT CARE CENTRE (RUGBY) 7H **75**
Hospital of St. Cross
Barby Road
RUGBY
CV22 5PX
Tel: 01788 663336

WARWICK HOSPITAL 7G **97**
Lakin Road
WARWICK
CV34 5BW
Tel: 01926 495321

WARWICK MYTON HOSPICE 1K **101**
Myton Lane
WARWICK
CV34 6PX
Tel: 01926 492518

WARWICKSHIRE NUFFIELD HEALTH HOSPITAL 2C **98**
The Chase
Old Milverton Lane
Blackdown
LEAMINGTON SPA
CV32 6RW
Tel: 01926 678478

ZOE'S PLACE - BABY HOSPICE 1C **50**
Easter Way
Ash Green
COVENTRY
CV7 9JG
Tel: 02476 361675